MORE THAN
A RUN

MORE THAN
A RUN

RICK MARKS

J.P. Tarcher, Inc.
Los Angeles

Distributed by St. Martin's Press
New York

Photos: Dick Bonneau, Chuck Foote, Rick Marks, Charlotte Perry,
John Rockwood
Design: John Brogna
Manufactured in the United States of America

Published by J.P. Tarcher, Inc.
9110 Sunset Blvd., Los Angeles, Calif. 90069
Published simultaneously in Canada by Macmillan of Canada
70 Bond St., Toronto, Canada M5B 1X3

DEDICATION

TO KIM AND GREG

CONTENTS

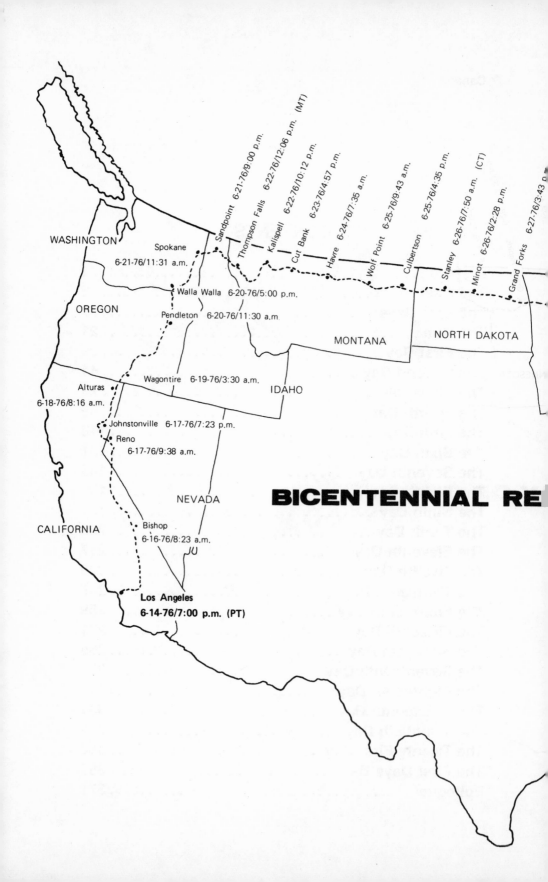

WASHINGTON

Spokane
6-21-76/11:31 a.m.

Sandpoint 6-21-76/9:00 p.m.

Thompson Falls 6-22-76/12:06 p.m. (MT)

Kalispell 6-22-76/10:12 p.m.

Cut Bank 6-23-76/4:57 p.m.

Havre 6-24-76/7:35 a.m.

Wolf Point 6-25-76/9:43 a.m.

Culbertson 6-25-76/4.35 p.m.

Stanley 6-26-76/7:50 a.m. (CT)

Minot 6-26-76/2:28 p.m.

Grand Forks 6-27-76/3:43 p.m.

OREGON

Walla Walla 6-20-76/5:00 p.m.

Pendleton 6-20-76/11:30 a.m.

MONTANA

NORTH DAKOTA

Wagontire 6-19-76/3:30 a.m.

IDAHO

Alturas
6-18-76/8:16 a.m.

Johnstonville 6-17-76/7:23 p.m.

Reno
6-17-76/9:38 a.m.

NEVADA

BICENTENNIAL RE

CALIFORNIA

Bishop
6-16-76/8:23 a.m.

UU

Los Angeles
6-14-76/7:00 p.m. (PT)

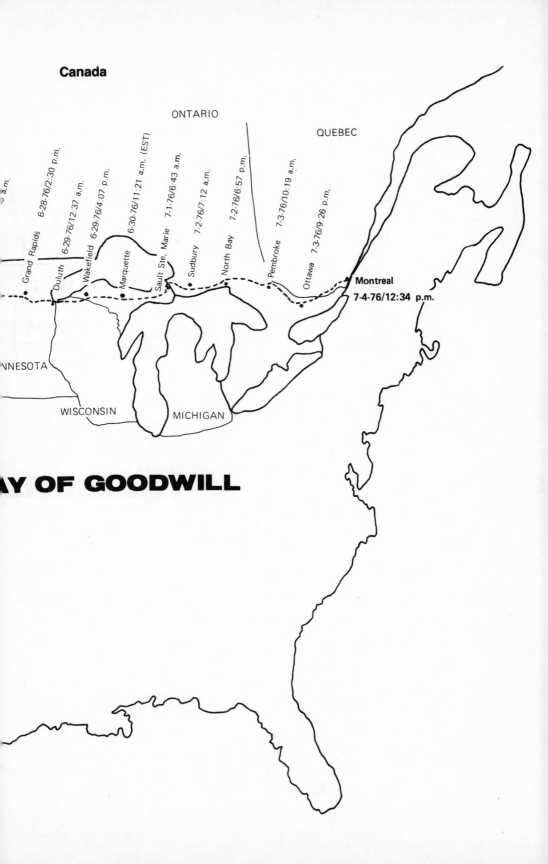

Canada

ONTARIO

QUEBEC

6-28-76/2:30 p.m.

6-29-76/12:37 a.m.

6-29-76/4:07 p.m.

6-30-76/11:21 a.m. (EST)

7-1-76/6:43 a.m.

7-2-76/7:12 a.m.

7-2-76/6:57 p.m.

7-3-76/10:19 a.m.

7-3-76/9:26 p.m.

Grand Rapids

Duluth

Wakefield

Marquette

Sault Ste. Marie

Sudbury

North Bay

Pembroke

Ottawa

Montreal
7-4-76/12:34 p.m.

NNESOTA

WISCONSIN

MICHIGAN

AY OF GOODWILL

PREFACE

This book was a two-year labor of love that began on a warm May evening in 1976 in the Los Angeles suburb of Canoga Park.

My next-door neighbor Frank McGinnis and I had just completed our daily three-mile run when Frank, an officer with the Los Angeles Police Department, casually mentioned to me that fourteen of his fellow policemen were going to run from Los Angeles to Montreal next month in honor of America's Bicentennial — each man running 10 miles at a time, the relay continuing 24 hours a day.

Frank told me about the ordeal and drama of past runs, sketched out details of the upcoming relay, and suggested that I might write a book about the epic undertaking.

I was receptive. At the time, my union was on strike against NBC in Burbank, where I worked as a news producer and writer. And I was also a novice runner. The strike, my running, and my friendship with Frank persuaded me to write the book.

My immediate problem was how to chronicle the adventures of fourteen runners and their sixteen support personnel, who would be traveling like a modern-day wagon train in four motor homes, a pace car, and a publicity car across almost 3,800 miles of North America in three weeks.

I finally settled on a plan that called for nearly total reliance on the tape recorder. The plan worked this way: Each day I would travel as much as possible with the men who were running,

1

joining them at about six or seven in the morning, and continuing with them until eight or nine at night. During that time I would tape the thoughts and recollections of each runner immediately following his 10-mile leg, tape conversations between team members, and conduct individual interviews.

Following each day's work, I would drive ahead about 100 miles to where I calculated the team would be the next morning, eat, sleep, and then rejoin the runners, quickly gathering information about what had transpired during the previous night.

I had help in the taping from Frank McGinnis, who accompanied me through the last two thirds of the run, and from Sgt. Dick Clark, one of the runners of Van Two, who carried a tape recorder across the continent with him.

In those instances when none of us was present during a critical conversation, the dialogue was reconstructed by the individuals involved. Otherwise, every conversation is as it occurred.

What remained after 21 days were more than 150 hours of tape recordings. It took nearly four months to transcribe those tapes and categorize the material.

I want especially to thank two people for their help and encouragement: Judi Marks, for her long hours of transcribing the tapes and her invaluable help in editing the manuscript; and Charlotte Perry, who did the lion's share of the transcribing, who contributed mightily to the editing, whose ideas for the form of the book were critical, and who typed and retyped the manuscript more times that she or I would care to remember. Charlotte lived this book more than her own life during the past two years.

Finally, I would like to thank fourteen magnificent cop-athletes and their support crew, who taught me the true meaning of courage, dedication, devotion, and respect during three memorable weeks of our lives.

Rick Marks
August 1978

THE CAST

Van One

SGT. BOB HICKEY, 38, 16-year veteran of LAPD, field supervisor in Hollenbeck Division. Fastest runner on 1974 Washington, D.C. to L.A. relay; wanted to repeat on Bicentennial Relay. The "man who runs through pain."

SGT. ALEX SHEARER, 47, 25 years with LAPD, investigator for L.A. Police Commission. Veteran of every LAPD relay. Team raconteur.

OFCR. BOB BURKE, 44, 20 years with LAPD, department athletic director. Creator of this type of run. Organized every aspect of Bicentennial Relay of Goodwill.

OFCR. JOHN ROCKWOOD, 34, five years with LAPD, physical training instructor at L.A. Police Academy. As member of Compton Police Department, once ran against LAPD.

OFCR. DICK BONNEAU, 35, five-year LAPD veteran, physical training instructor at Police Academy. Joined department and started running at 30. Shearer's straight man.

Van Two

OFCR. CHUCK FOOTE, 28, six-year veteran of LAPD, assigned to Juvenile Division. Team captain.

OFCR. JIM MURPHY, 36, three years on LAPD, patrolman in Hollywood Division. First LAPD relay. World-class runner and onetime Olympic hopeful. Holder of numerous national records for his age group. Considered egocentric by his teammates. Wanted to maintain image as "best runner" by compiling fastest average on relay.

SGT. DICK CLARK, 33, 11-year LAPD veteran, head of situation simulations unit at Police Academy. An alternate on this relay, replaced regular team member who dropped out shortly before run.

OFCR. FRANK JANOWICZ, 32, six years on LAPD, recruits women for department. Volatile personality. Trained religiously for nine months to be one of top runners on relay.

Van Three

OFCR. BOB JARVIS, 44, 17 years on LAPD, physical training instructor at Police Academy. Veteran of all LAPD relays. Part-time professional actor.

OFCR. PAT CONNELLY, 38, spent six years as LAPD reserve officer before joining department in 1971, assigned to Juvenile Division. World-class runner, alternate on 1964 U.S. Olympic team in 10,000-meter run. LAPD team coach.

LT. FRANK MULLENS, 54, 27 years with LAPD, head of department's robbery-hijacking unit. Started running at age 46. Former minor league baseball player.

OFCR. ED GARCIA, 33, seven years on LAPD, instructor at Police Academy. Along with Murphy, only "rookie" on team. Former boxer, viewed relay as another bout.

OFCR. CURT HALL, 37, nine years on LAPD, motorcycle officer in West Los Angeles. Runs average of eight marathons a year.

SUPPORT PERSONNEL

ANDY BAKJIAN, official of Amateur Athletic Union. Sanctioned the run.

ASST. CHIEF OF POLICE GEORGE BECK, highest-ranking member on run. Co-driver of Van Two.

CAPT. RUDY DE LEON, head of Hollenbeck Division. Helped drive pace car, "The Turtle."

INV. GEORGE DE WITT, team mechanic.

SGT. JACK GARRISON, co-driver, Van Three.

BOB HOGUE, Bob Burke's close friend. Los Angeles businessman. Only civilian team member. Chief fund raiser for run. Co-driver, Van One.

SGT. WALT KARPINSKY, co-driver of Van Two in early part of relay.

SGT. RON KISER, team trainer. Liked to call himself "Doctor."

INV. LOU McCLARY, chief publicity man for relay.

OFCR. JERRY MOWAT, driver of Van One in early part of relay.
SGT. J.P. NELSON, DeLeon's companion-driver in "The Turtle."
ASST. CHIEF CHARLES REESE, driver of Van Four, support vehicle.
SGT. ED WATKINS, shared Van Three driving with Garrison.
SGT. RICH WEMMER, McClary's assistant in publicity.

THE LAST DAYS

It was shortly after midnight when Clinton Street was jolted awake. Three blasts from a shotgun broke the calm. The bullets ripped through one of the small pastel houses that cover the hills and arroyos of East Los Angeles, the largest Mexican-American community in the United States. No one inside the house was hit; the police were notified by a neighbor, not by the intended victims.

Two police cars responded. The two officers who would handle the call rode ahead. Sgt. Bob Hickey rode behind, alone.

Hickey was a field supervisor. He worked the street, but he was no longer a street cop. And he missed it. The action, the chases, the questioning, the arrests. But above all, he missed helping people. Like the motto on the LAPD patrol cars says, "To protect and to serve." But "the street" was behind Hickey now. And after 16 years on the force, Hickey was seriously thinking of retiring from the Los Angeles Police Department in four years and joining another local police department, so that he could go back on patrol. Being a "Blue Knight" was a dream, not a nightmare, for Hickey.

Now his job was to observe the six men under him. To watch

7

how they deployed, questioned, acted, and reacted. Only in the rarest instance did he intercede. But his presence was felt. That was the whole theory behind field supervisors. Usually they worked the hot spots, those areas with high concentrations of minorities, or with special police problems, such as gays. There was more likely to be a citizen complaint about police behavior there. Supervisors could keep the problems to a minimum.

To most cops, field supervision is a promotion to a management-level job. To Hickey, it was like being retired. One look at him, and you could tell he wasn't ready for retirement. Thirty-eight years old, he had the athletic grace and physique of a man 15 years his junior and the face of a young Rex Harrison.

On this, his last night before vacation, Hickey performed his mission as he had so many nights before. He stood back and watched as the officers questioned the short, middle-aged Chicana whose house had been under attack just minutes earlier. But she would give no answers. She was protecting her oldest son, who was a member of the Clovers. No doubt, lowriders from the Hazards or the Avenue 18s or one of the countless other juvenile gangs that terrorize the barrio had decided to invade Clover territory this night. It might have been to retaliate for some earlier aggression, or simply to let the Clovers know they were there. Whatever it was, Hickey and his men got no cooperation from the woman.

To protect and to serve. It's difficult in the barrio.

Thursday, June 10, 1976   West Los Angeles

Curt Hall had been a motor cop for eight years. It was the reason he had joined the force. He loved the freedom of the bike. His job: ride the streets of West Los Angeles, stay visible, prevent traffic accidents, stop the carnage.

The Westside wasn't the tough Hollenbeck or 77th Street or Newton division. But things were getting worse in this upper-middle-class area, the home of UCLA. More shootings, robberies, rapes. As a motor cop, Hall wasn't assigned the hot call, but like all units, he was expected to respond. And because of his mobility, he was usually the first to arrive.

A couple of days earlier, he was the first on the scene of a 187 PC call — a possible homicide. But it was too late. The suspect was gone. The 25-year-old victim was sprawled in her own blood. She had been robbed, raped, and stabbed to death.

There were no hot calls this day, his final day before vacation. Hall worked his normal beat, Westwood Village, and the canyon roads that carry motorists between the San Fernando Valley and West Los Angeles. He settled on Beverly Glen Boulevard, a twisting stretch of pavement connecting Van Nuys with Bel-Air.

Some motorists like the challenge of Beverly Glen. They hit the straightaways at 50, 55 miles an hour, the curves at 35 to 40. Hall sat there, trying to be a visible deterrent. He wrote four tickets for speeding. There was grumbling, muttered swearing. But there were no accidents.

Friday, June 11, 1976   Downtown Los Angeles

Echo Park is an oasis in L.A.'s inner city. It lies one block off the crowded Hollywood Freeway, in an area dominated by Chicanos and dotted with poor, elderly whites. Sunset Boulevard forms one boundary of the park. But this is not the Strip, the Sunset of Schwabs' and Scandia. This is the Sunset of bleak old shops and cafes. Here every penny must go for the fundamentals of life. And so, Echo Park, with its giant, still lake, becomes all things to all people.

On this mild, smogless June day, the whole neighborhood seemed to be out, feeling the kind of wealth of the soul that comes from being engulfed in sunshine and greenery. For fifty cents an hour, they rented boats and plowed the green waters of the lake along with the swans. Lovers walked hand in hand. Mothers wheeled their babies in strollers. Children frolicked noisily on swings and slides. Joggers trotted along the rim of the lake, getting their daily workout. Old men laid claim to one park bench from sunup to sundown. They idled this day away thinking of other, fuller days.

At the extreme north end of the park, two men entered a rest room. One was short, blond, and well-built, with eyes older than his 35 years. The other man was taller, powerfully built, with black wavy hair and a moustache.

The shorter man entered first and walked to a urinal. Moments later, the other man took his place at a urinal about five feet away. Nothing was said. Ten seconds passed. Then the taller man turned slowly until he faced the other. His Levis were open and his hand was massaging his erect penis.

The shorter man said nothing, quickly zipped his worn, stained Levis, turned and left. Thirty seconds later, the other man left, too. But outside he was confronted by the man he had tried to seduce and his partner.

"You're under arrest," he was told.

"What for?"

"Lewd conduct."

Officer Dick Bonneau, on loan to the vice squad from his regular job as a physical training instructor at the Los Angeles Police Academy, had just performed his last piece of police work for a month.

Venice

A young man walked into the bank on Santa Monica Boulevard in the beach community of Venice shortly after noon. He surveyed the situation, taking it all in: the number of people, the tellers, the supervisors, the security guard.

Suddenly, he pulled a .38 caliber revolver from his waistband, charged across the bank, vaulted the tellers' counter and screamed, "This is a holdup! This is a holdup!"

By reflex, a bank employee triggered a silent alarm. Its recorded message poured out of the squawk boxes in the Robbery-Hijacking Section at Parker Center, 20 miles away in downtown Los Angeles.

The officer in charge of that ten-man section was Lt. Frank Mullens, a 27-year veteran of the force. The unit has two functions: It is responsible for dealing with all bank robberies and all truck hijackings in Los Angeles. Truck hijackings were relatively rare, but bank holdups were increasing.

Mullens called the FBI, which has federal jurisdiction in bank holdups. The FBI, in turn, called the bank to verify the squawk boxes' report. It was true. The bank was being robbed.

By now, the man had ripped open a cash drawer and emptied its contents into a paper bag. He had also seized the bank manager and threatened to kill him if he didn't open the vault. The manager led the man to the vault, which was already open. The gunman grabbed a fistful of money packets and tossed them into his bag.

Three miles away, Mullens' closest team had been alerted. It was on its way. So were the FBI and all available patrol cars in the area.

The robber had now gathered about $1,400. He leaped back over the counter, and as he did, his gun accidentally went off. A bullet crashed into the ceiling.

Minutes passed. The first patrol car arrived. Then came Mullens's men. Then the FBI. But they were all too late. The man and the money were gone.

A few hours later, in another section of the city, another bank was held up. This time there was no shouting, just a note.

Again, the suspect got away. Mullens had to work overtime. Just his luck. Overtime, on his last day before vacation.

Hollywood

Officer Jim Murphy — tall, lean, and strong — looked like the kind of cop you'd want if you were in trouble. But Murphy wanted to maintain a low profile as he patrolled the Hollywood area this day, his last before vacation. He knew he couldn't consciously avoid trouble. No cop could do that. But he wasn't going to look hard for it either. He didn't want to risk another disabling injury.

His right shoulder still had to be pumped full of cortisone because of that struggle in Griffith Park two months ago. Murphy and his partner were one of twenty-four units assigned to the park over Easter weekend. The police were anticipating trouble from youth gangs. So they were caught off-guard when a huge man in his middle 40s plowed his new Cadillac through two rows of barricades and past a no-left-turn sign, which had been put there to keep cars out of the now-full parking lots.

The confrontation developed immediately. Murphy had taken his baton from the patrol car and had secured it in his ring holder. It was standard operational procedure. But it infuriated the man, who had already leaped from his car, and was now pointing at Murphy's belt and shouting. He wanted to know what the hell the baton was for.

Murphy told him to settle down. But the man grew angrier. He moved toward Murphy's partner, who was writing a traffic citation. The man crowded close. Too close. He was on top of the officer now, almost touching him. Murphy told him to move back. The man refused. He knew his rights, he said. He could stand anywhere he damn pleased. But Murphy knew the danger. Policemen have had their guns taken away from them in these situations.

"If you don't step back I'll have to search you," Murphy warned. Again, defiance. So Murphy moved in. The suspect pulled away. Murphy's partner asked if they should cuff him. Murphy said no; maybe he'd settle down. But Murphy was wrong. And at that instant, a simple traffic infraction turned into a felony.

The man swung at Murphy. Murphy reacted quickly, grabbing and spinning the man around in one motion and placing a restraining hold on his neck. But he made a mistake. He didn't use sufficient force. He didn't want to get too deeply involved.

He didn't want the hassle, the probable citizen complaint, the possible injury.

The man broke loose, and as he did, Murphy felt the pain shoot through his body. A ligament torn in his right shoulder. His left thumb dislocated.

Finally, after a brief scuffle, the man was restrained and arrested. Arrested for the seventieth-plus time in his life. And Murphy would be off-duty from mid-April to mid-May, 33 days recuperating.

And so, on this June day, Murphy drove the streets of Hollywood as though it were the last patrol. Trouble would have to find him. He wrote just one ticket. And then he was gone. He would not return to Hollywood Division for more than a month.

The Police Academy

Getting straight. That's what Sgt. Dick Clark was trying to do, both here at the Police Academy where he worked, and in his personal life.

The divorce was draining him emotionally and physically. The kids were constantly on his mind. Those two beautiful, innocent little girls. He wouldn't raise them. He wouldn't watch them grow day by day. It was excruciating. But there was no going back. He knew he couldn't live there anymore. And he'd promised himself that he wouldn't try over and over again. That was too damaging to him, to her, to the kids, to everyone involved.

Clark had to call his attorney and some friends who still didn't know he was going to be out of town for five weeks starting Monday.

He knew he needed the change of environment that Monday would bring. But even that had its drawbacks. It might mean he wouldn't be there when the two vacancies were filled in the unit he headed at the academy. His four-member unit was responsible for setting up simulated field situations for recruits — homicides, burglaries, rapes, family squabbles. The idea was for the recruits to make all their mistakes at the academy, not in the field, where a mistake could kill them or their partner or some innocent civilian.

Clark made a couple of phone calls and checked out possible candidates for the two slots. But when he left that day, nothing had really been accomplished.

Everything in his life seemed unsettled and overwhelming.

The answers. Where the hell are the answers? Sometimes, he thought, there just aren't any.

Recruitment Division

Frank Janowicz came to work early. He was feeling good. There was no doubt about it: He was in the best physical condition of his life. He'd worked hard to get there. And on Monday it was all going to start paying off.

He knew what to expect this day. Little work, more worried talk about possible cutbacks here at the Recruitment Division, and a going-away party, probably at lunch.

Janowicz went over some reports and talked to two female recruits. That was his primary job — to recruit women for the department and then to get them ready physically for the Police Academy's tough training program.

Lunchtime arrived, but there was no party for him. He'd forgotten. It was the lieutenant's last day. He was leaving the division for good — not just for three weeks like Janowicz. They were taking the lieutenant to lunch. What the hell, Janowicz thought. They're saving my party for later.

The afternoon passed slowly. More recruits came by to check on their progress. And there was more talk about cutbacks, about recruitment, about pay, about promotions, about women, about the weekend.

But there was no party.

Janowicz: "Maybe if there hadn't been so many things going on, maybe then they would have thrown me a going-away party. Nothing big. Just some coffee and cake and best of luck. But there was nothing. Nothing."

Finally, Janowicz went home.

Eagle Rock High School

Officer Chuck Foote wasn't your usual cop on campus. He wasn't there to arrest students for drugs or vandalism or knifings or shootings. He was there to teach them. And this Friday, he was ending his assignment, filling out report cards for the 142 students he'd taught that semester at Eagle Rock High School, and getting ready for five weeks' vacation.

Foote and twenty-nine other Los Angeles police officers from Juvenile Division were assigned full-time to teach at Los Angeles secondary schools. The cops taught the kids how the law applied to them as juveniles and how it would apply to them as adults.

Crime prevention. For Foote, that was what the class was all about. That was how he rationalized being in a classroom and not on the street catching criminals.

All semester, Foote was amazed at how naive his students

were, not only about the law, but about the men and women who enforce it. "Most of them are as dumb as clay," he said. "I just tried to dispel their misconceptions and myths."

One of their biggest misunderstandings was about police shootings. It grew, he figured, from *The Streets of San Francisco*, *Police Woman*, *Adam-12*, and all the other Hollywood-distorted TV versions of police life. Police work is dangerous and demanding, he told his students. But it is not the knock-down, shoot-'em-up adventure being fed into their living rooms every evening.

Foote told them that in his six-and-a-half years on the force — five of them on the street — he had never shot anyone. And he said it was highly unlikely that the average cop would ever wound or kill anyone during his entire career. His students were incredulous.

On appearance, if anyone should have been able to get through to these kids, it was Foote. He was 28, but could have passed for one of them if his hair were a bit longer. He was athletic, glib and easygoing. But had he reached them?

"I don't think I changed any minds," he said. "You aren't going to do it in one school year."

Kennedy High School

When Officer Pat Connelly first arrived at Kennedy High School in the suburban San Fernando Valley, the kids called him "pig," and squealed "oink-oink," sometimes to his face, usually benind his back. Like Foote, he was a cop treading on hostile territory.

His looks were no asset. Tall, gangly, his face pock-marked, his eyes distorted by thick glasses, Connelly was hardly a figure to command fear, respect, or awe by sheer presence.

That first day he told his students that he was proud to be a cop, and that before the semester was over he hoped they would understand why. He told them there would be role playing. That some students would play police officers and others would play witnesses and victims. It was then that the handsome black youth interrupted him, shouting from his back-row seat, "I won't play no pig. I hate cops. I smoke dope. I've committed crimes. I've been arrested. And I don't care."

Connelly's first impulse was to throw the kid out of class. But he wouldn't pass his problems on to someone else. He'd handle them himself. Besides, this kid was only saying what most of his students were thinking. Even the affluent whites, who more and more these days were brushing up against the law over drug abuse, alcohol, cruising, curfew violations and vandalism. He would reach this kid. He would reach every one of them. Or at least he'd go down fighting.

And so, for the next nine months, he worked hard to gain their respect and confidence. He told them about himself, about his athletic, academic and police backgrounds. He was one of them, he said. He, too, had lived all his life in the San Fernando Valley.

Connelly told them about the tensions and dangers of the job. About officer survival. About never knowing if the person he'd just stopped on a routine traffic violation might suddenly whip out a gun and cut him down. Cops had to be guarded and cautious, he said, because they never knew with whom they were dealing.

Other cops came in, too, and explained their jobs. And for the first time the students began to see policemen as human beings, not as the faceless, humorless, constrained men in blue who patrolled their neighborhoods. Connelly's wife, Joan, spoke to his classes and explained the terrible strain police work puts on a family.

Connelly told his students to relax and enjoy the class and learn. And Connelly learned about them, too.

As the weeks went by, he made it a point to sit down and talk to each of his 180 students individually. At first the students were wary, uncomfortable. Most of the talk centered on the class curriculum. But slowly the kids began to like the skinny, "funny-looking" officer. And they began to trust him. Many began coming to him with their personal problems. He became a confidant, a counselor.

Connelly decided to reach out further. He stopped eating lunch and taking coffee breaks with the other teachers. Instead, he strolled among the students during his free periods, introducing himself, getting to know them.

He spoke at assemblies and to other classes. He began coaching the cross-country and track teams. He invited kids to his house. And finally, many of those young people called him their friend. Even a handsome black youngster who had once told him, "I hate cops."

And now it was time to part. It was graduation day at Kennedy High School. For Connelly, it was a sad, emotional moment, and it deflated his enthusiasm for the vacation he would start as soon as the ceremonies ended.

The senior class president, Nancy Wilson, began recounting

her class's fondest memories. Midway through her speech she paused, glanced at Connelly for a moment, and then turned back to her vast audience, gathered in the football stadium.

"I want to take this opportunity on behalf of the entire class," she said, "to publicly thank a very special man who was not only a teacher, but a friend. It gives me great pride to thank from the bottom of our hearts Los Angeles Police Officer Pat Connelly."

With that, the 828 seniors of Kennedy rose and gave Pat Connelly a standing ovation. And more than 4,000 of their parents and friends stood and applauded, too. The ovation lasted more than two minutes.

Pat Connelly swallowed hard.

Then a feeling of joy swept over him.

By God, he thought. I really did reach them.

Sunday, June 13, 1976   The Police Academy

Sunday. Eddie Garcia had planned to spend it exactly as the Lord had suggested — resting. Heaven knew he'd need it. Rest was going to be a rare and precious commodity during the next three weeks.

Garcia was supposed to have the day off. But at the last moment they needed someone to teach cardiopulmonary resuscitation to the reserve class at the Police Academy. Garcia was one of the few qualified instructors. And so his day of rest turned into an eight-hour day of work.

Garcia — taut and wiry, a former high school and college sprinter, an expert in the martial arts and an ex-boxer — was a self-defense and physical training instructor at the Police Academy. Normally he taught recruits. But the Los Angeles Police Department was faced with severe budget restrictions, and there hadn't been a recruit class at the Academy in three months, since March.

With recruit training nonexistent, the slack was being taken up by reservists. They were coming through the academy at an unprecedented rate — two forty- to forty-five member classes at a time. And Garcia and the other P.T. instructors were busy training them.

Reservists. They come from all sections of the community, from all walks of life. They receive 10 days of training each month for six months. And then for at least 16 hours a month they are police officers in every sense but one. Pay. Because no matter how long or difficult or dangerous their work, they get only $10 a month.

It takes a special type of dedication to be a cop for less than a dollar an hour. Garcia knew this. And it made this Sunday go by a little more easily.

Monday, June 14, 1976, 8 A.M. The Police Commission

Sgt. Alex Shearer typed his monthly report, which detailed the cases he'd handled during May for the Police Commission. Shearer investigated people who needed police business permits. In Los Angeles, if you want to run a movie theater, massage parlor, auto rental, lockshop, pool hall, or any of about forty similar establishments, you need a background clearance from the police department. The city doesn't want former prostitutes running massage parlors, or former burglars running lockshops, or smut dealers operating theaters.

From experience, Shearer knew that more than 90 percent of the applicants for police permits were legitimate businesspeople who'd already invested a great deal of time, money and effort in their ventures. Their final obstacle was here — the vast, sometimes intransigent bureaucracy of the police department.

"You know," said Shearer, "some guys down here like to hassle these people a week or so . . . but end up having to give them the permit anyway. There's no reason for that."

Shearer's philosophy was simple: Cut the red tape and get those on the up-and-up into business as fast as possible. "My greatest pleasure," he reflected, "is to shave a corner here and there — all legitimately, of course — and get them going."

Alex Shearer is different from most cops. He calls himself a rebel and a liberal, two terms seldom embraced by his fellow officers. Yet Shearer is universally liked and respected on the department. Part of the reason is his dry sense of humor, quick wit and unassuming ways. But primarily it is because Alex Shearer is a good tough cop who's done it all in his quarter-century on the force.

"People ask me, 'What do you enjoy about police work?' I tell them, 'What I'm doing right now. Helping people.'"

"You know," he said, "I never really got a great deal of enjoyment from putting some poor fool in jail, unless of course he really deserved to go. I just don't like to hassle anyone."

Sgt. Shearer had to work this Monday morning to help himself. He hadn't quite accumulated enough overtime to qualify for the three weeks he'd need off starting this afternoon. Now he had it. He signed his report, handed it in, and headed for the Police Academy.

8 A.M. to 7 P.M.   The Police Academy

At the Los Angeles Police Academy, officers John Rockwood and Bob Jarvis were busy loading four motor homes with food, beer, soft drinks, water, propane, towels, shotguns, ice chests and other items needed for a three-week trip across the North American continent.

Rockwood and Jarvis worked at the academy as physical training instructors. But today their job was to pack the giant vans — three new $30,000 Vogue motor homes and a new but smaller Commander van.

Inside his small office at the academy, Officer Bob Burke, the department's athletic director, was worried. For the past three days he'd slept a total of six hours. Most of his waking hours had been spent working on a problem that still wasn't resolved. The three Vogues being feverishly loaded by Jarvis, Rockwood, and other police volunteers, and painstakingly equipped with radios by the department's maintenance section, could be snatched from them at the last moment. And the last moment was fast approaching. It was now noon. The Vogues or three replacement motor homes would be needed before six that evening.

At 1 P.M. the word filtered down: The Vogues were out. The supplies and equipment were removed and loaded onto the replacements. At 3 P.M. the Vogues were back in. The unloading and reloading began anew. At 4:30 P.M. the Vogues were out — this time for good. The final transfer began.

During the afternoon, as the tension and confusion mounted, other officers began arriving. By 3 P.M., they were all there, all fourteen. Dick Bonneau from vice, on loan from Training Division. Jim Murphy from Hollywood Division. Curt Hall from West Los Angeles Division. Alex Shearer from the Police Commission. Pat Connelly and Chuck Foote from Juvenile Division. Frank Janowicz from Recruitment Division. Frank Mullens from Robbery-Homicide Division. Bob Hickey from Hollenbeck Division. Dick Clark, Eddie Garcia and Rockwood, Jarvis and Burke from Training Division.

The men began to load their personal belongings into the vans. Shaving gear, toothpaste, toothbrushes, civilian clothes, magazines, books, running shoes, arch supports, cotton and nylon running socks, running shorts, running shirts, sweats and jockstraps.

At 5 P.M., only one of the vans was ready, but the men had to leave for the Los Angeles Coliseum. Police Chief Ed Davis, members of the Los Angeles City Council, representatives of the

Canadian government and police agencies throughout Southern California, the news media, friends and relatives were there for ceremonies to honor the fourteen men.

At the Coliseum, there were brief remarks from the dignitaries, a prayer, wishes of good luck, and then, at 7 P.M., with just two vans ready, it began. A 3,765-mile Bicentennial Relay of Goodwill, a run that would test fourteen men physically, mentally and emotionally for the next 21 days.

THE RUN

A relay of nearly 4,000 miles involving thirty people doesn't just happen. It took Bob Burke and his wife Sue nearly two years to map out the run. It took Burke and his businessman friend Bob Hogue more than a year to raise $17,343 to stage the run, and months to procure the four motor homes, pace car, public relations car, food, beverages and equipment to house, feed and move the team. It took public relations man Lou McClary and his staff nearly a year to coordinate the voluntary receptions along the way. And it was supposed to take the runners at least nine months of training — 60 to 70 miles of running a week — to prepare their bodies for the physical challenge ahead. Half of them were unable to do that because of job demands, injuries or personal problems.

But on June 14, 1976, at 7 P.M., after 22 months of preparation, it looked rather simple.

The LAPD track team was formed in 1963 by a veteran Hollenbeck Division detective, Toby Medina. It wasn't much of a team then — just two men, Medina and Bob Burke. But six months later, it increased its membership by 50 percent. Bob Jarvis joined.

Slowly over the years the team grew. The men entered AAU meets throughout California, competing as individuals. But none fared too well.

21

Then in 1968, Burke and a few of the other runners got an idea. Perhaps they'd be competitive as a team — a relay team. The idea was kicked around.

None of them was terribly fast, it was agreed, but all were strong and durable. So any relay they entered should be long and the course itself as difficult as possible. That way toughness, endurance, and perseverance would take precedence over speed.

And thus was born a new kind of relay. One in which each man would be required to run more than once over difficult terrain, under any and all conditions, and at least five miles at a time.

In 1969, the LAPD cross-country relay team was formed. Eight men, each man running five miles three times. Rules were drawn up and sanctioned by the AAU:

"The run will continue under any and all weather conditions.

"Regardless of injury, no runner will run less than five miles at one time. If a runner is forced to quit running prior to completion of his leg, the next runner will complete the fallen team member's leg and will also run his own. But when the injured runner's turn comes again, he must run or be disqualified.

"If the injured man is disqualified, every man will move back one leg and now your team consists of seven men for the duration of the race.

"If more injuries follow, then the same procedure will be used. This means that either team could finish the race with less than a full team."

In early 1969, the LAPD team challenged a team from the Los Angeles County Sheriff's Department. The race was from Los Angeles to San Diego, a distance of 125 miles. The LAPD won.

Then came a 500-mile race from Los Angeles to San Francisco against the San Francisco Police Department. The rules were changed for this and all subsequent runs to allow for 10-mile legs, more runners, and to permit each man to run as many legs as necessary to finish the relay. Again, the LAPD won.

Next came a race against the Compton Police Department from Compton to San Leandro in Northern California and back to Los Angeles, a distance of just over 1,000 miles. Once more, the LAPD won.

The LAPD then tried to line up a race against another department, established track club or university. But none would bite. The team had become invincible at the form it created.

So in 1972 the LAPD ran alone, this time 2,000 miles from

Tijuana to Vancouver. The performance gained the team a paragraph in the *Guinness Book of World Records.*

Two years later the team nearly doubled that cross-country relay record. Again without competition, the men ran from Washington, D.C., to Los Angeles, 3,881 miles.

Shortly after that race, Los Angeles was officially designated one of the Bicentennial cities. Its theme was sports. At the same time, totally independent of L.A.'s Bicentennial plans, Bob Burke was planning yet another run, this one from deep in Mexico to Canada.

As Burke gathered information and data for his run, eight policemen were shot to death in Mexico City. A month later a bomb exploded at the Mexican Consulate in Los Angeles. Burke decided that police officers from Los Angeles, running along the roads of Mexico, might not be safe.

At about the same time, departmental pressure was growing for him to involve the LAPD in the Bicentennial celebration. Finally the two ideas merged. He would shift the run. It would now be from Los Angeles to Montreal in honor of America's 200th birthday and the Olympic games. The Bicentennial Relay of Goodwill was reality — at least on paper.

Then the work began. First Burke and his wife mapped out a rough course — from Los Angeles to Spokane, then a hard right turn that would carry the team along the northern edge of the nation to Sault Ste. Marie, Michigan, into Canada, and finally to Montreal. They contacted eighty cities along the route, requesting detailed maps. Then for four months they plotted the mileage from city to city, every right- and left-hand turn, every minute detail. Burke got paid for only eight hours of work a day, no matter how many hours he worked. On the maps alone, he and his wife toiled every night, four hours a night, for four months.

Finally, in the fall of 1975, the maps were complete. The relay would be 3,765 miles, just short of the record set in the Washington, D.C., relay. A presentation was made to Chief Ed Davis. He was impressed. And he issued an order: "Bring in the number one P.R. team." That meant Lou McClary, a detective who had become the department's public relations specialist over the years.

McClary, a close friend of Burke's, would have two assistants, Sgt. Rich Wemmer and Julia Nagano of the department's public information section. Over a nine-month period they sent out more than a thousand letters, soliciting cooperation from government, civic and business leaders, and law enforcement agencies in the ten states and two Canadian provinces along the route. The public relations staff was able to estimate when the relay team would enter a particular town because Burke, using the D.C. run as a guide, had figured each man would average 75 minutes per 10-mile leg. On that basis, it was calculated that the team would reach Montreal at precisely 12:34 P.M. on July 4.

So Burke had a route, and the P.R. people were coordinating ceremonies and celebrations. All the team needed was money. Burke knew that would be no problem. He turned to the man he called his brother — his closest friend, Bob Hogue.

Hogue is a young Los Angeles businessman with connections throughout Southern California. Together with Burke, he solicited 90 percent of the money, food and equipment for the relay. "Without my brother," Burke said simply, "there would be no relay."

There was one other matter to be taken care of — the team itself. When Burke talks of the team he means everyone — the drivers, the trainer, the AAU official, the publicity people, the mechanic, and, of course, the runners.

All team members, with the exception of Lou McClary, were making this run on their own time — vacation time. The department's only contribution was to "allow" them to work overtime and then trade that time for days off.

The runners would travel in three vans. Five runners and two drivers each in Vans One and Three, four runners and two drivers in Van Two. The assignments were made by Burke. "The key is harmony," he said. "You can't put all the hotheads in one van, and all the calm guys in another. You can't put Hickey and Janowicz together. You'd have to take out the blocks and let them play. And you can't put Connelly and me together. We're two strong personalities and on a run like this, in a tiny little van, it just wouldn't work."

Van Four would be the support vehicle. It would carry a trainer, Sgt. Ron Kiser, who referred to himself as a doctor; a mechanic, Investigator George DeWitt; AAU official Andy Bakjian, who would sanction the run; and driver Charles Reese, an assistant chief of police.

Two men were permanently assigned to the pace car (appropriately enough an AMC Pacer) — Capt. Rudy DeLeon of Hollenbeck Division and Sgt. J.P. Nelson — although others would share the job. The car, dubbed "The Turtle," would follow the runners, relaying messages, playing their favorite music over a loudspeaker, giving them water and oxygen when needed, serving as their protector from cars, trucks and unfriendly animals, and furnishing encouragement and humor. The drivers of "The Turtle" would never travel faster than 10 miles an hour. And they would perform their task round-the-clock for three weeks. The job required incredible patience.

The public relations men, Lou McClary and Rich Wemmer, would serve as advance men — contacting the news media and coordinating the festivities ahead of the team. They would sleep in motels.

And finally there were the runners. Fourteen of them. They ranged in age from 28 to 54. They spanned the ranks from policeman-two to lieutenant. Their average time on the department was 11.8 years. Two of the runners nearly made it to the Olympics. A couple more had run in college. But for the most part, these men had started running after they had joined the department.

In concept they all knew what lay ahead. They would run through the poisoned air of big cities. The cold of the mountains. The inferno of the desert. They'd travel through the mosquito-infested forests of Minnesota and Michigan, the soggy hills of Washington, and the debilitating altitudes of the Angeles Crest, and Conway and Deadman's summits.

They would run in pain. Sometimes in agony. They would run on blisters and with sore aching muscles. They would run whether they were fatigued or fresh. They would run no matter the time, place or condition.

And per Burke's projection, they would have to maintain at least a 75-minute-per-leg average. Seventy-five minutes for 10 miles. Repeated at least twenty-seven times, every 16 hours, for three weeks.

How tough is that? Take your car and drive 10 miles. And as you do, note the slope of the road. Note the temperature, the humidity, the smog, the altitude. A runner certainly does. Then go to a high school track and try running one mile — just one solitary mile — in seven minutes and 30 seconds. Don't be surprised if you can't. Less than 5 percent of the population of the United States can. Then imagine running 10 miles at that pace. Ten miles at night, up a mountain. Then 16 hours later, straight downhill, your body absorbing thousands of pounds of shock with each step.

The U.S. Army, most professional football teams and most physical fitness experts consider a man to be in top physical condition if he is able to run one mile in under six minutes. Every member of the LAPD team could do that easily. And more than half were capable of running 10 miles consistently between 60 and 65 minutes. These men were in the top 1 percent of the nation physically.

But the physical aspect was only part of their challenge. Perhaps even more demanding was their new and foreign environment. For the next 21 days, these men would be torn from their normal routine — six to eight hours of sleep in a comfortable bed, eight hours of work, moments of solitude, leisure time, the comforts of home, the companionship of family and friends.

Their new environment began with a new time frame — a 16-hour day. Sixteen hours, because that was approximately the time between a man's 10-mile legs. And everything — everything — would revolve around those 10-mile runs. During their "day" — the intervening 16 hours — the men would grab as much sleep as possible. Usually about four and a half hours, in rare instances as much as six or seven — sometimes none at all. They would eat one meal. Do laundry. Write letters. Make phone calls. Read books and girlie magazines. Try to adjust their bowels. And treat or be treated for sore muscles, blisters, and an assortment of other aches and pains.

There was another major problem the entire team faced. Cops in a well-publicized run, moving across the country at all hours, under the most vulnerable of conditions, would be easy prey for fanatics. Burke had received a warning of such danger. The Department of Justice of Montana wrote a letter which said, in part, "The American Indian Movement (AIM) has stated it will blow out the candles on our centennial cake. Inasmuch as your mission of goodwill is directly related to the Bicentennial celebration we feel you should be made aware of potential problems on the Indian reservations . . . The Montana Highway Patrol has no authority on said reservations."

But the team was ready. The men had accumulated their overtime, run their miles, and psyched themselves up for what Chuck Foote had called "the adventure that lay ahead."

And they carried fifteen shotguns — a precaution against the peril to that adventure.

But there was one other threat — one from within.

The seeds had been planted in 1972, when the LAPD team went unchallenged on its Tijuana to Vancouver run. Before that, the runners had been united against opponents. But starting in 1972, without outside competition, they had turned inward, some competing against their teammates, others against themselves.

This internal competition hadn't mattered much on the Tijuana or Washington, D.C., runs because there had been few obligations along the way. It hadn't mattered what time they reached a certain town. The men could run as fast as they wished, battling the clocks as they always had.

But this run was different. This was supposed to be a relay of goodwill. This time the team was supposed to be at a certain place at a certain time. The commitments were staggering. In 21 days, there were at least 100 dates to be kept — breakfasts, lunches, dinners, interviews, proclamations and runs past every law enforcement agency on the route — a tribute built into the relay by Burke.

And yet most of the runners did not seem to view themselves as goodwill ambassadors. When they spoke of their goals on the relay, they spoke in terms of their running goals.

And therein also lay the peril to the Bicentennial Relay of Goodwill.

Reason — as well as rifles — would be needed to preserve the adventure.

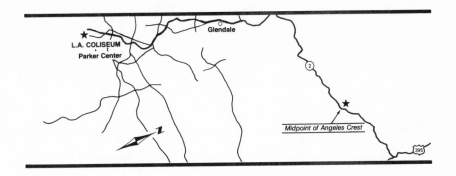

THE FIRST DAY
Monday, June 14, 1976,

Los Angeles Memorial Coliseum

Bob Hickey: *"I want the best overall average per leg on this relay."*

AAU official Andy Bakjian aimed his starter's pistol at the smoggy heavens and at precisely seven o'clock Monday evening, he squeezed the trigger. The Bicentennial Relay of Goodwill was underway.

With the Los Angeles Police Band playing the Olympic theme and sirens from patrol cars blaring, Sgt. Bob Hickey from Hollenbeck Division took the baton from Police Chief Ed Davis and darted from the L.A. Coliseum. Running along with him for the first mile was 13-year-old Sharon Hulse, one of thirty girls Hickey coached.

Hickey drew the honor of starting the relay because he had recorded the fastest overall time during the Washington, D.C., to Los Angeles run two years earlier. For thirty grueling 10-mile legs, across every imaginable terrain and in every weather condition, he had averaged 67 minutes per leg — a 6:45-per-mile clip. That is running, not jogging. And Hickey had done it every 15 hours for three weeks, because there were only thirteen runners on the team then. Curt Hall, a member of that team, recalled Hickey's performance with awe. "You would have had to be there to believe it," Hall said. "He was truly amazing. His endurance, stamina, strength . . . there was no doubt about it . . . he was number one."

Hickey's goal on this relay was to be number one again — to

record the fastest overall average time. He figured his toughest competition would come from Chuck Foote and Jim Murphy.

Nine of Hickey's girls would run along with him on his first leg. Each would run one mile and then all of them would join him for the final mile. Sharon Hulse, the first runner, was the best. Two days earlier she had set a new American record for 12- and 13-year-old girls with a 4:56.5 mile.

As Hickey and Hulse started down the Coliseum Drive, they were supposed to run between two rows of police from thirty law enforcement agencies from Los Angeles and Orange counties. The officers stood smartly at attention, saluting. Ahead of them were television cameramen and newspaper photographers who had positioned themselves for a perfect shot of Hickey, the honor guard and the Coliseum's Olympic torch.

But instead of running between the two rows of officers, Hickey ran behind them. As Hickey shot by, the startled cops turned halfway around, holding their salute. The cameramen dropped their equipment in disgust. And Investigator Lou McClary, the head publicity man for the run, dropped his composure and swore. Just minutes before, he and another officer had rehearsed Hickey, telling him exactly where to run. Hickey claimed no one had. But then Hickey often was in a world of his own.

Hickey's world. It was a world of energy and intensity. A world devoid of relaxation. A world of perpetual motion. Hickey's incredible energy seemed to take control of him at times, driving him, consuming him and often shutting him off from others. It made him a man of extremes who did things his way. Sometimes his way was humorous. Sometimes it was perplexing. But often it was annoying, maddening and even dangerous.

Running was a prime example of the latter. Two basic laws govern long-distance running — relaxation and concentration. Hickey was virtually incapable of relaxing. But as if to compensate, he was able to concentrate to the point of self-hypnosis. He could put pain out of his mind. Pat Connelly liked to say Hickey thrived on pain. But thriving on pain — thriving on any extreme — can be both a blessing and a curse. It had proved nearly fatal for Hickey in the 1972 run.

Hickey had just finished a tough 10-mile leg and handed the baton to Alex Shearer. As Shearer began running, he heard footsteps behind him. He thought it might be one of the UCLA doctors who were monitoring the runners' physical and emotional levels during the relay. No matter; Shearer hated anyone to run with him. He picked up the pace. But the footsteps continued. Shearer went faster. The steps pounded faster after him. Shearer began to stride out — about a 5:30-per-mile clip. So did the man behind him. Suddenly there was a commotion. Several of the runners and doctors had sprinted out and subdued Shearer's pursuer. It was Hickey.

He had locked in. Somewhere along those 10 miles Hickey had crossed into his own world. He was in "no man's land," as Bob Burke said later. After already running 10 exhausting miles, he was sprinting. His pulse, as monitored by the doctors, was more than 200 beats a minute. The doctors had shouted that he had to be stopped, or he would kill himself.

Hickey and Hulse moved past the derelicts and decay of Skid Row. Behind them was a caravan: the pace car, its two huge, blue lights whirling on top; a stream of black-and-whites, sirens wailing; two vans carrying runners and support people; and a bus transporting relatives and friends to the hand-off point.

Hickey wanted to run this leg in 60 minutes or better, which meant each of his girls would have to maintain at least a six-minute-per-mile pace. Most were capable of that. But two got tired running the hills in downtown Los Angeles. So Hickey told them to grab hold of his shorts — red-, white and blue-striped Bicentennial shorts he'd purchased especially for this relay — and he pulled them along.

At the end of his leg in Glendale, Hickey was clocked at 59:18. But there was a mixup in the distance. He'd run only 9.8 miles. Still, he was jubilant. "I feel great," he said afterward. "I could go again right now."

No one doubted he could.

7:59 P.M.

Alex Shearer: *"I want to run as fast as I can from point A to point B. I don't care about times."*

About a hundred well-wishers had gathered at the hand-off spot to cheer as Hickey passed the baton to Alex Shearer. "The old man of the highway," Hickey liked to call him. Actually Shearer wasn't the oldest man on the highway. He was 47. Frank Mullens, who would run his first leg early the next morning, was 54.

Shearer was in trouble from the start as he trudged through the streets of Glendale. The fumes from the motorcade were choking him.

He ran alone, as usual. The word was out: He didn't want any "ginky" people running with him. He didn't even want any "ginky" people waving at him along the way, although there was little that could be done to thwart a spontaneous outpouring of goodwill. And he didn't want to talk to any TV, radio or newspaper reporters, or any town officials, or any just-plain-folks along the way, either. His job was to run, he said. Not to fraternize. "I just want to get from point A to point B as fast as I can and get back in the van . . . and get a cold beer and a warm shower and write letters to my family and/or my loved ones."

Only Alex could get away with that type of attitude on a run of goodwill. But Bob Burke, coordinator of the relay, understood.

"You know, Alex and I have been receiving or passing off the baton to one another for 13 years — even before we had this kind of long distance relay. Alex signs on for one thing. Running. He doesn't like to go to receptions or talk to the press. If I really insisted, I think he would do those things. But then that would be depriving him of his feelings. And I wouldn't trade Al for ten guys."

Shearer is unique. "Cantankerous but lovable," his good friend Dick Bonneau says of him. Independent. Humorous. Candid. Creative. He's a complex man with a simple philosophy: "I don't like to be mediocre at anything I do. I like to be the best or pretty close to the best."

His innate curiosity drives him in many directions, making him a man of contrasts.

He loves the good life. He lives in a huge beachfront home with his wife of more than 20 years and the three youngest of their five children. He is a wine connoisseur (and had brought a small but well-chosen selection in the van), a collector of pipes, a voracious reader of English literature and poetry, a former theater arts major who still appreciates a fine play now and then, and an accomplished chess player.

And yet here he was — sweating and coughing in the heat, smog and fumes of Glendale. But this was Shearer, too. The physical fitness devotee who lifted weights, played a first-rate game of volleyball and basketball and who was a good long-distance runner even though he hadn't started until he was nearly 40.

He felt as if he were 80 as he reached the seven-mile mark. In addition to the fumes and the smog, altitude was becoming a problem. He ran up Foothill Boulevard and left onto Angeles Crest Highway. It was all uphill.

Two miles to go. He was exhausted. Sweat poured down his long, drawn face. He pushed himself forward.

One mile to go. His legs and chest ached. He was coughing with every step.

Half a mile to go. He spotted the camper and a huge crowd ahead, perhaps as many as 200 people. This was the last chance for friends and relatives of the runners and support people to root the team on. The curious from this affluent, well-manicured neighborhood had abandoned their televisions, drinks, and card games to join the throng. As Shearer handed the baton to Bob Burke, a cheer filled the warm night and the police band struck up, "California, Here I Come."

Just before his leg Shearer had joked with his campermates: "I can't believe I'm here again. I think God hates me." But at the end — 75 minutes later — he wasn't joking anymore. "It was brutal," he gasped. "The carbon monoxide, the altitude. I'm wiped out."

Shearer thought he knew what to expect. He was a veteran of these relays. The running was never the toughest part, he told himself. It was the living conditions. Those cramped vans. "That's gotta be the closest thing to being in prison," he told anyone who'd listen.

But it had been two years since his last relay. Perhaps age was making its move on Alex Shearer.

9:14 P.M.   The Angeles National Forest

Bob Burke: *"I want to keep all my legs under 70 minutes."*

Ever since the LAPD relay team was formed in 1963, it always seemed that Alex Shearer plodded up a massive mountain, only to hand the baton to Bob Burke, who would glide down the other side.

So there was a joke among the veterans of the team: Alex Shearer climbs the mountains so that Bob Burke can see the view. It was a friendly, ribbing remark. The men knew that in this type of relay, after twenty or thirty legs, everything would balance out. Each runner would get his share of uphill, downhill, heat and cold. Still, the joke was not funny to Burke.

Burke, along with his wife, had mapped out every mile of the Bicentennial Relay, just as they had mapped out every mile of every past run. But this time they made certain that Burke would climb the first mountain. And the first mountain was the mighty and defiant Angeles Crest. Thirty miles of pure hell.

Burke would be the first of three men to challenge it, so that the rest of the team could see the view.

Burke plowed his way up the Crest. Mouth open. Eyes straight ahead. Face expressionless. He was ready. He had come here countless times during the past nine months to rehearse.

Most runners view hills with the same singlemindedness that

a general might view a well-entrenched enemy — as an adversary to be leveled by brute force. But Bob Burke had developed a subtler strategy.

"I used to say, 'I'm going to beat you to death. I'm going to pound you into sand.' But I've been injured on hills . . . the last time about six months before the relay . . . right here on the Crest. So I've changed my approach. I realize they're not gonna move, that they've been sitting there for years. And they've had a lot of dumb guys try to run them and knock them down.

"So I just talk to them real nice. I say, 'You're a beautiful mountain. I'm just going to trespass on you for a while. Let me up easy. Don't hurt me. We'll be friends.'"

As Burke made friends with the Crest, Van One drove past him on its way to the next hand-off point. Dick Bonneau gazed out the window and nodded toward Burke. "You know," he said,"no ordinary man could do that. And when you realize you're not among ordinary men, it gives you a helluva boost."

For Burke, this run up the Angeles Crest was as much an escape as it was a challenge. The last month had been a tense, difficult one for him. The past few days had been nearly unbearable.

For once it had seemed the runners would travel in style and comfort. A Canadian firm needed three new Vogue motor homes. They were to be delivered to Montreal by the team.

But on Monday morning, just 10 hours before the firing of the starter's pistol, the Los Angeles bank that owned the Vogues announced it wouldn't release them without a note of credit from the Canadian firm. All day, frantic negotiations went on between the LAPD, the Canadian company, the bank, and even high-ranking Canadian government officials. But it was too late. The note could not be transmitted that quickly. Fortunately, during the afternoon, backup vans had been donated by police officers who had heard about the problem. Those smaller vans and their owners had saved the relay.

But there was still a lot on Burke's mind as he ascended the Crest. Van Two was only now leaving the academy after being equipped with radios. The condition of all these last-minute vans was suspect. And if that weren't enough, nearly $2,000 — about one-third of the expense money — was missing.

The ballyhoo of the city was far behind. Burke tried to relax. The night was cool. The sky filled with stars. Behind Burke, the pace car played his favorite music — bagpipes. It was eerie. One man running in the dead of night. A car trailing slowly, its blue warning lights illuminating the dark. And that music — that strange, plaintive music echoing off the canyon walls.

At the hand-off spot, Shearer and Bonneau were waiting for Burke with a cold beer and a towel. Burke handed the baton to John Rockwood, walked a few steps, and then took the beer. He had run his 10 miles in 82 minutes, 47 seconds. There was no way he could maintain his sub-70-minute goal on the Crest.

How tough was it, someone asked. "I really don't know," he said, his short red hair dripping sweat down his freckled face. "How do you say if it's tough or not? You're used to it mentally, and so what's tough to one person isn't tough to another."

His speech was soft and slow. This was a gentle warrior. He sipped his beer, wiped his forehead and added, "I enjoy it."

10:36 P.M.

John Rockwood: *"I want to keep all my times in the 70s."*

For the first six miles John Rockwood enjoyed it, too, despite the long, hard day he'd put in loading and unloading the Vogues and the backup vans at the Police Academy. "Every time I went up and down those stairs," he recalled, "I thought — there's another minute added to my first leg!"

Rockwood's first six miles were mostly downhill and he glided along, the night air cooling and refreshing him. But the Crest is deceptive. And just when Rockwood thought he had it licked, it turned. For his last four miles the Crest went up, gradually at first, then sharply. Rockwood's legs grew heavy. His breathing became labored. Despite the night air, sweat began to stream down his tanned face. His dark eyes seemed to recede. He was struggling.

Then at seven miles he felt it. Raw soreness on the bottoms of his feet and toes. All runners know the feeling, but as long as they keep running, there's nothing they can do about it. And Rockwood had to keep running another three miles. "Shit," he gasped. Seven miles into the first of twenty-eight legs, he'd developed blisters.

Of the fourteen men on the relay, perhaps none knew more about the physical pain and mental anguish of this type of running than Rockwood.

January 1971. John Rockwood was a member of the Compton Police Department. Bob Burke asked him if he could put together a team of ten runners that could race the LAPD from Compton to San Leandro in Northern California, and back to

Los Angeles — a distance of about a thousand miles. Each man would run ten 10-mile legs in turn. Rockwood said he'd get a team together and meet the challenge. It sounded like fun.

The Compton team had one month to prepare. That seemed like plenty of time. The men trained three days during the week, running between five and seven miles. And then on weekends they hit the beach. The plan was to run ten miles each day, Saturday and Sunday. Those would be the big workouts.

And so they'd be every weekend, a police car pacing them along the Strand from Manhattan Beach to Palos Verdes, five white and five black men running, and one of the blacks yelling, "The devil's after me . . . the devil's after me . . . he's making me do this!" And absolutely no one along the beach knowing what the hell was going on.

Usually at seven or eight miles half the team would quit running and plop into the pace car to drink beer while the others joked their way down the beach. The Compton cops were having lots of fun.

February 1971. The steps of the Compton Police Department. The race was about to start. The first leg would match the LAPD's Chuck Foote against Compton's Frank Aguilar, perhaps its best runner.

Aguilar stayed with Foote for the first mile. And that was the last time Compton saw the LAPD team. By the time Rockwood, Compton's second runner, got the baton, he was three miles behind Bob Burke, the LAPD's second man. And so it went. Compton falling further behind. But it was still lots of fun.

On Rockwood's second leg, he started to feel pain in both feet. When he looked down, his once-white running shoes were red. When he finished, his feet were covered with blood. Rockwood continued in the race. But another runner's testicles swelled as large as tennis balls and he had to drop out. So then there were nine, each still running 10-mile legs. With just a little less rest in between.

Rockwood's feet cleared up. But another runner developed severe ankle strain. He dropped out. There were eight. Two more runners became too exhausted to continue. There were six. Those six made the turn at San Leandro and headed back toward Los Angeles.

The race was only half over. And it wasn't much fun anymore.

The LAPD was now more than a day ahead of them, but the Compton cops continued. When they reached the Simi Valley, about 50 miles from the finish line at Los Angeles City Hall, an AAU official and the doctor who was monitoring the athletes concluded that two more runners were too fatigued to continue. So then there were four, each running every six hours.

Finally, mercifully, they finished — a full day-and-a-half behind the LAPD team.

"It was quite an experience," said Rockwood. "All of us thought we could finish it and maybe even beat the LAPD. But physically, some of us just couldn't do it. Mentally, some of us just gave up. We thought we were training for it properly, running 35, 40 miles a week for one month. But you have to run 75 to a hundred miles a week for a half-year or better. You have to watch your diet and work out.

"We thought we were training. But we were only playing. It was a disaster."

Shortly after that race, Rockwood decided to quit the Compton Police Department to join the LAPD. He would be giving up quite a bit: five years seniority toward a 20-year retirement and a good job working as a detective in robbery-homicide. But Rockwood was impressed with the LAPD: "I admired their professionalism as police officers and their spirit and camaraderie as competitors."

So Rockwood joined the LAPD in 1971, a rookie again. His goal was to work at the Los Angeles Police Academy as a self-defense and physical training instructor. In April of 1974 he made it.

But this night, the easy five-mile runs with recruits at the Academy were far behind. Rockwood was struggling up the Crest. He was coughing. His lungs were screaming for air. His legs felt dead. And he had blisters.

Rockwood was exhausted at the finish. The long day had taken its toll. And tomorrow would be worse. Tomorrow he'd face the Mojave.

11:53 P.M.

Dick Bonneau: *"I just want to be able to finish this thing."*

Officer Dick Bonneau was not ready for the relay. His life was in upheaval. He was selling his home, working on a number of critical projects at Training Division and applying for a new position on the vice squad. But more important, he was in poor physical shape. He had trained sporadically. For the first four months of 1976 he had run about 45 miles a week. It was a fair start. The next month he had trained hard — 10 miles in the morning, five in the afternoon every day. He was building.

But then Bonneau got his chance to work vice. And those long leisurely days at the academy that provided ample opportunity to run gave way to irregular hours of busting hookers, pimps, perverts, gamblers and gays.

The month before the run, he had trained only in spurts. In long-distance running a man's conditioning can vanish if he doesn't train for two or three weeks. That's what happened to Bonneau. He'd lost it.

But here he was, climbing the Crest at midnight. The final runner out of Van One.

Bonneau took the baton from Rockwood on a steep incline at about the 5,000-foot level. He felt dizzy almost immediately. His body wasn't getting enough oxygen. For two miles he ran uphill. Then the Crest leveled off and gradually sloped downward. But at about the five-mile mark, it made one final swing up. Bonneau would run those last five miles in perhaps the worst pain of his life.

Because of his lack of conditioning, Bonneau was working his muscles faster than he could supply oxygen to his system. Without oxygen, lactic acid was building up, causing pain and fatigue. In its advanced stages, lactic acid can cause severe cramps, or it can stop a runner completely. Bonneau hadn't reached that point, but he was hurting badly. His body was now starved for oxygen.

The 6,000-foot level. He pushed himself, talked to himself and convinced himself it was almost over. Only about a half-mile to go, he thought. He knew he could do that. But then the bitter reality came blaring through. The official word from the pace car: "Seven miles down, three to go, Dicky. Atta way to go, Dicky!"

"Oh, my God," he thought, "I'll never make it." Bonneau was laboring. Despite the crisp night air, the humidity was pronounced. He couldn't cool down. His perspiration system wasn't working correctly. Nothing was working correctly. Seven miles into his first leg, Bonneau felt he would never survive more than another two or three runs. He knew he could gut out the three miles remaining in this leg. Even with his muscles tightening and his body begging for air.

But what about tomorrow when he'd have to run in the suffocating heat of the Mojave Desert? And the following days when there'd be more desert and then mountains and extreme cold?

His mind wandered back to the academy. Back to his job as a physical training instructor. Back to what he'd taught the recruits about stress. And how running, especially long-distance running, could prepare a police officer to deal with the most trying circumstances.

Aside from its obvious physical benefits, running taught recruits to deal with pain, discomfort, fright, the unknown, themselves. There came that point during any long-distance run
when a runner could easily say, "I give up. I can't do it. It's too
painful." If a police officer could push himself beyond that, he
had conquered fear. And if he could conquer fear in one area, he
might not panic when faced with a life-and-death situation on
the job.

Bonneau wasn't about to panic, either, as he approached the
7,000-foot level. He had climbed nearly 2,000 feet in 10 miles.

When he finished, he knew he had to devise some kind of
strategy to get through the next three weeks. Otherwise he
would have to admit to his fellow runners what he was only now
beginning to realize himself — that he could become the first
member of an LAPD relay team ever to drop out of a cross-
country run.

It was about 1 A.M. when Bonneau handed the baton to Chuck
Foote. Van One had completed its first 50 miles. The other
runners had already showered and were relaxing or sleeping
when Bonneau entered the camper. He took a quick shower,
and then Van One shot up and over the Crest and headed down
toward the Mojave. It traveled 90 miles ahead, to where it would
pick up the baton for its next leg in about 11 hours.

As the days went by, those legs would seem to bunch up. And
the runners would feel that all they were doing was recovering
from their last run and preparing for their next one.

From 2:30 to 6 A.M. the runners and drivers slept. Burke and
Shearer shared a four- by seven-foot bunk in the back of the van.
Hickey and Rockwood shared an identical bunk on the right rear
side. Bonneau and one of the drivers slept in another such bunk
over the front section of the van. And one of the drivers slept on
the floor.

At six o'clock everyone woke up and ate. The runners had to
eat their one big meal between runs and at least three hours
before their first man took the baton. Otherwise there could be
severe stomach problems.

So Van One was the first camper to start getting acclimated to
its new environment. An environment of claustrophobic living
quarters, sporadic sleep, rushed meals and punishing 10-mile
runs.

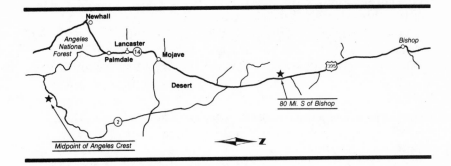

THE SECOND DAY
Tuesday, June 15, 1976

In late spring the Mojave is brutal. Motorists pass through it as quickly as possible, windows up, air conditioners on. Open the windows even a crack and the hot dry air explodes in the face. Walk outside for a moment and the body is enveloped in suffocating heat. Perspiration bubbles from under the skin. The mouth grows dry, the body weak. Five minutes here is too long. But nine runners would challenge this hell for more than an hour each this day. The fierce competition, innate in the team, would be set aside in the Mojave, replaced by a more basic instinct — survival.

Chuck Foote: *"I want to have a good overall average per leg . . . but I'm really here to have fun and enjoy my friends."*

Chuck Foote was the team captain, and, at 28, the only member of the team under 30. He would carry the baton over the summit of the Angeles Crest and start it on its journey to the edge of the Mojave.

As Foote climbed the last miles of the Crest, the follow car played "Sons of the Pioneers" music, his favorite. Santa Ana winds from the desert below met him head-on. But he traveled along easily, comfortably. His running was a mirror of his personality — smooth, even-paced, pleasant. His personality was the reason the other runners had elected him their team captain

41

two years earlier. And it was the reason Bob Burke had appointed him captain for this relay.

In most other groups Foote would have been unobtrusive. But among these men — some strong-willed and volatile, some insecure and petulant, some a bit eccentric — he was a standout. A standout because he was so relaxed, even-tempered and controlled.

Foote was also a fine runner. Not in the same class as Connelly or Murphy, but one who would lead by example, if not by strength of personality.

Foote did have the capacity to take charge, but more often than not, he seemed to be swept along by events and circumstances.

It had happened that way in college . . .

Foote had been an undeclared major for two years, "having fun," as he is fond of saying about so many aspects of his life. Finally, because he enjoyed government in high school, he decided to major in public administration.

It had happened in his college track career . . .

He'd been a fair runner in high school — a 4:55 miler and a 10:55 two-miler. But when he entered Cal State Los Angeles, he thought the competition would be too tough. So he didn't go out for track or cross-country. Then one day he picked up the school paper and checked the track results. He discovered he was fast enough. Foote competed for four years. His best time over the three-mile course was 14:39.

It had also happened in his career . . .

Foote was undecided about what he wanted to do after graduating from college in December of 1969. He'd been married for six months, and he had to make a decision quickly. A friend of his, an LAPD sergeant, happened to visit him one afternoon in late December. The conversation turned to work, and his friend casually suggested a career in law enforcement. "You're your own boss," his friend said. "You can ride around in a car and do as you please." Foote had never thought about becoming a cop. "But I said, 'It sounds like a lot of fun.'" And he joined.

It had happened as a recruit at the Police Academy . . .

In March of 1970, Foote and eighty other new recruits lined up to run the mile-and-a-quarter training course. The P.T. staff wanted to find out just how tough the new men were. An instructor yelled, "Go!" and the herd of young men moved out slowly, cautiously. Foote was baffled. He knew that a mile and a quarter was not a jog. So he flew past the herd and glided over the course.

Foote was on his way back just as the other recruits were

reaching the halfway point. When he crossed the finish line, a P.T. instructor screamed at him: "What the hell do you think you're doing? You ran the damn thing in seven minutes and two seconds." The department record at the time was seven minutes flat. The instructor thought Foote had cheated.

The next day the entire P.T. staff, including a captain and a lieutenant, gathered near the course to see if Foote's performance was a fluke, a deception or the real thing. This time Foote flew over the course in six minutes and 25 seconds. A new record.

Soon afterward Foote noticed a tall red-haired officer watching him every day as he ran with his recruit class. For weeks there was never a word from the man, never a change of expression. Finally one day Officer Bob Burke asked recruit Chuck Foote to join the LAPD's cross-country relay team, to run from Los Angeles to San Francisco against a team from the San Francisco Police Department.

The race was in June 1970, through the deserts of California. It was hot, miserable. But Foote never complained. He just ran as fast as he could. About midway through, the San Francisco cops quit, and then Foote and the others didn't have to run as fast anymore.

And so it went. Circumstances and events sweeping him along. Leadoff runner against the Compton Police Department team in 1971. Elected team captain for the Washington, D.C., to Los Angeles run in 1974. Appointed team captain for the Bicentennial run.

Over the years Foote did occasionally stop to evaluate the impact his almost casual choices had made on his life.

"You know," he reflected, "I think I got into police work the way most cops do. I backed in. But at some point I think most cops ask themselves, 'Is this what I really want to do?' A lot of guys say, 'No. Get me out of this ballgame. I'd rather lay bricks someplace.' But there's a lot of guys like me who say, 'Hey, this is a great profession.'

"As far as this type of relay running is concerned, you can't just drift into it. You have to understand what it is. Here you are, placed in a situation that says for 21 days you're going to be on the road living in a little shack on wheels. Get used to it, adapt to it, 'cause it's not gonna change. And you're gonna have to run every 16, 17 hours. Whether you like it or not. Whether you feel lousy or good. It doesn't matter. You gotta do it every 16 hours.

"You know, this whole thing is not just a run . . . it's an adventure."

Foote's first 10-mile adventure was nearly over. He was now

on the downward side of the Crest, running a smooth six-and-a-half-minute-per-mile pace. As he handed the baton to Jim Murphy, the follow car called out his time and mileage: 66:10 for 9.7 miles.

"Shoot," he said. "I wish they'd get it straight so I can run a full 10. None of these 9.7s. That means some other poor slob has to run three-tenths for me."

2:17 A.M.

Jim Murphy: *"I want to keep my image . . . I want the best average per leg . . . and the fastest single 10-miler."*

As a youngster in Southern California, Jim Murphy fell victim to Osgood-Schlatter disease, a painful, debilitating disorder of the knees which made physical activity impossible. One summer as a teenager, he spent three months in bed, his knees wrapped, his legs immobile.

Murphy was tall, thin and uncoordinated. And even when he overcame his childhood tribulation, he was unable to participate in any sport that required coordination and skill.

"If I slammed a car door, I'd dislocate my thumb," he said. "I was that kind of kid."

But during his high school years, Murphy began hiking between 20 and 25 miles every weekend into Southern California's rugged Castaic Mountains to dig for gypsum and oil shale in a mine he'd staked out. The hikes strengthened his legs. And finally, as a senior in high school, he decided to go out for track.

"The coach asked me what I wanted to run. I said I didn't know. He said how about the 880. And I said fine, what is it? And he said it's twice around the track.

"I got into running because it was the only thing I could do athletically. It doesn't take much talent. And I couldn't get hurt doing it. Anyone can develop into a distance runner. The thing is, very few people can develop into a great distance runner."

In high school, college and the service, Murphy was a mediocre distance runner at best. But during his three years in the army, he competed against some of the top American runners. And he learned from them.

"I thought running was just putting one foot in front of the other," he said. "But these guys were serious. They talked about conditioning and training techniques and different coaches." The coach mentioned most often was Mike Igloi, the Hungarian-born track genius who was training many of America's top distance runners at his track club in Los Angeles.

"So when I got out of the army I went to see Igloi," Murphy said. "I asked him to coach me. He asked what my goals were. And I said I just wanted to be a good runner." Although that was akin to an algebra student asking Einstein to tutor him because he just wanted to be a good mathematician, Igloi took Murphy on.

"I guess he saw raw potential . . . or maybe he was just fascinated by me," Murphy laughed. Whatever the reason, after one year of training, Igloi saw potential greatness. He concluded that Murphy had the speed, strength, rhythm and natural ability to be the best marathon runner in the world. And he even projected a time: two hours and 12 minutes. If Murphy could do it he'd be the first man to run that far that fast.

Igloi, whose innovations and scientific techniques had revolutionized long-distance running, was rarely wrong. But he hedged his projection with two qualifications: desire and absence of injuries.

Murphy trained under Igloi for 18 grueling months. Three, four, five hours a day. And then, during one three-week span in December of 1966 and January of 1967, it appeared he just might fulfill Igloi's awesome projection.

In mid-December he entered the Western Hemisphere Marathon in Culver City. Many of the top marathoners in the United States and Europe were there. Murphy, a virtual neophyte, finished fourth with an Olympic-qualifying time of two hours and 30 minutes. He was on his way.

Twenty days later — an incredibly short recuperative period — he was back. This time in the World Masters' Marathon in Las Vegas, Nevada. And this time the best long-distance runners in the world were there.

Igloi had plotted his student's strategy carefully. Murphy was to go out cautiously for the first thirteen miles, pick it up for the next seven, and then kick home in the final six. If Murphy did that, he would run the course in two hours and 20 minutes. He would also be on target for a 2:12 marathon. And more important, on schedule for a gold medal in Mexico City, 18 months away.

He ran the first 13 in 71 minutes, a blistering pace. And he wasn't even pushing himself. He was floating. He increased his tempo at 13 miles as planned, and glided along. Strong. Effortlessly. All the training, sacrifice and pain were paying off this scorching day on the roads around Vegas. He'd break 2:20. The speed, ability, rhythm and desire were all there.

He began to pick up the pace and shift into his final six-mile kick. His mind was prepared for the agony of those last six miles. But his body was not.

The side cramps came on slowly. At first he thought he could run through them, that they might even go away. But they grew worse. Murphy slowed down. It didn't help. He struggled on. The pain became excruciating. He massaged the aching area, altered his breathing, did everything he could. But there was no relief. He managed to make it to the finish line in the respectable time of two hours and 30 minutes. He finished tenth. Tenth in the entire world.

During the next six months he trained five hours a day, seven days a week. It was torture. But exquisite torture, for he still visualized that 2:12 marathon and gold in Mexico City.

Murphy doesn't remember exactly when he first felt the pain in his knees. But he sensed this was different from the natural pain he'd experienced as a long-distance runner. He was right. This was bursitis. The doctors told him there was little they could do. So he tried to overcome it himself. He altered his running style, but that only compounded his problems. In addition to bursitis, he developed hip problems.

Murphy backed off. Cut his training. Eased off on competition. But nothing worked; he was in constant misery. Finally in June of 1967 he'd had enough. He quit.

A 2:12 marathon. First in the Olympics. The best in the world. These would remain bittersweet memories of what might have been.

Most good athletes have a certain aura of confidence about them. They are proud of their bodies and how they perform. They realize they can do things that few people can do. And above all, perhaps, they thrive on society's romantic view of sports heroes. An athlete can come away from all that with a strong, healthy self-image. Or he can emerge vain, self-centered, egotistical.

When Jim Murphy joined the Los Angeles Police Department, there were many who thought he fit the latter description. One of them was Chuck Foote: "I've known Jim five years, and I've always felt he thought he was better than everyone else. And not just athletically." Another was Pat Connelly, himself a world-class runner in the mid-sixties. "I'll never forget his first day as a recruit at the academy," Connelly recalled. "I was in the P.T. office. And he was outside, telling the other guys, 'I ran this, I ran that.' And someone asked him if he knew Pat Connelly. And instead of saying, 'Yeah, I know Pat; we ran a lot of races back in the sixties,' instead of saying that, he told them, 'Yeah, I know him. I beat him here and I beat him there . . .'

"That was his nature. No humility. Always talking about himself. It was irritating. And the guys took offense to it. In fact he almost didn't make this relay because the guys were worried about his personality, about his inability to get along."

Murphy's personality was on Bob Burke's mind, too, shortly before the run.

"I sat down with Jim and talked to him," Burke said. "And I told him the guys are very proud that you are going to be part of the team because of your ability and your class. You're world class. But you, in turn, must think highly of them, too. Most of us never even competed in high school track.

"But I guarantee you at the end of this relay, you're going to be proud of them. And you're going to return to your Santa Monica Track Club and see those tremendous athletes and know that they could not do this."

Murphy had joined the Santa Monica Track Club in 1971, shortly after he came on the department. During his first week at the academy, he had shattered Chuck Foote's mile-and-a-quarter record for recruits. That seemed to release his old competitive juices, and Murphy, now in his early thirties, had decided to return to distance running. He began training under Joe Douglas, the successor to Mike Igloi. And he flourished.

"Douglas just hit on the right combination," Murphy said. "His workouts were less physically demanding than Igloi's. And my body was more mature. I began to do things I'd never done before."

Indeed he did. During 1975 and 1976, Murphy set American records for his age group — 35 years and older — in the mile (4:24.7), 3,000-meter, and distance medley relay. He began running every distance from the mile to the marathon. And with the exception of 10,000 meters and the marathon, he recorded personal all-time bests at every distance.

But once again he developed a serious ailment — tendinitis. This time, however, he was able to keep the inflammation under control by icing down the sore spots.

Ailments and injuries have plagued Murphy throughout his athletic career, throughout his life. And they've created a certain timidity in this big, powerful cop. That was the reason he was so cautious during his last day on the job. And that was the reason he was still worried about injuries going into the run.

A couple weeks before the relay his coach had taken him off the track and put him on pavement to toughen his feet. He and

Murphy were concerned about blisters. Murphy had a history of them. And because of his long layoff after the Griffith Park scuffle, the heels and balls of his feet were more tender and susceptible than ever before.

Murphy prayed that he'd stay sound, not only for the obvious reasons, but because running and competition had become his way of being accepted, of proving his worth to himself and others.

Acceptance. That was the most compelling factor for Murphy on this run because, despite his reputation and skills, he was a mere rookie on the team; he felt like an outsider. He wanted to become part of the team.

He hadn't helped matters himself since he'd qualified for the run. He attended the team's meetings only after constant goading by Pat Connelly and Bob Burke. He never trained on the hills of the academy with the other runners. Instead he trained "uptown" with the exclusive Santa Monica Track Club, under one of the best coaches in the world.

He'd refused to listen to any of the experienced LAPD runners, who tried to prepare him for the relay. They warned him that this was different from anything he'd ever done before. But Murphy only laughed. He'd done it all, he told them. His teammates finally gave up.

Outwardly Murphy stayed aloof. Inwardly he craved acceptance. But he'd win acceptance his way — by being the best. His goals were clear: He wanted the best overall average per leg and the best single 10-mile leg. "I want to keep my image as the best runner," he said simply.

It was cool and clear on the Angeles Crest as Murphy waited for Chuck Foote to hand him the baton. Murphy had checked with the pace car drivers about the terrain ahead. They'd told him the first two miles would be uphill and the rest down.

So he went out hard. He would bomb the first two, he decided, get a good time going and then blast home the last eight.

But he was to learn his first of many lessons about this type of running: Don't listen to anyone's description of what's in store for you.

As planned, Murphy went out hard on the first two miles. But the road kept twisting upward. Three miles. Four miles. Five miles. Still up. He was getting tired. And frustrated. When would it end? He ran the first five in 35 minutes and 15 seconds. A good time, considering the terrain. Finally after five miles, the promised decline. Murphy exploded. He lifted his long muscular legs, swung his arms and went full-throttle out. He ran the last five miles in 29 minutes and 30 seconds. An extraordinary pace.

When he finished he felt good and strong. He'd done it. And just wait until he got some flat land. Say around seven at night. After a good rest.

He was the best runner. His image was intact. Jim Murphy was on his way to acceptance.

3:21 A.M.

Dick Clark: *"I promised myself if I started I'd finish – even if I had to walk or crawl."*

Dick Clark entered the team through the back door. But it shouldn't have been that way.

A grandfather clause in the bylaws of the team states that if a runner participates in one relay, he automatically qualifies for the next one. Clark was a member of the LAPD squad that defeated the Compton Police Department so decisively in 1971. But he had fallen out of favor with Bob Burke, the man who decided all issues relating to the team. It was Burke who set up the grandfather clause, and it was Burke who ignored it.

Clark said two incidents did it. The first occurred after the Compton race, when Police Chief Ed Davis posed for pictures with the runners. In one photo, Clark made the mistake of putting his hand on Davis. "Somebody told me that pissed Burke off," Clark said. "I didn't know my place or something."

Despite that, the grandfather clause held for the Washington, D.C., to Los Angeles run in 1974. Clark was set to go. Then he was assigned to undercover work, a delicate assignment. There was no way he could run on a highly publicized relay for the department and work the undercover detail. So he turned in his sweats. And Clark believed that, along with the picture-taking incident with Chief Davis, poisoned his relationship with Burke.

True or not, when the Montreal run was set, Clark wasn't on the team. Some of the runners, including Pat Connelly, reminded Burke that Clark was an ex-member and that under the grandfather clause he should get a position on the team. Burke said no. Clark would have to earn a spot.

Two positions were open. Three men tried out: Clark, Jim Murphy, and Eddie Garcia. The test was two 10-mile runs three hours apart. It was January, but it was hot.

Clark knew that Murphy was a world-class runner. And he knew Garcia was a former sprint star who had made the transition to long-distance running. Both were better 10-milers than he. But he was going to try to psych them. His plan was to stay close to them in the first 10-miler and then perhaps scare them into overextending, panicking, maybe even injuring themselves in the second race.

The first 10-miler wound through the streets of the San Fernando Valley. The mercury was pushing 90. And by dogged determination Clark hung in. Murphy and Garcia pulled ahead of him early and ran together. But Clark set a pace and maintained. And after the first 10-miler he was only 45 seconds behind them.

They rested. Three hours. Clark tried to appear rested, relaxed, confident. More psych. The trio set out again. This time from Griffith Park to the Police Academy. The heat was still intense, the smog nearly unbearable, the pace brisk. Again Murphy and Garcia sprinted ahead. And again Clark set a pace and stuck to it. He was 100 yards behind them. They looked back at the five-mile mark and there he was, 100 yards away. Waiting. Stalking. Psyching. Six miles. Seven miles. Eight miles. The same scene over and over. Murphy and Garcia ahead, periodically glancing back. Clark chugging behind, waiting for the panic, the fatigue, the injury. If it happened he was there to take advantage. To grab his rightful place on the team.

Murphy and Garcia reached the top of the road that leads to the Police Academy. They looked back one last time in disbelief. Despite their blistering pace, there, 100 yards below them, just beginning the final incline, was Dick Clark.

There was no way he could beat them now, but he had done everything in his power to try. Murphy and Garcia would join twelve other experienced runners on the Bicentennial Relay of Goodwill to Montreal. Dick Clark would be an alternate.

Over the weeks, Clark kept in touch with Burke. There were often rumors that this runner or that runner was going to drop out. But nothing happened. Clark's training had all but ceased. He was out of condition. He had a terrible, nagging cold. He was going through a painful divorce. He was having trouble sleeping.

It was one month before the run. Clark was serving as narrator, actor and technical adviser on a police training film. He had toyed with an acting career and had done some modeling, both commerically and for the police department. It seemed a natural. He was tall, dark and handsome — a walking cliché. But Clark was also bright, articulate and witty. And he was tough. A former head of physical training at the academy and a certified expert in police defensive tactics. He was going through his triple acting-narrating-advisory role when he was called to the telephone.

"Hi . . . this is Bob," the voice greeted him. "I've got some bad news for you." But Clark sensed immediately that the news wasn't bad at all.

He was going. One of the runners had dropped out — too many personal problems. "Shit, I can't believe it," Clark thought. "After all the shit I've been through. After thinking about those guys running to Montreal without me. About me having to make the damn team. And then not being able to do it. And now this."

Are you in shape, Burke asked. Clark lied: "Yes." But it wouldn't be a lie, he told himself. Whatever it would take, he'd be ready. Burke was relieved and happy. Damn him, Clark thought, reflecting on how Burke had slighted him earlier. "He was in trouble and he needed a replacement. He knew I would do whatever it took to make the run."

Clark had one month to get himself ready. His primary goal was to condition his cardiovascular system. His legs were strong. His mental approach was, too. At least he knew what to expect.

But Clark had a terrible chest cold. And it's tough for a runner to build his cardiovascular system when his lungs aren't working properly. So Clark loaded up on antibiotics. And he ran. It took him one week to build up to 10 miles. That first weekend Pat Connelly talked him into running 15 miles through the San Fernando Valley and then up to Mulholland Drive. The run annihilated him. It was another week before he fully recovered. Two weeks down, two to go. The hell with coaching, Clark said. He decided to run on his own schedule, at his own pace. "Run comfortable — run within yourself," is how long-distance runners explain it. And so he did. But in this case it didn't work because he usually felt comfortable running only seven or eight miles. And that wasn't enough.

Finally, 10 days before the relay, a realization hit him: He'd have to run with the cold, and he'd have to increase his miles. He got up to 10 miles again, then overextended to 13, 15.

Clark was ready physically. But just barely. He had no time for that critical period of confidence-building, overdistancing, of proving to himself that he could make it. He wasn't sure he was ready for a really tough 10-miler if it came early.

And so, as he ran down the Angeles Crest, he was hoping that he'd have time to condition himself before he hit the leg that right now could break him. He prayed for time.

Clark had a sideache and cramps, but most of his run was downhill and he got caught up in the excitement. He picked up the pace. He pounded down the mountain. His calves started to tighten. But he went faster and faster. And then with about 100 yards to go, he lifted his knees, swung his arms, and sprinted. Like a damn fool, he sprinted. When it was over he felt as though someone had pounded both calves with a sledgehammer.

"How stupid," he said. "Twenty-six legs to go, and I try to ruin myself on the first one."

The follow car called out his time: 67 minutes.

"I shouldn't have done it," he said. "But the excitement of the moment and those clocks. They make runners do foolish things."

Clark knew he would not be so foolish again. "I'm not a fast runner," he said. "My job is to run consistently and finish 10 miles — to heck with times. I promised myself that if I started this relay I'd finish. That every mile assigned to me would have my name on it at the end . . . even if I had to walk or crawl. And that's what I'm gonna do."

4:28 A.M.

Frank Janowicz: *"I wanna be in the top five."*

There is nothing subtle about Frank Janowicz. It's all on the surface. His loves and hates, wants and needs, anger and tenderness. He's a man who never learned to be discreet. If he has a fault, that is it.

He was a star football, basketball and baseball player at Mt. Carmel High School in South Los Angeles. He had a tryout with the Dodgers. Played army and college football. And had aspirations to go pro.

He came on the department in 1970 weighing 190 pounds. But he lifted weights. Six months later, job jitters had turned him into a compulsive eater and he gained 60 pounds. He was powerful, intimidating.

When he started jogging in 1972 he looked like Gulliver among the Lilliputians. And even now at 170 pounds he looked out of place — too big, too strong, too awesome to be a cross-country runner.

Janowicz is ruggedly handsome. Dark, curly hair. Square jaw. And eyes that seem to have a life of their own. Dark. Expressive. These are the eyes of Rasputin. But Frank Janowicz is no monster. There is a streak of violence in him, yes. And the eyes express it. But they also express his love and pain and determination.

There is no better way to know Frank Janowicz than to listen to his own story:

"I'm an athlete-cop. I know I'm different from the average policeman. I'm doing something very few people can do. And I walk proud because of it.

"Being a cross-country runner is a big thing. A lot of these guys won't admit it. But anybody who runs cross-country has got to have a big ego. If they don't, then they're a fool. Nobody in his right mind would punish their body for nothing.

"What do I get out of it? It really helps my ego. Guys respect me. Out of 7,000 guys on the department, I bet 5,000 know my name. It's like being compared to Chief Davis. I'm in the same boat, 'cause they say: 'He's a runner.' And that makes me in a very special elite group.

"The best way to explain it is you're like a starlet. You're like an idol. They may not respect you because of the fact that you're a police officer. But they have to respect you for doing something that's almost impossible. Very few people can do what we're doing.

"I like the recognition, but I work for my recognition. I've trained nine months for this, the longest I've trained for anything in my life. I got up every morning at five o'clock, Monday through Friday, for nine months and ran 10 miles. If I could study the way I train, I'd be a straight-A student. It takes a lot of hard work, a lot of sacrificing, a lot of dedication. Like Chuck Foote says, 'A lot of dumbness.'

"This is a race. We're running against each other. I was number six (in overall team average) on the last run. This time I wanna be in the top five. It's expected of me. I psych myself up. I say, 'I'm gonna run these guys into the ground.' I make believe I'm competing in the world Olympics."

Janowicz wanted to psych out his competition early. And he saw an opportunity on his first leg. It was nearly all downhill. And so, with the pace car playing his favorite Johnny Mathis love songs, Janowicz thundered down the Crest — violating every principle of long-distance running.

On an intellectual level he knew how he should run: "Relax your entire body. Then just make believe you're walking fast. Increase your tempo. Let your legs do all the work. And you'll get some fast times. Just concentrate and relax."

But Janowicz didn't follow any of his own advice. Out of control, working his upper body and arms like a sprinter, he ran his first mile in 4:50, the first five in 27:30. A tremendous pace. But his head was rolling, his arms were much too high and his feet were pounding, pounding, pounding. His upper legs absorbed incredible shock. When it was over, he'd run 9.8 miles in 56 minutes and 40 seconds. Only one other leg during the entire relay would be run faster.

Janowicz could barely walk afterward. His thighs were sore and his calves were tight. He wouldn't recover for days.

"I ran stupid," he said later. "I was thinking more with my ego than with my mind."

Janowicz was suffering. But he would continue to run with his ego until circumstances would dictate that he could do so no longer.

5:24 A.M.

Bob Jarvis: *"I just wanna keep 'em all in the 70s."*

Janowicz charged out of the hills and handed the baton to Bob Jarvis, the first runner out of Van Three. Janowicz had completed the conquest of the Angeles Crest. Jarvis would be the first runner to challenge the barren desolation of the Mojave. It was 5:30 in the morning. Cool and quiet. Rolling hills ahead.

Janowicz rejoined Van Two, which now sped ahead toward Four Corners, 75 miles up Highway 395. There the drivers and runners would sleep about three hours, eat a hearty breakfast and get ready for their second leg late that afternoon in the desert heat.

Meanwhile, at the edge of the Mojave, Jarvis had set a comfortable seven-minute-per-mile pace for himself. Jarvis — compact and powerful, with a youthful vigor and appearance that belied his 44 years — had been a cop for more than two decades. Four years in Milwaukee, 17 in Los Angeles.

He had shared a patrol car with Joe Wambaugh during the Watts riots in 1965 and shot a man. He was knocked unconscious during the Century City riot of 1967. And since 1968 he'd worked as a physical training and self-defense instructor at the Los Angeles Police Academy. He was the perfect image for recruits — tough, conditioned, confident. A cop's cop.

He'd been an athlete all his life. A sprinter in high school and a star football player in high school and college. He'd been scouted by the pros as a possible defensive halfback. He was reigning judo champion of the LAPD. One of the original members of the department's cross-country relay team. One of only three runners to participate in every LAPD relay since the team's inception in 1967.

And yet . . .

"If it had come right before we left — and I'd had a really good offer — a part that woulda maybe changed my entire life — then I woulda backed out of this run."

If Frank Janowicz wanted to be known as an athlete cop, then Bob Jarvis wanted to be known as an actor-cop. And ultimately as an actor only.

He grew up in Milwaukee watching Bogey and John Wayne and vowing to himself that someday he, too, would "do those things."

In 1970 he got his first break. Joe Wambaugh, who knew of his acting aspirations, asked him to play a part in the movie version of *The New Centurions*. Jarvis jumped at the chance. He was typecast as a physical training instructor. It was a start. Soon Jarvis landed roles on *The Rookies*, *Police Story*, *Police Woman*, *Joe Forrester*, *Medical Story*, and *SWAT*. He even appeared on a soap opera, *Days of Our Lives*. Most of his roles were small. But the work was steady, and he was hopeful about the future.

"I like being a cop. But I'm getting into a whole new career. I want to get my 20 years in, retire, and then get into acting full-time, providing the door's open. Otherwise, I'll stay on the department. But one of these days I'm gonna get a big break. I know I am."

Jarvis finished his 10 miles in 69 minutes. He was a little tight. But it was nothing serious. He showered, carefully styled his hair with a blow dryer, dabbed on some aftershave lotion and then relaxed.

6:33 A.M.

Pat Connelly: *"I'd like the best overall average, but I'm not as strong as Hickey or Janowicz. I'll settle for the fastest leg."*

"I ran in high school and college. I ran for the Southern California Striders. I ran on a U.S. team that toured Europe. I ran in the Olympic trials in the 10,000 meters and the marathon.

"But I'd rather tell people I'm part of the LAPD relay team than any of my past achievements. I would have quit racing long ago, just enjoyed it as a hobby — but there is something about doing this that just fills me with pride."

More than anything in his life, Pat Connelly wanted to be a cop. His love affair with the department began in 1965. It took him six years to consummate the relationship.

In 1965, Connelly was working at Hughes Aircraft Company coordinating an assembly line. He was also sharing an apartment with an old college fraternity brother, a policeman in Hollywood Division.

Through his roommate he began to meet a lot of policemen. "I was fascinated by their work, their lifestyle. I liked to drink with 'em and hustle girls with 'em. And one day I decided I wanted to join the LAPD."

Connelly was 27 when he applied. He passed everything — except the physical. His eyes were bad. Twenty-forty uncorrected. As far as the department was concerned, he might as well have been blind. Connelly was shattered. "Have you ever wanted something and couldn't have it? Something just out of your reach? It makes you want it even more. That's the way I felt about becoming a cop. I wanted it desperately."

So desperately he decided to settle for second best. He'd become a reserve officer. The requirements weren't as stringent and the pay was nil. But he didn't care. He wanted to be a cop — any kind of cop. "My reasons weren't the most noble. For me it was the badge, the uniform, the authority, the respect, the prestige, the gun. Stop a guy on the street, then go down to the beach and hustle a gal. I don't care what most policemen tell you. Those are the main reasons they join. Then of course the honeymoon wears off. And either it's a happy marriage, or it dissolves. Me, I developed a real love for the job."

But in 1965 Connelly was simply infatuated. He became a reserve officer, hoping that someday the department would change its requirements and allow him to join full-time. Reservists are required to work at least two eight-hour shifts each month. But Connelly worked eight hours each Friday and Saturday night and every day of his vacation. He got $10 a month, no matter how many hours he worked.

In 1968, Connelly's life took a number of turns. He got married, was assigned to West Valley Division, where he met a watch commander named Frank Mullens, and struck up a friendship with his old physical training instructor, Bob Jarvis.

Jarvis knew Connelly's track background. And one day, as they were jogging at the Police Academy, Jarvis asked Connelly if he'd coach the LAPD runners who were preparing for the California Police Olympics. Connelly said he'd love to.

The following year he coached the team for its first long-distance relay, against the Los Angeles County Sheriff's Department. Connelly devised the training schedule. He got the runners onto asphalt so their bodies could adjust to the pounding and their feet would toughen up. He put them on longer distances and worked on their endurance and speed. And the LAPD won.

By late 1969 Connelly was getting more involved with regular policemen. "Burke, Mullens, Jarvis and my other friends tried to help me get on the department, but nothing worked." His eyes were the obstacle, but Connelly had another problem. His wife, Joan, didn't want him to join. "She was afraid I'd get hurt or killed," he said. "She didn't want to sit home every night and wait."

In early 1970 Connelly began to train the LAPD runners for their second relay — this one against the San Francisco Police Department. Two months before the run, Bob Burke came up with a surprise. "He asked me if I wanted to run. Not just coach — run. God, I was thrilled. I wasn't a regular cop. But I met the requirement. I was a sworn peace officer."

Connelly was the second runner out. When he got the baton in West Los Angeles, the LAPD was nearly a mile behind.

"I'll never forget it," he said, "I was so high, my feet never touched the ground. I passed the San Francisco runner about two miles into my leg. Twenty-five police cars were at that corner. Their sirens were on, red lights flashing, everybody cheering as I went by. That was the greatest thrill of my life."

Connelly ran that leg in a blistering 53 minutes, and the LAPD easily won the relay. But perhaps most significant for Connelly was that following the race, his wife began to talk to the wives of police officers. And she discovered they didn't sit at home worrying, that they went about their own lives with the realization that their husbands were doing something they wanted to do.

Two weeks after the run Joan Connelly told her husband, "Go ahead and take the eye test again. I hope you make it."

So once more he tried. But once more he failed. Then he got an idea. "I memorized the chart," he said. "And I went back and read 20-20. The doctor signed me over to personnel."

But even that wasn't the end of Connelly's battle. For seven long months he waited for the department to summon him. Nothing happened.

"I was upset and depressed. I told Joan I was going to start looking for another career."

Then in November of 1970 he got a postcard: "You are assigned to class 1270 at the Los Angeles Police Academy."

"I nearly cried," he said. "I'd finally made it. I became a policeman that day." Connelly's struggle was over.

But this day in the Mojave, his struggle to Montreal was about to begin.

Joan Connelly was waiting with Pat at the hand-off point as Bob Jarvis approached with the baton. Joan was the only wife along on the relay. She, Connelly, their two young daughters, and Mike Nocita, a friend waiting to be ordained into the priesthood, were traveling in the Connellys' camper. They'd go as far as Nevada together. Then Joan, the kids and Nocita were to head home, and Connelly would become a resident of Van Three.

Connelly ran his 10 miles with Nocita. The terrain was flat. The desert air was still and cool. They ran a relaxed seven-minute-per-mile pace, finishing in exactly 70 minutes.

7:43 A.M.

Frank Mullens: *"I want to average 75 minutes per leg."*

Frank Mullens was the oldest member of the team (54), the highest-ranking member (a lieutenant), and the senior member (27 years on the force). He began running in 1968 at the age of 46. The man who got him started had just handed him the baton — Pat Connelly.

Mullens had played baseball since he was a kid in Burbank. He'd played in high school and in the semipro and professional ranks. And he was still playing for the LAPD in 1968 when he suffered a severe back injury. That ended his baseball days.

What can a 46-year-old has-been baseball player do to keep in shape, he asked Connelly one day. Connelly, a runner all his life, had an obvious answer: run. He told Mullens to get a complete physical. Mullens did. He passed. And the training began.

"It's going to be simple," Connelly assured his aging pupil during their first session. "I want you to run as far as you can until you feel like you're going to throw up. Then stop." The nausea hit Mullens after a half-mile. He bent over, clutching his stomach and gasping for air. His coach was unmoved. "Frank," he said triumphantly, "we've now found out that you can run half a mile before you collapse."

Connelly was not being flip or cruel. He was being careful. "Half a mile is your limit," he told Mullens. "Now we'll cut that in half. You'll jog a quarter of a mile every day. That's your workout."

Mullens ran his quarter of a mile every day for three weeks under the watchful eye of Connelly. Then Connelly changed the routine to a quarter-mile jog, a walk until Mullens was fully recovered, and another quarter-mile jog.

There was a definite reason behind the Connelly method. He wanted Mullens to gain confidence in his ability to run. He wanted him to feel comfortable and relaxed. "Psychologically," said Connelly, "it's important for a runner — especially a beginning runner — to finish fresh every day.

"Too many people go out and buy a new pair of shoes and start running and they don't stop until they've driven themselves into the ground. They finish physically and mentally down, and they quit running altogether. The secret is to feel good at the end. That way they'll be ready to go out again the next day."

Connelly told Mullens to continue running on his own: first a half-mile, then a walk, then another half-mile. Do that for a couple weeks, he said, then up the mileage.

Mullens did. And very gradually, over a five-month period, he worked his way up to four miles. But at that point he seemed to hit a mental and physical barrier. He was simply unable to push himself any further.

"One day," Mullens recalled, "Pat took me out and said, 'Frank, we're going to run 10 today.' All I could say was I'd try." Connelly told Mullens to do three things: relax, stay close behind him, and above all, forget about how far he was running.

They ran around Balboa Park in the south end of the San Fernando Valley. Mullens grew tired. His legs heavy, his breathing labored. He felt like stopping several times. "But Connelly kept telling me to keep going. I did. I owe that one to Pat."

Ten miles. It took him 95 minutes. He felt as though he'd reached the stars.

"That was eight years ago," Connelly said as he watched his friend move toward the hand-off point, "and look at him now — his third long-distance relay."

Two years before, on the Washington, D.C., to Los Angeles run, Mullens had averaged 85 minutes per leg for thirty 10-mile runs. This time his goal was to cut that by ten minutes. As he breezed across the rolling hills of the desert he was right on schedule. Seventy-four minutes. Anddd thhe finished fresh and strong. The Connelly way.

8:30 A.M.   Near Four Corners, California

Further up the Mojave, the men of Van Two were asleep. These men easily had the best living accommodations on the run. It wasn't so much their van as their numbers. Only four runners and two drivers were assigned to Van Two. Vans One and Three each had an extra runner.

The drivers of Van Two slept in a four- by seven-foot bunk over the front section of the camper. Chuck Foote and Dick Clark slept together in a narrow three-and-a-half by six-and-a-half-foot bunk along the right side of the van. And Frank Janowicz and Jim Murphy shared a four- by seven-foot bunk in the rear.

A small American flag hung over Clark's bunk. It was the only wall decoration. Like the other vans, there was a refrigerator, an ice chest, a small kitchen and a cramped bathroom. The runners would rejoice whenever they got a chance to use other bathroom facilities, even those at a gas station or a jail.

The runners were scheduled to wake up in about an hour to eat and get ready for their second leg. Like the men of Van One, they were getting accustomed to their new environment.

The men in Van Three were having a more difficult time adjusting. Their van was built to accommodate three, possibly four adults. But seven men had to exist in its tiny confines up to 20 hours a day. The only "furniture" in the van was the bunks. They served as beds, sofas, dining areas, card tables, desks. When Connelly joined the van he would share a six-by-seven-foot bunk with Jarvis and Hall in the rear of the van. Above them was a four-by-seven-foot storage area that had been converted into another bunk. There were just 18 inches between the mattress and the ceiling. Mullens and Garcia had to squeeze into that area to sleep. It was uncomfortable for Garcia, torture for Mullens. He drew the inside. He was broader than Garcia, and he was unable to turn over. It was "like sleeping in a coffin," Mullens said.

The drivers slept on a bunk over the front area of the camper. That, too, was a storage area, seven feet long and four feet wide.

The camper was quickly dubbed Pigpen Three by the other vans. There was simply no place to store anything. Shoes, laundry, towels and other items were strewn on the narrow floor.

Alex Shearer had visited the camper earlier in the day. "I had to get out of there," he said later. "I felt like I was getting claustrophobia. You know, the Marquis de Sade would have felt right at home there."

8:57 A.M.

Eddie Garcia: *"You can't go into it like John Wayne . . ."*

Eddie Garcia and Curt Hall would be the final two runners out of Van Three. Seventeen hours earlier, amid tense preparations at the Police Academy, it appeared these two might destroy the fragile camaraderie necessary for the relay to run smoothly.

Their encounter began innocuously enough with some friendly pushing and shoving. Hall, a big, easy-going Texan, then asked his campermate to show him some karate kicks. Garcia did. But when Hall told him to stop, he wouldn't. The good-natured sparring suddenly turned serious. Hall hit Garcia with a hard punch to the jaw. Hall, at 6'3", 160 pounds, was five inches taller and 20 pounds heavier than Garcia. He was also a weight lifter. But Garcia was a karate and judo expert and a former amateur boxer.

It looked as though the skirmish might turn into a brawl. But Bob Jarvis, himself an ex-amateur fighter, quickly stepped in and stopped it. The two combatants shook hands, but the peace seemed tenuous at best.

"A great way to start a relay of goodwill," Jarvis said, as the runners returned to their more immediate task of loading vans.

Garcia's task this Tuesday morning was the Mojave. He was the first runner to catch the full intensity of the scorching desert. But in a way it suited him. Garcia thrived on challenges. He viewed adversity as part of the growing process. To him, fear and pain were an integral part of life. He welcomed them as opponents.

Garcia was complex, enigmatic. During the year-and-a-half he trained for the relay he often ran far ahead of his experienced teammates. And he told them that was exactly how he intended to run each and every leg during the relay. Full-throttle. All-out.

Jarvis, for one, was amused. "Go ahead, Eddie," he told his fellow P.T. instructor, "go ahead and burn every damn one of 'em. It's fine with me. But after two or three legs we'll be burying you under some rock in the desert."

Everyone who ran with Garcia during those months preceding the relay — Jarvis, Burke, Bonneau, Connelly, Clark — thought Garcia would self-destruct on the run.

But by the time it started, Garcia had carefully mapped out a strategy more befitting his cautious, controlled self. He would approach the run as he had once approached the ring. He would test his opponent. Probe its strengths and weaknesses. And at the same time discover his own. He'd jab a little, dance a little. But he would not go for a knockout.

"I'm entering the unknown," he said. "I've done that before. In the ring. In police work. A lot of strategy is involved in a run like this. It has to be calculated very carefully. You can't go into it like John Wayne and gun it down.

"My strategy is to take those twenty-seven or twenty-eight legs as one run. The heat, the cold, the mountains, the desert, the 2 A.M. runs, the uphills — all of those are obstacles. The ultimate challenge is the entire relay.

"You know, some of these guys take each and every leg as a

contest. They're running like there's no tomorrow. But tomorrow will come. Whether they're there for it is another question."

More than anything else, it was fear that dominated Garcia's approach to the relay.

"The reality of fear is there," he said. "Fear that I won't be able to finish. Fear that I'll hurt myself physically. Fear that my body simply can't continue, that my mind can't push me anymore."

So Garcia would run carefully. Prudently. Under control. Within himself. The Mojave had flattened out. But it was terribly hot. Garcia finished his 10 miles in a comfortable 73 minutes. He felt good despite the heat.

His opponent was tough. But the first round went to Garcia.

10 A.M.   Near Four Corners, California

As Curt Hall took the baton that morning, Dick Clark was talking with Sheriff Jim Green of Inyo County, further up the Mojave. Clark was concerned about the leg he would run later that day.

Clark: "When does it cool down around here?"

Green: "About five or six."

Clark was happy.

Green: "But the ground temperature stays around 150, 160 degrees until about 7:30."

Clark was not so happy. Blisters, he thought. Ground heat causes blisters.

Clark (brightening up again): "You know what I oughta do today? I oughta go chase lizards."

No response from Sheriff Green.

Clark (undaunted): "Is it true that those lizards out there carry little chips of wood on their backs so that they can flip them over and stand on them when the sand gets hot?"

Green (not giving an inch): "No. But they do carry little canteens on their sides."

Heat. No element is more dangerous to a runner. Anything above 85 degrees is considered unsafe. Even in cold weather, running generates tremendous body temperatures. In weather above 85 degrees, the body is often unable to cool down. The results can be dehydration, heat cramps, heat exhaustion, or heat stroke.

It was already 90 degrees in the Mojave.

And that was merely the cool of morning.

10:10 A.M.

Curt Hall: *"I wanted to have at least the fourth-best average overall — but that was before the injury."*

He didn't finish the ninth grade in Dallas, Texas, where he grew up. By the time he was 16 he was living alone in a boarding house, supporting himself as a delivery boy. His bicycle was his transportation. By the time he was 17 he had a police record. He called it joyriding. The cops called it auto theft. By the time he was 18 he was married. By the time he was 19 he had a daughter and a son and had moved to Los Angeles. By the time he was 24 he had worked as a welder, an upholsterer, an insurance salesman and at countless other jobs. Curt Hall was a man without roots or direction.

At 24 the army drafted him. Six months later he was assigned to the military police. "That changed my life," he said. "I loved the bike. I decided then that I wanted to keep riding it, but not in the army. As a cop. I'm a cop only because I was an MP. It's that simple."

But joining the LAPD wasn't simple at all. The department frowns on recruits with police records. Even "joyriding" records. It made Hall wait nearly two years before accepting him, and another year before allowing him to join the department's elite motorcycle corps. But at last, at 27, he had a career. He also had a new wife; he'd been divorced and remarried. Curt Hall finally had roots and direction.

"I've been a motor cop for eight years," he laughed, "and the only thing dangerous about it, at least where I work, is gettin' run over."

That's danger enough. On February 8, 1969, a car pulled in front of Hall's motorcycle in a supermarket parking lot. Hall swerved to avoid it. But he went down, his bike landing on top of him. His shoulder and leg were broken. The doctor told him he'd walk with a limp the rest of his life unless he exercised the damaged leg.

"So I just started jogging during my lunch hour," he said. "I finally built up to where I was running four miles every day, at a real slow pace. Within six months I was running seven miles. Six months later I entered a 'little marathon' — 13 miles. And a year later I started running marathons. I never had any real formal training. But it came easy. The only thing that made it tough was my weight."

When he started jogging, Hall weighed 220 pounds. Going into the Bicentennial run he weighed 160. Despite his six-foot three-inch frame he considered himself 10 pounds overweight.

His "overweight" condition was the result of another motorcycle accident. On May 3, 1976, a month-and-a-half before the relay, a car pulled out from a stop sign 50 feet in front of him. "I had no chance," he said. His bike went down on him again. This

time he bruised a shoulder, twisted an ankle and broke a toe.
The doctor told him he was lucky.

But the accident obliterated his training. He had hoped to
finish in the top four in the relay, behind Foote, Murphy and
Connelly. The injury ended that.

At the time of his accident, Hall had completed his distance
work. That was easy because he ran year-round. In fact, more
than any other member of the LAPD team, Hall loved to run
long, tough distances. Since 1972 he had averaged eight
marathons a year, twelve in 1973 alone. In 1974 and again in 1975
he was voted the outstanding long distance runner on the
LAPD. And every Friday for months before the relay, he would
stuff his gun and uniform into his locker after work, change into
his jogging clothes, and run from the station in West Los
Angeles to his home, 31 miles away. He'd cover the distance in
about four-and-a-half hours, better than an eight-minute-per-
mile pace.

So his distance work done, Hall was just starting to focus on
his speed. But after the accident he couldn't run on his sore
ankle. It wasn't until three days before the relay that he was able
to pick up his pace. By that time his physical condition had
deteriorated, he had gained 10 pounds, and he was depressed.
His goal on the relay would be to get into condition. He would
have to forget about times and racing and take things as
they came.

The first thing that came was the Mojave.

"I went out too fast," he said. "I took some water at about five
miles. But it didn't help. It was so hot my perspiration dissolved
into the atmosphere instead of cooling my body. The pavement
was burning. It felt like a hot griddle.

"Most of my training had been in the morning when it's cool.
To prepare for this kind of heat you've got to run in it for a
month-and-a-half. I wasn't ready for it."

Hall sipped a beer and wiped his forehead with a towel. He
looked at Bob Hickey, who had just taken the baton from him.

"You know," Hall said slowly, his moustache dripping sweat,
"I hate to run in the heat. I pity those guys."

His pity was well-placed. The next six runners out of Vans
One and Two would spend seven and a half hours under the
sun's most merciless rays.

11:27 A.M. BOB HICKEY
Air: 100° Pavement: 120° Altitude: 4,500'

"It was constant uphill. And so hot the sun just drained my
strength. It happened before I realized it. I started remembering

when I ran the desert in other runs. I remembered that feeling, and I remembered swearing to God that I'd never do it again. But there I was.

"And then the blisters. I knew they were forming. You know, the only thing that's gonna keep you going through twenty-eight legs is your feet. I said to myself, 'God, I can't afford to get blisters.' It goes through everybody's mind.

"I took oxygen twice from the pace car. And it seemed to help. But then the heat and the altitude and that steady climb got to me. I couldn't lift my legs. I was getting dizzy and dehydrated. My feet were burning. It was like I'd stuck them in a frying pan.

"I thought about running off the road on the rough surface, but then you take the chance of injuring yourself. So I stayed on the asphalt and hoped that the heat would subside. It didn't.

"Then I started thinking about quitting. Not the run. Just having Alex come back and get me. But that's not fair. He'd just have to run further. His own 10 plus what I didn't run.

"And then I thought, 'I'll walk . . . I'll walk . . . I'll walk. I'll crawl before I quit.'"

Hickey ran his 10 miles in 66 minutes.

"I wanted to get out of the heat," he said later. "And the only way was to get it over with."

Hickey did develop the blister he'd feared, on the ball of his left foot. It was drained and treated by "Doctor" Kiser, who told him it was in a sensitive area. But Kiser said if he soaked it, it wouldn't be a problem. Hickey felt the treatment could wait. He tidied up the camper and then slept most of the afternoon.

12:33 P.M. ALEX SHEARER
Air: 106° Pavement: 128° Altitude: 5,000'

"I didn't feel too bad the first coupla miles. But then the heat from the pavement started to burn through the soles of my shoes.

"Every once in a while, I'd come to a hot spot where the temperature would seem to go up five to ten degrees for about a quarter of a mile. It felt like I was running on coals. I actually tried running on the dirt. But that was too risky.

"I said to myself, 'You know, this is no place for someone who's lived on the beach all his life.' Rockwood and I live there and we train there. And I started thinking: From the Standard Oil pier to the Manhattan Beach pier is about two-and-two-tenths miles. And I tried to take myself out of the desert and onto that strand of beach. I said, 'Now I'm running down the sand, and that cool breeze is blowing on me.' But nothing seemed to help.

"At five miles my legs started cramping. I shoulda taken more salt. I took oxygen three times. I don't even know if it helped. It was just something to do.

"At seven miles I thought, 'God, I'll never make it. I'll have to stop and walk or something.' But I just kept plodding along, hoping for the best.

"I tried to put myself on the beach again. Thought about the sea breeze blowing in. And getting home and sitting down and having a cold beer . . . and about how good it was going to be to sleep in a comfortable bed."

In psychological terms, there are two basic running strategies. One is association: The runner stays in contact with the pain and discomfort of his run, constantly monitoring his body — his respiration, muscles, temperature, and other possible danger signs. Most world-class runners employ this technique.

The other strategy is disassociation: The runner mentally detaches himself from the pain by putting himself elsewhere — on the beach or in a comfortable bed, as Shearer had done. Hickey had employed this strategy when he locked in during the Tijuana run. And therein lies the danger of disassociation. It is a form of self-hypnosis, of self-deception. The runner ignores the warning signs of pain to complete his mission. The result can be pulled muscles, heat exhaustion, and even — as with Hickey — mental disorientation.

Most of the runners — like Shearer through the Mojave — would employ a combination of these strategies.

Shearer saw the camper. "I just put my head down and said, 'I'm not gonna look up until I get there.'"

When he got there, he bent over. Exhausted. The perspiration streamed down his face and evaporated as it hit the pavement.

"It was miserable," he gasped. "I didn't think it would ever end."

Later he confessed to his teammates that he had thought about quitting. But Shearer had never quit before. And he wasn't going to quit now, even on this day in the desert.

1:56 P.M. BOB BURKE
Air: 112° Pavement: 135° Altitude: 5,000'

"I tried to run as fast as I could and concentrate on my breathing and posture.

"I thought about home, the scenery, a cool drink, anything . . . anything to get my mind off it.

"And then at the end I got a hill. A bad one. I just relaxed, shook myself out and took it.

"And that was it. What can I say? I just got hot like everybody else."

Bob Burke, normally a man of few words, was even more taciturn after his 73 minutes under the desert sun.

3:10 P.M. JOHN ROCKWOOD
Air: 114° Pavement: 140° Altitude: 5,000'

Rockwood had developed blisters on his run up the Angeles Crest. But they'd been treated. And he was ready. As ready as a beachboy could be for the Mojave.

Shearer: "Hey, John, try to stay off the hot pavement."

Hickey (just awakened): "Good luck, partner. Keep your hat wet, and get water on your neck and shoulders every two or three miles."

Shearer: "And John?"

Rockwood (half-annoyed): "What?"

Shearer: "Try to run fast so you can make the breeze blow around you."

Rockwood was not amused.

Moments later he took the baton from Bob Burke.

"The heat hit me hard from the start. It was reflecting off the ground, hitting me right in the face. I couldn't see anything.

"At five miles the sun had drained me. I couldn't lift. I couldn't breathe. It felt like there was a constant pressure on me, holding me back. I wanted to go faster but I couldn't.

"At six miles it became a matter of just trying to survive. I felt like walking. But for some reason I just kept putting one foot in front of the other.

"The last two miles were total agony. I shoulda taken oxygen, but I didn't. And I couldn't drink the water from the pace car 'cause it was hot.

"I asked them to play some music . . . anything to take my mind off the running, the pain. But it just got worse. I thought it would never end. I said to myself, 'What am I doing out here?' At that point, I had no answer."

Rockwood had about 400 yards to go when the residents of the van, sans the slumbering Hickey, formed a welcoming party outside, a ritual after most runs, especially tough ones.

Shearer: "Bonneau here, he's the luckiest runner. Always gets the good conditions. We go to races, and he always gets the downhills. Now look out there. He's not only got downhill, he's even got some wind to his back. What more could you want?"

Bonneau: "About 10 degrees cooler."

Shearer: "It will be by the time Rockwood gets here."

Rockwood now had 100 yards to go.

"I saw the camper and Bonneau standing there," he recalled, "and I said to myself, 'God, I made it!' But there was a mixup in the mileage. Bonneau kept moving down the road away from me. That was a real psychological mess-up for me."

Fifty yards to go.

Driver Jerry Mowat: "Look at him! He looks like he's about dead."

Rockwood staggered in. His face reflected his agony: His eyes shut from the burning sweat that had poured down his forehead. His mouth half-open. His complexion bright red. Burke put a cold towel around Rockwood's shoulders. Rockwood bent over, choking for breath.

"Miserable . . . miserable . . . miserable," he whispered. Someone handed him his favorite drink, a 50-50 mixture of Tab and water, a personal blend designed to keep him from feeling bloated. He sipped it and wiped his face with the towel.

"I'm really hurting. I thought it would never end."

Rockwood thought it would take him only a few hours to bounce back.

4:31 P.M. DICK BONNEAU
Air: 108° Pavement: 130° Altitude: 5,000'

Bonneau was worried. He was out of shape and still feeling the effects of his bout with the Angeles Crest. He wasn't at all certain he'd be among the survivors when the team reached Montreal. But during the past 16 hours he'd devised an approach that he hoped would get him through.

"I decided to stop thinking about everything except the next 10-miler. And I decided to run each leg the way I felt. If I had to slow down, I'd slow down. If it took me an hour and a half, I'd take it. I decided to stop thinking about Montreal and all the 10-milers in between."

Bonneau's leg was slightly downhill. "The heat was almost unbearable, but it wasn't my main problem. It was fatigue from my lack of conditioning.

"I was exhausted. I just kept telling myself, 'Finish the leg, put one foot in front of the other, and finish the leg.'

"My thighs were tight, and I got dehydrated. I took water, which I rarely do. But it didn't help.

"I never felt in control the whole 10 miles. It was a struggle. But somehow I did it."

Bonneau handed the baton to Chuck Foote. The agony was finally over for Van One. A deputy from the Inyo County Sheriff's Department invited the runners and drivers to his house. They swam in his backyard pool, barbecued steaks, drank wine and then headed up the road. The baton would be theirs again in 11½ hours.

5:42 P.M. CHUCK FOOTE
Air: 95° Pavement: 115° Altitude: 5,000'

"The follow car was spraying me with water. I was drinking water. I put ice under my hat. I put ice in my mouth. But nothing helped. I got dehydrated.

"I've run this area on two other relays. I thought I was mentally prepared. But I wasn't. You can't be. It's too darn hot. You can't train for it. You just don't normally run in that kind of heat.

"Toward the end I felt I was operating on about 15 percent efficiency. I was sloppy. My legs were heavy. I ached all over. I got a blister from the hot pavement.

"You have to take a run like that mile by mile. And just keep going. 'Cause if you stop and walk you'll never get going again, and you'll be out there for two hours. You'd probably die."

6:58 P.M. JIM MURPHY
Air: 85° Pavement: 110°

The temperature was sinking with the desert sun. But the pavement still held the day's heat and the threat of blisters. Murphy, a competitive runner for 19 years, felt butterflies as he waited for the baton, even though his only competition would be himself.

"It's like I'm going into a race," he said. "To me there is no difference between running in the nationals or in Europe and out here. I've got the same nervousness. My stomach is jumpy and the adrenalin is pumping. But that's good. Getting up for your leg has a tendency to override any problems you have. You see, for a conditioned athlete, unless he has severe structural problems, this is all mental, because physically you know you can run 10 miles."

Murphy asked the follow car to call out his times at three, five, seven, and nine miles. It would give him an indication of his tempo and help him judge how to pace himself. He ran his first three miles in 17 minutes, a remarkable pace considering the heat. During his next seven miles, he hit three tough upgrades. His thighs tightened a bit, and he developed a blister on his right heel.

While Murphy was running, his campermates were discussing the competition that was already developing between Hickey and Murphy.

Clark: "Hickey is such a veteran, and he's a master of self-hypnotism or something. It just seems like he doesn't feel the pain. The more painful it is the better he likes it. He just seems to lock in."

Janowicz: "Murphy is faster. For any one race he can take ya. He'll probably run the fastest leg. But I don't care how fast Murphy is; he won't beat Hickey overall."

Murphy had run his first nine miles in just over 54 minutes. He had a chance to break 60. He picked up his pace.

Clark was limbering up as he waited for the hand-off. Two college students drove up. They were wearing running shoes and shorts. They strolled to the hand-off point.

Clark: "Looks like I might have some company."

Janowicz: "A couple of kids. You'll run 'em into the ground."

Foote: "Yeah, hot shots."

The students introduced themselves. They'd heard about the relay on the radio.

First runner (to Clark): "Mind if we run along?"

Clark (immodestly): "No, not at all. As long as you don't slow me down."

Second runner: "I don't think we will. I've run a 2:30 marathon. And my friend here has broken three hours."

Clark (who had never broken three hours in the marathon, to himself): "They won't slow me down."

Murphy finished his leg in 59 minutes and 58 seconds. He was on schedule toward being number one.

7:58 P.M. DICK CLARK

Clark was having difficulty being number one on his own leg. "I had trouble keeping up with that 2:30 marathoner," he confessed. "I probably shouldn't have run so fast. My legs knotted up. They felt like hamburger."

Inside Van Two, Murphy carefully recorded his time on a piece of paper next to those of Hickey, Janowicz, Foote, and Connelly. He was keeping close tabs on the competition.

Clark: "It was so flat that I could see just about my whole 10 miles in front of me. I hate that, 'cause then you just run, run, run . . . counting telephone poles. I felt lousy the whole way."

Afterward, Clark could barely walk. His calves and right knee ached. And his thighs were still tight from his foolhardy charge down the Angeles Crest. He struggled up the steps of the camper.

Clark's 10 miles completed a 130-mile stretch of desert that Jarvis had begun early that morning. The Mojave was behind them.

9:16 P.M. FRANK JANOWICZ

Frank Janowicz, who had run 10 miles of downhill at 5 A.M., would now get 10 miles of uphill. He would climb into the foothills that lead to Bishop, California, 90 miles away. Unfortunately, he had been misinformed about the terrain before his leg.

"The sheriff here told me my first five would be up and the second five would be flat. But they were all up.

"I got real pissed at the sheriff, but I was even more pissed at that hill. I started cussing it. I always cuss hills. I called it every name I could think of. I challenged it. I said, 'Hill, I'm gonna lower you. I'm gonna make you flatland. Get out of my way!'"

Janowicz climbed 1,500 feet during his 10 miles. On the last five he ran into headwinds up to 25 miles an hour. Still he finished in 70 minutes and 19 seconds. His goal was to finish among the top five runners. And he wasn't about to let a hill and some wind slow him down.

His thighs and calves ached. But it was the sheriff who was uppermost in his mind. "I'm not gonna ask anybody anymore what it's like ahead, 'cause they don't know. They drive, and that's a helluva lot different than running."

Janowicz checked his time against his competitors' and limped around outside the camper, trying to loosen his leg muscles. He looked like a cripple. He was running much too hard. It didn't seem possible that he'd be able to run again in just 16 hours.

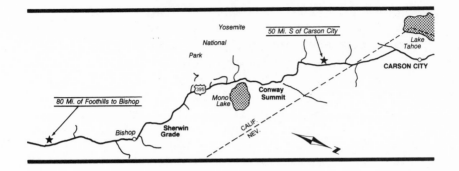

Yosemite National Park

50 Mi. S of Carson City

Lake Tahoe

CARSON CITY

395

Mono Lake

Conway Summit

80 Mi. of Foothills to Bishop

Bishop

Sherwin Grade

CALIF. NEV.

THE THIRD DAY
Wednesday, June 16, 1976

10:26 P.M. — 7:45 A.M.

The five runners of Van Three and the first three runners of Van One carried the baton through the desert night to Bishop. They ran their hilly 80-mile course in just over nine and a quarter hours.

Curt Hall took the baton at 3:32 in the morning.

"I had to push myself almost from the beginning, and I couldn't understand why. At about the three-mile mark I told the follow car that I was getting real tired. And they said, 'No wonder . . . you've been going straight uphill.'

"I didn't even know I was on a hill, it was so dark. It felt good to get that leg under my belt. Night . . . a hill . . . it gives you confidence."

7:30 A.M.   Bishop, California

Bishop — population 3,500, quiet and clean, located in California's high desert; average mean temperature in June, 90 degrees. It was the first "major" city the runners had hit since leaving Los Angeles.

By 8 A.M., all the runners with the exception of John Rockwood, who was just starting his leg, had gathered in Bishop City Park in the center of town. There, the twelve men of the Bishop police force, their wives, and thirty retired L.A. policemen sponsored a breakfast of fresh trout, eggs, hash browns, orange juice, and coffee. The runners were treated like conquer-

ing heroes. Radio and television crews were there and so were
scores of townspeople who had learned about the run.

For most of the runners, it was a chance to relax and bask in
glory. For Frank Mullens it was a reunion with old colleagues.

"We talked about old times, and I got to wishing that I were
retired like they were," he laughed.

Frank Mullens is normally a man of few words. He is a cop of
the fifties. His delivery and demeanor are reminiscent of that
decade's most famous TV cop, Jack Webb. But familiar faces
jogged his memory and loosened his tongue.

"Back in the fifties . . . it was sure different back then," he told
his friends. "Few shootings. Twenty-seven years and only shot
at once . . .

"I'll never forget old Walt Herberso. Remember him? Dope
peddler, robber . . . Christ, got to know him over the years.
Busted him four or five times. The last time was after he'd
escaped from sheriff's deputies.

"We traced him to an apartment in Glendale. This guy hiding
him says, 'Come right in and search the place if you'd like . . . I
don't know where Walt is.'

"I figured something was screwy and I said, 'Where's your
car?' I don't know why I asked. But anyway, I walked over to the
car. And there was old Walt, huddled up on the floor, trying to
hide.

"He'd taken a deputy's gun during his escape, so I just put my
knee right in the middle of his back, and I said, 'Walt, I want to
see your hands come out — and they'd better come out empty,
because I have my gun right at your head.'

"He didn't have the gun. We got it later from his apartment.
But on the way to jail I said to him, 'Well, I guess you won't get
away this time. This is it.'

"And Walt said, 'Yeah. I guess so.' Then he kinda smiles and
said, 'What the hell are you gonna do now? You've made a
career out of busting me.'"

Mullens and the others laughed. He continued.

"You know, old Walt was wrong. I busted Oscar Monroe even
more often. Oscar was an old-time bookmaker, and he could
never figure out how me and my partner kept knocking off his
bookie joints.

"Well, it was all a simple tail job. I'd go over to Oscar's house
in the morning and hide out. He'd get into his car and drive off to
meet his partner. And I'd follow him. They would meet someplace, exchange some notes and then separate . . . and I'd follow
one of them to the phone spot where the bets were taken. Then

I'd go back to the office, pick up my partner and knock the place off. Oscar could never figure out how we did it . . .

"I remember I was working Memorial Day one time with Bobby Matthews. And I said, 'Hey, Bob, let's go call on Oscar. I found his new spot.'

"So we went over to this apartment building. The only problem was we didn't know what apartment he was in. But Oscar always smoked a cigar . . . a little, heavy-set guy with that cigar always stuck in his mouth. I said to Bobby, 'Just start sniffing under the doors. We'll find cigar smoke, and we'll find Oscar.' And sure enough, we got him.

"I musta busted Oscar six or seven times. He was a congenial guy. And he'd just shrug. He'd bail out, pay his fine and go on. But he never did figure out how we busted him."

8 A.M.   On the road to Bishop

John Rockwood was still exhausted and suffering the effects of dehydration from his bout with the Mojave the day before.

He ran the first mile and a half with Larry Kramer, one of the drivers of Van One, and the next four with Bishop Police Chief Jerry Galvin and one of Galvin's deputies. They ran together until they reached Bishop City Park, where 400 people had gathered to root Rockwood on.

"It was really something," he said. "All those people clapping and cheering for me. Galvin and his deputy dropped out there, and I went on alone. It started to get real hot. And I started hurtin'. I got dehydrated again and I couldn't get enough air. And then it just hit me. I fell apart. All those people — and then nothing. All the physical pain. I got really depressed. I felt like crying. Like quitting."

Rockwood pushed on. His body was near the breaking point. His mind began devising schemes of escape. "I started to get some real weird thoughts during the last few miles. I started to think, 'God, if I could just find a way to get out of this whole thing I'd do it.' I thought, 'Wow, if I got hit by a car, that would be the end of it.'"

His agony was compounded by another problem. He'd fractured a toe on his right foot four days before the run during a karate workout.

Karate was as important to Rockwood's life as running and police work. And at times all three merged.

When Rockwood joined the Compton Police Department in 1966, all patrol officers operated alone, in one-man cars. Compton was — and still is — a tough, high-crime area just south of

Watts. "So I got into karate pretty heavy. In 1967 I took fourth in the California Police Olympics.

"Some of the guys used to kid me. They'd say, 'Rockwood doesn't really need a backup when he's on a tough call, 'cause he can take care of himself.' And sometimes, when I really needed a backup, it took a little longer for me to get one. Sometimes I wouldn't get one at all.

"I remember one time . . . there was this ex-football player — an ex-Marine who was terrorizing Compton Junior College, hitting people and threatening 'em. He was about six-foot-three, 220 pounds . . . and a complete psycho. They asked him to leave the campus, and he refused. So I was sent to get him off. They told me I'd have a backup.

"But when I got there, there was no backup, and there was my man sitting on a bench in the middle of campus. I told him he was bothering the people, and he'd have to leave. He said, 'I'm not leaving.' And he started to take off his jacket.

"I figured, 'Well, instead of fighting this guy, I'll spray him with Mace, and that will be that.' Wrong. I sprayed him right in the face, and all he did was shake his head and say, 'You shouldn't have done that.'

"I figured I'm in trouble now. But luckily, he took off running. So I chased after him, and I could hear the kids laughing and saying, 'Man, that's the slowest policeman I've ever seen.'

"Hell, I wasn't trying to catch him. I was just trying to get him off the campus. Besides, I still didn't have my backup. Anyway, as I was chasing him, I took a swing at him with my baton and caught him on the right side of his head. He started bleeding and stopped running, and I figured he was giving up. So I started to put my baton away. But he grabbed it and came at me.

"That's when I used my karate. I used a front kick to the stomach and a front punch to the face, and he went down. I handcuffed him.

"And right then, here comes my backup, strolling along, drinking a McDonald's Coke, and he says, 'What's going on?'

"I said, 'Where have you been? I needed help!'

"And he said, 'I figured with your karate you could handle it.'

"It blew my mind . . . that whole karate thing was getting out of hand."

Rockwood's last mile was uphill. It took him 10 torturous minutes to complete it. Afterward, his teammates started pumping water into him.

"I must have drunk half a gallon in five minutes," he said later.

Rockwood was completely exhausted. He was scheduled to run again at three the next morning.

Two years earlier, during the Washington, D.C., to Los Angeles run, Alex Shearer had spotted his short, blond, baby-faced teammate Dick Bonneau sitting between two elderly gentlemen on the tram that carries people from Dulles Airport into the nation's capital. Shearer, his imagination working overtime, conjured up the image of a kid being taken for a train ride by his two elderly guardians. When the men left, Shearer walked over to Bonneau and said, 'Sonny, now that your guardians have left, it looks like I'll have to take care of you. You'll be my ward." And so a whole routine was born. Not in the same league as Martin and Lewis or Abbott and Costello. Still, it was original, and it kept everyone loose. Soon all the runners joined in.

Bonneau was christened The Kid. They bought him toys and ordered him cookies and milk at bars. They even held his hand when he crossed a street. Bonneau played his part, too, jumping up and down when he was excited, or breaking his toys when he was unhappy.

In Bishop, Bonneau's campermates bought him a toy windmill, which he broke. He claimed it was an accident. His teammates claimed it was a tantrum, because he wanted a Hostess Twinkie instead. Bonneau wanted to carry the broken windmill on the run, but he finally decided that in his beleaguered condition, a baton was enough.

He took the baton at 9:37 A.M. about five miles out of Bishop. It was 95 degrees. It would be another scorcher as the team moved over mountainous desert terrain.

"The first seven miles were fairly level," Bonneau said. "But the last three were the Sherwin Grade. Three miles straight up. It was brutal in that heat."

At the end, Bonneau was dehydrated and fatigued — "sore all over." He put a cold towel around his neck.

"My only consolation is that my next one will be at night. I just hope it's good terrain, because at this point, I'm in real trouble physically."

Heat and blisters were becoming the twin enemies. Nothing could be done about the heat. But "Doctor" Ron Kiser was being kept busy treating blisters.

"A blister is like a burn," he theorized, "except that nature covers a blister with a layer of skin and a thin cushion of liquid. The skin protects it from infection. The liquid is a healing agent.

"The only problem is that a blister needs time to heal. So you can't run on it, 'cause it'll rupture. But these guys gotta run. So what I try to do is speed up nature. I take the healing fluid out with a hypodermic needle and replace it with my healing agent — a water solution containing 5 percent mercurochrome. It's dry, not liquidy, so you can run on it without busting open the skin on top.

"The key is to get all the fluid out, or it'll start building up again during a run, and that's trouble. Sometimes you have to go very deep to get it out, and that can hurt. But the only way to keep a guy with blisters going is to get the liquid out and dry out the area."

The relay was not yet two days old, but already a number of runners had undergone the Kiser treatment. And some were not happy with it.

9:45 A.M.   **Outside Van Two**

Shearer: "My feet are killing me. My blisters are real painful."

Clark: "Did you do anything for them before your run?"

Shearer (in wry form): "Yeah, I did. I stayed as far away from 'Doctor' Kiser as I could. And every time he asked me how I was feeling, I'd say, 'Fine, fine, Ron, just fine.'"

Clark: "Is he a quack?"

Shearer: "Well, I would say that 'Doctor' Kiser reminds me of the doctor in *King's Row*, who performed unnecessary amputations on his patients and other sadistic practices. I would say that his greatest pleasure is to inflict pain on some poor runner and hear him scream."

Clark: "Are you going to have your blisters treated at all?"

Shearer: "Not by Kiser. I guess I'll just run on them. I don't think they're going to get any better. I'll probably run in pain all the way to Montreal. [Then, turning to publicist Wemmer and warming to one of his favorite subjects:] And that's why I don't want any of those ginky high school or college kids running with me, Wemmer. Not with my toes the way they are. Absolutely not!"

Wemmer (to Rockwood): "How are your feet, John?"

Rockwood: "I've got blisters on both feet. Kiser worked on them, and now they're worse. They're full of fluid."

Shearer: "See what I told you! I just hope the good 'doctor' has malpractice insurance."

Rockwood: "I'm gonna drain 'em myself."

Hickey: "Hey, I'll drain them for you, John."

Rockwood: "Okay, I'm switching to Hickey. He'll be my doctor from now on."

Wemmer: "What can you do about blisters anyway?"

Rockwood: "Well, the best way to prevent 'em is to wear nylon socks. Wear a double pair. Unfortunately I didn't. But once you've got blisters, my only advice is to stay away from Kiser. Hide if you have to. But stay away."

Shearer: "Amen."

10:57 A.M. CHUCK FOOTE
100°

Dick Bonneau had handed the baton to Chuck Foote on the Sherwin Grade. As Foote began his seven-mile journey to the summit, Van One regrouped and drove to driver Larry Kramer's cabin in nearby Mammoth. The main attraction of the cabin was its Jacuzzi. The runners took turns letting the jets of water massage their worn bodies and feet. Then they barbecued steaks, drank wine from Shearer's private stock, and hit the road once more.

Foote's journey up the Sherwin Grade had started at the 4,000-foot level. "And it went straight up from there," he said. "It was like running up the side of a building. And it was hot.

"I took a lot of water, ate ice, got sprayed by the follow car. I wasn't gonna chance getting dehydrated again."

Foote climbed 3,000 feet during his 10 miles, one of the steepest inclines of the relay. Trucks crawled over this grade in their lowest gear, groaning in distress. Foote traveled along stoically, silently. He was tired and drenched in sweat at the end. Still, he recovered quickly.

"I feel good," he said five minutes after his leg. "I'm getting in the groove. It's great to be out here with this bunch of guys. They're all my friends. It's lots of fun."

12:18 P.M. JIM MURPHY
105°

Murphy was now running. Foote was outside the camper, cooling down. Clark was inside getting ready for his next leg. And Janowicz was sitting on his bunk in the rear of the camper, talking to no one in particular.

Janowicz: "Christ, everything hurts. My thighs, my calves, my feet. What the hell am I doing here? I must be crazy. We're all crazy."

Janowicz asked driver George Moore to check on Murphy's time.

Moore: "Roadrunner Two to the Turtle. What is Murphy's time?"

The pace car: "Murphy has run his first five miles in 30:15."
Moore (to pace car): "Roger, Turtle."
Janowicz: "Christ, good time!"
Moore (to pace car): "We'll get Clark ready."
Janowicz: "You'd better get out there now, Dick. Murphy'll probably run his last five in 20 minutes."

Murphy's first six miles were downhill into the desert. But his last four were into the foothills. That slowed him down a bit. When he finished, the pace car called out his time again: 66:40. The announcement blared across the CB radio in Van Two. Janowicz shook his head. "Good time," he muttered. "Jesus . . . good time."

Murphy entered the van and began stuffing ice cubes into his socks. He did it after each of his runs to cool down his Achilles tendons. It kept his tendinitis from flaring up. "If my Achilles go," he said, "I'm gone. Crippled."

1:24 P.M. DICK CLARK

Clark was on the road now. Inside Van Two, Foote, Murphy and Janowicz drank beers and relaxed.

Foote: "Well, three legs down and twenty-four to go."

Murphy: "Yeah, I'm not really thinking about that. It's so awesome. [Then, turning to earthier matters] Clark's been farting like a buffalo."

Janowicz: "We all are."

Murphy: "It must be the lousy food. I had a sideache last time out, and Dick told me he had one on his second leg."

Janowicz: "So did I. It's the food, the hours, the living conditions. We gotta be crazy. I'm crippled, and I gotta run in an hour. I'll never make it. I can't even move my legs, and I gotta run. Christ. Shit."

Clark ran his first five miles uphill into a strong headwind. "It was real bad," he said. "I felt like I was running in place." But the terrain leveled off for his last five. He was relieved. "For a while I thought it was gonna be all uphill. I was thinking, 'This could be the tough one I'm not ready for.' Now I have a little more time."

Clark had two miles to go when Janowicz limped through the narrow camper and gingerly descended its two steps backwards, as though he were climbing down a ladder. His legs were too sore to stretch forward.

For 10 minutes he walked around slowly, limping, cursing and stretching his painful muscles. Then he broke into a slow,

girls would say, 'Oh, poor Pat. Look at Pat.' It wasn't the kind of attention I would have liked, but it was still something. You gotta understand, I was a bad student, a lousy athlete, and part of a crowd of thirteen kids at home. I liked any attention.

"One afternoon I tried out for the C hurdles. That was a joke. I broke a couple of hurdles. Kept falling over them. So I gave up in frustration and started to jog around the track real, real slow.

"I went around three, four, five laps. And I said to myself, 'I'll just keep going . . . see how far I can go.' Pretty soon everybody from the track team started watching me, and they were saying, 'Look at Connelly. He's still running.' And they started counting. And the attention of them counting got my adrenalin going. I did seventeen laps. No one could believe it. I was a celebrity."

Connelly won letters in cross-country in both his sophomore and junior years. But he was too slow to letter in track. His fastest time for the mile was a dismal 5:08.

"You don't have to be fast in cross-country," he smiled. "You just have to be able to run a long ways. I could do that. But I didn't have the speed to compete in the shorter distances.

"I remember the late Dean Cromwell, the USC track coach, came to one of our track meets when I was a junior. He sat next to my uncle. And my uncle said to him, 'That's my nephew down there running last, 180 yards behind. But he sure likes to run. Runs everywhere.' And Cromwell said, 'Well, you just tell him to keep running and be patient. If he really likes it, he'll develop and do well.'

"That inspired me."

During the summer between his junior and senior years, Connelly ran every day. "I musta run a thousand miles," he said. "I'd run very long distances, up to 12 miles, and my friends and family would just marvel at my endurance.

"I remember, we went down to Fontana to visit the family one weekend. And my dad said, 'You see Pat here? He can run an hour without stopping.' And one uncle said, 'I don't believe it!' So the whole family piled into a car and followed me while I ran down Fontana Avenue. They followed me for an hour-and-a-half. I just kept running to show them how far I could go. To me it was a great deal — all that attention."

That summer Connelly sprouted, adding three inches in height and 20 pounds in bulk. Now he looked like a runner, six-foot-two, 145 pounds. He'd also picked up strength and speed. He ran a 4:29 mile his senior year and placed fifth in the city championships. And he won the city cross-country title at the varsity level.

He began grooming himself like an athlete, too. His duck-tail had given way to a flat-top. His clothing was more subdued. "And my friendships changed," he said. "I started hanging around with athletes — the kind of kids my mom liked me to bring home."

With high school graduation near, Connelly was worried about his future. He wanted to keep running but he wasn't sure how to do it.

"I asked my coach, 'What do I do? Where do I go?' He said, 'You go to college.' I said, 'College? You gotta be kidding.' The word had never been mentioned in my home. My parents had enough trouble putting food on the table for thirteen kids. They didn't motivate us academically. In fact only three of us made it through high school."

Connelly barely made it. There were 65 students in his graduating class at Birmingham High School in 1957; he was number 63 academically.

Instead of going to college, he went into the navy, and after his hitch he enrolled at Pierce Junior College, not far from his old high school. His coach was Bob Chambers, later to become one of the best long-distance coaches in the nation. But at the time, Chambers was from the old school. "Monday, I'd run quarter miles," Connelly said, "Tuesdays, half miles. Wednesday, I'd jog. Thursday, a light workout or sometimes nothing at all. Friday, the meet. Formwise I was pretty much the same kid who'd run in high school. Terrible. Sloppy. I ran on my heels, leaning back and straining. Bob did nothing to change that."

Still, during his two years at Pierce, Connelly ran a 4:23 mile and a 9:51 two-mile. That was a pretty good double in those days. But as in high school, his real forte was cross-country. He won the conference cross-country championship in both his freshman and sophomore years, cutting his time over the three-mile course from 15:30 to 14:30. But most important, Connelly was gradually picking up speed in shorter distances. For the first time in his career, he was able to break two minutes in the half-mile. He was looking forward to competing at a four-year college.

In the fall of 1960 his life fell into disarray. Connelly was nearly killed in an auto accident. He broke his kneecap, fractured three ribs, and suffered a severe concussion. While recuperating he was accepted by Arizona State University. But his father died before he had a chance to enroll. The family business, a newsstand, needed tending. The responsibility fell to Connelly, the oldest unmarried son. He never ran in college again.

By 1962 the newsstand had gone bankrupt, and Connelly had gone to work for Litton Systems. He had also returned to college to pick up the first of two bachelor's degrees. And he had resumed his track career, this time with the Southern California Striders.

"I trained on my own," he said. "I didn't do very well. My times were the same as they were at Pierce. I was the same old Connelly — lousy form. And just like high school and college, no one ever told me."

Finally one man did. Pete Petersens. Born in Latvia, survivor of a German concentration camp, refugee from the communists in his homeland, a graduate of USC. Petersens had learned coaching from Mike Igloi.

Connelly was at a crossroads when he met Petersens, who was coaching the Striders. "I was either going to slide downhill or become a decent runner," he said.

"One afternoon as we were jogging, Petersens told me, 'Pat, you know your form is terrible, just terrible. Shorten your stride. Get off your heels. Get up on your toes. Lean forward. Get your arms up.' I did that. It felt good, natural. But the most important thing he did was teach me how to relax. He took the stress out of running."

Two weeks later Connelly ran a 4:19.3 mile in a Strider time trial. It was his best ever. "I'd laid off all winter. I wasn't even in shape. I'd done it on form alone. That race instituted my faith in Pete. I owe everything to that man. I owe him my life, really."

By the end of 1963, Connelly ranked in the top dozen in the nation in the three- and six-mile. And this once-skinny kid with a duck-tail who got attention because he ran so poorly suddenly had thoughts of the Olympics.

In early 1964, Connelly placed in the top six at the Olympic semifinal tryouts at Rutgers Islands, and that qualified him for the finals at the Los Angeles Coliseum in June of 1964. The top three would go to Tokyo later that summer.

The favorites were Billy Mills, Ron Larrieu and Gerry Lindgren. Connelly was the slowest man in the field.

"I was sick before the race," he recalled. "Sick from nervousness. But I said to myself, 'I'm gonna go out and do the best job I can. If they beat me, they're gonna know they were in a battle.'"

Fifty members of Connelly's family jammed into one section of the Coliseum as Connelly lined up for his once-in-a-lifetime shot. He remembers every inch of those six miles.

"Mills, Larrieu, Lindgren and I ran the first mile together in 4:30, a real fast pace. Every time I came around the south curve, my family cheered and screamed for me. That really juiced me up, lap after lap.

"The four of us came by the two-mile mark in nine minutes. I ran those two miles as fast as I'd ever run any two-mile race in my whole life. I was really moving.

"We were still together at three miles. We were running an incredible pace. At four miles my time was 19 minutes. I was still with them. At that point I thought, 'Maybe I can do it. Maybe I have a chance.'

"With one mile to go I was third, ahead of Larrieu, and behind Lindgren and Mills. With the excitement of the thing . . . my family . . . I was just flying.

"I was about 200 yards behind Lindgren when I heard the gun lap go off for him. Larrieu was 10 yards behind me. I started my final kick. I probably started too soon. I should have waited about another hundred yards, until I had 500 to go, because I was already tired.

"As I came around the curve into my final lap, I was losing form. Getting sloppy. I was just hanging on. I couldn't get enough oxygen. I had reached my limit.

"With 300 yards to go, I kept saying to myself, 'Hang on, hang on . . . beat Larrieu.' But at that point, 300 yards from the finish, Larrieu came flying past me like I was standing still. I couldn't stay with him . . . and I knew it. I knew it. Larrieu beat me. I finished fourth."

The race led Billy Mills to Tokyo and a gold medal in the six-mile. It led Pat Connelly to disillusionment. By the end of the year he had quit running altogether to coach high school students.

Three years later, in 1967, Connelly was working full-time at Hughes Aircraft Company. He was also a police reservist, a college student and a newlywed. His reputation as a coach had spread. He was coaching high school students from all over the San Fernando Valley six days a week — for no pay.

His life was busy, but he felt something was missing.

"One day," he laughed, "the Lord just spoke to me in my dreams and said, 'Pat, you shall run tomorrow.' So I got out of bed, dug out my running shoes and some old shorts, and I was gone.

"I ran up into the Santa Monica Mountains. I was really hurting. But I went 14 miles that day just on instinct and experience. It took me three days to recover."

Connelly has been running ever since.

Connelly tied his shoes and strolled to the hand-off point. Two minutes later he took the baton from Bob Jarvis. It was 5:20 in the evening, but still 90 degrees. Connelly ran with his friend, Mike Nocita. For two miles the terrain was flat, and they were cooled by the gentle breezes off dark blue Mono Lake, to their right. But Nocita and Connelly could see their bliss was temporary. The route wound its way to the base of the majestic Conway Summit, which rose 2,500' in eight miles.

"It was tough," Connelly said, "uphill all the way, very steep. I couldn't get enough oxygen. Neither of us could. It was like carrying a 150-pound weight on your back.

"Mike and I talked to each other all the way. I'd say, 'C'mon Mike. Let's hit it . . . let's go . . . let's take this hill.'

"You have to concentrate when you have that kind of struggle. You can't be daydreaming or looking around at the scenery. You have to think and keep telling yourself, 'Lean forward . . . get your arms up . . . bring your knees up . . . get good knee-drive.'

"I'd tell Mike, 'Don't look at the top of the hill. We've gotta take a little at a time.' I'd point to a sign 30 yards away and say, 'Let's take it.' And we'd get there, and I'd say, 'Great, great. Now, you see that post there? Let's get there.' And that's the way we went up the hill. One section at a time, not the whole thing, 'cause God, it would destroy you.

"We tried everything to get through that leg. Back home we run a nice, flat 10-mile course every day. So we pretended we were there. Changed our environment.

"We ran about a nine-minute-per-mile pace. Very slow, but we were hurting. Just couldn't get enough oxygen. We took our heartbeats near the end. Mine was 130 even though I was just jogging. At rest my pulse is 50, 52. So you can see how difficult it was."

Connelly always checked his pulse following his runs. Two minutes after handing the baton to Frank Mullens it was 100. Five minutes later it was 80. A remarkable recovery.

Fifty-four-year-old Frank Mullens ran the last three miles of Conway Summit. "I climbed about 500 feet, but I knew it would be downhill from there, so it wasn't so bad. The roughest part was the downhill, though. All that pounding. I got stiff, tight."

The desert heat gave way to cool mountain breezes as Eddie Garcia and Curt Hall completed the team's third leg.

The next day, the Bicentennial runners would once again spend most of their day in the hot, uninhabited desert, except for brief excursions through Carson City and Reno, Nevada.

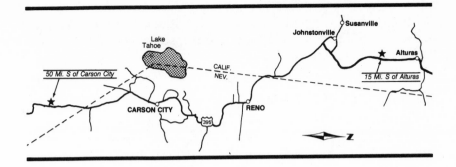

THE FOURTH DAY
Thursday, June 17, 1976

Three days of the relay were now complete. The runners had covered about 10 percent of the territory between Los Angeles and Montreal. In terms of running, each man had clearly defined his goals.

For Bob Hickey, Jim Murphy and Frank Janowicz, the Bicentennial Relay of Goodwill was a race, pure and simple. Each wanted the best overall average. Bob Burke, John Rockwood and Frank Mullens knew they couldn't compete for "number one." But they had set personal time objectives. The others, for the most part, simply wanted to run as fast as possible, with no real time objectives in mind.

Despite their varied approaches, all shared one common bond — the pressure of the clocks. The clocks were an ever-present barometer of individual performance. A constant means of comparison. And though it made no sense to compare 10 miles of uphill with 10 miles of downhill, that's exactly what was happening.

After each leg, the time was broadcast immediately to all the motor homes. None of the runners wanted it flashed across the radios that he'd been "out there" for 80 or 90 minutes.

So each of these men fought the elements and terrain as best he could. With nearly 3,500 miles to go, pain, injuries, and fatigue were already factors. Virtually every problem could be traced to the pressure of the clocks.

The goodwill aspect of the run had withered in the heat and desolation of the desert. In that vacuum, survival and the clocks became all-consuming.

10:48 P.M. BOB HICKEY

Bob Hickey was thinking of more than clocks as he waited for the hand-off from Curt Hall late Wednesday evening on the mountain road that leads to Carson City. Hickey, Burke, and driver Rudy DeLeon remember vividly what happened that night.

Burke: "Marines from a mountain warfare unit were on maneuvers in these hills all morning. Afterward, they had started drinking beer. There were eight of them — a colonel, a lieutenant, a gunnery sergeant, a lance corporal and four PFCs. A couple of us had driven ahead and bumped into them at about six o'clock. The colonel asked us when we'd be running by this point (about 15 miles out of Bridgeport). We told them around midnight. He said he and his men would like to go the full 10 with our runner. We said fine. At that time we didn't know the runner would be Hickey."

Hickey: "I'm not a jarhead fan myself. I mean, I respect them, but I'm an air force boy. When they arrived, we began kidding each other, and they named me 'Air Force One.'

"I didn't know what to expect. A couple of them were black, and they looked like sprinters to me. But all of them said they had run some distance. And of course their type of unit runs a lot through these hills. I didn't want to be embarrassed. I really got up for it."

Burke: "About five minutes before the hand-off to Hickey, the lieutenant — a young guy — stuck his finger down his throat to get rid of all that junk he'd been eating and drinking."

Hickey: "I took the baton, and I was sky-high. All I heard was Rudy yell, 'Show 'em, Bobby!' I just sprinted out of there. One of them lasted a half, maybe three-quarters of a mile. That's the last I saw of any of them."

DeLeon: "I ran the full distance with the marines, 10.4 miles. The lieutenant was just bound and determined not to let his colonel beat him. We were out about four or five miles, and all of a sudden he shit right in his pants. Totally. But he wouldn't stop and clean himself because he wanted to beat that colonel."

Hickey: "I went down about 1,200 feet, and that's quite a decline. My body took an awful jarring. I ran it in 65 minutes. That's pretty good for 10½ miles."

DeLeon: "The lieutenant and I finished together. We were

about six miles behind Hickey. Then the colonel came in. He was real tired, but he was a lot cleaner than his lieutenant."

Burke: "One of the PFCs collapsed. But his buddies got him going again."

Hickey: "Yeah. I was sorry to hear that. I believe that's fine dedication, but I don't believe anyone should be made to do that. But when you're in the service, your body belongs to God. Someone tells you to do something, it's an order. You do it."

Burke: "Eventually all of them finished. You know what's interesting? That's a mountain warfare unit. It's unique. It should be able to handle these mountains. But Hickey just dumped those guys. We should take that unit and trade it in."

Later that day, Van One driver Jerry Mowat told Van Two, "Those marines challenged the wrong guy when they challenged Hickey. Fuckin' Hickey. That turned him on. Hickey got a hard-on."

Bob Hickey: "No, I'm not your typical cop."
Anonymous teammate: "He's not your typical human being."

Bob Hickey, the man who "runs through pain," who had the best overall average in the last relay, who supervises six men in the tough Hollenbeck Division, is also a devout Christian Scientist who occasionally takes muscle-relaxing pills, is a member of a "cop family" who nearly became an outcast on the department, and is a fierce competitor who once grabbed the hand of an exhausted opponent so that they could cross the finish line together.

To most of his teammates, he is an enigma, a contradiction.

Shearer: "I love Bob Hickey. But Christ, he just doesn't think about the other person sometimes. I mean, I come back from a run, and who's in the shower? Hickey. And he's been back for an hour already. We all want to eat, and who's writing a letter? Hickey. We want to do laundry, and who wants to make a phone call? Hickey. I know he's basically a considerate person. But I think he has a tendency to live his own life as though he were alone in the van. He just doesn't really think about other people."

Burke: "Bob would jump in front of a bullet for you."

Foote: "Bob Hickey would give you his right arm."

Janowicz: "Hickey could be dying, and if somebody came along and said, 'My legs hurt,' he'd come alive just so he could take care of him."

Clark: "I can see Hickey droppin' dead in the roadway, crawlin' on his hands and knees with a smile on his face . . . realizing that he's gonna get the Runner of the Year award posthumously.

"I remember on the San Leandro run, the camper got lost, and Hickey ended up runing four extra miles on a bum hamstring. At the end of his run he was so forlorn. But he was so happy he got the chance to sacrifice himself, he almost died. He's a trooper. And he's also a martyr."

Connelly: "He's a Christian Scientist, but he takes pills all the time."

Bonneau: "Bob's a good friend. But the pills — that is one thing I've never quite understood."

Burke: "Some of the guys wonder why he goes to the doctor so much for his feet and why he takes pills for this and that. For Bob, that's a relaxer. It's a crutch to make him go faster. It's all mental."

Kiser: "I don't give him pills. He takes 'em."

Shearer: "I'll tell you one thing. Hickey is a regular little sweetheart — great to have around the camper. Always picking up, dusting things off. It raises my spirits to see all that cleanliness and neatness."

Kiser: "We call him Mother because he's very finicky. Always picking up socks, putting things in their right place, cleaning up, cooking. He's even got a little vacuum. He's a regular little housecleaner, see? And some of the guys — it just drives 'em crazy."

Bob Hickey: "When I was growing up I did everything with my mother. Things a daughter would do with a mother. I shopped, cooked, sewed with her. I can do all those because my mom taught me how to do them.

"My dad was a police officer. My family was very religious. I either wanted to become a cop or a minister. I've always enjoyed working with people and helping them.

"Finally I decided I wanted to be a minister. I was Christian Scientist, but I started visiting every church to find one that really pacified me — Mormon, Episcopalian, Catholic, Presbyterian. And I found that the people who went to these churches went there to show off a new dress or hat or to find out the latest gossip, or just to keep their next-door neighbor from gossiping about them. These people were hypocrites. Dammit. They were hypocrites.

"So finally I decided I would have my own church, my own congregation. The church would be nondenominational. When people had problems, we as a congregation would help them. I would teach the word of God as I thought it should be taught. That God said love Him. That God said talk to Me, pray to Me.

"For some reason, you know, people laughed at me."

"Finally I decided to go back to Christian Science and give up on the idea of becoming a minister. I said, 'I'm not gonna impose my religion on anyone. I'm just gonna do what I believe in. And I can serve people and help people by being a policeman.'

"So I became a policeman. And my six and a half years in accident investigation were probably the happiest of my life. I threw all my energies into helping people. People involved in traffic accidents need a policeman. I loved that job.

"Sure, I wrote tickets. And sometimes people would get real upset when I wrote them up. They'd say, 'Hey, why don't you go out and do what you're supposed to do? You know, arrest a criminal?' And I'd say, 'Do you know that more people die on the highways every year than are killed by crime?'

"And so I put my total efforts into writing citations, arresting drunk drivers and handling traffic accidents."

"I'm not an extremist in my religion. I believe that God gave men doctors and knowledge of medicine for practical reasons, primarily because there are a lot of people who don't have the strength to pray and be cured. You know, not everyone's Jesus Christ either. So I don't criticize people who go to doctors.

"Now my daughter broke her arm once, and I didn't just sit there and pray. I said, 'Dammit, let's get her to a hospital and have them set her arm. Then I'll pray. Pray there'll be no pain. Pray that it'll heal properly.'

"But cancer, a heart attack — no. A doctor would only postpone death."

"The last time I had something seriously wrong with me was in 1972. I was in San Diego competing in the Police Olympics. In the morning I competed in the pentathlon, and in the afternoon I came back and ran the mile. Then the next morning I ran the four-mile cross-country, and that afternoon I ran the marathon.

"All of a sudden I couldn't control my body. I must have dehydrated. It felt like someone was sticking me with pins and needles. I just collapsed to the ground and started shaking. I was almost in convulsions. This friend of mine called an ambulance. And when it arrived, his wife got in with me. She was a Christian Scientist, and bless her heart, she just kept talking to me all the way to the hospital. She kept saying, 'This is not happening to you. You can't accept this. God's with you.' And I said, 'Gee, that's terrific. Maybe I can handle it myself.'

"And all of a sudden I started coming out of it. And then I felt fantastic. The doctor came in to examine me in the emergency room. He said, 'What's our problem?' And I said, 'I have no problem. I'm fine. I don't know what it was, but I'm fine now.'

"He still wanted to examine me. And I said, 'Hey, I told you I'm fine . . . and I'm leaving.' He said, 'You can't leave.' And I said, 'Watch me . . .' And I got up and walked out. It is amazing what prayer can do."

"I was a frustrated athlete all my life. I couldn't make the basketball or track team in high school. I did make the football team, but I got into just one play. I was so thrilled I just stood around smiling and laughing. Some guy knocked me cold.

"In 1967, I entered the Police Olympics in tennis. I had practiced real hard. But I drew the top-seeded player and was eliminated in straight sets. I was shattered. Alex Shearer tried to comfort me. He asked me to run in the four-mile cross-country race the next day. I had never run cross-country, but he talked me into it.

"I had no idea how to run. I just stayed as close to the other runners as possible. I finished just behind Alex. I couldn't believe it. After all those years, I'd finally found something I could compete in.

"I owe a lot to Alex."

"My first assignment as a police officer was at 77th Division, virtually an all-black area. I just didn't fit in. My attitude was not the same as that of the general police officer who worked 77th. I never used the word 'nigger' until I had over two years on the job. The guys used to laugh at me and ridicule me 'cause I used to use words like golly, jeepers-creepers, gosh, colored or Negro.

"I felt that people should be treated equally. My attitude just wasn't accepted. The guys had very little to do with me. I was almost banned from the locker room. When I came in there to change uniforms, I'd hear people talking about me.

"They thought I was an ass because of the way I felt, because of my religion, because of the way I was raised.

"But I wouldn't let them change me. After a while, though, I no longer changed my uniform at the station. I'd just dress at home.

"I had problems with some of the officers, but they couldn't find anything they could dismiss me on or fire me for. I did my job. I was slow on my reports because I tried to be neat, and my supervisors always used to jump on me. They made it very difficult for me. I really didn't develop any close friends the whole time I was in 77th.

"Now when you work with different officers for a while, you develop some of their idiosyncracies, whether you like it or not. You try to maintain your individuality, but sometimes it's hard.

"And that's how I finally came to say the word, 'nigger.'

"I was in roll call, and the sergeant was reading off a list of guys we should be on the lookout for. And he named off this one guy who was raping and beating old women. And I just said out loud, 'goddamned nigger.' And then I turned around, and there was a black officer right behind me. I almost died.

"I said, 'I'm sorry.' He just said, 'I know.'

"But it really wasn't the cops that changed me. It was the people. The bad people. You go into homes and see cockroaches all over the place, and the house smells of defecation, and the parents don't give a goddamn about their kids. All they're interested in is getting money from welfare.

"I walked into a house once — I couldn't believe it. There was this kid sitting in a crib, defecation all over him. Maggots in his eyes — I'm serious, maggots. You see things like that, you cry. How could anyone treat their own child like that?

"There's only a few who do this. But when you see it, it upsets you. Man, you see kids lying in their urine, and that stench is so bad it turns you sick.

"Whites do it to their kids, too. But the problem was I was working in a black area, and that is where I saw it being done. To me, that parent was a nigger. But the kid wasn't. To me, that same white parent would be white trash. But the kid wouldn't be."

"When I first got to 77th, I worked with almost all old-timers, a vanishing breed. I worked with one guy who took gratuities. Nothing corrupt — just cigarettes and a quart of milk once in a while. Maybe a loaf of bread.

"And then I worked with a sleeper. This guy used to pull over every night, jump in the back seat and sleep for a couple hours.

"One night he said, 'You drive. I just got a vasectomy. I'm real sore.'

"I musta hit every bump that night. And it really made me feel good to watch him suffer.

"I don't like sleepers. That's not what we're being paid for. We're being paid to go out there and serve the public."

"Even today I have problems. I don't get along with all my supervisors in Hollenbeck. I'll give you an example. We had a gang member who'd been beaten up in a gang war.

"Officers told him, 'We've called an ambulance.' And he said 'Hey, I don't want any medical treatment.' When the ambulance arrived, one of the police officers told the crew, 'Hey, this guy's an asshole, and he's refusing treatment.'

"So the ambulance crew said, 'Do you want treatment?' The guy said no, and they just walked away. Didn't even try to examine him. And there's a sergeant right there, too. And it's his function as a policeman to protect and serve. I don't care if that guy's a gang member or what his attitude is toward police.

"So I went up to the guy and said, 'You need medical treatment. You get in my car and I'll take you to the hospital.' He said, 'I'm not goin'.' I said, 'Hey, look at your mouth — just look at it! You gotta get your lip sewn up. It's bad, really bad.'

"His girl friend came up 'bout this time and said, 'He's right. Go with him. You need it.' And so he went with me to the hospital.

"But my fellow supervisor completely blew his cool, blew his mind about that. And two policemen wound up thinking I'm an asshole."

"How many close friends do I have on the force? Real close friends? Probably none.

"Do I love my fellow officers? Yeah. I'd die for 'em."

11:52 P.M. ALEX SHEARER

"I ran through Devil's Canyon. Five miles downhill. Everything was going along very smoothly when I heard this dog barking. Then this thing just sort of appeared out of the brush. It was the size of a small bear. Huge. [According to more dispassionate observers, it was a German shepherd.]

"I kind of veered around it, holding the baton up. But I said to myself, 'Man, this baton isn't going to do me any good.' So I ran back to the follow car for protection, and they chased the beast away. After that, all the guys in the camper thought it was pretty funny to go by me and bark."

When Shearer got back into the van, he felt pressure under the nails on two of his toes. Blood was building up beneath the toenails.

1:04 A.M. BOB BURKE

Bob Burke carried the baton across the California border into Nevada.

"There were a million little gnats along the way. One of them got in my mouth."

After the run, Burke pressed ice packs onto his feet for half an hour. "But there are no real problems," he said. "My feet bother me, just like everyone else's."

2:17 A.M. JOHN ROCKWOOD

He had run three tough legs — one up the Angeles Crest and two across the Mojave Desert. But for the past 16 hours he had fought his dehydration with liquids and had slept and/or rested for 12 hours. John Rockwood felt he was ready.

"The worst part was the cold. I couldn't even bend my fingers, they were so cold. I kept alternating the baton from hand to hand so I could stick my free hand in my sweats.

"But I felt great. I thought I was hauling a good seven-minute-per-mile pace. But as I handed off to Bonneau, the van read off my time — 85 minutes. I was really disappointed."

It was the slowest leg anyone had run. But there were some encouraging signs for Rockwood. He was feeling stronger. And he had won his battle with dehydration. "I'm looking forward to the next one," he said. "If I get the right conditions, I'll start to get my times back down. I'm ready to go now."

3:42 A.M. DICK BONNEAU

Dick Bonneau was expecting the worst. Like Rockwood, he had struggled through his first three legs.

"I figured this would be another tough one. So I went out slow. But after a couple miles I felt really good. I couldn't believe it.

"It was nice and cool — about 55 degrees — and it was all downhill. Without a doubt, that was my easiest leg. I knew then that I'd make it to Montreal. I ran it in 68 minutes. I really surprised myself."

Dick Bonneau had a long history of surprising himself and others. Small and youthful, he didn't really look like a cop. Yet he was one of the department's best.

He hadn't started running until he was 30. Yet he was one of the team's most dependable members.

He'd nearly flunked out of high school. Yet he later picked up a bachelor's degree and nearly a master's.

He was a wild kid who "didn't give a damn about anyone or anything."

And yet . . .

Connelly: "Dick Bonneau is the type of guy you like to be around. You say, 'Hi, Dick. How are you?' And you mean it."

Shearer: "He's a good friend. He's probably the most likeable guy on the team."

Burke: "He never says anything bad about anyone. He hasn't got an enemy in the world. You talk to Dick for two seconds, and you like him."

Hickey: "He's good people. Beautiful."

Dick Bonneau: "I was interested in two things in high school — chasing girls and making trouble. I did what I wanted to do and to hell with everyone else. And I was a bad student, mostly D's and F's. Finally the principal called me in and said, 'Either you straighten up, or you're out.'

"At that point I began to change. I began to study. In my senior year I got straight A's. That showed me I could have done it all along."

Bonneau got married during his junior year in high school. After graduation he went to work at North American Aviation.

"But I always wanted to be a policeman. My behavior in high school was inconsistent with that goal. But I just couldn't see any relationship between school and what I wanted to do.

"Police work fascinated me. It seemed as if cops were always involved in something exciting. Then there was job security and the fact that it was a well-respected job. And you didn't need college for it."

In 1961, when he turned 21, Bonneau made a serious effort to get into police work. He checked with several departments, including the LAPD. But the answer was the same all over: At 5 foot 7, Bonneau was two inches too short.

His job at North American was becoming a bore. "It was a menial task. I wanted out. But I realized I wasn't going to become a policeman, so I started looking around for another profession."

Bonneau decided to go to college to become a teacher. He picked up a bachelor's degree, a teaching credential, and completed all his course work for a master's degree. But then he "pulled a lazy." He didn't write the thesis. Still, Bonneau had learned more about himself.

"I realized that if I applied myself, I could do almost anything. I just had to be self-motivated."

It took him seven years to complete his college work. During that time he continued to work at North American, "hating every minute of it." But now he had a new and challenging profession to look forward to. Or at least he thought he did.

"I student-taught for one semester," he recalled. "And I didn't like it. After all that college, I decided I didn't want to be a teacher after all."

Bonneau was in a quandary. He was nearly 30. He had a wife and two young children. But he had no career.

"About this time, my brother, who was an officer with the LAPD, mentioned something about the department changing some of its requirements. He really didn't know for sure. But we checked, and as fate would have it, they had made some changes."

The department had decided that if an otherwise qualified applicant possessed something it considered valuable — such as a college degree — it would grant a waiver. The department had also dropped its height requirement from five-feet-nine-inches to five-feet-eight.

"I was able to trade my degree for an inch," Bonneau laughed.

But he wasn't in completely. Ahead lay the Police Academy and its strenuous physical training program. Dick Bonneau had never done anything athletic in his life. He was short, overweight, and out of shape. And he was 30.

"My brother told me I'd better get in shape," he said. "I had six months to do it. I was worried.

"That next weekend I walked to the park near my house, about a half-block away. It was a fifth of a mile around. That first day, I ran one lap, and I thought I was going to die. I was barely able to walk back to my house. My heart was pumping so fast I thought it was going to jump through my chest. It was 10 minutes before I got my breath back."

But every day Bonneau went to that park. Every day he ran.

"I didn't know anything about running, anything about training," he said. "I just settled on a very simple technique. I ran the same distance for one week. Then on Monday each week, I increased my distance one lap. It took me six months, but I finally worked my way up to three miles."

Bonneau had also started a calisthenics program — pushups, situps, pullups. But he worried about his condition until the day he arrived at the Police Academy. He shouldn't have.

A recruit at the academy is graded in three areas: physical, academic, and marksmanship. On combined scores Bonneau finished number one in his class.

"I gained tremendous confidence in my ability to handle even the most difficult challenges. After all, I'd gotten into something completely different, and I'd excelled."

Running now became an important facet of Bonneau's life. "I realized it was important to stay in good shape in order to perform well at my job and be able to take care of myself on the street. So I continued to run about five miles a day.

"In 1971, I read in the department newspaper about the Tijuana to Vancouver relay. I wasn't running far enough yet to try out for the team, but I told myself if they ever ran again, I would be ready. I wanted to be part of the team.

"So I started increasing my mileage. One afternoon I met Bob Burke and Chuck Foote at the academy and began running with them. In 1973 Bob told me that the team was going to run from Washington, D.C., to Los Angeles the following year. He told me a spot was open. I tried out and made it."

For one of the few times in his life, Dick Bonneau wasn't surprised.

4:30 A.M.   **15 miles outside Carson City**

The residents of Van Two couldn't believe it. Someone actually had worse sleeping accommodations than theirs. An Automobile Club driver and his two mechanics, who had volunteered to service the campers and pace car for three days, were now crammed into the front seat of their truck, sleeping. Dick Clark began a running commentary on the men from his vantage point in Van Two.

"The bright morning sun is shaking them from their slumber. The guy in the center is now awake. He has a blank stare. He doesn't know where he is. The guy to his left has his mouth open and appears to be snoring. The guy on the right is snuggled up to the guy in the middle. The guy in the middle doesn't like his companionship. He's trying to move him away. They're all awake and hurtin' now. They can't believe they're here."

Clark broke off his commentary, walked over to the truck and offered the men the comforts of Van Two. But they declined. They had to hit the road again.

Shortly before his leg, Jim Murphy put in a call to Van One. What was Hickey's time? Sixty-five minutes. Murphy wrote it down in his ledger, then listened carefully as the follow car broadcast Foote's progress.

Four men were clearly in the race for the best overall average on the relay — Murphy, Foote, Hickey, and Janowicz. At this point, only a couple of minutes per leg separated them.

5:53 A.M. JIM MURPHY

Murphy ran through Carson City, Nevada, named for Kit Carson, founded in 1858, elevation 4,660 feet, population 15,468, the nation's smallest state capital. When he passed one of the town's many casinos, the guards waved. They were the only people outside on this chilly morning.

Four years earlier, on the Tijuana to Vancouver run, the team also ran through Carson City. Several of the runners decided to visit the Green Lantern brothel. (Prostitution is legal in Nevada.) None of the runners partook of the Green Lantern's hospitality. But they did give each of the ladies an autographed picture of the team posed with Chief Ed Davis. One of the prostitutes proclaimed, "I'm gonna hang this on my wall and tell all my clients I screwed the whole LAPD team, including Chief Davis!"

Murphy ran his leg in 62:30. But he had a problem. It had started about midway through his run. Just as he and his coach had feared, his lack of conditioning had made his feet susceptible to blisters. And now he had one. It covered most of the heel of his right foot. It was ugly, painful, and serious.

6:55 A.M. DICK CLARK

Like Murphy's run, Clark's was mostly level. But he was tired. "I ran like a snail."

Toward the end there was a steep hill. Clark relaxed, shook himself out and started to take it. About half a mile up he saw the camper. It's almost over, he thought. But the camper shot ahead. "They made a mistake," the follow car announced. "You've got two more miles to go."

It took Clark nearly 20 minutes to struggle up those last two miles. He barely made it.

Clark's legs were aching. He was coughing hard. He still needed time to condition himself for the "tough one." But time had finally run out.

8:13 A.M. FRANK JANOWICZ

Clark and Frank Janowicz bridged the short distance between Carson City and Reno. Janowicz ran his leg in 67 minutes across rolling hills. "I knew that Hickey, Murphy and Foote had all run good times," he said afterward, "so I knew I had to stay in the 60s to be competitive."

8:15 A.M.   Carson City

Back in Carson City, the runners from Van One were eating a huge breakfast, compliments of the Golden Nugget casino. The other vans had been scheduled to be there, too. The team had expected to arrive in Carson City at precisely 7:16 Thursday morning. But during the night the runners had taken advantage of the cool weather and relatively flat terrain and had picked up their tempo. Murphy had blazed through Carson City 45 minutes early. For the first time since leaving Los Angeles, the team was ahead of schedule. So only Van One got to enjoy the hospitality of the Golden Nugget.

9:20 A.M. BOB JARVIS

"God, another hot bastard," Bob Jarvis groaned as he took the baton toward Reno. Jarvis had drawn the same assignment in the Tijuana to Vancouver run, and Frank Janowicz had handed him the baton then, too.

"Frank is really pissed," Jarvis laughed. "He says all he ever gets to do is run where people ain't."

An interview with Dick Clark on KOLO radio had alerted Reno to the run, and Jarvis received a warm welcome as he ran past the casinos and hotels that fill the downtown area. Along the way people waved, cheered, shook his hand, or sounded their car horns. Behind Jarvis, the pace car blared out his favorite bagpipe music. It was now 95 degrees.

9:30 A.M.   Reno

In Reno, "Doctor" Kiser treated his latest patient, Chuck Foote. As he shot his water-mercurochrome solution into Foote's blister, the team captain howled.

"I never heard an Indian yell so loud," said Clark, who liked to ignore the fact that Foote was only one-sixteenth Indian.

During the next hour Kiser worked on the other three runners of Van Two. "He just about amputated our footsies," Clark said later.

10:35 A.M. PAT CONNELLY

The temperature was edging toward 100 degrees as Pat Connelly and his friend, Mike Nocita, ran their final leg together. They maintained their usual seven-minute-per-mile pace, seemingly oblivious to the heat. Immediately afterward, Connelly took his pulse. It was 88.

Joan Connelly sat nearby, a soft drink in her hand, and talked about her husband and their life together.

"When Pat was working the street, he'd come home late and

just take off for a 10-mile run. It gave him a chance to really unwind. A lot of policemen unwind in front of the TV set or go out and have a few beers with the boys. Running is his way.

"Running has been a family experience for us. Sometimes I feel I spend half my life sitting on benches with a stopwatch, waiting for him to come over a hill. But I love it, because he's doing something he wants to do.

"Even these three and a half weeks away from the family. It's rough, but it would be worse for him to be home and see the guys leave. The unhappiness he would feel would be harder for me to live with than being alone. I think most of the wives feel that way.

"You know, Pat has run all his life, but after his first couple of runs with the LAPD, he was just amazed at the feeling generated by being part of the team. He told me, 'You know, they're all competitive athletes, but no one is out for himself. They're really and truly a team.'

"As a police family, we discuss matters a lot of families don't talk about, like what we'd do if anything happened to him. He said, 'Well, if anything happened to me, the pallbearers would have to be the runners. These are the people I feel closest to.'"

Soon afterward, Joan, the children and Nocita were on the road back to Los Angeles.

11 A.M.   **Reno**

Ron Kiser liked to call himself "Doctor," but he ignored the confidentiality of the doctor-patient relationship as he talked about his "practice" with the men of Van Two:

"Mullens is having trouble sleeping, so I gave him something. I'll see how he feels later. Everyone else in Van Three is okay. But I'm waiting for that asshole that's with Connelly to get a big blister on his foot. The preacher or whatever the hell he is. He can go fuck himself.

"Let's see. In Van One, Rockwood, Shearer and Hickey have blisters. Nothing serious. And Bonneau has athlete's foot. But Mowat won't tell me where they are so I can treat 'em. All he'll say is they're somewhere in Reno. He said everyone threatened to break his neck if he told me. I know Bonneau and Hickey want to see me. But fuck 'em. I'm not out drummin' up business."

11:20 A.M.

Jim Murphy was upset with the amount of money allotted for meals. "Five dollars a day just isn't enough," he told Rudy DeLeon. "You've got to eat a lot of food when you're punishing yourself physically like we are. And we just aren't getting enough money."

11:45 A.M. — 3:50 P.M.
Van Three   North of Reno

Frank Mullens, Eddie Garcia and Curt Hall got hills, headwinds, heat, and altitude during their 10-milers through Nevada's parched desert. The temperature was now over 100 degrees.

Mullens' right hamstring, which he'd injured four months earlier, was aggravated during the run. He alternately applied ice and heat to it for an hour afterward. But it was still sore.

Garcia's 10 miles were the toughest he'd run so far. "My feet felt numb," he said. "Every part of my body still aches. The pavement was so hot [about 135 degrees], and my feet just burned."

And Hall ran 10 miles of uphill. "But I felt strong," he said. "I'm getting into condition." Hall paused a moment. "I'd probably feel like Superman if I wasn't in this heat."

12 Noon   Reno

"Doctor" Kiser was still fuming about Van One.

"Usually you can't find a doctor," he told Chuck Foote. "But I can't find my patients."

3:50 P.M.
Van One   45 miles north of Reno

They ran the Angeles Crest, and twice they ran the Mojave during the heat of the day. Finally, last night on leg four, they got a respite. But that's all it was — a respite.

Hickey: "Leg five was hell. I thought I was gonna die. It was so hot, and I had a steady incline. My feet were just killing me. I never thought they'd hurt this much. But the worst thing is the blister on my left foot [a souvenir of the Mojave]. Kiser's been draining it for two days now, but it just won't heal up."

Hickey ran his leg in 67 minutes.

Shearer: "What a horrible run that was. It was hot, hilly. And there was a real bad pitch to the road. That puts tremendous strain on the feet, and it causes blisters. I was real tired. Couldn't drive, lift my legs. And my toes were real sore. The blood is really building up under my toenails.

"Some of my teammates are saying I should have an operation to relieve the pressure. But I think at least some of them are suggesting it for their own selfish reasons: They want to hear me scream. I think I'll try to live with it for now.

"One real nice thing about the run was that Larry Kramer, AKA Snow White, ran along with me. But I had some trouble because he kept trying to hold my hand."

During the past two days, the runners and drivers of Vans One and Two had chosen nicknames for one another. In Van One, the runners named themselves after some of the Seven Dwarfs and had dubbed Larry Kramer as Snow White. In Van Two, Chuck Foote and Dick Clark were teamed as Tonto and the Lone Ranger. Jim Murphy was Mercury. And Frank Janowicz was Batman. Van Three went with the names that were on their birth certificates.

6 P.M.
Outside Van One   55 miles north of Reno

Clark: "I think a lot of people might hang up their hats or their jockstraps after this run."
    Kramer: "No. If Burke said at Christmas time you're gonna run to the North Pole and see Santa Claus, you'd all fuckin' go. And I'd go along and drive."

6:19 P.M. BOB BURKE

"A bicyclist came out and rode along with me. He has a two-and-a-half-acre farm just outside Johnstonville. And he said to me, 'Wanna see heaven? Take a look to the left.' And there was his farm. Lots of pine trees and horses and a real nice house. It was heaven."

7:30 P.M. JOHN ROCKWOOD

Rockwood had been struggling for four days. His first run had left him with blisters, his second and third with dehydration, and his fourth with the poorest time of any runner so far. But he had slept six hours, eaten a big meal, and drunk plenty of liquids.
    "The fifth leg was a great one," he said. "I finally turned it around. I ran it in 73 minutes. You know, all my other runs were in the 80s and that psychs you out. You feel like you're letting everyone down."

8:43 P.M. DICK BONNEAU

Bonneau's turnaround leg had come 16 hours earlier. He felt strong again this evening.
    "It was real nice — cool, easy road conditions. I ran it in 70. So I've put two good ones back to back. I feel real good."

9:56 P.M. BONNEAU to FOOTE
The hand-off

A conflict erupted over how far Bonneau had run. Van One accused Van Two of parking a tenth of a mile beyond the correct pass-off point. Van Two, driven by Assistant Chief of Police George Beck, insisted it was actually a tenth of a mile short. Van One finally admitted it was wrong.

An anonymous runner in Van Two: "The Chief is never wrong."

Two hours before Foote's leg, the city fathers of Susanville had hosted a dinner for the runners at the local high school.

"I tasted that dinner the whole way," said Foote.

Foote's blisters had been treated by Kiser earlier in the day. "I don't know what he gave me," he said, "but whatever it was, it worked pretty well. I don't feel my toes."

11:02 P.M. JIM MURPHY

For Jim Murphy, Thursday had been a day of agony. He, too, had been treated in Reno by Kiser for the giant, painful blister on his right heel. Kiser had drained it and injected the Mercurochrome-water solution. He said it should be fine — in a couple of days.

But Murphy found it impossible to sleep. The pain was excruciating. He returned to Kiser and got a sleeping pill. It did no good. His foot throbbed. It kept him awake all afternoon and evening. Suddenly he felt a surge of panic. "The enormity of what was ahead just overwhelmed me. I thought, 'My God, I've got twenty-two or twenty-three more 10-milers to go, and I've got severe blisters. It's gonna be impossible to make it.'

"But then I kinda pulled myself together, and I thought, 'I hold three American records for my age group. I hold a cross-country record for the LAPD. I've been a national champion. There's no way I'm gonna just make it to Reno and then fly back home! I couldn't live with myself.'"

Murphy thought about the pain he'd suffered in past races. And how he'd driven himself and risen to the challenge then. He thought about his first big marathon in 1965, running for the Santa Monica Athletic Association at the AAU team championship in Yonkers, New York.

"Six miles from the finish I got a heel blister — the same place as this one — and I had to run all these steep hills, up and down like a roller coaster. That's death on a blister. Toward the end I was leaving bloody footprints.

"The skin came completely off the blister — it was raw — but I kept running. I knew I had to keep going because if I stopped even for a moment, the pain would stop me dead. Finally the nerve endings got numb. But at the finish I felt like it was the end of the world, it hurt so much.

"I finished tenth. And that gave our team first place.

"After the run, I couldn't sleep, I couldn't sit still, I couldn't do anything. The pain would just well up, and I'd have to get up and hobble around. That lasted about four days."

Murphy tried to use that experience as a touchstone as he prepared for his fifth run. But the situations in Yonkers and here in the Nevada desert weren't parallel.

"I realized I only had to endure the pain in the Yonkers marathon up to a certain point. I knew it would end, and then I could rest and wait 'til my blister healed. In fact I didn't run again for two weeks.

"But in this type of relay, you can't sit around and wait for something to heal. You have to run and then stop, run and then stop. And there is nothing, absolutely nothing more painful than doing that with a blister.

"Finally I thought to myself, 'My God, I might not make it. I've got an injury that could be terminal.'"

Murphy was doing a lot more than just thinking. He wrote a letter to his wife telling her of his doubts. And his teammates sensed his anxieties.

Clark: "He was makin' noises about what happens if you don't go out, if you don't make your leg."

Foote: "He was really hurting, and he was talking about sitting out a 10-miler."

Clark: "Chuck, Frank, myself . . . we told him kinda jokingly, 'Well, if you don't go out, we beat you half to death and throw you out of the camper.'"

Foote: "Without bluntly saying, 'Hey, if you sit out a 10-miler we'll take a shotgun and put a hole in your head,' I just told him, 'Look, even if you have to crawl, you finish. You finish your 10 miles. These guys don't care if you run fast or slow. All we care about is having a good time and everyone doing his job.'"

Clark: "I told him there's no way you just arbitrarily hang up your track shoes on this team. Because there's a lot of people depending on you. And I told him how I feel about it. I said, 'If my feet were bloody, and I had to run on stubs there's no way anybody would run any of my miles. I didn't come here to set any records; I don't have that much ability, and I'm not in great condition. But I am an integral part of the team.'"

For the first time Murphy began to understand what Burke and the others had meant months ago when they told him that this type of running was different from anything he'd ever done before. And yet now, as then, a part of him rebelled. Foote, Clark, and Janowicz could philosophize all they wanted about "the team" and the fact that "no one cares how fast you run," he thought. Fine concepts. But he had the kind of blister that can doom a runner. They were dealing in a world of fantasy — of heroics and gallantry. He was dealing in the real world — the world of pain.

"I was depressed and confused," he'd say later. "Normally I would not have run on that blister."

But he did.

"I couldn't even put my foot down before the run," he said. "And I thought, 'My God, what am I doing to myself?'

"I went out there, and the whole 10 miles was up and down — hills all the way. I ran the entire leg on the ball of my right foot, flat-footed on the left. That caused muscle problems in my right leg because of the unevenness. But I didn't dare test the sore spot even once.

"I kept talking to myself, pushing myself. I said, 'I know I can do it. I know I can drive myself mentally. I trained under Igloi, four, five tough hours at a time. I've run on bloody feet. My background has prepared me for this. I just have to drive myself mentally.'"

Murphy hobbled up and down the desert hills in 75 minutes and 37 seconds, 10 minutes slower than any of his previous legs. Afterward, Kiser drained the blister and shot it with Mercurochrome and water. Again it throbbed. Again Murphy took a sleeping pill. Again it did no good. His next 10 miles were about 14 hours away.

12:19 A.M. DICK CLARK

For four days, Clark had literally been running scared. Fear was his companion. He knew at some point he would have to face fear head-on and overcome it. He prayed that the confrontation with "the really grueling 10-miler" could be delayed. But shortly after midnight, on his fifth leg, the confrontation arrived.

"I started at the base of a mountain," he said. "I felt lousy from the start. I was tired. My legs hurt. And I just started going up — straight up.

"After the first mile I was worried. It was steep. I had no energy. I just kept plugging away.

"After the second mile I was real worried. I was getting very tired, and I was hurtin' — all over — my legs, my ankles, my knees. My left hip joint almost locked up on me. I figured if it did cramp up, I'd just drag that one leg. I was determined to keep going.

"After about two-and-a-half miles, it got even steeper — about a 45-degree incline. And it was windy. I just kept going around those curves and kept going up. Around curves and up. And I kept hoping and thinking and promising myself that around the next curve there was gonna be a downgrade. But it never came.

"About the third mile I figured, 'Shit, I've gotta lock in here. I can't keep praying for something that isn't gonna happen. This fuckin' hill isn't gonna end.'

"I told the follow car to play all the psych music I could think of — the Olympic theme, bagpipe music — anything that could psych me into making it.

"But it didn't seem to help. About the fourth mile I was feeling crushed by the whole thing — the pain, the fatigue, the uphill, the wind. It was all getting to me. And I thought, 'Christ, if I don't do something really quick, I'm gonna be in real trouble.' So I went into really heavy super-psych. I made that run, that one 10-mile leg, everything. I said, 'If I can finish this leg, I'll finish the whole relay.' I just collected everything and focused it on that one run. This was it.

"I concentrated on every step. I prayed. And I did a lot of deep thinking.

"I thought about the reasons I was on this run. My personal reasons, not the aesthetic reasons of 'goodwill.' At midnight, climbing a mountain to nowhere, who're you gonna show goodwill to? Some farmer who sees you in the roadway and honks at you and flips you the bone 'cause you've caused him some inconvenience? Nobody knows or even cares who you are or what you're doing. At that hour, under those circumstances, you focus on your own personal reasons for running.

"For me there were a couple of things. First, my ex-wife had said I wasn't gonna make it. And I figured I'd die before that happened, just to prove her wrong. And then I thought about my kids. I was doin' it for them, someone I care about. You know, I felt even stronger ties with my kids now than when I lived at home, 'cause I'd just lost them.

"I'd gone through this same mental process just before the run. I thought then, 'What the hell am I doing this for?' And at that time I thought about the glory of wearing USA sweats and crossing an international border. But I can remember thinking,

'I've lost everything. The family is breaking up. The kids are gone. Nothin' means nothin'. Not even this run. It means nothin'.

"I needed something concrete, something tangible. And that's when I thought about the best friend I ever had, Phil Barbutis. We were like brothers — one of those one-in-a-million relationships.

"In 1970, Phil was killed in an auto crash while serving in Germany in the air force. It was a helluva loss for me.

"Just before the run I went to his grave. It was a real emotional thing for me to sit there thinking about him, reflecting on his death.

"It was the day after Memorial Day and two flags were stuck in the ground on the grave. I took one of the flags, and I said, 'Phil, I'm gonna run this relay for you.'

"On the day the run started, I put that flag above my bunk as a reminder of my pledge to Phil.

"So that's what I focused on. Phil, my kids — and even the negative statement of my ex-wife. Personal things, things that really meant something to me."

Clark continued to climb. Five, six, seven miles. And then it happened.

"It started to level off. I knew I'd made it. I'd handled the worst possible conditions that could be thrown at me. And I'd made it. I knew then that nothing could prevent me from makin' it to Montreal.

"On that leg I came of age. I finished physically tired and mentally tough. And I said, 'Phil, we did it.'"

It took Clark 78 minutes and 30 seconds to conquer leg five. To conquer fear.

1:37 A.M. FRANK JANOWICZ

Frank Janowicz was hurting, but he was determined to beat Chuck Foote's time of 67 minutes on his fifth leg. So he went out fast, finishing the first five miles in 32 minutes, and then coasting home in 33:15. It was good terrain — gentle, rolling hills.

Afterward, Janowicz came up with a new ailment. "My shoulder hurts," he said. "I'm probably swinging it too much. My legs are improving, although my thighs and calves are still sore and my Achilles hurts a little."

Ten minutes after his leg, Janowicz was limping.

Overshadowing all else on this run was the fact that this was a team of police officers whose work was as much a brotherhood as a profession. They were comrades in arms, set off from the rest of society most conspicuously by their uniforms, but most importantly by their shared experiences. There are not many people who are asked to face death in their daily work.

Their sharing starts as recruits at the Police Academy — a combination boot camp-fraternity hell week. And it continues through their first assignment on the street — baptism under fire. The bond strengthens as the years wear on, as they encounter the darker side of life — the drunks, pimps, prostitutes and drug dealers, the child abuse, robberies, rapes, and murders.

From the start they are taught simple, basic rules. "Officer needs help" is a call to arms. A fallen officer is never to be abandoned. A slain officer is to be mourned and avenged. After a while the rules become second nature.

Their sharing creates a tremendous sense of understanding and compassion for one another. And it creates a bond among seemingly inharmonious cops. The bastards are still "their bastards." The oddballs "their oddballs."

Above all else they are taught never to let one another down. Their partners might be old or inexperienced, well-conditioned or flabby, deadly shots or just passable. They might be drunks, or sadists, or bigots, or saints. It doesn't really matter. Because their lives depend on one another. There's nowhere else to turn.

Not surprisingly, this attitude carried over into this run. Despite the competition between members, there was always an underlying assumption of cooperation and teamwork. Here, teammates might be complainers or stoics, speedsters or plodders, strong or injured. But again, it didn't matter. Because all they had was one another. And, as in the street, their survival depended on one another.

Perhaps Bob Burke explained it best one afternoon before the run at the Police Academy. How can these men run across the North American continent, he was asked. Without saying a word, Burke reached into his back pocket, pulled out his badge, and tossed it on the table.

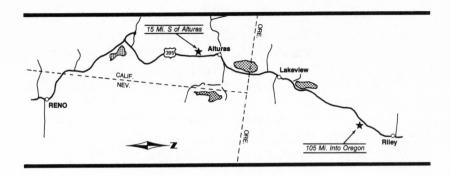

THE FIFTH DAY
Friday, June 18, 1976

2:42 A.M. - 9:16 A.M. BOB JARVIS
Van Three   15 miles south of Alturas, California

"The run was very tough. The first two miles were flat. The rest was straight up. And for the first time in any of these relays — and I've run in every one of them — I got blisters. A lot of pain. I'm Catholic, and I wear a rosary around my neck when I run. And sometimes I pray the rosary. I did it on that one. Just talked to the good Lord. Makes me stop thinking about how badly I'm hurting.

"You know, on every one of these relays I've hit the 'pain barrier' on at least one of my legs. Every bone, every muscle in my body just ached. I remember one relay, I was going up a mountain, and it started to rain, and I just let everything go. I mean, I just started bawling about three miles into my run, and I was still bawling when I passed off the baton.

"Most men just hide their emotions. But there's a really close feeling among the runners here. We can all identify with a guy who's crying at the end of his run. I see tears in a guy's eyes, and I understand. Now some of them will hide it — like Eddie Garcia. Those guys won't let go. But believe me, once you let it out, it's a great relief.

"I thought I was gonna hit that barrier — the pain barrier — on this leg, but I didn't. But it'll come. And then I'll just bawl like a baby and get it all out of my system. And then I'll be all right."

113

The pain barrier. Every long distance runner has experienced it. All dread it. It waits for them like an inevitable Delilah, ready to sap their strength and render them helpless. It hits marathoners at about the 18- to 20-mile mark. Every one of the LAPD runners has run a marathon, and they've all felt it. Most have also experienced it on these relays because of the cumulative effect of so many 10-mile legs with so little rest.

Jarvis: "It starts in your legs, then works up to your arms, your shoulders, your joints, and even your neck. It's as though you had a severe toothache from your toes to your head. The pain is so severe you can't put it out of your mind. Some runners can get by this barrier and continue on. Many can't."

Hall: "We call it rigor mortis. In the marathon I hit it at about 18 miles. Basically, you run out of blood sugar and when that's gone, your energy is gone. You feel like you're starving to death.

"You see, once you use up your blood sugar or glucose you start burning body fat. Now the average marathoner doesn't have that much fat, so he starts using pure muscle. That's like running into a wall, because the muscles can't make it by themselves. They've got to have blood sugar piped into them. Only the most extraordinary men can keep going on muscle alone."

Connelly: "It's like you have a big anvil on your chest and your mouth is full of cotton . . . your throat sandpaper . . . and every step you take is like someone putting a knife in your calves and thighs. That's agony . . . that's the pain barrier . . . that's rigor mortis.

"Let's say I have to run uphill for 10 miles. I know it's gonna be painful, grueling, difficult. But I'm looking forward to it, because the pain makes it satisfying after it's over. You look back and say, 'What a great thing I did.' If it wasn't difficult, none of us would probably do it."

Garcia: "I don't care who you are — even Frank Shorter. If you're a runner, you feel pain. Now a friend of mine told me, 'You know, I really don't like to run, but I sure like what it does for me.' And I totally agree with that. When you run and you're in pain, there's no way in hell that you're gonna say, 'Well, I love this type of pain.' But when it's over, you feel the benefits of running. It's beautiful, not only physically, but emotionally as well."

Foote: "Pain — the pain of running, but really any pain — lets you know who you are, lets you know yourself. It gives you an idea of your limitations. Now this pain barrier — I think it's a physical as well as a psychological thing.

"Take a novice runner who runs four, five, six miles. He gets winded, his legs get weary, and he'll say, 'Man, that hurts.' And he stops. What you've gotta do is get right up to the pain barrier every time. Do it consistently over a period of months. For some people it takes years, but finally you'll be able to push yourself through it."

Hickey: "I hit the pain barrier in the marathon at about 20 miles. You're going along beautifully, and at 20 you just start breaking down physically and psychologically.

"I once ran a marathon and at about 20 miles my body just went into orgasms — and not good orgasms. My whole body felt like it was gonna rip apart. But I finished.

"I once saw a film about an Olympic marathon runner. It showed him take the lead away from all these fantastic Olympic runners, and he was doing a beautiful job. And he entered the stadium first — about a hundred-yard lead. He had to run just 365 more yards to win. All of a sudden it looked like he was running in slow motion. Two other runners passed him, and he finished third. It looked as though someone had hit him with a two-by-four.

"That's the pain barrier. Your whole body is drained. Everything hurts. And your body is just screaming for you to stop. Even if you've got just 365 yards to go."

Shearer: "The legs, the lungs, the arms, the body — everything hurts. I've felt it on these relays. A lot of guys describe it as being 'wrapped in a blanket of pain.' What you have to do is push into the area where the pain is and stay there until you can't stand it, and then back off."

Bonneau: "When everything's going right you have this floating feeling. You can relax and drop your arms. It feels like you belong there. Running becomes a continuous motion, a natural rhythm and tempo.

"But when you hit the pain barrier you feel every step. You feel like quitting, but you can't let yourself quit. You can't be a long distance runner and not have the determination to deal with the pain and finish."

Rockwood: "You know, some doctors say running is one of the worst things you can do. Someone asked me, 'How do you know you're not destroying yourself?' My answer is, 'You don't.' You get lower back pain, knee problems, sore feet. You hit the pain barrier, and you think your entire body is going to come apart. But I think the benefits offset the problems."

Clark: "Long-distance running is like beating your head against a wall. It feels so good when you quit. But it also makes you enjoy things a lot more. Like just sitting down, being motionless — or having a simple glass of water. Those are glorious things after 10 or 20 hard miles or a marathon.

"Once you've experienced the pain barrier, you know what you can stand, what your limits are. You're dealing from experience, not coping with the unknown. A lot of people would quit if they felt that kind of pain. These people have not had the opportunity to condition themselves to push beyond the pain barrier. In other words, to feel pain, accept it, deal with it, and push past it.

"During a marathon you actually hurt to where your mind isn't functioning properly. You're not getting enough oxygen to the brain, and you start gettin' rummy in the head. Even Frank Shorter has said it — the last six miles are where the marathon begins. The first 20 are just background.

"I can remember the last six miles of my first marathon. I was getting numb in the head. I was trying to explain to the guy next to me what the five events were in the police pentathlon. I tried six or seven times to tell him, but I kept forgetting what we were talking about. I kept losing my train of thought. Finally it got so embarrassing I just quit talking.

"What happens is all your energy, particularly your mental energy, is focused on putting one foot in front of the other. It takes an incredible amount of concentration because of the pain. Everything else becomes secondary.

"The pain of the marathon, or any long-distance running, trains you to push yourself mentally — forces you to rise above discomfort and pain. The only reason that I went back to school and knew I could make it through college is because I finished a marathon. Most people might not see the correlation. But to me school was a mental marathon.

"Let's face it. What stops people from doing things or becoming something is the obstacles they put up in their own minds. Well, if you are schooled and conditioned to the point where your mind completely controls your body, then you have the ability to sit down and read a book and concentrate for 10 hours at a time, just as you have the ability to push yourself to run a marathon or run 10 miles every 16 hours for three weeks. To me, it goes from the mental and athletic to the mental and academic."

Foote: "Pain — the pain barrier — teaches you not to give up. It's a great training ground for a cop. Me, Connelly — Christ, we're not fighters. We're skinny guys. But I'll tell you something: I've got into scrapes with guys much bigger and stronger than me, and so has Connelly, and we've never been taken. We're fully prepared to fight for our lives."

Connelly was not only able to fight for his life when necessary, he was also able to combine cunning with running to avoid fights.

Connelly: "When I worked patrol I often got tangled up with guys bigger than me. Everyone in the division used to call me the 'gopher.' I was the runner, and they'd say, 'Go for this guy or go for that guy.' I got in some real wild foot pursuits.

"One afternoon my partner and I spotted these two guys, robbery suspects. We said, 'Halt!' And they took off on motorcycles. After about two blocks they ditched their cycles and took off on foot across an orange grove. I bailed out — I was the passenger. And here I am, coming right down on top of these guys real quick. I coulda caught 'em easily. But I said, 'Wait a second. I'm not gonna be a dummy and nab 'em while they're still fresh. They're much bigger than me.' So I just stayed about 10 yards back and let 'em run as far as they wanted.

"And they're looking over their shoulders and panting. We're about a mile into this orange grove now, and they're starting to stumble. They're exhausted, and I'm right behind 'em, about 10 yards. In fact, I'm slowin' down to stay 10 yards behind.

"They come to a six-foot chain link fence, and they just stop. Couldn't move. Exhausted. I just pulled my cuffs out and slapped 'em on.

"One of the guys says, 'How could you keep running like that? You're not even breathing hard.' And I said, 'I run 20 miles a day.' And the other guy says, 'Just our luck. We get in a cop chase, and the cop is just using us for a workout.'"

4:02 A.M. PAT CONNELLY

"It was the first leg I'd run without my family cheering me on. I thought about how much I love them. How much I wish they were here. How long it would be until I saw them again.

"I climbed about a thousand feet during the 10 miles, which was pretty tough. But the worst part was the loneliness."

5:20 A.M. - 8:30 A.M.

The desert had given way to rolling hills and farmlands as Mullens, Garcia, and Hall carried the baton back into California to the town of Alturas.

Alturas, in Modoc County, population 2,799, is located in the extreme northeast corner of the state. Its inhabitants call it "the last of the West." They hosted a breakfast for the runners at the local high school — pancakes, scrambled eggs, sausage.

The whole town contributed. The napkins were provided by the Modoc County Cow Belles, a group of ranchers' wives. Each napkin listed the founding families of Alturas and displayed their cattle brands: the Flournoys, the Webers, the Critchensons — all descendants of the first settlers of Modoc County back in the 1800s.

Mayor Neil Phillips welcomed the runners: "You're one of the greatest bunches I've ever met."

Later, Phillips table-hopped. He fingered one of the paper napkins and read off the names of the founding families, then pointed out their descendants around the room. "You know," he said proudly, "they're the backbone of America, these people."

Dick Clark was impressed. "You're right. This is what America is all about. You know, running through these small towns, we're finding out more and more who Mr. and Mrs. America really are."

At another table, Chief George Beck was being interviewed by a local radio station.

Beck: "My main project now is keeping these guys from dreaming up another one of these runs. They're killing us."

Not only was the breakfast a chance for the runners to meet "Mr. and Mrs. America," it was a rare opportunity for them to socialize with each other, exchange gossip, swap stories, and compare notes on aches and pains.

Burke: "Nobody's able to lift in our van right now. Everyone's legs are heavy."

Mullens: "I don't feel any power in my legs either. My thighs are killing me."

Hall: "I feel real weak. I can't break 80 minutes.

Mullens: "Yeah, my times have been lousy, too. So far I've run a 74, 76, 84, 82, and an 86. But I'll psych myself up."

Garcia: "I'm a little disappointed in my times, too, but I feel good. I'm getting used to that bunk. I'm sleeping a little better."

Mullens: "Well, I'm not sleeping so great. And I've gotta have my rest. And I'll tell you something — I really don't appreciate it when Chuck Foote comes in and wakes up my camper every morning. I enjoy Chuck's company, but not when I'm trying to sleep."

Clark: "This is great country up here. I'd like to come here and do a little hunting and fishing."

Bonneau: "I did a little hunting last night when I was running."

Clark: "Oh, yeah? What'd you hunt?"

Bonneau: "Bugs. I ate a lotta bugs."

Rockwood: "Yeah. I ate so many I'm not even hungry this morning."

9:16 A.M. BOB HICKEY

Bob Hickey took the baton five miles north of Alturas. The conditions were ideal: Gentle rolling hills and relatively cool, 80-degree temperatures. But Hickey ran one of his slowest legs — 72 minutes.

"This was the first time I had a chance to slow down," he said. "I've been trying for the last three runs, but I haven't been able to. I'm used to running at a certain tempo, and it's extremely hard for me to change. I'm competitive.

"But I saw Frank Janowicz this morning before my run, and he was limping around. He could barely walk. He's competing with me for the best overall average. And I know he's hurting himself. I don't want him to compete with me, because I don't want him to get hurt. So I decided I'd bring my times up — slow down a bit and ease the pressure on Frank. He'll see my times, see I ran a 72, and then he won't have to push himself.

"I finished with the best overall average two years ago. This time I don't care. I feel I could do it, but it just doesn't matter. It matters a whole lot more to Frank than it does to me.

"Frank's a big, strong tough guy on the outside. But he's really a very sensitive person. I love him like a brother."

So Bob Hickey, the fierce competitor who began the relay with the goal of being number one, changed his priorities on leg six. But if there's anything consistent about Bob Hickey, it's his inconsistency. He's a man of impulse and emotion. Because of that, his explanation for slowing down was believable. One past incident lent further credence.

"In 1972 at the national Police Olympics I broke a tradition as a competitor," he recalled. "I was running my sixth race of the Olympics — the six-mile cross-country. I was running in second place alongside this black guy from the New York City Police Department. We had about a half-mile to go, and there was no way either of us was going to catch the guy ahead of us.

"I knew I had second place locked up because this guy running beside me was tired. Every time he tried to pick up, I would pick up. He couldn't shake me.

"Finally he said, 'Hey, would you mind going in together?' And I said, 'No, I don't mind.' So I grabbed his hand, and we came in that way across the finish line — hand-in-hand. We both got a silver medal. I got three gold and three silver during the Olympics that year.

"So you see, winning is important to me. But when it's a teammate — and I consider all policemen teammates — it's not that important."

10:28 A.M. ALEX SHEARER

"The worst thing was the pain in my big toes. The pressure is really building up under the nails where I have two blood blisters. Hickey wants to operate tonight, but I'm afraid. I've undergone that operation before, and it's excruciating. In fact there's a tape recording of me screaming and all my teammates laughing in delight."

11:47 A.M. BOB BURKE

For thirteen of the fourteen runners, the major concerns were running, sleeping, eating, laundry, and injuries. Everything else had been taken care of for them. But Bob Burke's focus was wider. For nearly two years this relay had been his life. There had been countless crises along the way. And it wasn't until this day that one of the biggest ended.

Eighteen hundred dollars — money for hotel rooms in Montreal and plane flights home — had disappeared. Burke had thought that in the confusion of loading and unloading campers, the money had been lost — or worse. He had searched each camper without luck during the past three days. Finally he began to search his mind. It was then he realized the money was probably still in his office at the Police Academy. He called to check. And to his great relief, the money was in an envelope on his desk.

"That was the last of the mental problems," he said after his sixth leg. "The Vogues, the uncertainty over the condition of the substitute campers, and finally the money — it's all behind me now. It's going to be enjoyable running from here on out."

Burke sat on the edge of his bunk and popped open a beer. His voice, always soft, was nearly a whisper. There was a sense of calm about him. "Thank God we found that money," he said. "Thank God no one stole it."

There have been much deeper crises in Bob Burke's life than 1,800 missing dollars. And there have also been great moments of joy and compassion.

You might have seen what you are about to read. Millions of people did. Because Bob Burke was on Ralph Edwards' *This Is Your Life* television program in January of 1973.

Host Ralph Edwards: "How does a man become a police officer? What are the qualities that spin from brain to heart? That make a man knowingly face danger and death every day, and yet allow him to serve his fellow man? One day you are mediating in the Watts riots. On another, you are on a dawn raid of a suspected arsenal."

Voice of Ron Robinson (offstage): "And on another, he was holding the hand of a fellow officer who was badly shot up."

Ralph: "What had happened to you, Ron?"

Ron: "I had gone out on a 'family dispute' call and was shot right below the eye. I was taken to the hospital, where it was feared I'd lose my sight. I was lying there all alone, and when I looked up, I could vaguely see someone standing over me. It was Bob Burke. I had been in such pain before, and so alone, and suddenly there was Bob holding my hand. There were tears in my uninjured eye, and I remember seeing there were tears in his eyes. Somehow, in that moment, I knew I was going to make it. He kept holding my hand and saying to me, 'Hang in there, champ! It's going to be okay. I'll be right here with you.' And he was — all through the night. He came to see me in the hospital every day, and I found out that he went to church every day to say prayers for me. Thanks, Bob."

Ralph: "Thank you, Ronald Robinson. But let's come back to today, Bob. What is your present assignment?"

Bob Burke: "I'm athletic training officer at the Los Angeles Police Academy."

Ralph: "What are your duties?"

Bob: "I set up all athletic programs for the police department."

Voice of Daryl Gates (offstage): "And he does it well, Ralph."

Ralph: "The voice of a man who knows your record — acting police chief of the city of Los Angeles, Daryl Gates!"

Daryl: "Bob, Police Chief Ed Davis wanted to be here himself for this occasion, but as you know, he's out of town. Ralph, on Officer Burke's last fitness report, he received an 'outstanding' in the four categories that judge a police officer's qualities. This is the highest rating he can receive. And it is only the most outstanding officer who would ever receive 'outstanding' in all four. Officer Burke is a credit to our force, and in the work he is doing, is a credit to his community and to the nation."

Ralph: "Thank you, acting police chief Daryl Gates. Bob, your actual police career begins after you return from two years of military duty with the air force police, stationed in North Africa."

Voice of Sgt. Warren Aronson (offstage): "Bob Burke joined the L.A. Police Department in February, 1956, and I was in charge of his boot training."

Ralph: "A man who has been associated with you throughout your entire duty with the police force, Sgt. Warren Aronson! Yours and Bob's lives have been intertwined for 17 years, haven't they, Sgt. Aronson?"

Warren: "Yes. He and I have answered many calls together. And we've had some hairy experiences."

Ralph: "You and Bob received a commendation for one of them, didn't you, sergeant?"

Warren: "We had a call reporting that a man had barricaded himself in his house and was threatening to kill his wife and daughter. We tried to reason with him, but he was armed with a rifle. We put on armor-proofed vests, and then Bob and I crept in. We had our guns, but fortunately, we were able to disarm him when we got up to the door. It turned out he was an escapee from San Quentin."

Ralph: "Thank you, Sgt. Aronson. When did you first decide that you wanted to be a police officer, Bob?"

Bob: "From the time I was a kid."

Ralph: "While you're in high school, you are assigned as deputy police chief for a day at one of those boys' day affairs where kids take over various city jobs."

Voice of William Burke (offstage): "Bob came home all impressed and talked a lot about it."

Ralph: "A familiar voice, Bob. Your dad, William Burke! How did you and your wife feel about Bob's wanting to become a policeman, Mr. Burke?"

William Burke: "Well, we weren't too sure. We didn't want to see him hurt. I think that's a natural reaction. It was like the time Bob first joined the force and was directing traffic in downtown Los Angeles. He was hit by a car going 40 miles an hour — squarely in the back."

Ralph: "How badly were you hurt, Bob?"

Bob: "Pretty bad shape. When I came to after the accident, I couldn't move my legs. Had absolutely no feeling."

Ralph: "What did the doctors tell you?"

Bob: "I'd probably never walk again."

Ralph: "What was Bob's reaction to that, Mr. Burke?"

William: "Bob said, 'To hell with that verdict. I'm going to walk again.'"

Ralph: "Each day, as the doctors and nurses run a pencil across the bottoms of your feet, you can't feel anything. But you are determined to walk. Then one day, after many weeks and pencil scratches, you yell out: 'I can feel it!' And when you're released from the hospital, you're assigned to Central Division, where you begin to walk a beat. And those legs of yours are to carry you to a world's record that has been hailed internationally!"

Voice of Dan Patman (offstage): "I was in high school with Bob, and still consider him my best friend. Hey, 'Moose,' how about coming over for dinner?"

Ralph: "Another voice from the past, Bob. Now treasurer of the Patman Meat Company, Donald Patman! You called Bob 'Moose,' Don?"

Don: "Well, he was a pretty big kid, weighing about 225 pounds."

Ralph: "Was Bob a good student in high school, Don?"

Don: "No, Bob was just an average student. And in athletics, although he was on our football team, he never made more than the second or third string. A lot of guys would have given up. But not Bob. I wish a lot of us had Bob's willpower and his heart power. Where does it say that a man needs a college degree or financial wealth to be considered successful? I point to my friend 'Moose' Burke as a man who has it all. His work has often exposed him to violence and meanness — and yet he has remained the kindest, most understanding, gentle man you'll ever know. And he's turned out to be the best athlete of us all."

Ralph: "Thank you, Don Patman. Bob, all through your years on the force, you had one ambition — to be the athletic training officer for the Los Angeles police force. And it happened in 1967."

Voice of Sgt. Bob Hickey (offstage): "No other guy has devoted more of his own private time to helping other guys than Bob Burke."

Ralph: "A friend of yours on the force, Bob, Sgt. Bob Hickey! You talk about 'private' time, Sgt. Hickey?"

Bob Hickey: "Yes, Ralph. You see, Burke here has thought up and organized athletic events for his fellow officers to participate in. But this is all done on our own time, if we care to do it. And he has made us care. I guess the most exciting thing we've done happened last May."

Ralph: "What was that, Bob Burke?"

Bob Burke: "The Tijuana to Vancouver memorial race."

Ralph: "Why did you call it a memorial race, Bob?"

Bob Burke: "We did it in honor of our fellow policemen in Mexico, the United States and Canada who had been killed in the line of duty."

Ralph: "How was the race run, Bob Hickey?"

Bob Hickey: "Twelve of us, including Bob Burke, started in

Tijuana, Mexico, on May 9, 1972. We ran 1,720 miles in 10 days.
It was a grueling pace. But at the end of it, we set a new world's
record for a long-distance run, and we understand this is being
entered in the next edition of the *Guinness Book of World Records*."

Ralph: "And here, Bob, are the other 10 members of the
long-distance relay team — all officers of the Los Angeles Police
Department. Pat Connelly, Bob Jarvis, Tom Holroyd, Alex
Shearer, Ed Esqueda, Dennis Humphrey, Frank Mullens, Frank
Janowicz, Chuck Foote, John Rockwood. Thank you all for being
here. I know the world will be watching for your next run. For
your work in organizing this long-distance run you and the team
receive national publicity. And a commendation from the President's Council on Physical Fitness.

"We could have filled your life, Officer Bob Burke of the Los
Angeles Police Department, with stories of raids and riots and
shoot-outs. But there's another side to a police officer's life, not
mentioned on the front pages, that is as concerned with the
constructive side of a human being as it is with the protective
side. There are Bob Burkes in some fashion on every police force
in America. But for tonight, 'This Is Your Life.' Thank you, Bob,
and good night."

12:55 P.M. JOHN ROCKWOOD

John Rockwood took the baton five miles south of the Oregon
border. The temperature was in the mid-80s. "It was real nice
until I reached the border. Then it seemed like every mosquito in
Oregon was there to greet me."

Rockwood ran across the rolling hills in 75 minutes. It was his
second good leg in a row.

The northern part of California is barren and desolate. But just
across the border into Oregon, the terrain changes dramatically.
The brown sloping hills turn green and picturesque farms dot
the landscape.

"Beautiful," said Larry Kramer. "Those guys have got it made
now."

2:11 P.M. DICK BONNEAU

"That was a bad one. One of my worst. It's just accumulated
fatigue — you know, working your muscles over and over again
so much. They get to the breaking point. And you get down
mentally, too.

"On the Washington, D.C., run, I remember sitting out in the
middle of the Utah desert. It must have been about 100 degrees,

and the wind was blowing about 90 miles an hour. I was sitting there writing a letter to a friend. And I wrote, 'What in the hell am I doing here?'" And sometimes there's just no immediate answer. I mean, I know why I want to be here: loyalty to the team and the personal challenge. But once the fatigue and the mental depression set in, you have to be able to explain it to yourself again and make yourself believe it."

Bonneau ran through the town of Lakeview, tucked away in green mountains. About 300 people lined the sidewalks, cheering and shaking his hand.

Outside Lakeview there was another disagreement between Vans One and Two over distance. Chuck Foote kept moving up the highway as Bonneau got closer and closer. Van One claimed Bonneau was running too far. Van Two claimed he wasn't running far enough.

Murphy: "Well, the chief won again."

Kramer: "That's bullshit. That pisses me off. Same thing happened last night. Van Two doesn't give a fuck."

Shearer: "Why's everyone getting so excited? Now, John and I don't care if Bonneau has to run more than 10 miles, do we, John? It's good for him. He's young."

Rockwood: "Yeah, but he might get mad and throw one of his temper tantrums and break all his toys and spill his milk."

Shearer: "If he does, we'll just take away his crayons and won't let him go to the party in Lakeview."

2:30 P.M.   Lakeview, Oregon

The Jaycees of Lakeview sponsored a late luncheon for the runners. And so, for the second time in six hours, most of them got a chance to catch up on the latest news from the campers.

Shearer: "Bob Hickey wants to perform a major operation on my toenails. Do you think I should let him?"

Clark: "By all means."

Burke: "No."

Shearer: "Thank you, Bob. I've been waiting for somebody to say no."

Hickey (angrily): "Who said no?"

Shearer: "Burke."

Hickey (to Burke, slightly hurt): "Okay. Would you want Kiser to do it?"

Burke: "Yup."

Shearer: "Ah, if I had my choice I'd take Hickey."

Clark: "Well, it is your choice, isn't it?"

Shearer: "Yeah. And I'm taking Hickey. He's more gentle.

Take a look at this toe here on my right foot. This is the most painful."

Burke: "If I had a hammer, I'd fix it real quick."

Shearer (annoyed): "Where's Bonneau? He should be sitting right here next to me. Otherwise he'll get in trouble."

Rockwood: "He went wandering off. I think he's shopping."

Shearer: "Shopping? I didn't give him any allowance because he broke that windmill."

Clark (to Connelly): "How's everyone doin' in your camper?"

Connelly: "Great. 'Cause no one's killing themselves like Murphy or Janowicz or Hickey. We're running slow. We start our runs feeling great, and we finish feeling great. That's our philosophy. You've got a lot of racers in Vans One and Two, and that's too bad. Takes the fun out of it."

Clark: "How are Hall and Garcia getting along?"

Connelly: "Fine, fine. They only shadow box now. Don't really hit each other."

Clark: "How 'bout Mullens?"

Connelly: "Well, you know — not enough sleep, not enough to eat. Then I hear him snoring up there and see him piling down the food. He's all right."

Clark: "How's the fossil? Look at him over there. Thinks he's still a gay blade."

Connelly: "Yeah. Well, Jarvis has a little problem — gas. We have a green mist in our camper most of the time."

Hall: "That's for sure."

Clark: "Joan and the kids get back to L.A. all right?"

Connelly: "Yeah. I talked to her this morning. You know, she said she missed me. And man, I just welled up with tears. I couldn't even talk.

"God, when they left me yesterday — I've never felt anything like that. We've been married almost 10 years, and I've never experienced anything as emotional as that in my life."

Clark: "It's good to have a relationship like that. I'm envious."

Connelly: "Yeah. I couldn't even say goodbye. It was just so emotional."

3:24 P.M. CHUCK FOOTE

"The sun was just pounding down. No breeze. Nothing. The pace car needed gas, so the camper followed behind me the whole way. All I felt was the heat from the sun and the hot air from the radiator. It felt like some lion was breathin' down my neck. But the worst thing was no music, 'cause there was no pace car. And man, I gotta have my music."

Foote ran along a flat stretch of pavement that literally melted under his feet and stuck to his shoes. The air temperature was 83 degrees; the pavement, 110 degrees. He was dehydrated and fatigued at the end. His time: 68:10.

Afterward, Clark handed him a Salisbury steak sandwich from the Lakeview luncheon.

Foote (disappointed): "I was thinking ham and Swiss cheese on rye all the way."

Clark: "Don't complain. It's not often that the Lone Ranger feeds Tonto. And I'm doing it only because I've never seen such a pale-faced Indian before."

4:32 P.M. - 7:12 P.M. JIM MURPHY – DICK CLARK

For two days Jim Murphy had been in a constant state of pain and depression. The blister on his right heel was nearly unbearable. It had throbbed all night, and even sleeping pills had failed to provide him with the rest he desperately needed.

He still felt he might not be able to make it to Montreal, but for the time being he kept these thoughts to himself. He felt that the key to his continuing in the relay was the much-maligned "Doctor" Ron Kiser.

"Kiser had to be the one to get me through this. But at this point, I just didn't have the confidence in him yet."

Four times during the past 15 hours, Kiser had drawn fluid from the blister and replaced it with his Mercurochrome solution. The treatments were extremely painful. About an hour before Murphy's sixth run, Kiser drew the fluid out and injected Xylocaine, a pain killer, which deadened the area slightly.

The pavement was 115 degrees when Murphy took the baton. He ran cautiously; he feared more blisters.

"For the first seven miles, I strongly favored my right side, never coming down on my heel. Both calves and my right quadraceps got very tight. And my left Achilles tendon ached from the strain. But at seven miles, all that worked out, and I started to relax.

"I began to put a little weight on my right heel. It hurt at first, but slowly it started to get sensitized. I think I might have gotten used to the pain, or maybe just pushed myself past the threshold of pain. I really can't explain it medically."

At the end of his leg, Murphy was told by the pace car that he had run 10.1 miles in 80:46. Murphy exploded. "Ten-point-one on this fuckin' blister!" he yelled. "Couldn't they get their goddamn mileage right? Shit! No one gives a shit."

Murphy stormed over to Van Four, where Kiser treated his

blister once more, drawing out an enormous amount of fluid.

A short time later, Murphy limped back to Van Two. He took the piece of paper on which he'd been recording times of the top runners, crumpled it and threw it into a wastebasket. The "race" was over for Jim Murphy.

But it was far from over for Frank Janowicz, who was contemplating strategy for his next run.

"I know that Hickey has run a slow time (his 72-minute leg earlier in the day). And of course Murphy is hurt, and Chuck Foote has just run a 68. So this is the time to pick up some time on all of 'em."

5:52 P.M. DICK CLARK

Clark ran in barren foothills along a glistening lake. It was hot and the road conditions couldn't have been worse. Gravel covered the highway for his entire 10 miles.

"I was afraid I'd slip and twist an ankle or pick up a blister," he said. "It was just murder. The butcher [Kiser] had worked on a couple of small blisters and fixed 'em up, and he had told me that I was worrying about injuries too much — that I was putting too much weight and stress on the wrong places. So anyway, the resident quack told me to relax. I did, and it worked. I felt pretty good.

"But then, as I was skipping over that gravel, nearly dehydrated, the follow car says, 'You've got just nine tenths of a mile to go.' So I picked it up and started to bring it home. I figured I was going to see all my campermates and be wrapped in a warm blanket of friendship right around the next corner. Well, that corner came and went, and so did the next corner, and the next corner, and the next corner. There was no camper. Finally the follow car shut off the music and said, 'We don't know how to break this to you, Dick, but you've got over two miles to go. We made a mistake.' It was the second or third time it had happened to me. It was like somebody took a shovel and hit me right in the face."

Back at the camper, Janowicz was still debating how to run his next leg.

"I hope it cools off, but I know it won't. I'll have to run my whole leg in the heat. [Despite the hour, it was 86 degrees.] I should try to beat Foote's 68, but I could get blisters. The pavement's hot, and the gravel could cause a lot of problems. But to hell with it. I'm gonna go out and run hard. I think I can beat Chuck's time, and I know I can beat Hickey's."

7:12 P.M. FRANK JANOWICZ

"It was hot, very hot. Lots of upgrade. I got dehydrated. I kept taking water, and the follow car watered down my whole body. My calves were sore from the steep climb. And I got a blister. I ran it in 68:58."

As Janowicz tried to walk off the tightness, he began to reevaluate: "I'm mentally tired. I've been pushing myself too hard. I've got 22 or 23 more to go. I've just gotta back off."

9:43 P.M. PAT CONNELLY

"It was the nicest run I've had so far because it was the first time I was able to run level. I've had three summits in a row. I ran a comfortable 67.

"I still miss my family, but I'm over the real hard part now. You know, what's happening here is not unlike boot camp or basic training. The military makes you forget about Mom, home, your pastor. They tear you down completely, disrobe you of everything, and then they rebuild you into a tool of the military. Well, that's what we're sorta doing here. You leave home, you leave the good life — meals served by your wife, sleeping in your own bed, all that. It takes some time to get acclimated to a new routine. It takes time for the body to respond to x-amount of sleep, x-amount of food, x-amount of running. The heat and the mountains have made it just that much tougher. And some guys compound the problem by overextending. But I've run comfortably, and I'm getting acclimated."

12:10 A.M. EDDIE GARCIA

"Frank [Mullens] ran out of the foothills, and I caught the desert. I didn't even realize there was a desert in Oregon. It was a totally miserable run. My worst so far. Very painful. I was very tired. It was my second run that day, and that does something to you. I didn't get much rest because I finished the first one at about nine this morning, and it's real hard to sleep in the daytime. To run at this hour of the morning, you really have to push yourself. You push yourself to the point where you really just exist on will."

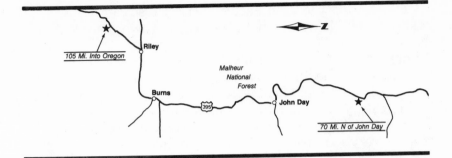

THE SIXTH DAY
Saturday, June 19, 1976

Van One

An hour and a half before his seventh leg, Alex Shearer couldn't get his shoes on. The blood building up under his toes was causing too much pain.

For two days, he had postponed the inevitable. Now he looked over at Bob Hickey and announced, "Let's operate."

His teammates cheered.

Hickey was prepared. He heated a paper clip to a white-hot intensity over the van's stove, and then approached his patient.

Shearer: "The gentlemen in the camper — gentlemen being my fellow runners — held me down. I closed my eyes. I couldn't watch. I'm very weak."

Hickey: "What you do is take the heated paper clip and press it gently against the nail. The clip is supposed to pierce the nail and release the pressure. There's a pillow of liquid between the nail and the tissue underneath. The needle isn't supposed to touch that tissue. If it does, it can cause incredible pain."

Shearer: "Dr. Hickey performed his surgery on my first toe with absolute perfection, much to my delight, and much to my teammates' dismay."

Hickey: "The first one went perfect. But the second toe had so much pressure built up that I had to put a lot more pressure against the nail with the paper clip. I accidentally pressed just a fraction too much. That did it. He cried."

Jerry Mowat: "He didn't actually cry. He screamed."

Rockwood: "It was pathetic hearing a grown man wail like that."

Shearer: "As I said, I wasn't watching, but the gentlemen in my camper tell me there was quite a bit of smoke. I screamed in agony. All that I could hear were the cheers of my teammates."

Bonneau: "We were all cheering for blood."

Shearer: "Hickey was the only one who felt sorry for me. He seemed very remorseful. I know he didn't want to hurt me, although the gentlemen wanted him to. It would have been easier for a person of less character to have succumbed to the wishes of the mob."

Hickey: "It's called 'Morton's foot.' I have the same problem. It's when the index toe is much longer than the big toe. It jams into your shoe as you run, and causes a buildup of blood underneath the toenail. I've had it before, and I could really sympathize with Alex."

Bonneau: "There's an old saying on this team: 'You'll find sympathy between shit and suicide in the dictionary.'"

There would be no sympathy on this relay, but there would be empathy. Sympathy, these men felt, bred weakness, a self-destructive emotion on a mission that demanded strength.

There would also be a kind of gallows humor. It beat crying.

3:53 A.M. ALEX SHEARER

"Thanks to Hickey, I was able to run. I just took it real easy. Stayed under 80 minutes. It was real pleasant."

8:47 A.M. CHUCK FOOTE

Once again, there was a dispute between Vans One and Two over mileage. This time, Van One complained that Bonneau had been "shorted" two tenths of a mile.

Clark: "They're being petty."

It was humid but mild as Foote took the baton on a steady decline. He ran at an even six-and-a-half-minute pace.

Inside Van Two, Clark, Murphy and Janowicz relaxed on their bunks.

Clark: "Only a policeman would live like this, run like this."

Murphy: "Right. Only person dumb enough."

Clark: "Yeah. A policeman has his brain taken out before he gets to the academy."

Janowicz: "I feel really wasted. I don't see how I can do my next 10."

Murphy: "All I'm trying to do is make it through this part of the run. My blister still hurts, and my muscles are sore from trying to compensate and keep the pressure off the heel. It's mentally discouraging. The only thing I can think about is making it through this and getting well again."

Clark: "We've already made that decision for you. You will make it through. Otherwise, we'll strap you to the back of the pace car and drag you 10 miles."

Murphy tied his shoes, hobbled out of the camper, and waited for the hand-off. About an hour earlier, Kiser had once again drawn the fluid from his frightful heel blister and injected the Mercurochrome solution.

"I just didn't know if Kiser knew what he was doing," Murphy said later. "Burke kept telling me, 'Don't worry. Kiser is great with blisters. He'll get you through.' But I just didn't know how much longer I could stand the pain and continue running. I'd run my last leg in 80 minutes, which is like walking for me."

Murphy ran his leg in 85. Worse, he developed another blister on the same foot.

"I was in a complete mental depression, 'cause I was running so slow. I was embarrassed, frustrated, and angry. Blisters have absolutely destroyed me in the past. And I thought, 'That's what's gonna happen to me now.'"

10 A.M.   Burns, Oregon

Hickey donned a chef's hat and barbecued steaks for the men of Vans One and Three in a tiny park in the center of Burns, a dot on the map of southern Oregon.

Mullens: "We finished running at the ideal time, around midnight. We all got a good night's sleep, six or seven hours. Now we're having a good meal. That's the two most important things on a run like this — sleep and food."

Dick Bonneau had wandered over to say hello. He caught Mullens's last remarks.

Bonneau: "He's right. We finished at about nine this morning. Now it's pushing toward noon. Our first man's gonna run at around seven or eight tonight. That means we have to grab some sleep this afternoon, and that's difficult. It's hot, humid — and it's daytime. But we've gotta sleep at least two or three hours."

Mullens: "It seems that this thing runs in cycles. One good night's sleep, then two bad ones."

Mullens walked over to a drinking fountain, rinsed his mouth out, pulled out a small container of dental floss and carefully cleaned between each tooth.

Connelly: "He's in great shape, considering his age. But Christ! He complains a lot. 'I didn't eat enough, I didn't sleep enough.' I think he's getting senile. And he's preoccupied with his appearance. He thinks he can stay young forever. He's vain. I mean, he won't wear glasses, even though he can't see. And he won't wear a hearing aid, even though he can't hear. I say, 'Frank, nice run.' And he says, 'No, I don't want any food right now.' I say, 'Frank, turn around and look at me and read my lips.'"

Meanwhile, a couple of the other runners from Van Three had heard about Shearer's operation earlier that day. They wanted to get the details first-hand.

Shearer: "They held me down forcibly, and then Hickey plunged this paper clip through my toe. He didn't mean to. But my other campermates cheered as I yelled in agony."

Hall: "Did you take it personally?"

Shearer: "By all means, no. I prefer to think that it wasn't me that they enjoyed seeing in pain. I would say it was any fellow human being who happened to be suffering. It could have been anyone. It could have been that kid over there playing with his mother, or an orphan, or a cripple."

Jerry Mowat: "Hey, I never did see what you were crying and complaining about. Let me see what it looks like."

Bonneau: "You'll be surprised. I bet you thought Hickey had amputated it. Look at it."

Alex removed his shoe and sock.

Mowat: "That little thing? That little thing?"

Everyone burst into laughter. Except Alex.

Shearer: "Well, I'll be putting my shoe back on. I mean, that's the typical reaction."

Burke: "Wait a second, Alex. Leave your shoe off. [To Rockwood] C'mon. Let's go over and step on it."

Rockwood walked over to get a slice of watermelon.

Shearer: "Hey, Rockwood! Would you get me a piece of watermelon and a spoon?"

Rockwood (half-annoyed): "Oh yeah, sure."

Shearer: "And hurry up about it."

Rockwood: "Would you like an end cut or . . ."

Shearer: "I don't want an end cut. I hate end cuts."

Mowat: "Being very difficult . . ."

Bonneau: "Bitch, bitch, bitch . . ."

Shearer: "Now be quite, Bonneau, or you'll go without dessert. Rockwood, get me a spoon and hurry up . . ."

Rockwood: "What happened to your spoon? You're supposed to have a fork, knife and spoon."

Shearer: "I didn't take a spoon. Get me one."

Rockwood: "I don't know where they are."

Shearer: "Then give me yours."

Rockwood: "Here. Anything to quiet you down."

11:17 A.M. DICK CLARK

"I've decided to start dedicating my runs to famous Americans of the past. This one was dedicated to Jim Bridger, a great American. An Indian fighter and guide. He was the one who warned General Custer about the Sioux. But Custer didn't believe him, so he got wiped out.

"I didn't tell Tonto [Chuck Foote] what I did. I was afraid to. But Tonto told me I needn't worry about Indians out here. This is not good ambush country. I trust Tonto."

Clark ran through flat farmlands. The first six miles were down, the last four up. "That was a little disheartening," he said. "It was hot, and I felt like I was chasing the clouds because they kept moving away from me. They were usually a little faster than me, which means they were like jackrabbits. So I didn't get much of a cooling down."

In Van Two, Janowicz was thinking about his upcoming leg. With about one quarter of the relay complete, he had the second fastest time per leg — just one minute and 20 seconds behind Bob Hickey. Chuck Foote was third, and his times were steadily improving. Moreover, he wasn't struggling like Janowicz, and he didn't have blisters, like Hickey. Jim Murphy was in fourth place, but his blisters had eliminated him from the competition. Bob Burke was just two seconds behind Murphy.

The average time-per-leg, as compiled by the pace car: Hickey (after seven legs), 66:07; Janowicz (six), 67:37; Foote (seven), 69:46; Murphy (seven), 72:18; Burke (seven), 72:20.

Once again Janowicz was grumbling about his physical condition as he got ready to leave the van for his 20-minute warmup. Cursing under his breath he backed down the steps carefully. He was unable to walk down forward. He was furious at himself for the pain and discomfort he was inflicting on his body.

But Janowicz had always been explosive, undisciplined, volatile.

"I was a wild kid in high school. Very adventurous. They called me the Mad Polack 'cause I had a quick temper, and I was very physical. I had a reputation for being vicious, of being an animal.

"But you know, I never got in a fight in high school. I came close, though. One time I was at a party, and I started bouncing this Volkswagen that was parked in the street blocking my car. Bouncing it up and down. So this guy twice my size comes out, and he says, 'What the hell are you doin' with my car?' And I say, 'Look, just get out of my way.' I don't know why I was so mad, but I was. Now this guy could have buried me right there in the street. But somebody says, 'That's Frank Janowicz.' And the guy just backed off. That's the kind of reputation I had."

"I come from an athletic family. My uncle won the Heisman Trophy — you know, Vic Janowicz. My big dream was to play professional baseball. I played all nine positions, but my best was third base. I had one tryout with the Dodgers. I got ten or fifteen swings at the plate, and that was it. I didn't think that was fair. I was a good defensive player. I had no fear of the ball. I'd stop it with my body. The scouts said two things about me: This guy shows a willingness to work, and this guy has a quick temper. In fact, they said I was like Jimmy Piersall."

"After the army, I went to Long Beach State College and played football. I was playing second-string end. I was pretty fast and had good hands. I thought about playing pro. But I got hurt, and that ended that. Also, I was 25. I was really livin' in a fantasy world."

"I joined the department when I was 27. And I really had to control my temper. I wasn't a very good shot in recruit training, and this one instructor was always getting on my case. I'd shoot lousy, and he'd say, 'Janowicz, give me forty-five pushups.' That was easy for me, but the way he told me to do them got me mad. This one time, I just looked at him, and he could just see in my eyes that I was saying, 'Why don't you go get screwed?' I talk with my eyes a lot. So he said, 'Watch it, Janowicz. If you don't change your attitude, I'm gonna bounce you out of the academy.' I respect that guy now. He got me to shoot expert."

"My first night on the job — fresh out of the academy — I was working with this real nice black officer.

"It was raining. We saw this guy asleep in his car, right near the Coliseum. My partner walked over to him and woke him up, and the guy took a swing at him. But my partner's able to subdue the guy and handcuff him. He pats him down real fast — checking for weapons — and then I get in the back seat with him.

"We're bringing him back to the station, and my partner says, 'Look, this is your first night on the job, and I want you to book this guy 'cause it'll look real good on your record.'

"So when we get to the station, I put my gun in the officers' box, 'cause you can't carry a gun when you book a guy inside a jail. So we're standing in front of the booking officer, and I tell this guy, 'Okay, take everything out of your pockets and put it up on the shelf there in front of you.' So the guy pulls everything out of his front pockets, and then he takes about eight or ten handkerchiefs out of his back pocket. Then he pulls a gun out.

"I grabbed it from him. As I did, I had this mental flashback of this officer that they'd told us about at the academy. This guy got shot his first night on the job. And I just saw his face and everything in that split-second that I grabbed the gun.

"The booking officer says, 'Did you search this guy?' And I said, 'My partner searched him.' And the booking officer says, 'Janowicz, if you don't choke this guy out in three seconds, I'm gonna choke you out.'

"The guy was about chest-high on me, and I put a choke hold on him. I wanted to kill him. All that kept going through my mind was, 'I'm gonna break his neck. I'm gonna kill him.' I kept screaming at him, 'You fuckin' bastard. You goddamn fuckin' bastard.' I kept choking the guy, just kept choking him. Finally, he shit in his pants.

"But I kept choking him. Finally, I thought I'd better let go. I did, and he dropped to the floor.

"I shook all night. I was still shaking when I got home. I could have got killed my first night on the job."

"A short time later in Southwest Division [a predominantly black area near where Janowicz grew up], we got a 415 call — man with a gun. This guy was drunk, and he was going up and down the street saying that he was gonna kill somebody. You know, blacks are very violent people.

"Anyway, I spotted the guy as he drove into a dairy. I was still a rookie and overreacted. I jumped out of the car and ran over to his car. And I stuck my gun through the window at his head and said, 'Don't made a move, asshole.' The guy was sitting behind the wheel and . . . I saw him reaching for his gun. I said to myself, 'This is gonna be it. I'm gonna shoot him.'

"But for a split-second, I waited. I don't know why. My finger was just squeezing the trigger. And all of a sudden he grabbed his gun and threw it out the window. I had all the p.c. — probable cause — in the world to blow this guy up. But something told me not to. It's close as I've ever come to killing a man."

"I'm lucky. Most guys are fortunate to find just one good woman all their lives. I found two. I just thank God for that. Because I'm very demanding. I'm quasimilitary.

"I married my wife in 1975. She's always been 100 percent behind me. What we've got going is communication. You know, sex is a big thing, because if you're an athlete and in good shape, you got a cravin' for it. But as you get older, you start lookin' at different things, and your wife's gotta be almost like a friend. You gotta enjoy talkin' to her. That's what I enjoy. I really miss the fact that she's not gonna be in Montreal to see us run in there.

"When we were going together, she told me she wanted to be a reserve cop. I told her no. That's bullshit. One cop in the family is enough. But then I started thinking, 'What would it be like if she told me that I couldn't work out or be on the cross-country team?' So I kind of revamped my thinking and let her join. This is something she wanted. And I figured, if she becomes a reservist, she might understand what I have to go through sometimes.

"I'm real proud of her. When she started through the Academy I told her, 'Hey, you gotta run.' I coached her. Taught her to relax, to run on the balls of her feet — you know, everything I don't do. She was the third fastest woman in the class. Ran the mile-and-a-quarter course in about 10 minutes, which is really fast for a woman.

"She's worked vice outside. She worked one bar to see if they were serving after-hours — and of course most of the customers were policemen, which is typical. She's also worked as a decoy prostitute. I don't mind her working inside. But outside is bullshit. Because, hey, look, it's dangerous for me, and I'm a man. I'm twice her size, plus I carry a gun. She can do whatever she wants inside. But working the street is bullshit. There's a lot of trouble out there."

"The first woman I ever loved was Jo Ann. She was 10 years older than me: She was 31; I was 21. We did everything together. We were like a team. She backed me 100 percent. She actually talked me into becoming a cop. And she backed my athletic endeavors.

"We were gonna get married. I'd just joined the force. It was

1971. She kept havin' this cough. Finally she went into the hospital. They took a couple of x-rays and ordered exploratory surgery.

"I was in the waiting room when the doctor came out. His first words were, 'I'm sorry — she's a lovely girl. In the prime of her life.' I said, 'What the hell are you talking about?' He said, 'She has cancer. A tumor on her lungs. It's terminal.'

"He said she might live two weeks, two months — he didn't know. I went in to see her. She didn't say anything about it. And I didn't either. I just said, 'Everything's gonna be okay.' She said, 'Yes. I know.' But deep down, I think she knew.

"Over the next few months, she kept going back and forth from her home to the hospital. Finally she said, 'I wanna go home.' She wanted to die at home.

"I had to go to the store one morning. I said, 'I'll be right back.' She didn't say anything. She had this special little wave for me which meant, 'Okay.' So she waved as I went out the door. I was gone about a half-hour. When I returned, she was dead. It was eleven o'clock in the morning. November 14, 1971.

"I never thought I'd replace her. Thank God I did."

12:25 P.M. FRANK JANOWICZ

"I knew Chuck Foote had run a 64, so I wanted to run my leg in the middle 60s. I ran the first mile in six minutes. And I felt good for the first five because there was a tailwind pushing me. I was just coasting. But I couldn't maintain it. After five, I started dying. It started to go uphill. The humidity got me."

Janowicz ran his leg in 72 minutes. Five minutes later he proclaimed it his "worst run of the relay." He walked around outside the camper, trying to work out the tightness. Ten minutes passed. "I feel really wasted," he said. "I think the run yesterday over the rocks took a lot out of me, because I really blasted that. I pushed myself too hard. I'm paying for it."

He walked and stretched for another five minutes. "But this one I just ran—this one was my worst yet. In fact, it was the worst 10 miles I've ever run. My worst leg ever. I've gotta slow down. I gotta think about finishing these babies. I got two more weeks to run. I gotta stop competing with Foote. He's unbelievable."

4:32 P.M. FRANK MULLENS

The road to John Day, Oregon winds through a hilly, wooded area. The team had passed through there four years earlier on its Tijuana to Vancouver relay. The people of John Day had heard the runners were coming then and decided to stage a welcome befitting their town's frontier image. About fifteen men, dressed like Indians and bandits, had lain in wait as Pat Connelly came around the final bend that leads into the city of 1,500.

Without warning, they streamed out of the hills, shouting and firing blanks from their rifles and pistols. Connelly nearly had a heart attack.

Later the town threw open its doors to the "city slickers," hosting a huge barbecue and entertaining them with a honky-tonk piano and can-can dancers.

So as Frank Mullens and his close friend, Rudy DeLeon, ran toward John Day on this afternoon, they were expecting some sort of welcome.

Mullens: "We covered about five miles. Then all of a sudden these guys dressed like Union and Confederate soldiers jumped out of the bushes and started shooting at us."

DeLeon: "They say I jumped six feet in the air."

Mullens: "Scared the hell out of me. I wasn't expecting anything that far out of town."

DeLeon: "I told Frank, 'I'm dropping back. You're the celebrity here.' He's the one who sacrificed and trained hard for this. Not me. I'm just a driver. He deserved the recognition. But he said, 'No. Get up here. These guys are gonna take my picture, and I want you in it.'"

Mullens: "I told Rudy to stay with me. That there was gonna be a lot of fun. Then I see this cannon right in the middle of the road. They set off three sticks of dynamite. Scared the hell out of me again."

DeLeon: "About twelve guys were around the cannon, dressed in uniforms. They shook our hands. I wanted to drop back again, but Frank kept telling me to run with him."

Mullens: "And then these girls came swarming out of the bushes, dressed like saloon girls."

DeLeon: "I dropped back a little when these can-can girls jumped out on the road. I pointed to Frank and said, 'He's the runner. He's the runner.' And I ran across the road."

Mullens: "I ran toward them and then just fell into their arms. There must have been about eight of 'em. Pretty little things."

By now about 200 people from John Day had gathered around the team. Publicist Lou McClary introduced the runners as Mullens continued toward the town, alone.

McClary: "This is Pat Connelly, the team coach. Ran in the Olympic trials in 1964. And this is Bob Burke, an original member of SWAT. He's the department's athletic director. He's responsible for the run. And this is Chuck Foote, the team captain. And this is Frank Janowicz, who's recorded the fastest 10-miler so far — an incredible 56 minutes. And this is Bob Jarvis. He's an actor . . ."

"A what?" asked one of the teen-age girls, frowning.

McClary: "He's an actor. He's had parts in *Police Woman, Joe Forrester, Medical story . . .*"

Jarvis pulled himself up to his full 5 feet 10 inches and tried not to look annoyed.

"C'mon," another girl interrupted. "We don't believe it."

McClary persisted. "He's even acted in television movies."

"Are you really an actor?" one of the girls asked, punching yet another hole in Jarvis's fragile ego.

"Yes," he said brusquely, "I am."

"We don't believe it," they giggled. "You can't buffalo us. He's not an actor . . . c'mon!"

All the girls joined in the laughter. McClary looked at Jarvis and shrugged.

7:12 P.M.   **John Day, Oregon**

In addition to his medicine cabinet, Ron Kiser brought a motion picture camera along on the relay. Every so often he liked to stage events to show the folks back home.

Connelly: "There was this gal who was riding a horse during the 'ambush.' She was really gassed. She'd been drinking whisky all afternoon with the guys. Kiser talked her into taking off her clothes and then running out of the camper just as Garcia handed the baton to Hall. She was supposed to come out screaming like she'd been raped."

But the best-laid plans of Van Three went astray when the elderly editor of John Day's only newspaper and his wife showed up at the camper to take some pictures.

Connelly: "We couldn't do it. But after they left, we shot ahead about a mile and parked. And Kiser talked the gal into taking off her clothes again and hiding behind a willow tree. She was supposed to jump out and run along with Hall, as though it were nothing."

Hall: "I knew they were gonna do something with this gal, 'cause I'd seen her earlier. But I didn't know what. As I ran past the camper, John Rockwood started hollering at me to slow down. I turned around to see what was going on, and there was the gal about 15 feet behind me. She didn't have a thing on. She ran about 10 or 12 feet, then turned around and ran back into the bushes."

Connelly: "She was so damned drunk, she could barely move, much less run."

Mullens: "A couple of truckers saw her. I thought sure as hell they were gonna drive off the highway. She came back toward the camper, and she had to con old DeLeon into givin' her her clothes back. He's standin' there with her bra and panties, handin' them to her as she's walkin' to the van. Then she said, 'It's such a great thing you're doin.' You're such a fantastic bunch of guys. I wouldn't do this for just anyone.'"

Connelly: "No, she wouldn't. Just some strangers running through town . . ."

Clark: ". . . only on a Saturday night."

Later the incident made the national news wires and was carried by many of the radio and television stations in Los Angeles. The story of John Day's Lady Godiva upset a lot of wives and girlfriends of team members.

Hall's run was one of the most brutal of the relay. His 10 miles were all uphill. "It took me 80 minutes. You know, I like hills. But there was no letup in that one. It was tough."

The bushwackers of John Day, officially known as the Whisky Gulch Gang, along with the city's police department and the sheriff of Grant County, Oregon, hosted a steak fry for the team at the Original Sells Brewery.

For two and a half hours it was like the Old West revisited. There was a honky-tonk piano, dance hall girls, and some of the townfolk even staged mock gunfights.

8:32 P.M. BOB HICKEY

Bob Hickey carried the baton through Oregon's scenic Malheur National Forest.

"I kept hoping it would stay light so I could see the mountains and trees and streams. It was just beautiful. But about halfway through it got completely dark."

Hickey pushed himself his entire 10 miles. His time on the uphill course: 69:04. "That's the hardest I've run so far," he said afterward. "I found out that guys like Janowicz and Murphy have injuries, and I can't slow down 'cause that would impair the team's overall time. I slowed down a few days ago so Janowicz wouldn't injure himself anymore. But now, two of our fastest runners have injuries, so I have to pick it up."

9:41 P.M. — 2:32 A.M.

Shearer, then Burke, Rockwood and Bonneau, breezed across the hills of Oregon as Saturday gave way to Sunday. It was cool, quiet and dark. All the runners felt good. Burke's leg had carried the team to the 1,000-mile mark.

On the surface, despite five days of ravaging heat, everything seemed to be going smoothly. But the men were going too fast. Ahead lay the major ceremonial commitments of the run of goodwill. The team was now about one and a half hours ahead of schedule.

At the time it seemed like a blessing. But it would prove to be a curse.

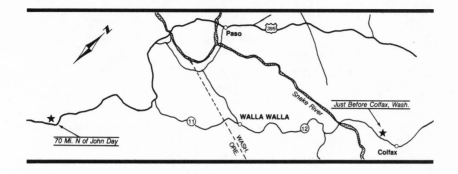

THE SEVENTH DAY
Sunday, June 20, 1976

2:32 A.M. CHUCK FOOTE

After starting the relay slowly — but comfortably and sanely — Chuck Foote was going to the whip. He ran his eighth leg in 61:55 — the fifth straight time he had broken 70 minutes. In the battle for the fastest overall average, he was still in third place behind Bob Hickey (66:44) and Frank Janowicz (68:04). But his eight-leg average of 68:33 had been built without strain or injury.

3:34 A.M. JIM MURPHY

Murphy limped through the forests of Oregon, his heel blister slowing him to 89:42, the worst leg of the relay. But during the past two days, Murphy had undergone something of a transformation.

"I was still depressed and hurting bad," he'd recall, "but I was gaining confidence in Kiser. He was getting me through my 10-milers. The skin wasn't coming off the blister. He knew what he was doing."

Before and after each run, Kiser continued to draw fluid from Murphy's blisters and then inject them with the Mercurochrome solution. He also gave Murphy pills — "muscle relaxers so I could sleep." And he built cushions for the heel and ball of Murphy's foot to relieve the pressure on the sore areas.

"Thanks to Kiser, I began to think I'd make it."

Alex Shearer had likened him to a doctor in "King's Row." John Rockwood had castigated him. Bob Jarvis had said his knowledge of athletic medicine was "superficial."

But Bob Burke swore by him. And even Dick Clark, who had called him "our resident quack," said he was "keeping everyone on the road."

He was Ron Kiser, a 41-year-old sergeant assigned to the police commission. Tall, muscular, he had the ego and self-assurance of a cop-athlete, which he was.

Kiser: "I was a pharmacy major in college, and it just wasn't my bag. I worked in drugstores, and I didn't like it. I never went back to school after that.

"But I've always been involved in athletics, and a lot of my friends are doctors and trainers and pharmacists. I've picked up a lot of helpful hints — maybe witch-doctor techniques.

"In dealing with athletic injuries, you learn from the experience of being an athlete and treating athletes. Most doctors can't comprehend what you have to do. In the past, we've had doctors go along on these relays and run a little, and I ended up treating them.

"On the Washington, D.C., run, the American Podiatry Association had its people come out and see if they could treat us. They'd look at a blister and their comments were, 'Oh, yes. Why don't you come into the office tomorrow?' Or, 'Stay off your feet a few days; it'll be all right.'

"Well, that's absolutely ridiculous. We can't treat things like a podiatrist would. We have to get the guy back on the road every 16 hours.

"Physical problems lead to mental stress. I have guys sniveling to me for sleeping pills. But I won't give them to 'em until I am absolutely sure that without those pills they can't sleep."

"We've tried to line up relay races against top-flight competition. But they won't bite. One of the top track coaches in the country told us, 'Sure, I could get a great team together, and we'd run your asses into the ground during the first two or three days. But the first blister that a guy got, he'd stop. First muscle strain a guy got, he'd stop. That's what they're used to doing. And the discomfort of the whole thing would eventually stop everyone.'

"You know, there's a lot of runners that would like to do this. But they'd do these legs five or six times, and then they'd say, 'That's enough for me.'

"Well, these guys don't have that luxury. They've committed themselves to the run. And that's their feeling — that they're gonna do it whether they have to crawl. There isn't one guy here who would give up unless he absolutely had to — unless he passed out, or you grabbed him and took him off the run."

5:04 A.M. DICK CLARK

The sun was just beginning to illuminate the Oregon sky as Dick Clark took the baton in farmlands about 70 miles from the Washington border.

"It was a beautiful morning, beautiful country," he said. "I felt real good. And then someone in the pace car said, 'Happy Father's Day.' And from that point on I just reflected on all the shit in my personal life.

"The main thing I thought about was that somebody else was gonna raise my kids. I thought about how Kimmie, my three-year-old, and Cindy, my six-year-old, cried when I said good-bye to them at the Coliseum. How Kimmie wouldn't let go of me. How I took her and Cindy to the next hand-off point and tried to say goodbye again. And then ended up taking them up another 10 miles, to the Angeles Crest, where Joan Connelly finally took them. They were both crying and holding on to me.

"I thought about how deeply I felt toward them. What a terrible loss that I wasn't gonna be with them as they grew up.

"I just thought about how shitty everything was. Here it was Father's Day, and this was the first of many I was gonna be away from them. I just vented my emotions by running hard. I laid down a 6:30-per-mile pace, which is real fast for me."

Inside Van Two, Foote and Murphy were relaxing on their bunks. Foote had two children and Murphy's wife was eight months pregnant.

Foote: "Hey, it's Father's Day. We're gonna have to celebrate. Even oncoming fathers."

Murphy: "Yeah. Maybe some wine . . ."

Foote: "No. This is special. Cherry brandy."

Murphy: "Good. Good."

The conversation rambled for a few minutes, and it became obvious that Murphy no longer was thinking about sitting out a 10-miler.

Foote: "A couple hours ago the local sheriff caught up with one of the campers and announced there was an emergency phone call."

Murphy: "Yeah. When I heard that I said, 'Damn. The little rascal's come out already.'"

Foote: "Emergency phone calls scare the daylights out of me when I'm away from home."

Murphy: "I've run four of these 10-milers on this blister. Probably one or two more, and I'll be okay. I don't wanna be going back home. I hope the baby doesn't come early. Then I'd have to go, and I'll never know if I coulda made it to Montreal."

Clark pounded over the asphalt. He wished he could stay out there forever. Just running and running toward Montreal, and away from Los Angeles and his problems. The other runners might moan and groan about their new, foreign environment. But Clark welcomed it. It was so much better than what he had left behind.

For a moment the images of Kimmie and Cindy passed from his mind, and he began focusing on his surroundings.

"I thought how beautiful the sunrise was, how beautiful the landscape was — and yet how sad I felt."

"For some reason, sunsets, sunrises — when they're really beautiful, they make me feel sad. They're only temporary. It's like a beautiful moment in your life. It ends. And that's sad."

Clark finished his 10 miles in 67 minutes flat, eclipsing by 27 seconds his fastest previous leg — his first, down the Crest. But he felt "bitter and depressed" as he entered the camper.

"Then I saw this little package lying on my cot," he said. "I opened it, and there was a little bag inside. And attached to it were two cards that said, 'To Daddy.' I started to read the cards, but the other guys were in the camper, and I just felt I couldn't handle it. I was gonna take 'em outside and read 'em. Then I realized if I did that, I might really lose the whole thing. So I just put them away and started talking about something else.

"I knew how the package got there. Pat and Joan Connelly had taken my kids out shortly before the run. Pat's my kids' godfather. So I knew the Connellys had helped them buy the gifts and the cards.

"After I got myself together, I got on the radio and said, 'Camper Two to the Pigpen. Thanks to the Easter Bunny for the cards.'

"I had a hard time keeping myself together."

Clark himself was the product of a broken home. It was one of the major forces that shaped his life.

"The last time I remember us being a family was when I was six or seven, sitting around the table playing Monopoly. My parents finally broke up when I was 14. But they'd been breaking up all that time. It was a constant strain on me. I loved both my parents, and it was painful to watch them ripping each other apart all the time.

"I envied my friends who came from a stable family background. There was little peace of mind at my house. I couldn't have friends over because of the possibility that violent arguments would break out, causing a humiliating and embarrassing situation. I think I could have focused more on academics, athletics, personal relationships if I had a stable family life. It seemed that friends who came from such a background had a concrete foundation to build their abilities.

"When my family did break up, my two brothers decided to stay with my mom. She was much less the disciplinarian than my father. But I felt someone should stay with my dad, so I went to live with him.

"He was a switchman for the railroad, who had definite ideas about life. He felt education was a waste of time. He felt it was important to learn responsibilities — to come home and do chores instead of wasting time around school playing team sports and such. And he felt joining the military was the only way to become a man. In fact, he drove me to the recruiter."

"I started working when I was 15. It was at a nursery, four hours after school and eight hours each day on Saturday and Sunday. It was the only way I could afford a car and the tuition for parochial school, where all my friends were.

"I guess in effect I was a very young bachelor. Not the 'Fonz,' but close. I had a lot of freedom along with my responsibilities. And I had a lot of friends."

"In school, I was a motivated screwoff — the school clown. I regret it now, because when I started applying myself [Clark has a bachelor's degree in biology, which he earned after six years at the age of 32] it was too late. I think if I had applied myself earlier, I might have gone to medical school. I love the sciences. But all through high school I got poor grades, and I thought I was stupid. I remember I aced a geometry test in college. That was the first time I realized I had a brain."

"Work and my size made it impossible for me to do anything athletically in high school. The one time I did go out for football, I was cut because I was so small the insurance wouldn't cover me. They let me be the team manager, but after the first game I quit. I figured out that manager was another word for water boy."

"I was in the air force four years. They tested me, and I excelled in three areas: cook, fireman and air policeman. I chose policeman. It was then that I first began thinking about becoming a police officer. I figured I could have a career in a respectable profession.

"My background investigator told me the main reason recruits don't make it through the Police Academy is physical training. So two months before I started, I began running and doing calisthenics. I finished first in my class physically. I was surprised. I was afraid I'd flunk out physically."

"When I came back to the academy in 1970 as a physical training instructor I started running distances. I had to, to stay ahead of the recruits. In those days you'd take the recruits on very long runs, up to 10 miles. That's considered cruel and unusual punishment now.

"Most of my co-instructors were members of the cross-country relay team. They'd run marathons, and they'd been in the early relays. I got caught up in the enthusiasm. My first relay was the San Leandro run."

"My wife and I loved each other deeply when we got married. Then we drifted apart. We tried a marriage counselor. Marriage encounter. Finally a trial separation. Nothing worked.

"We never fought in front of the kids, because of my experience. And I wouldn't stretch out the divorce for 10 years for the same reason. I felt it should be done quickly. It's scary. It's considered a social failure. But I wouldn't want my children to suffer through years of tension and turmoil like I did. I feel the divorce was the lesser of two evils for my children. They could adapt. Still, it's very painful. It's like losing a limb. The two things that matter most in my life are gone. Life has little meaning for me now."

Clark masked his agony well during the relay. He clowned and joked his way through, always careful to conceal his true emotions. It was a protective device he learned early in life.

6:11 A.M. FRANK JANOWICZ

For the first time since the relay began, Janowicz's leg muscles were starting to loosen up a bit. And for the first time, he followed his own advice and ran under control. But it was a struggle.

"Everything was ideal. Cool. Downhill. I coulda broken 60. But I just kept sayin', 'Slow down. Slow down. You got twenty more of these. You gotta take it easy.'"

Still, Janowicz ran his 10 miles in 60:59, his second fastest leg.

7:12 A.M. — 1:25 P.M.
Van Three

The runners of Van Three carried the baton across the farmlands of northern Oregon. Bob Jarvis ran through two small lumber towns, the blister on his left foot giving him minor problems.

Pat Connelly glided over rolling hills that led into and out of the town of Pendleton, population 13,197, home of Pendleton wool and one of the west's most famous rodeos, the Pendleton Roundup.

It was midmorning when Mullens took the baton. The heat and humidity were rising, and to make matters worse, Mullens caught three steep upgrades. Still, he ran his leg in 77:45, one of his fastest times yet.

Eddie Garcia felt like he was on a roller coaster as he navigated 10 miles of rolling hills toward the Washington border.

And Curt Hall broke 70 minutes for the first time (67:59) as he ran the final 10 miles of Oregon. Bob Hickey was standing just inside Washington as Hall handed him the baton.

1:25 P.M. BOB HICKEY

Three state police cars escorted Hickey as he ran over green hills toward Walla Walla, Washington. His blistered left foot hurt from the start.

Inside Van One, the talk turned to Indians.

Burke: "Well, we'll be making our big right-hand turn pretty soon, and then we'll go through Idaho and Montana."

Rockwood: "Where did you say we might have the Indian problem?"

Burke: "Montana. That's where we got the letter from, warning about possible trouble from AIM. But really, we could have trouble anywhere. We're advertising that we're policemen. Any group of extremists could try to blow up a bunch of cops running across the country."

Shearer: "Well, we've got that cute little Indian, Chuck Foote. He'll get us through the reservation."

Burke: "Yeah. But you know what he said about us: 'When arrow comes through air, me no know you, sucker paleface.'"

Everyone laughed. Burke grew serious:

"But if it works out for us it'll be real nice. I want to give the Indian chieftains a flag. I want them to take part in this celebration. They were the first Americans. We should give them our respect. Remember the Mojave? That's the kind of land we gave 'em to live on. It's a disgrace. If we were them, we'd be angry, too. I just hope everything works out. If it doesn't, we might have to skirt 'em."

Hickey and his escort were now inside the city limits of Walla Walla, population 23,619. Sirens blared. People waved.

Inside Van One:

Burke (to Shearer): "Hey, I saw you talking to reporters at the border."

Shearer: "That's right. My public relations image is improving. In fact I'm thinking about getting an agent to handle my appearances before the media. Maybe Bonneau."

Hickey was now north of Walla Walla, about eight miles into his run. His blisters burned with each step. "I began running on the heel of my left foot to take the pressure off," he said, "but that caused leg cramps, because I was running so unnaturally.

"At about nine miles, I saw the camper ahead and figured, 'Good — it's almost over.' But the camper was all screwed up in its mileage and it moved four times. Every time I got close, it moved. I thought, 'God, what are they trying to do to me?'"

Hickey's blisters were more serious than Murphy's. They covered the entire ball of his left foot. And they went nearly to the bone. Hickey was undergoing much the same treatment as Murphy. But he completely ignored Kiser's most important instruction — to soak his blistered foot in Epsom salts and water to prevent infection.

"The blisters don't look like they're gonna go away," he said shortly after his run. "There are blisters under blisters under blisters. I'll have to go to Montreal on them. But I can do it. I'll crawl if I have to. I'll pray. I'll do it on faith. But I'll do it."

There is a standard on the team against which all blisters are gauged: "Humphrey's blisters." Denny Humphrey was Bob

Burke's young assistant at the Police Academy during the early 1970s. A weight-lifter with bird-like legs, he decided that as a once-in-a-lifetime adventure, he would be part of the team on its Tijuana to Vancouver relay.

Humphrey worked for months to build his endurance and stamina. But his feet weren't ready for the severe pounding. On his first run, he developed blisters on the balls of both feet. By his second leg, the skin had come completely off the blistered areas. For the next week and a half, Humphrey ran on those open wounds, blood soaking through his socks and shoes.

The pain must have been maddening. But Humphrey never complained — not once.

That stoicism had also become a standard for the team.

2:31 P.M. ALEX SHEARER

"This one was unbelievable. It was hot [91 degrees]. The pavement was burning. It was all uphill. And I had this tightness in my diaphragm. I felt like there was a little ball in there that was expanding. It hurt. It must be some kind of muscle problem."

At the five-mile mark, driver Larry Kramer got out and ran with Shearer. "I started getting dizzy after just two miles," said Kramer, a tough, well-conditioned athlete himself. "It was real hot and the altitude was pretty bad. Alex had a real hard time breathing. His chest was hurting. Also, a lot of cars were coming by, and the exhaust was choking us. It was a lousy run. I'm glad I didn't go the full 10."

But Shearer had to, and at the end he was pale and drenched in sweat.

"I don't feel too good," he gasped. He walked a few feet and sat down on the bottom step of the camper. "I'm getting very nauseous. Better stay right here. I'm very dizzy."

Five minutes passed. Slowly his color returned. "I feel better," he said. "Boy, that's the worst I've felt after any leg. Even after the Mojave."

3:56 P.M. BOB BURKE

The temperature was 93 degrees. And the pavement melted under Bob Burke's shoes, sticking to the soles. At the end, he was drained. "We didn't get enough summer training," he said.

Burke drank a beer and gazed at Rockwood, now about three-quarters of a mile down the road.

"We've had nothing but heat since we left Los Angeles — a week of it. But they tell me it's raining up ahead. I hope so. These temperatures are draining a lot of guys."

5:04 P.M. JOHN ROCKWOOD

The temperature was still in the 90s, and the pavement was nearly 130 degrees as Rockwood carried the baton toward the town of Dayton, Washington, population 2,500.

"It was real tough — straight uphill. I could feel that heat off the pavement from the beginning. The cars were throwing off carbon monoxide. And my legs just didn't have a thing."

In Van One, Alex Shearer was lying prostrate on his bunk, a pad and pencil in his hands.

"I feel like I'm dead," he said. "I'm making out my last will and testament. I'm giving Rockwood my Adidases. Burke will get my running shorts and shirts. Hickey gets my dental floss. Kramer, AKA Snow White, gets my comb [he's nearly bald]. And my little ward, Dick Bonneau, will get something personal — maybe some wine."

The last two miles were hell for Rockwood. He couldn't get enough oxygen. His chest ached and his feet were numb. He was on the verge of tears — the agony was so great.

He handed the baton to Dick Bonneau and then leaned over, hands on his knees. He was breathing hard. "Ssshew. Oh, Lord. Feel bad. Legs are so heavy. Horrible. Just horrible."

He walked into the camper to fix a Tab and water. "It's been hot every day. Even in the mountains. There's been no relief. This hot weather is just killin' us."

Rockwood spotted his beach buddy, Shearer, lying on his bunk in a state of exhaustion.

Rockwood: "Disgusting run, Alex. Just disgusting."

Shearer: "They're all disgusting."

6:23 P.M. DICK BONNEAU

As Bonneau took the baton, Dick Clark was talking to a local law enforcement official at the next hand-off point.

Local cop: "We have information that there's a group of Indians riding this way, and they're threatening to kill one policeman a day. They're armed with AR-15s. One car has Colorado plates. We're not sure if they're with AIM. Some are out of the Dakotas — Wounded Knee country, you know. They're picking up people as they go."

Clark: "We're out on the road at all hours. We're easy pickins. But we do have some rifles."

Local cop: "Good. Just be careful. Real careful."

Two days earlier, Alex Shearer promised a steak dinner to the next runner in his van to break 65 minutes. Dick Bonneau had everything going for him as he ran his ninth leg. It was relatively cool — 83 degrees — and all downhill.

"I kept careful track of my times along the way," he laughed. "At five miles, I was at 32:25. I just held that pace, and at 10 miles, I had a steak dinner. I ran the 10 in 64:13."

Shearer: "Congratulations. I just hope I'm alive to deliver."

Bonneau: "Why don't you just give me the money now, in that case. I'll buy my own steak."

Shearer: "Shut up and go to bed."

The team was now about 100 miles south of Spokane. The road wound its way across steep green hills.

7:27 P.M. CHUCK FOOTE

Chuck Foote had a habit of blowing his nose hard when he ran. About two miles into his ninth leg, he blew it too hard, ruptured a blood vessel, and gushed blood. "I couldn't stop it with tissues," he said. "So I tried to suck air into my nostrils to dry them out. But it didn't help. I ate blood for eight miles."

At the end, he was covered with blood.

Clark: "Christ, it looks like the Indians decided to attack but got their own man."

Despite his nosebleed, Foote ran his leg in 63:30.

Janowicz: "He's a regular little Jim Thorpe."

Foote: "I feel like Chief Running Nose."

8:30 P.M. JIM MURPHY

An hour before his run, Murphy's blister was drained again. A half hour later, he took an Empirin compound to kill the pain.

For seven miles he ran carefully. Then he decided to test the blister for the first time since his fifth leg, three days before when it had worsened.

"It felt all right," he said, "but my right ankle is real sore. I'm worried about it now. I have to be real careful. I can't push. These physical problems are just mounting. One leads to another because each one makes you run unnaturally and causes more injuries.

"I'm real down mentally. I'm out there an hour and a half every time now. It's just real frustrating."

Murphy ran his 10 miles in 88 minutes.

8:45 P.M.

Back in Van One, the men had eaten, downed some of Shearer's wine, and were now getting ready for a normal night's sleep. They wouldn't take the baton until about six or seven the next morning.

Shearer was thumbing through a *Penthouse* magazine, when he came across the letters to the editor, letters that could be politely described as offbeat. There were a couple about men who were strongly attracted to women with missing limbs. Another about a woman who had discovered a midget with a prodigious penis. Another about a woman whose favorite sexual partner was her dog. And so it went.

Shearer began to read the letters aloud. The runners and drivers gathered 'round, attracted as much by Shearer's deep voice and theatrical delivery as the content. He read on, like a perverse Mother Goose, and the men laughed and yelled for more.

And thus was created Uncle Alex, who would put his nephews to bed each night with dramatic readings of "Letters to *Penthouse*."

Soon the other campers learned of Uncle Alex, and they clamored for readings, too. There was some talk about putting his performances "on the air," on the CB radio hookup. That was vetoed.

If anyone wanted to hear Uncle Alex, he had to go to Van One. The pilgrimage was to be made many times during the next two weeks.

9:58 P.M. DICK CLARK

Clark took the baton in rugged wilderness at the edge of Washington's mighty Snake River, near the base of a tree-covered mountain. And he went up. Ten miles straight up.

"It was miserable," he said. "At about six miles, a guy in a pickup stopped and asked me where I was going. I said 'Canada,' and plugged on. He probably thought I was an escapee — probably from a nut house."

11:18 P.M. FRANK JANOWICZ

The climb continued for Janowicz, despite assurances from a highway patrol officer that it would level off after a couple of miles.

"He was wrong. Nothing unusual," Janowicz said later. "Those guys don't know nothing. They ride around in cars and have no idea what a hill is. I'm not gonna ask anymore about the terrain."

Janowicz ran the leg, his ninth, in 69:27, remarkable considering the physical challenge involved. But the most significant aspect was neither the time, terrain nor strain. It was something that occurred about midway through.

"It was about midnight. And it was real humid. And all of a sudden I felt water falling on me. At first I thought it was some farmer sprinkling his crops. Then I realized it was raining."

Rain. After seven days of insufferable heat, it was starting to rain.

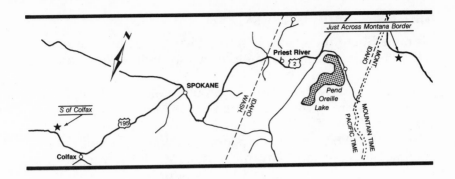

THE EIGHTH DAY
Monday, June 21, 1976

12:28 A.M. BOB JARVIS

Bob Jarvis ate two steaks, a huge salad, topped that off with strawberries, then downed a can of beer and two glasses of wine. An hour later, in a light drizzle, he took the baton over hilly country outside Colfax, Washington.

"That was a bad one," he told his campermates afterward. "I felt like my whole dinner was in my throat. I cursed the hills. I cursed the valleys. I cursed myself. I said 'Oh, shit!' a thousand times. I felt really bad."

Connelly: "Well, you ran it in 91 minutes. Real slow."

Garcia: "And he sniveled all the way."

Jarvis: "Yeah. I sniveled and cursed and cussed, and I should have upchucked, but I didn't."

Mullens: "He should have run it in about 63 minutes."

Garcia: "He's too old to run any course in 63 minutes."

Jarvis: "Shut up, you dumb-ass Mexican."

Garcia: "Too old. You've had it. Ninety-one minutes. Christ, we thought you were never gonna come back."

Jarvis: "I shouldn't have."

1:59 A.M.

It was still raining as Pat Connelly and Frank Mullens moved the team to within 40 miles of Spokane. Connelly called his leg "great." Mullens said it was his "best yet."

4:21 A.M. EDDIE GARCIA

"It rained hard the whole 10 miles. I liked that. But it was very hilly. And it was in the middle of the night. Those are the worst."

Garcia had now completed nine rounds against his opponent. "I know his strengths and weaknesses. And I'm beginning to know my own. The key is never anticipating. Roll with his punches. When you see an opening — a long downhill, rain, a cooling breeze — any advantage, take it. But never go for a knockout. Don't try to blast 10 miles of uphill. Don't fight the clock. Don't fight yourself."

Garcia's penchant for challenges — for testing himself — was the primary force driving him on: "This relay is a small but important part in developing myself as a total human being. The challenge, the discipline, the fear will make me reach down deep into myself and make me know myself better.

"It will help me as a police officer, an athlete, a man. It's a beautiful test."

He had grown up in the roughest section of Tucson, Arizona. A scrawny, homely kid, he had one exceptional attribute — speed. It would save him from the young toughs who chased him home after school nearly every day. And later, it would propel him into athletics, and away from the perils of the street.

By high school, Eddie Garcia was a strong, well-conditioned athlete — an amateur boxer and a champion sprinter who finished second in the state in the 440-yard dash. He had no trouble with the neighborhood toughs anymore.

It was boxing that supplied him with his first great "test."

"I fought this friend," he recalled. "I was dancing around, jabbing him — really dishing it out and having a good time. Well, this guy could hit like a mule. And every time he hit me, I felt pain from the top of my head to the bottom of my feet. In the second round, he caught me with a roundhouse punch, right in the jaw. I don't remember a thing, not a damned thing. The next thing I knew, I was on my knees.

"The thing about boxing is you gotta learn how to lose before you learn how to win. You can't be a good fighter unless you get knocked on your ass, see stars and feel pain. Only then do you learn how to control fear. It hurts like hell. But slowly the fear goes away. You handle that fear once, you'll always be able to handle it."

He had wanted to be a cop since high school. But he was particular. He wanted to be part of a big-city police department. He wanted decent pay, high professional standards, a good chance for upward mobility. He chose Los Angeles.

And from the beginning, Garcia planned his strategy carefully. Just as he planned every other aspect of his life.

"I decided I wanted to be an instructor at the Police Academy the first day I walked in there. It's funny, but with God's help, it worked out that way.

"Education is crucial for advancement. I have a bachelor's degree in police administration and police science. My immediate objectives are to get a master's degree and promotions in the department — first to sergeant, and then . . .

"I like being a police officer. It's challenging. It's an opportunity to help others."

But many of Garcia's days on the street were spent simply surviving. As a cop, Garcia has come face-to-face with the ultimate fear — death. And as he did in the ring, he faced that fear, and conquered it, too.

Friday, April 13, 1973

"I was working the daywatch in Hollenbeck Division. We got a radio call. A 415, man with a gun. The suspect was impersonating a police officer in downtown Los Angeles. He allegedly was sticking a gun in people's faces, searching them, pushing them around.

"When we spotted him he was walking down the street. He was about three car lengths away, coming right toward us. We leaped out of our vehicle with our guns drawn. It was like *Gunsmoke*. The guy just kept walking right at us. We told him to stop, get his hands in the air. Instead, he went for his gun.

"He got it about halfway out. I shot him. He lived. He was found guilty of assaulting a police officer.

"You know, a cop walks a thin line. You have to make split-second decisions. But they'd better be right or you pay the price: You could lose your job if you overreact; you could lose your life if you underreact.

"I'm not ashamed of what I did. But I'm not proud of it either. It's something I had to do, to preserve not only my own life, but other people's, as well. I was the victim of an attempted murder. I'd do it again. No question about it.

"That was the closest I ever came to killing a man."

Garcia's boxing and martial arts background prepared him for another challenge.

"This other time in Hollenbeck, my partner was in court, so I was alone, and there was another 415 — this one a male mental right in front of the county hospital.

"It was raining. The first thing I saw was a huge crowd standing across the street from the hospital; a lot of doctors, nurses, hospital employees and people from the area. And right in the middle of the street, I saw this individual.

"He was black, about 6 feet 2 inches, 180 pounds and solid. He was wearing brown pants, a hat — and that was it. He was out there swinging a piece of wire cable about three feet long with a one-inch hook on the end — swinging it at cars that were passing by. The traffic was going every which-way. Somebody told me he'd been chasing people around the street, trying to hit 'em with that hook.

"I didn't want to get him excited. I was trying to buy time, hoping some help would arrive. But, of course, everybody in the crowd was waiting for the man in the blue uniform to do something about this monster who had been terrorizing them.

"I got in my vehicle and drove past the suspect, who was sitting on the sidewalk in front of the hospital now. I wanted to keep his emotions down. I sensed that if I hurried too much, I would rile him up. I made a U-turn and parked about 10 feet from the suspect. I got out of my black-and-white, and put my baton to rein. I wanted to keep as low a profile as possible.

"I walked up to him and tried to talk to him in the most kind, gentle, humane voice I could muster. You know, like I was his long-lost brother. I just tried to pacify him and lower his anxiety level.

"I musta conversed with him for about 10 minutes. It seemed like an eternity. I was saying anything I could think of: 'How you doin'?' Anything.

"After about 10 minutes, I walked back to my car to request another unit, code two. But every unit was tied up.

"I walked back to the guy and started talking to him once more. He hadn't said a word yet. Then slowly he looked at me, very cold, without any expression on his face, and he said, 'Man, I'se gonna kill you.' There was no doubt in my mind that he meant it.

"Finally another black-and-white arrived. And that did it. He jumped up and ran toward the wall that surrounds the hospital. He put his back to the wall and held that wire and hook out in a fighting position. So I took out my baton to do battle with him. Him with the hook, me with the baton.

"I could hear this cheering from the crowd across the street. The fight was like an old-time movie. Him swinging at me, and me darting in and out with the baton. He was smiling, laughing. Coming at me. Swinging that chain.

"I musta hit him everywhere with that baton. But it didn't have any effect. He just kept on coming with that wire and hook —and swinging. He caught me once, right across the cheek, and cut me.

"I kept hitting him with the baton. But the more I did, the more he seemed to like it. You could tell by the look on his face. There was no doubt about it: He was a psycho.

"Finally I swung the baton as hard as I could across his shins, hoping to drop him. But the baton went flying. He came at me with that hook. And I had to resort to my hands. I was able to hit him once, across the face. He came at me again, swinging that hook. I got in close, hit him about three times with my left — quick jabs — then with a right, and then I used a front kick to the solar plexis. It lifted him up, and he came down on his face.

"Behind me, I heard another cheer. I jumped on him and handcuffed him. He was lying on his stomach. Grass and mud on his face. He looked up at me and said, 'You're bad, man.' He was still smiling. He was a psycho. A stone psycho. Right out of Ward Three — the psychiatric ward at the hospital."

Once more, on this run, Garcia was being challenged. And once more, he would be a better and stronger man if he survived.

"It isn't injury that I fear," he said, relaxing after his ninth leg. "My fear is that somewhere in the middle of the run, I'll hit a brick wall — physically and psychologically. In other words, I won't be able to finish. Me. I won't have the inner strength to do it. The determination.

"I've run a marathon, but this is the ultimate test in terms of physical and psychological stress. If you can conquer this type of ordeal, you have really accomplished something. This is more than a run . . ."

6:56 A.M.
BOB HICKEY   20 miles south of Spokane

Bob Hickey, the "man who ran through pain," cried in pain his entire 10 miles.

"I cried and prayed," he said. "I just kept telling myself, 'This pain is not real. It's not happening to me. I can overcome it.' I prayed for the strength to put it out of my mind. To keep going."

Despite his agonizing blisters, Hickey ran 10.1 miles in under 67 minutes.

Over and over again during the run, Hickey had whispered his favorite prayer, "The Lord is my shepherd, I shall not want..."

"It helped me overcome the pain," he said. "It helped me finish."

Hickey had relied on the Lord's Prayer before on these relays. On both the Tijuana and Washington, D.C., runs, he had brought a vocalist's version of the prayer, and had the follow car play it four or five times on each leg. "It wasn't just that it was the Lord's Prayer that turned me on. It was the tempo. I'd get myself locked into the tempo. It was fantastic."

In 1974, on the Washington, D.C., run, the follow car played the Lord's Prayer continuously for Hickey on an entire 10-mile leg — a total of twenty-two times. The team was coming through New Mexico at the time. The incident is another "Hickey legend."

"The pace car is equipped with a ton of radio gear," Hickey explained. "During my run, that equipment came crashing down on the floor, near the accelerator. Both the driver and the passenger in the pace car reached down to pick the stuff up.

"All of a sudden, I felt the car bump me. I thought, 'Well, they're playing games.' Then the car hit me again and I said, 'Hey, c'mon — knock it off.' And then they realized the car was bumping me. And they hit the brakes. But when they did, the car lurched downward and caught me on the backs of my calves and knocked me down. It was like somebody had hit me with a baseball bat across the calves.

"I laid there for a few minutes — more in shock than anything. And Bob Hogue, who was the passenger, jumped out of the car and said, 'You all right?' I said, 'Don't touch me.' I was in tears. I said, 'My God, I'm gonna be out of the run.' (Under AAU rules, if a runner is touched, he can be disqualified.) And I got up and started moving around. I said, 'I've gotta finish.'

"I think I had about four or five miles to go, and they started calling ahead to the van to come back, and I said, 'No. I'm gonna finish it. I've gotta finish it. At least let me try.' And they said okay.

"I'm very emotional at times. I was crying so hard at that moment. I don't think I was crying from the pain, but from the fear. I knew I had to finish the leg. Because if I didn't, and I was unable to run the next time, then I would be dropped from the run. So I figured if I could just finish this one, then I could miss the next one and recuperate, and the guys would understand.

"For the last five miles they played the Lord's Prayer for me. I knew it was tough on 'em, because it was repeated every three minutes, and they were going crazy. But I repeated it—and sang it and screamed it. I did everything I could to finish that run.

"After I handed the baton to Alex Shearer, I went over to a small resting place, and I did nothing but pray. I thanked God that I wasn't hurt, and that nothing was broken. And I prayed that I'd have the strength and courage to continue running if I could.

"I had a real bad bruise and a bad charley horse. I packed my upper calf in ice for five hours.

"The next day, Bonneau, who passed the baton to me, probably had the toughest run on the whole relay. He brought the baton up over the 10,000-foot mark, just outside Taos, New Mexico. It was about 30 degrees, three in the morning.

"I don't know if I could've run those 10 miles. I was just lucky. My 10 was almost all downhill. It was still cold, and I was bundled up like a teddy bear.

"Well, I took the baton, and they started off playing the Lord's Prayer for me. And they played it the whole run. That seemed to set my rhythm. I hit the five-mile point, and I started feeling strong. And I no longer wondered if I'd be able to continue running.

"I started taking off all my heavy clothing. Finally, I got down to my shorts and my T-shirt like I normally run. And I ran my last five miles in 32 minutes.

"It never ceases to amaze me how prayer, a strong belief in God, and a belief in yourself can help you overcome just about anything. It's fantastic."

When Hickey finished his tenth leg, just 15 miles outside Spokane, Ron Kiser quickly drained his blister and deadened it with an injection. But once again Hickey ignored Kiser's admonition to soak the raw, blistered area to prevent infection.

8:03 A.M. ALEX SHEARER

Just 16 hours earlier, Shearer had been making out his last will and testament after a brutal run through the heat and humidity of Oregon. He had suffered severe chest pains during the run.

A self-analysis had determined those pains were probably the result of "too many fried foods." So Shearer put himself on a strict diet. And he felt "100 percent better" as he took the baton on the outskirts of Spokane, Washington.

"Yesterday I couldn't have run another step," he said, "but this time I could have run several more miles. It was outstanding. Light rain. Good terrain. Perfect running conditions. In fact, the van could see I was enjoying it so much that they let me run an extra seven-tenths of a mile. [The van got lost.]

"After my 10.7-miler, Lou McClary and I split a bottle of champagne to celebrate the fact that we were now about a third of the way to Montreal."

McClary's part of the celebration was tempered somewhat, however. The team had been scheduled to arrive in Spokane at 11:31 A.M. Monday. But Shearer had reached the city limits at about 9 A.M. — two and a half hours early. For the first time, hurried adjustments had to be made in the welcoming ceremonies, sponsored by police and city officials.

McClary had worked with Rich Wemmer and Julia Nagano for nine months, setting up these "goodwill" ceremonies. He had done it on the basis of Burke's projection that each runner would average 75 minutes per 10-mile leg. And he had done it on orders from Chief Ed Davis, who wanted the Bicentennial Relay of Goodwill to live up to its name.

McClary had done his work dutifully. He had set up more than 100 welcomes and ceremonies along the relay route. But suddenly a luncheon had turned into a breakfast.

McClary could see the problem mushrooming if the runners continued their blistering pace. Makeshift adjustments in scheduling. Vans quickly returning to a town they had shot through two, three, four hours ahead of time. A quick dinner and welcoming ceremony. Then a madcap ride up the road — now 110 or 120 miles instead of the normal 80 or 90 — to catch some sleep and wait for the baton.

It would put added strain on everyone, but most importantly, it would drain the runners, as well as the goodwill theme of the run. McClary could see the problem clearly. But at this point, he would say nothing. He would adjust and hope.

"The runners are the stars," he said. "We're the support." And then ominously, "I would never suggest that they slow down. You can't tell trained, competitive athletes to slow down because of a breakfast in some town in Idaho.

"It's just not compatible to have competition and planned events. But that's my problem. I sent letters to those towns a year ago. And somehow, I'll have to see that all their preparations don't go to waste."

McClary and Wemmer had their work cut out for them.

9:10 A.M. BOB BURKE

Bob Burke was elated. "We're two and a half hours ahead of schedule and really moving," Burke said after his tenth leg. "Just about everyone's running consistently under 70 minutes. Everyone's getting stronger. We're finally out of the heat. And just wait 'til we hit the flatlands of Idaho and Montana. We'll just fly!"

Clearly the "running" and the "goodwill" aspects of the Bicentennial Relay of Goodwill were on a collision course. But at this point, the man in charge was oblivious to that.

10:15 A.M. JOHN ROCKWOOD — DICK BONNEAU

Bob Burke was absolutely right. Everyone did seem to be getting stronger. For the first time, John Rockwood broke 70 minutes.

And even though Dick Bonneau had a "miserable run," he finished his leg in 73 minutes.

Now even "miserable" runs were being completed under the projected 75-minute-per-leg pace.

11:35 P.M. CHUCK FOOTE

As Chuck Foote blazed across the rain-soaked hills of Washington, Bob Burke was pressed into service as Jim Murphy's substitute doctor. Kiser was working on other patients. And Hickey, who would normally replace Kiser, was sleeping. So it was up to Burke to treat Murphy's blisters, and he took mock, devilish delight in doing so.

Burke: "Where's the whiskey for my patient?"

Clark: "Forget the whiskey. Just have Alex come over and tell Jim one of his bedtime stories."

Burke: "No, whiskey. Then aspirin. I think all my patients should at least have an aspirin before I operate."

As Burke inserted the hypodermic needle into Murphy's blister, Clark broke into play-by-play.

Clark: "The needle is going in. The fluid is coming out. Murphy's eyes are closed. Hey, wait one second here! That's the needle we were playing darts with last night. No matter. The needle will still be good for darts tonight."

Three miles into his leg, Foote's nose began to bleed again. "I began sucking that stuff into my throat. And finally I got a big glob of it, and it damn near gagged me. Disgusting."

Shearer entered the camper: "How're you doin', doctor?"

Burke (with mock fiendishness): "I love my new job. But if Hickey finds out I'm doin' this, he'll kill me. At the very least, he'll stop cooking for us in revenge. We'll all be surviving on peanut-butter-and-jelly sandwiches."

Murphy: "Burke doesn't know how much I enjoy this. But just wait 'til he feels all my wet poop on his neck."

Burke drew out a cc-and-a-half of fluid.

Burke: "The operation is a success. You'll never run again."

Murphy: "Great. I'll see you guys in L.A. Best of luck."

For seven days, for 1,310 miles, the LAPD runners had been traveling north. But during his 10 miles, Foote gradually began to make the big right-hand turn that eventually would take the runners across the northern-most section of the United States, into Canada, and to Montreal.

Foote made the turn without even knowing it.

In Van Two, Murphy was preparing for his tenth leg. He had been unable to break 80 minutes his last four times out. Blood was now building up inside the painful blister that covered the entire heel of his right foot.

"It's frustrating to run this slow," he said, tying his shoes. "But it's just a matter of riding out this period, letting the blister heal, and then running the way I can again."

Murphy stepped from the camper and gazed down the road. His pain and frustration were evident. "The last few runs seemed like they'd never end." His voice faded. He spotted Foote down the road, completing another sub-65-minute leg. Murphy knew what he should do. But pride and ego had blunted reason.

He grabbed the baton from Foote's outstretched hand and bolted down the road. For the first time in five days, he would run like the Murphy of old.

Chuck Foote looked more like he'd just fought ten rounds with Muhammad Ali than run 10 miles through the scenic forests of northeastern Washington. His face, shirt and trunks were covered with blood.

Foote: "I figure I only lost about a tablespoon of blood."

Clark: "Looks like you lost a gallon."

Janowicz: "Christ, you ran the damned thing in 62 minutes."

Clark: "He's a tough little Indian. But he's also a deceptive little critter. You know, last night I thought Tonto and me came to an understanding. I dedicated my run to Jim Thorpe, and he told me that the good spirits in the sky would smile upon me. And I had 10 miles of uphill . . ."

Foote: ". . . and it rained on your ass."

Clark: ". . . and I had headwind."

Foote: "Sometimes the good spirits like to pull a paleface's leg."

Clark: "Well, Tonto told me he was gonna run for Davy Crockett today, in honor of my running for Jim Thorpe."

Foote: 'Yeah, and look what happened. I swallowed blood for seven miles."

Clark: "That's because the paleface spirits got even."

Foote: "Just wait 'til we get your white ass in AIM country. You'd better wear a feather and dedicate your soul to Geronimo."

1:37 P.M. JIM MURPHY

Murphy was floating. He reached the three-mile mark in just over 19 minutes. He knew it was only a matter of time before the blister would begin to throb and ache. He didn't care. He was tired of spending 85 minutes on the road. He was frustrated and humiliated. He would run hard. To hell with caution and reason.

At eight miles, the pain came. First slowly. Then in a rush. It was excruciating. Every step was like coming down on hot coals. There was no way to avoid the fire. It would be with him the last mile and a half. He slowed down. Thought about past glories. Past agonies. It helped — a little. At the end, his blister had filled with liquid and the pain was unbearable. "But at least I broke 70." He had run his leg in 67 minutes.

2:44 P.M. DICK CLARK

Murphy had crossed a 20-foot bridge that connects Washington and Idaho. The countryside where Clark began his 10 miles was breathtaking: pine-covered mountains dipping into a lush green valley, a fast-moving river gurgling alongside. The sky was overcast, the temperature cool.

"I dedicated the run to Daniel Boone," Clark said, "and it was a good choice. The scenery and everything put me in mind of trapping and hunting and Indians and canoes."

The road sloped upward for about a half mile, then leveled off and dropped down toward the town of Priest River, a logging community of 1,500. It seemed as though the entire population were outside, waiting for Clark.

At the edge of town, two young girls held up a 5-by-10-foot banner that read, "Welcome LAPD." As Clark approached the banner, five youngsters broke from the crowd and began running with him, slapping his hand and grabbing at his shirt and shorts.

To them he was the sports hero of Sunday afternoon television and the Los Angeles policeman of *Police Story* and *Adam-12*.

In one important respect, these were not the cops portrayed on television. Many of those portrayals deal with drinking, mental breakdowns, suicide — the result of the tensions and stress of police work.

The runners — indeed, most cops — talk about tension and stress from a gut level. But two men who have studied the problem are Dr. Martin Reiser, the director of behavioral sciences for the LAPD, and Dr. Hans Selye, perhaps the world's foremost authority on stress.

They offer some interesting insights into the relationship between running and reduction of stress.

Dr. Reiser: "In police work, perhaps more so than most other jobs, you'll find men turning to alcohol, heightened sexual activity outside marriage, or compulsive work activity. In other jobs, compulsion about your job, while not necessarily a healthy thing, is rarely harmful to anyone else. But a compulsive policeman can be dangerous.

"In our stress management training seminars, we teach nutrition, certain relaxation techniques such as hypnotism or meditation, and running.

"I view long-distance running as accepting a challenge — testing oneself physically, mentally and spiritually to reassure oneself that he is still adequate physically, and still has sufficient motivation to achieve.

"The beauty of running long distances is that it involves a lesser degree of risk-taking than most other activities where you test yourself — such as auto racing or skydiving. The risk in running is usually at the beginning, in the training. And then it actually becomes a healthy thing."

According to Dr. Selye, stress is the response of the body to any demand made upon it. Stress, says Selye, is a normal part of life — in fact even necessary. "Complete freedom from stress is death."

The critical point, according to Selye, is that there are two kinds of stress. One is negative — such as that caused by a death in the family, a final examination, a combat mission. One is positive — that caused by a surprise birthday party, a promotion, running. A positive stress can be used to wipe out a negative stress. Says Selye, "Stress on one system helps to relax another." Put another way, heavy exercise can burn up energy that otherwise might be channeled into depression, nervous tension or anxiety.

And so running, aside from its obvious physical benefits, has a psychologically therapeutic effect, too. It can help a cop — it can help anyone — cope with the demands of modern life.

At the moment, it was providing Clark with an ego boost. People clapped and cheered, and motorists honked their horns as he ran down the street. Good luck, we're with ya, they yelled. Clark waved and smiled.

"They get a lot out of this," Clark would say later. "But I think we're getting a lot more."

3:55 P.M. FRANK JANOWICZ

Janowicz ran a sub-70, and afterward, he declared he felt absolutely great.

Clark (incredulous): "Nothing bothers you?"

Janowicz: "No. I feel great."

(Pause.)

Janowicz: "My legs are a little sore, though."

(Pause.)

"And my blister hurts."

(Pause.)

"And my groin is sore. My right calf is tight. My thighs are stiff. Shit, I can't get loose. One hundred miles and I can't get loose. I'm running like a cripple."

Clark: "Jeez, Frank, for a moment I was worried about ya."

5:02 P.M. BOB JARVIS

Bob Jarvis, who 15 hours earlier had run the slowest leg that would be logged on the relay, regained his form and charged across the tree-covered hills that lead into the fishing community of Sandpoint. The town of 4,144 is dwarfed by lofty, snow-capped mountain peaks and graced by nearby Lake Pend Oreille, one of the largest and most beautiful freshwater lakes in the Pacific Northwest.

In Van Two, the runners and drivers were toasting their 100th miles. Clark opened a chilled bottle of cold duck, poured the contents into six paper cups, and then offered a sober salute:

"We're toasting the bravery of six tough men in this camper for finishing 100 miles each."

The men pressed their cups together and downed the cold duck.

The reception at Priest River was repeated in Sandpoint. As Jarvis ran through the town — bagpipe music blaring behind him — people began to stream out of their houses and run alongside him, shaking his hand and wishing him good luck. Four blocks into the city, seven members of the high school track team joined Jarvis for about a mile. As they passed the local police station, five members of the department came out to shake Jarvis's hand.

"How far do you guys run?" one of the cops asked Pat Connelly.

Connelly: "Ten miles."

Sandpoint cop: "How long does it take you? Two, three hours?"

Connelly: "Oh, no. Eighty minutes, at the most. But we're averaging about 68 minutes now."

Sandpoint cop: "Jesus! My God!"

Jarvis breezed out of the town. The blisters on his left foot still bothered him, but he was exhilarated. "It feels great to run through a town like that. Everybody's so friendly. It should be like that from now on."

Priest River, Idaho

The Lions Club and Chamber of Commerce of Priest River hosted a dinner for the runners. All the vans were supposed to attend, but the relay was now two hours and 45 minutes ahead of schedule. Van Three was already 25 miles past the town. And Van One was parked ahead, too, catching some sleep. So only Van Two was able to stay behind and enjoy the hospitality.

Nancy Thomas, a local resident: "You fellas have devised a wonderful way to see the country."

Clark: "I've driven back and forth across the U.S., and I've done a lot of bike riding. But nothing compares with running. Taking time to see the scenery, talking to the citizens, getting feedback. It's fantastic."

7:19 P.M. FRANK MULLENS

The terrain and weather were ideal, but Mullens was struggling. After 90 miles on the road and sleeping under the worst conditions dealt any runner, the 54-year-old lieutenant confided to a friend: "I'm just getting too old for this stuff. My legs are not what they used to be. This is positively my last relay."

Mullens could barely climb the two steps into the van. His legs were sore and weak. "I felt like I wanted to give him a little shove, a little help," one of his teammates said, "but Frank's too proud a guy. He doesn't want any special treatment."

9:47 P.M. CURT HALL

As Curt Hall took the baton, Bob and Pat Woods, two residents of Sandpoint, handed Pat Connelly and Frank Mullens two jars of homemade jam. They'd driven 20 miles to make the delivery.

Pat Woods: "It's for breakfast tomorrow morning."

Connelly: "It'll never last 'til then."

The runners and the Woods talked for about half an hour. Then the couple left. The cop-athletes of Van Three were amazed at the Woodses' gesture.

Connelly: "Could you see that happening in L.A.? Someone driving 20 miles at night to deliver jam to a bunch of strangers?"

Hall ran his fastest leg yet — 65 minutes. Three miles into his run, he crossed into Montana.

Montana: Throughout the years, it had been a home to countless trappers, traders and ranchers. It had also been home to the Plains Indians, as well as the site of the Little Big Horn, of Custer's Last Stand, of Chief Joseph's courageous but futile attempt to reach a Canadian sanctuary.

Now it was a different kind of home to thousands of Indians who lived on the nomadic waste of its vast badlands, a breeding ground for despair and disillusionment, for anger and extremism.

Photos by members of the team and accompanying personnel.

Top photo, Site of the 1932 Olympics and the starting point for the 1976 Bicentennial Relay of Goodwill.
Bottom photo, The first hand-off: Chief Ed Davis to Bob Hickey at the L. A. Coliseum.

Eddie Garcia gets in another round against his "opponent."

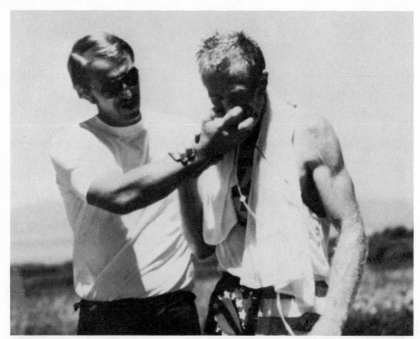

Top photo, Driver Walt Karpinsky administers oxygen to Bob Burke in the Mojave.
Bottom photo, Bob Hickey after his 66-minute encounter with the Mojave.

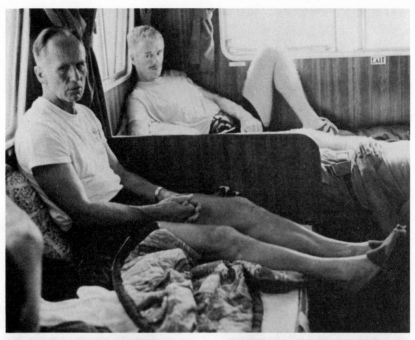

Top photo, Frank Mullens pays a visit to Bob Burke in Van One.
Bottom photo, Pacer's predicament: Rudy DeLeon and author try to extricate pace car after Curt Hall's detour backfires.

Top photo, The hand-off: Jim Murphy to Dick Clark.
Bottom photo, Frank Mullens after a tough 10 miles: "He looked every one of his 54 years."

Alex Shearer "running on coals" in the Mojave.

Top photo, The author interviews Bob Burke in Van One.
Bottom photo, Fill-'er-up: Team coach Pat Connelly and Asst. Police Chief George Beck.

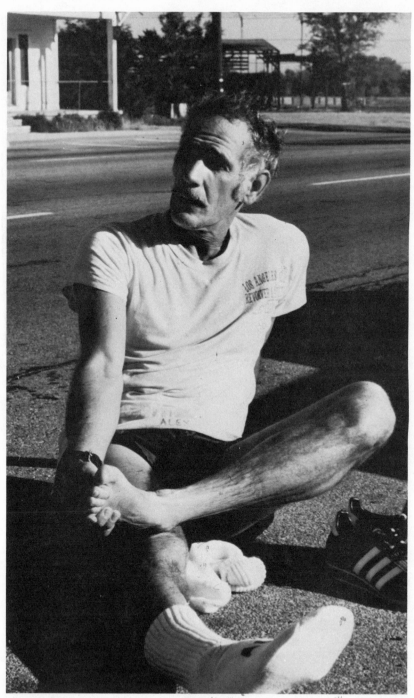
"The Old Man of the Highway," Alex Shearer.

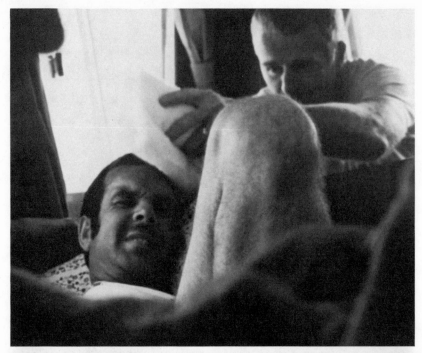

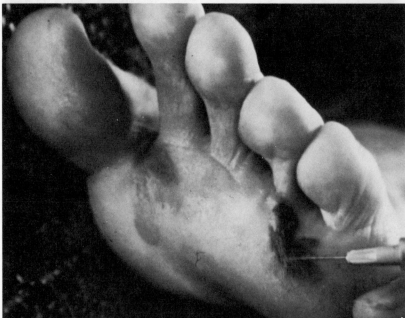

Top photo, The agony of the feet: John Rockwood undergoes "surgery" for blisters.
Bottom photo, Ron Kiser performs Mercurochrome surgery on John Rockwood's blisters. Blisters were minor compared to those of Hickey and Murphy.

Top photo, We're Number One! (L–R) Burke, Murphy, Rockwood, Connelly, Mullens, Foote, Garcia, Clark, Bonneau, Shearer, and Hall.
Bottom photo, Curt Hall: He loved to run long, tough distances.

Pat Connelly flies through Sault Ste. Marie, Michigan: "I can't go any slower."

Top photo, Art Linkletter is interviewed with Bob Jarvis near Grand Forks, N. D. *Bottom photo,* Moving into their fourth state: (L–R) Hickey, Karpinsky, Kramer, and Garcia.

Top r. photo, Team captain Chuck Foote minutes after a 10-miler in Michigan.
Top l. photo, Dick Bonneau in the Mojave:"I never felt in control . . . but somehow I did it."
Bottom photo, Welcome, runners! An unexpected sight in Canada. The woman made the flag as a greeting for the LAPD team.

Top photo, The Bicentennial Relay moves into Canada across the International Bridge.
Bottom photo, Hickey, Shearer, and Rockwood enjoy the hospitality of the Pembroke police.

Top r. photo, John Rockwood in Montreal after his last 10-miler. He doesn't know another brutal run awaits him moments later.

Top l. photo, Frank Janowicz at the end in Montreal.

Bottom photo, LAPD runners with Canadian hosts on the last three miles of their nearly 4,000 mile journey.

Top photo, A gift in Montreal. Olympic banner is presented to Burke, Clark, Hickey, and Jarvis.

Bottom photo, LAPD team and Canadian runners in consul-general's office in Montreal: "It was the best of possible endings."

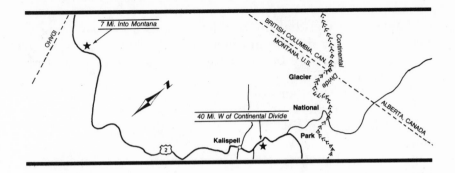

THE NINTH DAY
Tuesday, June 22, 1976

10:52 P.M. — 5:40 A.M.
Van One

The night was cool but comfortable. The course — gentle, rolling hills. The countryside — sparsely populated Montana prairie-lands.

Hickey covered his 10 miles in 66:47, on throbbing blisters. Afterward, Kiser gave him aspirin and a muscle relaxer. Once again, the blisters were drained. And once again, Hickey did not soak them.

Shearer covered similar terrain in 76 minutes. Burke ran his leg in 68. Rockwood in 75. And Bonneau in 70.

And so, during one brief turn, Van One picked up another 19 minutes on the projected time of 75 minutes per leg, pushing the team nearly three hours ahead of schedule. And the Montana flats, along with the innate competition among the runners, were certain to keep pushing the team further and further ahead.

Inside Van One, "Uncle Alex" picked up a ragged issue of *Penthouse* magazine. His "nephews" quickly gathered around, and Alex began reading — this time about the delights of sex with a midget.

Rockwood: "Hey, Sonny. Do midgets have as much fun as normal people?"

Kramer: "Yeah, do you feel your sex life is stunted by your size?"

Bonneau: "I feel that my development as a human being is being stunted by this environment."

Shearer: "Huh! We buy him toys, games, candy — and no appreciation."

Burke: "Read another story, Uncle Alex. Read another story."

Everyone: "Yeah, yeah. [Then in chorus, to the tune of "It's Howdy Doody Time"] "It's Uncle Alex time, it's Uncle Alex time . . ."

So Alex read another letter. This one about the secret joys of incestuous relationships. It was a smash.

Shearer: "I think all my nephews can go to bed now. Uncle Alex is real tired. And he is going to have to run again later today like all his nephews. So we should all get some sleep. Give me my bottle of wine, Bonneau. Uncle Alex would like a little nip before bedtime."

Everyone: "We would, too! We would, too!"

Shearer: "Okay. Get your glasses."

Alex and his "nephews" drank their wine and then went to sleep.

5:40 A.M. CHUCK FOOTE

"What a way to start the day. Somebody coming over to your bunk before five in the morning shouting, 'On the road! On the road! Get your ass up! You gotta run!'

"I didn't see a soul for 10 miles. Just some mountain sheep along the road eating.

"My nose itched but I didn't dare touch it. First time in three runs I didn't have a nosebleed."

6:45 A.M. JIM MURPHY — DICK CLARK

After running four consecutive legs in 80 minutes or longer, Murphy had broken 70 minutes his last time out. His blistered right heel was a mass of pain. But he had decided to run hard again. "I felt I was letting down the team and myself," he said. To hell with the physical pain. Pride and image were more important.

He ran over the Montana flatlands in 73 minutes.

Afterward, his heel was on fire.

While Clark was waiting for the hand-off, he chatted with the editor of the weekly newspaper of Plains, Montana.

Clark: "What's the terrain like ahead?"

Editor: "All uphill . . ."

Clark: "I wish you hadn't said that. But it really doesn't matter, 'cause I'm the toughest guy around."

The editor was wrong. It was only nine miles uphill.

Clark: "It was miserable. On top of that, I kept asking the follow car to play John Denver records, and they kept playing Olivia Newton-John. Andy Bakjian, the AAU official, tried to convince me it was John Denver. I thought I was going nuts.

"Finally, comin' up the last hill, I went back to the follow car and told them to please play John Denver. And Andy said, 'It is John Denver.' I said, 'Dammit, Andy, it's Olivia Newton-John.' Finally, with about 400 yards to go, they put on a John Denver record. I got half a verse as I finished."

9:21 A.M. FRANK JANOWICZ

The Montana flats had suddenly given way to tree-covered mountains. But Janowicz was oblivious to the scenery. "My mind was blank. I couldn't think of anything but the pain. My groin, thighs, and right calf hurt."

Van Two was parked just outside Hot Springs, Montana, beside an open field. Driver George Moore spotted some old broken-down farm equipment about 50 feet off the road and began walking toward it.

Foote: "What in the hell is he doing?"

Clark: "He says he's interested in antique farm equipment."

Moore eyed a 1929 Harvester hay-loader and then looked back at the camper and scratched his head.

Clark: "He's trying to figure out some way to stick that thing into this overcrowded camper."

Murphy: "He'd better also think about some farmer coming out and filling him with buckshot."

Moore began kicking the tires of a 1932 pickup truck.

Clark: "George Moore is not from this planet."

Janowicz picked up the pace as he reached the end of a five-mile climb. His groin and thighs had loosened up. He decided to try to break 65 minutes.

Moore had smuggled a carburetor off a 1922 Model A and brought it back to the camper.

Moore: "This is a very rare item."

Clark (looking directly at Moore): "Speaking of rare items . . ."

Moore: "Hey, seriously. You can't find these anywhere."

Clark: "Yeah, except out here. You know, I think they're gonna get a posse together and come after you."

Foote: "They're gonna hang you, boy."

Clark: "Takin' parts off their Model Ts is a hanging offense in this part of the country."

Moore: "It's only a Model A."

Clark: "For that, they're gonna make you a eunuch."

Janowicz was running his miles in slightly under six minutes each. "Everything hurt, but I just kept pushing myself. I wanted to break 65."

In Van Two, Clark recalled an incident on his last 10-miler:

"About halfway through, a couple of cowboys drove past me with a horse trailer attached to their truck, and there was an old quarterhorse inside. And that old horse just about broke his neck turnin' around and watchin' me . . . probably wonderin' what the hell I was doin' out there."

Murphy: "He probably never saw anything so slow."

Janowicz pounded across the asphalt. His groin was pulling, but he ran hard anyway. He finished in 64:30. In the battle for best overall average, he was now indisputably in third place, behind Hickey and Foote.

Janowicz walked around outside the camper trying to loosen his muscles and cool down. "I can't believe how much I hurt," he said. "My groin is just killing me."

He walked for another five minutes.

Janowicz: "Did you see those cows on the side of the road? I thought they were gonna come after me."

Clark: "Yeah. I wonder how they escaped."

Janowicz: "I thought maybe they were lookin' for a stud. But I think my stud's all worn out. They were all females, too. They had that misty-eyed look."

12:55 P.M. FRANK MULLENS

Frank Mullens took the baton in Montana farmlands. Cattle were grazing in the fields behind barbed wire fences. One cow had managed to escape and walked along the road. The weather was cool, the sky threatening.

"I had a good course. A lot of downhill. A tail wind. I ran it in 75 minutes. I should have gone faster, but I'm just tired. Rudy DeLeon ran with me. We got a couple of hills, and Rudy pulled me along."

DeLeon: "I like to run with Frank. Of all the guys, he's probably the one whose friendship and companionship I enjoy the

most. I guess it's because we have the most in common. We're
the two oldest guys.

"Our conversation is usually very low-key. We talk about the
elements and the problems that affect us. We talk a lot about
hills. We cuss 'em out. On this run we yelled, 'You fuckin' hill.
You sonofabitch. When are you gonna end?'"

Once back in the camper, Mullens fixed a peanut-butter-and-
jelly sandwich and drank two glasses of grapefruit juice. He sat
on an ice chest, shoulders slumped, head down, his face drawn
and pale. He looked every one of his 54 years.

Mullens: "I'll go for a half mile and feel great, and then I'll feel
lousy. Why do I feel good and bad, good and bad?"

Connelly: "I can't explain it physically. It must be something
mental. Do you feel shitty going uphill?"

Mullens: "Terrain doesn't make any difference. It can happen
anytime during the leg. Except my last two miles. I always feel
pretty good on my last two miles, you know — coming in. That is
psychological."

Connelly: "What bothers you?"

Mullens: "I get a tired feeling. And a lot of times it isn't
everything at once. Sometimes I can't get my breathing together. That's the way it's been on every leg."

Connelly: "It's gotta be psychological."

Mullens: "I suppose so. But this last one was one of the worst
yet. I felt lousy most of the way."

Mullens put an ice pack on his right knee. "I twisted it a couple
years ago playing that lousy slow pitch. It started bothering me
two days ago when I had a lot of downhill. All that pounding
really irritates it."

A great deal in Mullens' life — his injuries, his running, even
his career in law enforcement — can be traced to baseball. When
he talks of his life, he talks of baseball:

"I played ball in high school, and at the same time, I started
playing semipro ball in various leagues around Burbank.

"I remember one day, I went to watch the old Lockheed
Aircraft baseball team. They had a pretty good semipro team.
Well, they were short a ballplayer that day, and they asked me if
I'd like to play.

"They stuck me in the outfield. It was great. But my high
school coach found out about it, and I lost a couple of games
eligibility. I don't know how he found out about it, 'cause I
played under an assumed name.

"Just before my senior year in high school, in 1939, I got an offer from the St. Louis Cardinals organization. They wanted to sign me. My parents were against it. They wanted me to finish high school. But I promised them I'd go back and finish.

"So I signed, and the Cards sent me to their Albuquerque team. It was a Class D league in New Mexico and Arizona. I got down there in the middle of the season and played part-time. Kind of a utility ballplayer. I was only 17. I thought it was fantastic.

"When the season ended, I came back and finished high school.

"In 1940, I went to spring training with Sacramento and got shipped to Pocatello, Idaho. It was a Cardinal farm club in a C league. I didn't do very well there, and they sold me to Twin Falls. I did poorly there, and they sold me to Idaho Falls. And I did poorly there. Finally, I became discouraged and went home. I didn't finish the season. Instead, I got a job at Lockheed."

During the next three years, Mullens worked at Lockheed, got married, and joined the air force when World War Two broke out.

"I was in the service for two years. I played ball the whole time. I was stationed in Texas. Played in Victoria, Houston, Amarillo, all over Texas."

When the war ended, Mullens went back to work at Lockheed. In 1946, the Seattle club of the Pacific Coast League held its spring training in nearby San Fernando. Mullens tried out, was signed as an outfielder and optioned to Vancouver of the old Class A Western International League. "I had a good season. I even got a chance to play a few games with Seattle when Vancouver's season ended. I felt real confident. I felt I had a chance to play major league ball. That's what I wanted to do. That's what any professional ballplayer wants to do. I thought I had a shot."

Mullens had an outstanding year with Vancouver in 1947. He felt he was nearing the majors. "I hit around .322. Had about thirty home runs. Stole a lot of bases and made a lot of assists from the outfield. Again, I went to the parent club, Seattle, at the end of the year. I got into several games, and I hit a couple of home runs. I felt very confident."

But in 1948, the dream ended. "I went to spring training again with Seattle, and again they shipped me to Vancouver. I was real disappointed. I started to contemplate my future. I was 26. I had two small daughters. And I was on the road most of the time. I had to make a decision. If I'm not going any higher in baseball, I'd better get out now and start a new career.

"So I made a decision to join the police department. I joined in February of 1949.

"At the time, the department had a ball team made up of a lot of ex-professional ballplayers. Most of us were recruited by the same guy, Vic Penny. He ran the LAPD ball club. He told me, 'Hey, come on the department. You can play ball, and you've got yourself a job. You can have a lot of fun.'

"I said great; I need a job. And I could do something I really wanted to do — play ball.

"I played for the department two or three times during the week. We played the Los Angeles Angels and the Hollywood Stars of the Pacific Coast League during their spring training, and we traveled around to San Diego and Las Vegas and played a lot of other teams.

"During this time, I was working vice, which was great because it really allowed me to get away to play ball. But finally, Bill Parker became chief, and the team folded. He didn't want policemen going out and playing ball and getting paid for being policemen.

"The team hung together for a while. We still played on Sundays, and we played in a couple of tournaments. But we never could regain our popularity on the department. I guess Parker was right; after all, we were playing on police time."

"I never planned to become a policeman. If I could have continued playing baseball on another job, I probably would have done so. It's just that I met Vic Penny. If I hadn't met him, who knows where I'd be today.

"But looking back, I wouldn't have wanted anything else. I am completely satisfied. I have almost 27 years on the department. I'm almost at the end of my career. I have been very happy."

2:12 P.M. EDDIE GARCIA

Eddie Garcia was thinking about possums. Not the furry kind, but the ones he often found inside boxing rings. As opponents, possums are notorious, feigning injury, lulling their prey into complacency, then springing to life, snatching victory from what seemed like certain defeat.

Garcia was starting to believe that his opponent on this cross-country relay might be playing possum. On this, his eleventh leg, he was feeling strong and relaxed. He ran along the shores of Flathead Lake, a breathtaking expanse of water tucked away beneath tree-covered mountains that, in their skyward advance, dissolved into snow-capped peaks.

Flathead is the largest natural lake west of the Mississippi —
28 miles long, 5 to 15 miles wide, and mesmerizing in its beauty.
As if that weren't enough, the sky was overcast, the temperature cool, and the terrain flat. Absolutely ideal conditions.
Suddenly the run was more like a training session with a
paunchy, punched-out sparring mate than a full-scale battle
with a finely tuned opponent. Garcia was confident.

"I think I've figured my opponent out," he would say after his
run. "He's a possum. Just when he thinks you're complacent, he
throws a hill at you, or heat, or humidity. He wants you to think
he's hurting, that you're getting the best of him. Just like in the
ring. The possum's always looking for a sucker. This opponent
is looking for a sucker, too. But I know his game. I don't think I'll
have any problems with him. I'm sure I can beat him."

3:18 P.M. CURT HALL

Curt Hall had severe stomach cramps. Suddenly he darted off
the road and into the forest. Fortunately he'd had the foresight
to carry some toilet paper.

4:36 P.M. BOB HICKEY

There was wind, rain, even snow flurries as Hickey ran toward
the town of Kalispell, Montana, population 10,526. Hickey's
blistered foot was protected by a cushion especially built for him
by Ron Kiser. Along the way some hardy folks braved the
elements and ran beside Hickey, waving, grabbing his hand,
and taking his picture. Hickey was a celebrity.

Inside Van One, Alex Shearer was getting ready for his
twelfth leg.

Shearer: "I'm going to wear a hat. I don't want people to
mistake me for Leonard Nimoy."

Rockwood: "Leonard Nimoy is too smart to go on a thing like
this."

Shearer: "You have a point. Still, I'm going to wear a hat,
because I am going to run through a town, and my hair isn't
combed."

Rockwood: "Just watch. After you take it through town,
Burke will get 10 miles of downhill, which will end as soon as I
take the baton. I'll get Mount Whitney. Just watch."

Shearer: "Yeah. You're right. Burke has been running downhill since this thing started. I don't think he's had a hill yet. Of
course, that figures since he planned the whole run."

Burke: "That's right. The Angeles Crest isn't a hill. And Billy

Barty plays center for the Lakers."

Shearer: "Great rebounder."

At the end of his run, Hickey sprinted toward a couple standing off to the side of the road. When he reached them, he fell into
their arms, and they embraced. They were close family friends,
Bob and Maxine King, who had moved from Los Angeles to
Cider Lake, Montana, to retire a couple years earlier.

Maxine: "Your mother sent us the schedule of the run, but we
found out you're ahead of schedule, so we got here early."

Hickey: "Yeah. We must be about three and a half hours
ahead."

Bob: "How's the running?"

Hickey: "Tiring. No, not really. The people and the receptions
have been great. The country is so fantastic."

The conversation drifted from running to police work. And
Hickey decided to entertain the Kings with a foot pursuit story:

"I'll tell you about the only foot pursuit I ever lost. My partner
and I were looking around for a burglary suspect in a residential
area. I spotted him first, across the street — about 50, 75 feet
away. Young black guy. I said, 'Halt! Police officer!' He didn't do
anything but rabbit. Went. And I said to myself, 'Here we go.'

"He went between two houses, and then circled back to the
front. Then I heard this 'smack.' I figured he hit a wall or
something. And I figured I had him. Well, I came charging into
the front, and I ran right into a huge rose bush. It caught me right
under the nose and across the eyes. I never saw it. The thing
decked me. And then I heard the guy scamper over this fence
and make his escape. That's the only pursuit I ever lost."

5:41 P.M. ALEX SHEARER

Shearer carried the baton through Kalispell, the rain soaking
through his hat and dripping down his moustache.

"I felt good for five miles, then I got real tired. It was like
running out of gas halfway through a trip."

Shearer's legs were "heavy" but his chest felt fine. "My no-
fried-foods diet's working," he announced shortly after the run.
"But every time I see a French-fried potato, I froth at the mouth. I
don't know how much longer I can hold out."

During his entire 10 miles, no one had mistaken him for
Leonard Nimoy. The hat apparently had worked.

6:57 P.M. BOB BURKE

It was cold and raining as Burke headed toward Glacier Point,

Montana. The terrain was slightly downhill, just as Rockwood had jokingly predicted.

Burke ran his 10 miles in 67 minutes and 31 seconds. He was now firmly established among the top runners. The standings: Hickey (after twelve legs), 66:23; Foote (11), 67:06; Janowicz (11), 67:29; Burke (12), 70:29.

8:04 P.M. JOHN ROCKWOOD

And just as Rockwood had also predicted, he got a hill. It was slight, but nonetheless, it was a hill. Rockwood's journey carried him through West Glacier, near the base of the Rocky Mountains. The city is the gateway to spectacular Glacier Park — more than a million acres of valleys, lakes and rugged, tree-covered mountains carved by glaciers during the last Ice Age. This is the lush richness that was America two centuries ago. Now it is an anachronism — a reminder of a paradise lost.

Rockwood ran along the magnificent "Going to the Sun Road," one of the most scenic in the world. Some 50 miles long, it connects the east and west sides of Glacier Park and crosses the Continental Divide at Logan Pass — altitude 6,664 feet.

As Rockwood passed through the small communities along the way, scores of people stopped what they were doing to wish him luck and urge him on. "People came out of their houses, out of bars and stores. A couple of little kids called me 'Super Runner.' I got a great feeling there."

Inside Van One, Hickey was still talking to his friends, Bob and Maxine King. The Kings asked for another pursuit story. Hickey was off and running.

"Twice during these relays I've helped run down suspects. The first time was in 1972, just after we'd completed our run to Vancouver. The whole team was going out for a late dinner, and myself and another runner were waiting for everyone just outside our hotel.

"This guy comes rushing by me, and he's holding something. And then I hear someone yelling, 'Help, I've been robbed, I've been robbed!' And I just knew who the suspect was. So I run into the hotel and try to catch the guy, but he steps into the elevator, and the doors close. I start watching the numbers. They stop at six, and I run up the stairs to the sixth floor. But I'm too late; no one's there. I try listening at different doors to hear any commotion, but nothing. So I go back down the stairs and outside, and I start walking through the parking lot, and I'm almost hit by this purse. Someone threw it out the window. I look up, and there's the suspect on a sixth floor terrace. He jumps back, but now I know where he is. I notify the local police, and we go up and they bust a gang of purse snatchers.

"Then two years later, the team had just arrived in Washington, D.C., for our run to Los Angeles, and we go to this Italian restaurant. We finish eating, and we're walking out of the place, and this guy comes rushing past us, and then we hear the restaurant manager screaming, 'Help, help, I've been robbed! Stop that man!' I take off after the guy with a couple of the other runners, and we chase him about a block, and he jumps into this car with his friends — about seven other people. We surround the car, and just then, a plainclothes D.C. car pulls up. They arrest the whole bunch of 'em for theft. They'd left without paying their bill."

The chill had turned to bitter cold as Rockwood headed into Glacier Park. But the people and scenery had made it his best run yet.

9:14 P.M. DICK BONNEAU

Bonneau continued along the "Going to the Sun Road," but there was no sun. It was pitch dark. He was passing through America the Beautiful, but he might as well have been in the Mojave.

The temperature was near-freezing and rain was pouring as Bonneau finished eight miles of straight uphill and began his final 100 yards. Despite the hour and the weather, most of the members of Vans One and Two had gathered at the hand-off point.

Clark: "Here comes Dickie, chargin' up the hill like a little kid bringin' home the paper."

As Bonneau finished and handed the baton to Foote, Clark gave him a banana. And Rockwood presented him with a toy windmill on behalf of Van One.

Rockwood: "We take care of our kids."

Bonneau was dripping wet.

Clark: "You looked like a little wood nymph running out there."

Bonneau: "Well, I'm gonna get out of this cold, get a shower, and listen to some stories from Uncle Alex."

Clark: "Dickie, I don't know how to break this to ya — but you already missed out on Uncle Alex's bedtime stories. He's asleep."

Bonneau: "Well, he's gonna have to wake up and repeat 'em."

Clark. "No. Impossible. He and Burke are cuddled up together like a couple of old bears. Disgusting sight. Disgusting."

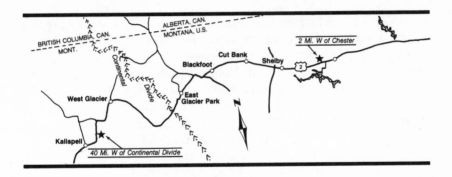

THE TENTH DAY
Wednesday, June 23, 1976

East Glacier, Montana

There's a bar in the town of East Glacier, and in the bar, there's a ragged piece of paper tacked to the wall behind the bartender. It issues a warning: "The following people are prohibited by court injunction from entering these premises. If they do, they will be arrested." Below the warning is a list of some 30 names — names like Judy Running Bear, Phil Black Fox, and Ben Red Cloud.

The bartender, a woman in her early 40s, with coarse blond hair that falls unevenly around a tough, lined face, points to the names in disgust. "He threw a bottle of beer at me. Missed, but smashed the mirror. This one hit a customer over the head with a chair. Damn near killed him. These two took a guy outside and beat him with a cue stick. We don't want these bastards around here anymore. If they step on these premises, they're gone. Jail. That's it."

East Glacier is just outside the Blackfoot Indian Reservation in east Montana. At about seven in the morning, Frank Mullens would carry the Bicentennial baton onto the reservation. No one quite knew what to expect.

10:27 P.M. CHUCK FOOTE

"It was like running in a snow tunnel. Mist was coming off the road. It was dark. Eerie. I expected Sherlock Holmes to come out and say, 'Dr. Watson.'"

In Van Two, Murphy was massaging his calves, getting ready for his next leg. Clark was reading the autobiography of Audie Murphy, *To Hell and Back*. And Janowicz was sleeping. The two drivers, Assistant Chief of Police George Beck and Officer George Moore, were sitting at the front of the van, chatting.

Clark heard a car. He sat up in his bunk, pulled back the window shade and gazed out into the darkness.

The car drew closer, then slowed to about 15 miles an hour. Now it was beside the van, barely moving. Six Indians were inside. They were looking at the huge van. Its signs told the story: "The Los Angeles Police Department Bicentennial Relay of Goodwill." The car crept past the van, and suddenly its engine stopped. "They've parked," Clark thought. He sat on his bunk, paralyzed, hoping to hear the engine start and the car resume its journey. Seconds went by. He heard nothing.

"Where the hell's the shotguns?" he shouted.

"What for?" Murphy asked.

"A car full of Indians just pulled ahead and stopped."

The shotguns were in a locker above the driver's seat. Clark pulled one down and loaded it.

"Christ! Foote's out there alone!" Clark said, as he moved back to the window above his bunk. "That follow car isn't even armed."

Foote was about halfway through his leg. He asked the follow car to play a tape his daughter had made shortly before the relay. Within moments, the night was filled with Jack and Jill and Little Miss Muffet.

Clark peered out the window. He saw nothing. Heard nothing. Moments passed. Everyone in the van, except for the slumbering Janowicz, was staring at Clark.

Off in the distance, a car door opened, then closed. Clark swallowed and pulled the rifle to his chest. Everyone was frozen. Listening, waiting. Then a noise.

"Something's moving out there," Clark whispered. "Sounds like just one person."

"Crunch . . . crunch . . ." The sound of footsteps shattered the stillness. Murphy shook Janowicz awake.

Foote sped across the fog-shrouded mountains. The tape of his daughter ran out. Rudy DeLeon searched for a Statler Brothers tape — Foote's next request. "I really felt the loneliness when the music stopped," Foote would say. "I felt like the loneliest man in the world."

Clark pulled back the window shade and narrowed his eyes, trying to pick up the movement outside. He saw nothing.

"Crunch . . . crunch . . ." The footsteps drew closer. A lone figure moved toward the van. It stopped for a moment about 10 feet away, apparently gazing at the signs.

"I can see him," Clark whispered. "He's just standing there."

"Is he armed?" Beck asked.

"I don't think so," Clark said. "But it's so damned dark . . ."

The figure walked toward the van.

"He's coming," Clark whispered.

Then three sharp knocks. George Moore looked at Beck and Clark. Moore was closest to the door. He wanted guidance.

Beck nodded.

Clark quickly hid his shotgun along the head of his bunk. Moore opened the door.

The girl couldn't have been more than 16 years old. Dark eyes. Clear, bronze skin. Black hair that tumbled to her shoulders. She was beautiful.

"Hi," she said softly. "We heard you were coming this way. Welcome."

Clark pushed the shotgun under his blanket.

Indian girl: "My friends are too shy to say hello."

Clark: "They shouldn't feel that way. Tell them to come in. We've got beer, coffee, soft drinks, food. Want something?"

Indian girl: "No, thank you. Where are you going?"

Clark: "Canada. We started in Los Angeles. We'll end in Montreal." The words spilled from him. He was almost giddy with relief and excitement. "Each of us runs 10 miles every 16 hours. We do it for three weeks. Hey, really — your friends are welcome . . ."

Indian girl: "No. We gotta get going anyway. We live on the reservation. It's about 40 miles from here. When will you get there?"

Clark: "Around seven or eight this morning, I guess."

Indian girl: "I hope I'll see you later. Good luck."

Clark: "Thanks for stopping by."

The girl left. The men of Van Two relaxed and laughed. The first confrontation with the "Indian problem" was over.

At nine miles, the follow car broadcast Foote's progress to Van Two: "Our little Indian friend here has got just one more mile to go. He has run his first nine in 55:10."

Murphy (sarcastically and jealously): "He's moving right along."

Beck: "That little Indian fart."

Janowicz (disgustedly): "He's run sub-65s his last nine legs. I didn't think he was in that kind of shape."

Clark: "Chuck is tough."

Van Two: "We read you, Turtle. Mercury Murphy is ready to go."

11:30 P.M. JIM MURPHY

"It was pitch dark. I stepped out of the camper, and I didn't even know what direction I was facing. I knew it was beautiful country. I could hear the waterfalls and streams running beside me. But it was so dark and cold [near-freezing], and it was 10 miles of uphill. Miserable. Horrible. I never thought I'd get to the five-mile mark. It seemed like I was running forever.

"I was thinkin' — won't it be nice when I'm home and I'm warm and comfortable. I tried to think of good things, warm things, things that comfort you for the moment. But I kept wondering: 'What the hell am I doing out here? Why am I on this run?' I couldn't answer those questions. I just knew I had to finish those 10 miles.

"You know, I've run with snow on the ground in 30-degree weather, and I've run marathons in the desert when it was 90 degrees. But at least it was daylight, and I was competing against someone. This time it was just me against the darkness and cold and hills and myself. Distance, time, terrain — there was nothing to relate to. It was like being in outer space. My feet kept hitting the ground, but other than that, I could have been on the moon. I didn't know where I was or how far I'd run. I swear — that was the longest 10 miles I've ever run in my life.

"Normally, on a tough run, I'll keep saying, 'C'mon, push yourself. Push yourself.' But on this one, it wasn't a question of pushing myself. I was just trying to keep my mind off the nothingness out there and from going nuts."

For 84 minutes, Murphy ran in the "nothingness" of Glacier National Park. The terrain, darkness and cold hampered him. But it was his blistered right foot, which he'd ignored during his past two runs, that slowed him.

At first, the heel blister merely ached. He could deal with that. By the seven-mile mark, it throbbed. And by eight miles, the pain had welled up and consumed him. But in this bitterly cold vacuum, at least he finally had something he could relate to: pain.

12:55 A.M. DICK CLARK

"It was cold and very dark, but I enjoyed it. I like to run in the darkness. You can create your own world. Let your imagination run wild. Be kind of a loner against the world."

Inside Van Two, Foote to Janowicz: "Clark dedicated his run to Jim Bridger, the Indian fighter, and he got all uphill. Serves him right. He's gonna need a grappling hook to get up that mountain."

There was almost a ghostly aura about it as Clark seemed to materialize out of the rain and mist of Glacier National Park and closed to within 150 yards of the hand-off point. He had run 10 miles of uphill. His pace: a steady eight and a half minutes per mile. Finally, the hand-off.

"You've got 10 miles of uphill, Frank!" Clark yelled to Janowicz as he handed him the baton.

"Shit," Janowicz replied.

2:19 A.M. FRANK JANOWICZ

"It was early in the morning. Raining. Cold. I was tired. And everything hurt, from my feet to my groin. But I got this motion picture going in my mind — my kids, my wife, home. And that helped."

But at six miles, the film ran out. And the reality of the run took over.

"The last five miles were a real mental battle. I kept praying it would level off. But it never did. Every time I came to a turn, there was another hill. I tried to relax and just keep my feet moving. It was a struggle."

Inside Van Two, Clark told Foote he hadn't dedicated his run to Jim Bridger, after all.

Clark: "It was Jim Bowie."

Foote: "Well, he probably killed a few Indians in his day, too. That's why you got rain, fog and 10 miles of hill."

Clark: "I gutted it out, like I always do."

Foote: "Don't give me that shit. The Great Spirit ate your ass."

At eight miles, Janowicz reached the Continental Divide. "I wish it had been daylight," he said. "I woulda liked a picture of that. I was so pissed off. But I felt like a real pioneer going over it. Like a real Viking."

Afterward, he took inventory again. His groin, thighs and calves hurt. And he had a severe blister on his right heel. "It's just like Murphy's," he said, shaking his head. "Just like Murphy's."

Janowicz walked into the bathroom and closed the door.
Clark: "The strong, silent type."
Murphy: "Yeah, absolutely stoic. Never a complaint."

The policemen from Los Angeles were now 22 miles from the
Indian reservation in Montana's badlands. The temperature was
in the low 40s. The rain was coming in torrents.

3:32 A.M. BOB JARVIS

"I wore a full rain suit and ran as fast as I could to get out of that
miserable weather."

Inside Van Three, the talk was predictable.
Connelly: "Well, Frank, you'll take it onto the reservation."
Hall: "They won't lay a hand on ya, Frank."
Connelly: "We'll be right behind you, Frank. Right here. In
the van. Warm and safe. But we'll be with you in spirit, Frank."
Watkins: "I've got an idea! Let's change Speedy Gonzales's
[Eddie Garcia's nickname] name to Eddie Featherhawk. He'll be
our token Indian. He'll get us safely across the reservation. If
they find out his real identity, we'll just give him to 'em as a
fucking slave."
Clark: "Maybe we could make a trade. Get some horse blan-
kets and a squaw or something."

Jarvis moved out of Glacier National Park and down the
barren, rolling hills that lead to the Blackfoot reservation —
home to some 10,000 Indians. His blisters had almost healed,
and his muscles were loose. But the rain, the slippery pavement
and the raincoat slowed him to about eight minutes per mile.
Jarvis handed the baton to Pat Connelly 12 miles from the reservation.

4:50 A.M.

Van Three had sped ahead and was now parked alongside Van
One at the next hand-off point, about two miles outside the
reservation. Eight Indians approached. Three of them wore
badges. A somber Bob Burke slowly emerged from Van One.
First Indian (extending his hand): "I'm one of the tribal chieftains. These are the reservation police. We'll be escorting you
across the reservation."
Burke: "Thank you. Thank you very much."

Second Indian (a reservation cop): "From L.A., huh? How far have you run already?"

Burke: "More than 1,700 miles. We're nearly halfway. We really appreciate you helping us."

Third Indian (also a reservation cop): "Anything for a fellow police officer."

Everyone laughed. The second confrontation with the Indian problem — here on the Blackfoot reservation — had vanished. Like a smoke signal in the night.

6:08 A.M. FRANK MULLENS

Frank Mullens carried the baton onto the Blackfoot reservation. Officially, the temperature was 43 degrees, but with the wind-chill factor, it was near-freezing. And rain was falling.

When they reached the reservation, Mullens and the pace car were joined by two tribal patrol cars. The patrol cars flew the reservation flag; the pace car, the American flag. The reception along the way was subdued.

Despite leg weariness and fatigue, Mullens ran his first five miles in just over 35 minutes.

Inside Van Three, a reporter from a newspaper in nearby Shelby, Montana, asked Eddie Garcia if he was looking forward to his next run.

Garcia: "No. Obviously not. Don't even ask me. Look at it out there. Would you be looking forward to it? I never thought winter would come on June 23rd. It didn't get this cold all winter in L.A."

Three teenage Indian boys joined Mullens at the halfway point. It was obvious that despite their age, they were good, experienced runners.

Mullens and most of his teammates were ambivalent about being joined by other runners. They enjoyed the company; it was part of their mission of goodwill. But because of the rigors of the run, they preferred to set their own pace. Too often their companions pushed them beyond their limits. That was what was happening to Mullens. His young companions wanted Mullens to break 70 minutes. Everything was on schedule as Mullens entered his eighth mile.

"He said he was getting real tired," one of the Indians said afterward, "but I told him, 'Let's break 70 . . . c'mon, let's break 70.' He said, 'I don't think I can.' But we kept pulling him along. Kept the pace up."

At the end, Mullens's face was flushed. Perspiration mingled with the rain and poured down his forehead and cheeks. The near-freezing weather didn't cool him. He walked around outside the camper for several minutes, then slowly climbed inside.

Drivers Eddie Watkins and Jack Garrison recognized his agony, but ignored it — for Mullens's sake.

Watkins: "You looked real good out there."

Mullens: "Tired. My legs are sore. Shouldn't have pushed myself like that."

Garrison: "You broke 70. First time. You're getting in the groove. Getting stronger."

Mullens: "Man, I'm hungry."

He walked slowly to the kitchen, slapped together a peanut-butter-and-jelly sandwich, grabbed some crackers and cheese, and finished his raid by snatching a can of grapefruit juice.

Garrison: "A real gourmet."

Watkins: "Diamond Jim Mullens."

Clark and Murphy entered the camper.

Clark: "My legs are bionic. I could run forever. When we get to Montreal, let's just keep going. Whaddya think, Frank?"

Mullens: "I think we could, but the accommodations would have to be better. We couldn't live like this. If we could hire a cook, he could keep something going all the time. Then when a runner got through running and showering, he could eat. The camper would be eating continuously. And each runner could set up a routine."

Murphy: "You'd have to get a piece of ass once a week, too."

Mullens bit off a huge hunk from his sandwich and washed it down with a swig of grapefruit juice.

Mullens: "Oh well, sure. Hell, yeah. But eating — I've gotta eat. I eat everything in sight. I feel better when I eat. We sure could use a cook."

Mullens finished his sandwich and dug into the crackers and cheese.

Clark: "I think a masseuse wouldn't hurt either."

Mullens: "Oh, yeah. I could use one of those."

Jarvis: "I think we could run indefinitely."

Clark: "Think we could run around the world?"

Jarvis: "Maybe you could, but I'm not. This is my last one."

7:18 A.M. EDDIE GARCIA–CURT HALL

Garcia ran his first two miles at a slow, careful pace. Then, his muscles warm and loose, he moved out. The third and fourth miles sped by. He was running close to a six-minute-per-mile pace. And then it happened. First a twinge, just below the right knee. "Oh, God," he thought. He continued to run hard, hoping the discomfort would vanish. But he knew better. By the sixth mile, the discomfort had turned to pain. His opponent had landed a haymaker.

"I knew what it was right away," he said. "I've had it for years. It's a stretching of the nerves and tendons in the knee, caused by running on uneven surfaces. It feels like a bone's loose in the knee, rubbing against the other bones and joints. You can't take a step without feeling it. After a while, the pain settles in one spot, and it feels like a migraine headache. Every step becomes pure hell."

Garcia limped through his final two miles. Suddenly he was back in the ring, being pounded to the canvas. Then he was back in Hollenbeck Division, facing a drawn gun. His past had prepared him for this moment. He was not afraid.

Through the years, Garcia had discovered two sure-fire remedies for the inflamed knee. One was to stop running and let it heal. The other was to strengthen the muscles and tendons by exercising with foot weights. The first remedy was impossible. So Garcia would have to get some weights, and quickly, to prevent the knee from getting worse.

Once back in the van, Garcia converted his traveling bag into a makeshift weight, filling it with about 10 pounds of clothes and shoes. Then he stuck his foot through the carrying straps and tried to lift it. It was awkward. The bag kept slipping off.

He decided to apply heat. He boiled a hydrocollator and wrapped it around the afflicted area. After 10 minutes, he tried to walk. The pain was still there. He needed weights and complete rest. But he'd get neither for the next week-and-a-half. Halfway through his bout, Garcia had been suckered.

Curt Hall was tight and uncomfortable as he ran through the cold and rain. Huge trucks barreled by him, eclipsing the 55-mile-per-hour speed limit by 20 to 25 mph. Their fury blew him along the road like a rag doll. He was a motor cop, but his bike and badge were 2,000 miles away. And there were no "smokies" around to slow down the big diesels.

10 A.M. - 4:02 P.M.
Van One

The runners were now in the famous Big Sky country of Montana. The sky looked like a huge blue dome covering flatlands for hundreds of miles in every direction.

Bob Hickey had a tough run into and through the town of Cut Bank, population 4,004. The wind seemed to switch directions from moment to moment, and the rain and cold added to his discomfort. But the biggest discomfort came from his blisters. They had to be drained twice a day now. And Hickey was filling his body with aspirin and muscle relaxers to ease the pain.

Shearer and Burke ran through flatlands, Rockwood carried the baton through the town of Shelby, Montana, population 3,111, and Bonneau shot back onto the Montana flats once again.

When its thirteenth leg had ended, Van One had picked up another 35 minutes on the clocks. And so the team approached Chester, Montana, nearly four hours ahead of schedule.

4:02 P.M. CHUCK FOOTE

It was raining again as Chuck Foote began his thirteenth leg. But the terrain was flat and the wind was to his back. He decided to go all-out.

Publicist Rich Wemmer stopped by Van Two to visit.

Wemmer: "You know why there was no official reception in Cut Bank?"

Clark: "No. I was wondering about that."

Wemmer: "The sheriff there is a woman, and I understand she said we were just a bunch of freeloading policemen looking for a handout. So she didn't make any preparations."

Clark: "That was a disappointment. That's the first time any law enforcement agency hasn't greeted us."

Foote felt strong and loose. He wanted to break 60 minutes. He pushed his tall, lean frame past the three-mile mark in 17 minutes and 45 seconds.

Back in Van Two, Jim Murphy was getting ready for his leg. "I kept hearing them call out Chuck Foote's times," he said, "and that made me determined to go out and burn one — really burn one."

Foote broke 30 minutes for his first five miles. He didn't seem to be putting out any extra effort. His smooth, fluid style belied the strain.

At seven miles, Foote's time was relayed back to the van: 41:25.

Janowicz: "Cheee-rist! He's not human."

Murphy: "You know what's really remarkable? Any real good runner will tell you that you should run one hard and then back off — hard, easy; hard, easy. But he just keeps burning 'em — 60, 61, 62 minutes. And he doesn't even seem to be putting out."

Clark: "He must've sold his soul to the Great White Spirit for fast times. When we end this run, he'll suddenly turn old and senile and die."

Foote was hurting as he entered his final mile-and-a-half. "I had to talk to myself, push myself. Concentrate on my pace, breathing — and get myself past the pain. The other runs were relatively easy on this relay. It's funny the amount of extra energy needed to push yourself from a comfortable 62-minute leg to a sub-60-minute leg. It's just a couple of minutes, but there's a world of hurt and concentration in-between."

Outside Van Two, Murphy was stretching his long, powerful limbs and testing the ball of his blistered right foot. It felt good. The blister had "toughened up." Murphy was ready.

Foote entered his final mile. His time was 53:52. If he could maintain a six-minute-per-mile pace, he would become the first runner since Murphy — more than a week ago — to break 60 minutes.

The wind was gusting up to 35 miles an hour, hitting Foote at about a 30-degree angle from the back. The Montana night was chilly. Huge diesel trucks flew down the lonely road, pushing him back and forth, disrupting his pace and rhythm. Several trucks were carrying gravel to a construction site. As they shot by, some of the gravel spilled onto the road, bouncing off Foote's legs and chest. One piece shot past his head.

Foote was breathing hard. His mind was unable to get off the pain. His legs were numb. But from the pace car, he looked controlled and strong.

Pace Car: "Chuck, 10 miles — 59:50. Atta way to go."

Foote ran an extra tenth of a mile and handed the baton to Murphy.

Foote: "Wheeh! That was a tough little sucker."

He walked around near the van, drawing in the cool night air.

Janowicz: "Nice going, Chuck. You, me, Hickey and Murphy are the only ones to break 60 minutes."

Clark: "Who else do you think will do it?"

Foote: "Connelly can do it."

Janowicz: "That would be a heckuva race. Murphy, Connelly and Foote for 10."

Clark: "My money would be on Tonto. He's never let the Lone Ranger down. He'd run their white asses into the ground."

5:03 P.M. JIM MURPHY

"I wanted to break 60 minutes. I tested the blister for the first three miles, and it felt good. So I picked up the pace. I was under 30 minutes at the five-mile mark, and I just maintained a good hard turnover."

At the five-mile mark, Murphy's blister began to fill with fluid, but it was withstanding the pounding. "I knew I could do it. I felt like a coiled spring ready to let loose. I'd been holding back for a week. I was ready to explode."

And explode, he did. His muscles were loose, his stride free and easy.

The pace car shouted encouragement: "You're on schedule for breaking 60 — 47:30 for eight miles. You got it, Mercury. You got it."

Murphy was well under 54 minutes for nine miles. This is the way he had wanted to run. The way he was capable of running. He finished in 59:18. As Clark headed across the Montana prairielands, Pat Connelly walked over from Van Three.

Connelly: "Well, Murphy, you've re-established your image."

Murphy smiled and threw an arm around Connelly's shoulders.

Later, Murphy would reflect on the episode: "Connelly knew what the hell he was talking about. He's an experienced runner; he teaches, coaches. And he's perceptive. He understood I was out to prove to myself that I still had it, that I could still do it. He knew I had to make sure that my body was still responsive, that I still had the conditioning, that nothing was wrong with me.

"You know, three or four days of running slow like I did really affects you mentally. Especially when you're competitive and used to running good times, like I am."

But Murphy — the self-styled egotist, hotdog, braggart — had gained even greater insights into himself. Those insights had not come in a flash. They had come slowly — painfully so. Now, on a rainy Montana night, they crystallized.

"You know, I came on this team with a reputation. I felt that in order to gain acceptance — to become part of this team — I had to live up to that reputation.

"But then I started to realize — if you're an outsider, being the best won't automatically gain you acceptance. In fact, it might be better to lose. 'Cause sometimes people don't really accept you until they've seen you defeated. And after the fall, if you can come back to the top again, they can accept you 'cause then they're living your victory, too.

"I've run in other team endeavors, but I've never had the feeling I've had here. It's because we're all police officers. We have the same basic concepts, same ideals, same basic goals, same experiences, same background, same love of righteousness.

"On all the teams I've competed on, everyone was more of an individual, only concerned about himself and his performance. But in this situation, everyone really is interested in everyone else. It's unique.

"If I were just running for myself, I wouldn't have kept running on these blisters. But when the pain came, I didn't just think about how bad it hurt me. I thought about how it would hurt the thirteen other guys if I stopped. The team spirit, the team effort, really comes to the fore. And a large part of it is being cops. We want to show people how policemen feel about each other, how we can accomplish things as a team, and how we never let one another down.

"It took me a long time to realize what this relay was all about. But I think I have. I've shown them I'm not just running for Jim Murphy. I'm running with them and for them. I'm part of this team.

"You know, I've probably learned more about myself and running in the past week and a half than in my entire life. But that's the hell of it. Just when you think you've learned some great lesson in life, you have to learn something new."

Clark and then Janowicz ran across muddy, gravel-strewn roads toward Chester, Montana. Clark ran his leg in about 72 minutes, Janowicz in 63:10.

Janowicz's blister now covered his heel, and there was danger of the skin coming off. He had been running hard from the start. Nothing had slowed him down. Not tightness and soreness in his calves, thighs, groin and shoulder. But a blister is different. It can lay the toughest runner low. It had nearly destroyed Jim Murphy. It was having a telling effect on Frank Janowicz.

But its most damaging impact was yet to come.

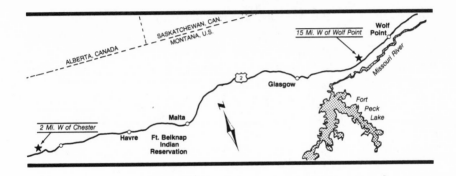

THE ELEVENTH DAY
Thursday, June 24, 1976

There is nothing mystical about running long distances. For hundreds of thousands of years, man was a running animal, using his two legs for everything from basic transportation to chasing down his food and escaping from his enemies.

Ever since the invention of the wheel, there has been an accelerated decline of man's function as a "self-transporter." But his basic instincts remain. Perhaps it was inevitable, then, that in this, the Golden Age of Transportation, millions of people would suddenly feel a need to run.

Most experienced coaches and runners — like Pat Connelly and Jim Murphy — will tell you that a healthy human being should be able to run long distances. All it takes is determination and correct technique.

In his coaching, Pat Connelly emphasizes natural rhythm and tempo. "If you want to learn to run correctly," he says, "watch a child run. He runs free, light, easy, relaxed. What happens after that is the child goes to school. His gym teacher says, 'Okay, everyone line up. We're gonna see how fast you can run.' It becomes a test. The kid tenses up. He knots his fists, clenches his jaw, tenses his shoulders. Running is no longer natural. I teach people to relax. Keep the fingers loose, shake out the arms, and keep the jaw loose. In fact, I say smile while you're running. It's an indication of how loose and relaxed you are."

If running is natural and the gift is given to nearly everyone, then speed is like Garbo's looks, Caruso's voice, Cliburn's touch, Einstein's genius —it is parceled out to the few. Among these fourteen men, only Pat Connelly and Jim Murphy received the gift. And even they could only be described as above-average athletes in this day of the "superstar."

Perhaps a new definition of greatness is needed. Perhaps greatness should be measured by how we fill the gap between our promise and our limits.

Today these men would cross the halfway mark of their remarkable journey across the North American continent.

They were closing the gap. They were approaching greatness.

Van Three

Bob Jarvis ran through the mud and rain of Chester, the blister on the ball of his left foot giving him only minor discomfort. Several teenagers joined Pat Connelly for about five miles of his leg. Frank Mullens — on advice from Connelly — slept seven hours after his exhausting twelfth leg, then ran a strong 75-minute 10-miler through rolling farmlands. And despite his knee problems — or perhaps more accurately, because of them — Eddie Garcia set out to become the fifth runner to break 60 minutes for a leg. "The knee felt a lot better than I expected it would," he said. "I figured I'd better go for broke now, 'cause there's no telling how bad it might be tomorrow."

He was on target for a sub-60, entering his final two miles. Then the "possum" sprang to life again, throwing a steep, intractable hill at him. It slowed Garcia to an eight-minute-per-mile pace. He ran the course in 64 minutes. His knee ached afterward.

Curt Hall, the last runner out of Van Three, took the baton around two o'clock in the morning. He expected a quiet run through Havre, population 10,558, one of the larger cities in this area of Montana. Like Chester, Havre was undergoing massive street construction. Rain made the going even more treacherous. As he ran through the dark streets, Hall looked like an oversized sprite, jumping over holes and loose gravel.

Hall reached the downtown district at about 2:30 A.M.. "I couldn't believe it," he recalled. "I thought the place would be dead at that hour, being a farm community and all. But it was jumpin'. Every other building was a bar. And every one was doing a booming business. Drunks kept coming out to greet me. I even had a drunk reporter try to interview me. He had a tape recorder, and he was trying to talk to me as I ran, so I slowed down. We ran about a quarter-mile together. I was just about walking at the end."

The runners of Van Three were a testimony to the Connelly philosophy of how to run in this type of relay. They ran comfortably, careful not to overextend. There were no Murphys, Hickeys or Janowiczs in Van Three.

Still, all were concerned about their times. Mullens, who wanted to average 75 minutes per leg, was now doing exactly that. But he was paying the price in mounting fatigue and muscle strain. Garcia was consistently in the 60s, but in constant pain from the injury to his right knee. Hall was routinely breaking 70 minutes every leg. And despite his blister, Jarvis was still running in the low 70s. Connelly's calves were tight, but he was averaging around 65 minutes for his last five legs.

So even Van Three, which had the least competitive nature and the slowest overall average of the three vans, was now averaging well under Bob Burke's projected 75-minute-per-leg pace.

Curt Hall had carried the baton through Havre five hours ahead of schedule. The team was supposed to arrive there at 7:35 A.M. for a breakfast hosted by local citizens' groups and the Havre Police Department. The team was 40 miles outside Havre when a citizens' committee caught up with Van One and presented fourteen Bicentennial pins — one for each runner.

Meantime, Van Two, which was parked 50 miles east of Havre, got a frantic call from publicist Lou McClary shortly before 6 A.M.. Could they cut their sleep short and return to Havre for the breakfast? Sure.

So the runners shot back, gulped down eggs, orange juice and coffee, talked with local officials and law enforcement people, and then headed back up the road. It was a frenzy of activity that was to be repeated again and again as the team moved further and further ahead of schedule.

While all that was going on, Van One was running its fourteenth leg across the rolling prairielands of central Montana. Hickey, despite "burning blisters," ran his 10 miles in 63:37. And Bob Burke ran his ninth consecutive sub-70-minute 10-miler. The standings: Hickey (after fourteen legs), 66:06; Foote (13), 66:18; Janowicz (13), 67:34; Burke (14), 69:51.

The sun was just coming up in Big Sky Country as John Rockwood glided across the Montana flats in 69:33. And Dick Bonneau carried the baton onto the Ft. Belknap Indian Reservation. Once again, Indian officials greeted the team, forming a three-car escort for Bonneau.

The area was infested with mosquitos, and Bonneau felt tired and "a bit sick." Still, he broke 70 minutes.

The team was now nearly five-and-a-half hours ahead.

8:17 A.M. CHUCK FOOTE

"I was just shootin' along, trying to concentrate on my music, when all of a sudden a pheasant came runnin' out of the brush, squawkin' and screamin'. It scared the dogshit out of me. Damn! I hate bein' scared like that when I'm concentratin'."

9:20 A.M. JIM MURPHY

Murphy may have "re-established his image," as Connelly had said after Murphy's thirteenth leg. But he had also aggravated his blister. "I just moved my arms, gritted my teeth and hobbled across the reservation."

Murphy ran his leg in just under 90 minutes. It was his second slowest leg of the relay. But his depression was gone. He hadn't let his teammates nor himself down. He was part of a grand effort. "I was at peace with myself," he'd say later.

Back in Van Two, Chuck Foote and Dick Clark were discussing the scheduling problem.

Clark: "Things are getting a little hectic here. Shooting back to Havre, scarfing down food, riding like hell to get the baton on time."

Foote: "You know, on the D.C. run, we had just thirteen guys. This time we have fourteen and at least five or six of the guys who ran last time are in much better shape now. That's why we're running faster. I told Bob [Burke] before the run that we'd average better than 75 minutes for 10 miles. He said no way."

Clark: "Okay. We're more than five hours ahead. We're supposed to arrive in Montreal on the Fourth. That's what this thing is all about. What are we gonna do if we arrive a day early?"

Foote: "Then we arrive a day early. That's all."

Clark: "Wouldn't it be a shame to run all that way and get no fanfare?"

Foote: "Oh, we'll get fanfare. Once we get into Canada, officials there will know exactly what time we'll hit Montreal. But I don't think we should plan to hit Montreal on the Fourth."

12:06 P.M. FRANK JANOWICZ

"The fourteenth leg was the longest 10 miles I've ever run in my life. My heel blister was killing me. I was really afraid of breaking it open. So I ran all 10 miles on the balls of my feet, which I'm not used to doing. Every once in a while, I'd hit that heel, and the pain would just shoot through me. I kept telling myself, 'You gotta run 10 miles. You're not a quitter. You're too tough a guy to be a quitter.' I got mad as hell at myself for getting the blister in the first place."

Halfway through his leg, Janowicz reached the outskirts of Malta, population 2,195. Malta was small but significant. It was the midway point of the run.

"It was like runnin' through the desert. I thought it was a ghost town. No reception. Nothing. The people just stared at me. They musta thought I was some kind of freak or some guy runnin' away from the sheriff."

Janowicz charged through town and out into the Montana plains. "My main concern was the time," he said. "I wanted to keep my average under 70 minutes. So I figured as long as I broke 75, I could always increase later on." Janowicz's time was 71:03 for 9.8 miles. (Later, Pat Connelly would label Van Two's runners as "Beck's Boys." "He always took care of 'em," Connelly said. "They never seemed to run a full 10. Always 9.8s, 9.7s. Beck's Boys.")

1:17 P.M. BOB JARVIS

Until a week ago, Bob Jarvis had never had a blister during an LAPD relay. Now, on his fourteenth leg, the blister on the ball of his left foot that had been nagging him for days flared up, and two other smaller blisters formed underneath. "They were throbbing," he said, "just killing me."

Inside Van Three, coach Pat Connelly was talking about the two oldest members of the team — 54-year-old Frank Mullens and 47-year-old Alex Shearer.

Connelly: "Frank's getting more confident. He's put four or five of these sub-75s back-to-back. He's beating this thing psychologically. He knows he can do it.

"Now Alex . . . he likes to run as a hobby. He won't run any further than he has to. If I said, 'Alex, the race ends at that telephone pole,' he would stop right at that telephone pole.

"But when Al wants something, he'll get it. I'll give you an example. In the Police Olympics a few years ago, Al was entered in the mile run. I was coaching him, and I told him, 'Al, you're going against a bunch of guys that are a lot faster and a lot younger than you. But you can beat them if you want to. Here's what you have to do: Stick with those guys and let them do all the work for the first three laps. Then, 50 yards before the gun lap, jump 'em. Take off. Don't wait for the gun before you go into your kick. Surprise 'em. And believe me, before they get their wits about 'em, you'll be 30 yards ahead of 'em, and they're gonna have to play catch-up, and they're not gonna be able to do it.'

"Well, he just kinda nodded his head, like he always does, and you're never sure if he's heard you or not. But he gets in that mile race and runs the first three laps in third place. He comes around the curve on the third lap, and with one lap and 50 yards to go he takes off.

"He gets 60 yards on them right away and wins the thing in 5:01. Now Alex is not a 5:01 miler. But he did it. I'll tell you something, though. He'll never do it again. He did it once and that's it. That's Alex."

2:32 P.M. PAT CONNELLY

Connelly took the baton about 15 miles east of Malta. A soft breeze caressed his neck and back as he ran over rolling hills. "I ran my final mile in less than five minutes. I ran the whole thing in 67. Didn't even push myself."

3:39 P.M. FRANK MULLENS

Connelly was right. Frank Mullens was getting mentally stronger. For eight miles, across rolling hills, he maintained a steady seven-minute-per-mile pace. But this time he wasn't overextending. He was relaxed. Confident. Strong. After the eighth mile, he hit several sharp inclines, as the farmlands turned to mosquito-infested marshes. He took the hills at a slower, but steady, pace.

Inside Van Three, Bob Jarvis' blisters had transformed him. Normally fast-talking, wisecracking and cocky, he was now sullen, depressed.

Jarvis: "I've never had any trouble before. A few small blisters, but they always went away themselves."

Garcia: "You old depressed fossil. You're getting old. Your whole damned body is getting old, Jarvis. Your face, your gut, your feet." Garcia laughed — a high, maniacal laugh. It angered Jarvis.

Jarvis: "Screw you, you dumb wetback. Your face looks like a goddamn roadmap."

Garcia: "You're old, Jarvis. Hell, they're gonna start casting you for wheelchair roll-ons in those movies you act in." Again, Garcia let go with his high-pitched laugh.

Jarvis: "Can't anyone do anything about him — send him back to Juarez or wherever the hell he came from? Why don't you go lift something with that damn foot of yours?"

Garcia laughed again and then went into the bathroom.

Jarvis: "I'm feeling great except for these damned blisters. They're driving me up the wall. Kiser drained them [about a half-hour earlier]. I don't know if he's doing me more harm than good."

Connelly: "I haven't used Kiser on this run. One run I did, though, and he got me through it. Same thing as yours, on the ball of the foot. But we made a mistake that time. We cut all the skin off the blister. Since then he's stopped doing that."

Jarvis: "Well, I'm not letting him cut at all. Just drain 'em. I'll go through the pain of running on 'em. I'm going to do it."

Jarvis' tormentor, Garcia, had wrapped his right knee tightly with an Ace bandage, and was now standing outside the van in the middle of Montana marshlands, a swarm of mosquitos keeping him company.

For two days, Garcia had tried without success to use his traveling bag as a weight to strengthen his right knee. He'd also resorted to heat and ice. But nothing had worked. "The knee hurts," he said shortly before his fourteenth leg. "The way it feels now, I won't be running another good time for a while."

4:54 P.M. EDDIE GARCIA

Mullens completed another sub-75-minute leg and handed the baton to Garcia.

"The terrain was level, which helped the knee. I passed through several real small towns. Everyone seemed real curious and friendly."

A photographer from the Associated Press followed Garcia in her car for about a mile. She would drive ahead of him, park, jump out of her car and shoot four or five pictures, then jump back in. Six times, she repeated the routine. The attention had its effect on Garcia. Despite his sore knee, he ran a respectable 73-minute leg. "If I can run 73s the rest of the way," he said afterward, "I'll feel pretty good."

6:07 P.M. CURT HALL

Curt Hall carried the baton over rolling hills, toward the town of Glasgow. At eight miles, he hit a steep upgrade.

Dick Clark came by to visit Van Three. As usual, there were
shoes, socks and towels on the floor. Eddie Garcia was sitting on
an ice chest, waiting for a hydrocollator to heat on the van's
stove.

Clark looked around at the crowded, unkempt camper.

Clark: "You know what's really bad about this place?"

Everyone burst into laughter.

Watkins: "How long you got?"

Clark: "No, I'm serious. You've got room for a dance hall out
here in the middle. And you got a lotta cupboard space. But you
don't have any sleeping space."

Watkins: "Hey, three dwarfs couldn't live in here comfortably. What the hell are you talking about?"

Clark gazed at the pile of running shoes near the back of the
camper.

Clark: "There must be 25 pairs of shoes there. It must be fun
trying to find your pair when it comes time to run."

Watkins: "Oh, we play a game. We see who can find his shoes
and get 'em on the fastest. The winner gets an orange."

Clark: "I was wondering why Pat here has been running
barefoot the last couple times."

Watkins: "Yeah. We take his glasses away, and he has to feel
for his shoes. If he can't find 'em, tough shit."

Hall power-drove the last 50 yards of the hill and then coasted
down toward the hand-off point. There, ahead of him, was Bob
Hickey, warming up for his fifteenth run in 11 days.

Hickey does everything with a certain quickness. He moves,
talks, runs, and even warms up quickly. As he waited for Hall,
he sprinted about 40 yards, stopped and walked back to the
hand-off point, rolling his head and swinging his arms. He bent
down, touched his toes, swung his hips, jumped up and down
lightly, his hands on his hips, then rolled his head again and
sprinted for another 40 yards.

Connelly, who rarely warmed up at all, watched in amaze-
ment.

Connelly: "You'd think he was getting ready for the Olympics."

Hall was now about 30 yards from the hand-off point. Hickey
was still limbering up, jumping up and down, rolling his head,
kicking his feet and swinging his hips. He was still gyrating
when Hall handed him the baton.

7:25 P.M. BOB HICKEY

Lightning crackled across the gray, overcast sky as Hickey took the baton on the hills of eastern Montana.

"The fifteenth was my best run so far. I could have pushed it any time I wanted. I just floated. It was a great feeling."

Hickey's blisters still hurt, but he ran the leg in 61:58, his fastest since his opening 10-miler out of the Los Angeles Memorial Coliseum. Later, Kiser drained the blisters, and told Hickey to soak his feet. Once again, Hickey ignored the advice.

8:27 P.M. ALEX SHEARER

Crusty, cantankerous Alex Shearer didn't like to run through towns. He hated people to wave and make a big fuss over him. But once again, Alex ran through a town. This time, Glasgow, population, 4,700, once a trade center for pioneers, located in the heart of Montana's scenic river country. The temperature had dropped into the low 50s as Shearer ran through the streets of Glasgow, a police escort in front of him, people waving, looking and shouting along the way.

Shearer wound his way past the police station, the customary gesture of camaraderie worked into the relay by Bob Burke.

And then he swung out of Glasgow, into the barren Montana hills once more. He was feeling good. He had kept his pledge to lay off fried foods, and his legs were loosening up. Uncle Alex handed the baton to Bob Burke and got ready for his nightly reading, a tiny snort, and a good night's sleep.

9:43 P.M. BOB BURKE

Bob Burke ran over barren spaces about 110 miles west of the North Dakota border. The first five miles were flat. He set a fast tempo. If the hospitable terrain continued, he had a chance to break into the low 60s.

Back in Glasgow, the runners were chatting with some of the local police officers.

Local cop: "You know, we feel like we know you guys. Every TV program about cops is about the LAPD."

Bonneau: "Except *The Streets of San Francisco.*"

Local cop: "San Francisco's just a suburb, isn't it?"

Bonneau (laughing): "Yeah. That's right."

Connelly: "What's your biggest law enforcement problem here?"

Local cop: "Oh, we have some problems with Indians. Robberies. Nothing real serious, though. Nothin' like L.A. No homicides."

Clark: "Of course, you wouldn't know it for a year if one of those ranchers out there in the boondocks was killed."

Local cop: "Probably not."

Meantime, Hickey was talking to another Montana cop about Hollenbeck Division.

Hickey: "It's a nice little division. Predominately Mexican-American. Our biggest problem is with Chicano youth gangs. A lot of fights, a lot of killing."

Local cop: "You guys must be real demons on the street there. You ever chase down any of those punks on foot?"

Hickey: "Oh, yeah. I had a real funny one once. I was working in downtown Los Angeles as a sergeant. My partner and I were looking for some kids who were going around vandalizing coin machines — you know, the kind you put paper money into to get coins.

"Anyway, we spot these five kids. I stopped the car, and I said, 'Can I talk to you guys?' And they took off — split — in five different directions.

"I said, 'Sonofagun,' grabbed my nightstick and took off after one of 'em. About a 17-year-old kid. Very muscular, very strong.

"I chased him about a mile right through downtown L.A. I wasn't really going hard, though. I just wanted to tire him out. But I was yelling at the people on the street, 'Would you stop that fella — stop him for me, please.'"

The local cop laughed. "You asked people to stop him?"

Hickey: "Yeah. But everyone was real apprehensive. It was funny. I'd see guys put their foot out and try to trip him, or take a half-assed swing at him. Things like that."

Local cop: "And you're yelling ahead, 'Stop this fellow, please'?"

Hickey: "Yeah. Finally the kid jumped a wall into a parking lot and went around three or four cars and jumped back out. And I just followed him. He went into another parking lot and started going around these cars again. And I said, 'Friend, sooner or later you're gonna get tired, you know?' And he turned around and just went, 'Uh, uh, uh, uh . . . ' Panting sounds, you know. Then he said, 'You're right.' But he kept on going."

The local cop laughed again. "He discovered it wasn't Cannon who was chasing him, huh?"

Hickey: "No. Well, finally he just stopped. He was totally exhausted. I put him up against a car and told him to spread his feet. I searched him and cuffed him, and I said, 'Son, since you

like to run so much, we're gonna run all the way back to the car.'
He said, 'I can't run another foot.' I said, 'Friend, you're gonna
run, or I'm gonna drag your ass.' And I just kept shoving him all
the way back. Every time he'd stop, I'd just shove him, and I'd
say, 'C'mon, I thought you liked to run.'

"You know, the guy was black. But I would never put anyone
down by saying, 'Well, I thought you guys could run,' or anything like that. I just said 'You like to run. Let's go.'

"And that's what we did, a mile-and-a-half back to the car. He
was just about dead when we got there."

The local cop was near tears from laughter. His belly shook.
He was at least 50 pounds overweight.

Local cop: "I'd love to do that to one of these Indian bastards
around here."

Burke was on schedule for a sub-65-minute leg. But "the man
who never runs hills" suddenly ran into a mountain. For five
miles, he went straight up. "It must have been the only mountain in Montana," Burke said afterward. Still, he was able to run
his tenth consecutive sub-70 leg — but by the slenderest of
margins. His time: 69:59. The standings: Hickey (after fifteen
legs), 65:50; Foote (fourteen), 66:03; Janowicz (fourteen), 67:49;
Burke (fifteen), 69:52.

12:07 A.M. DICK BONNEAU

When Rockwood completed his leg and handed the baton to
Bonneau, the LAPD runners had covered exactly 2,000 miles.
The team was now more than five and a half hours ahead of
schedule.

Tomorrow, according to plans drawn up months earlier, they
were supposed to enter the town of Wolf Point, Montana, at
precisely 9:43 A.M. They were to be guests of honor at a breakfast
hosted by the Wolf Point Junior Chamber of Commerce, the local
police and sheriff's departments, and the Indian tribal police.
But at 9:43 A.M., the team not only wouldn't be in Wolf Point — it
wouldn't even be in Montana.

It was cold and raining as Bonneau completed the eleventh
day of the relay and began the twelfth. He scooted over the
rolling hills toward Wolf Point in 67 minutes.

Once back in Van One, Bonneau took a quick shower, and
then in chorus with the other runners, chanted for Uncle Alex to
read his fabled bedtime stories.

Chorus: "It's Uncle Alex time, it's Uncle Alex time . . ."

Shearer: "All right. All right. But Uncle Alex is very tired, so his nephews will get only two stories tonight. The first is about a young female librarian who can achieve orgasm with her partner only while reading a thesaurus. I like that one, because it might teach you a little culture. The other is about a young man who gains satisfaction by engaging himself with several varieties of fruit — watermelons and the like. You get the idea? I thought that one might teach you a little about man's relation to nature."

Shearer read the stories, then shared a little wine with his "nephews," and everyone went to sleep.

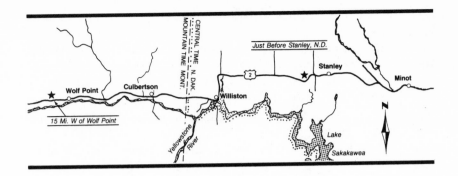

Just Before Stanley, N.D.

15 Mi. W of Wolf Point

THE TWELFTH DAY
Friday, June 25, 1976

1:14 A.M. - 6:11 A.M.
Van Two

Chuck Foote roared through the cold Montana night in 62:32, "mosquitos itching the life out of me. They don't sleep."

And shortly after 3 A.M., nearly seven hours ahead of schedule, Jim Murphy carried the baton through Wolf Point, population 3,095, mostly Sioux and Assinboine Indians.

As Dick Clark took the baton, the sun was just beginning its 18-hour excursion across Montana's Big Sky.

Inside Van Two, the talk was about Wolf Point.

Murphy: "When I hit Wolf Point, I heard a lot of dogs howling and a couple of people stumbled out of their houses to see me. Right in the middle of the night."

Foote: "It's a thriving metropolis, isn't it?"

Murphy: "Sure is."

Foote: "Hate to see it in the daytime, but I think we will."

In the rear of the camper, Frank Janowicz added a few wrinkles to his now-familiar pre-run routine. Instead of merely cursing and questioning his sanity for participating in the run, Janowicz began to express himself physically. He threw a towel to the floor and slammed his fist into the wall of the camper. "I don't know what the hell I'm doing here," he said. "I must be crazy. I've got a blister that's killing me. And now I gotta run 10 miles at five in the morning. I can't believe I'm not at home in bed, instead of out here in the middle of nowhere, like a big, dumb idiot . . ."

With that out of his system, Janowicz took the baton outside the two-street town of Poplar.

"This might be a dumb thing to say," Janowicz said, "but about halfway through the run, I was actually glad I got my blister. I said, 'Okay, here's one more ailment that will test me and show how tough I am.'

"At about eight or nine miles, I started to feel strong. I said, 'Damn, I'm running better because of this blister.' The blister was making me run up on the balls of my feet, and it was taking the stress off my thighs. My thighs were actually starting to feel good for the first time since my first leg. That blister kinda turned out to be a blessing."

For years, Pat Connelly had been telling Janowicz to run on the balls of his feet. It is Connelly's theory that the lower leg — the calf — can sustain the shock of long distance running much better than the upper leg.

Connelly: "When you run on the balls of your feet, the bone of the lower leg and the calves take the shock. The calves will be sore for a while, but they'll loosen up. The bone can absorb the shock forever. But when you run on the heels or flatfooted, the thighs take the shock. That's mostly muscle. And those muscles will ache for a long, long time. If you have a choice between putting pressure on bone or muscle, take the bone. It's a lot more resilient. The bone is not going to ache and get sore like the muscle."

It took Janowicz a long time and a lot of unnecessary pain to learn that simple lesson.

7:40 A.M.

Back in Poplar, the runners of Van Two were in jail. Voluntarily. Showers had been arranged there by the local cops. They were preferable to the one in the camper.

Foote: "This water is freezing. Oh, Christ! It's hot now. It's burning my butt!"

Clark: "The temperature control is not the best."

The cops, a little giddy from their nearly two-week ordeal, began to pretend they were on the other side of the law. They hatched an escape plan.

Clark: "Chuck here can slip his skinny little body through the bars. No problem for him."

Murphy: "And Janowicz can run through the wall."

Foote: "We'll just call the jailer and tell him that Murphy's blister is killing him, and he has to see a doctor."

Murphy: "Clark could just start farting. They'd let him loose for sure."

As the runners began to dry off, publicist Lou McClary entered the dreary cellblock.

McClary: "How'd you like those showers I arranged for you guys?"

Clark: "Wonderful, Lou. You know of a hospital where they treat burns and shock?"

McClary: "Whaaa?"

Murphy: "The temperature control was a little fucked up."

Foote: "I got a feeling you're a little fucked up, also, Lou. Wolf Point?"

McClary: "Could you? Listen, I'm real sorry. Real sorry. I hate to do . . ."

Foote: "You want us to shoot our asses back there for the breakfast."

McClary: "It's up to you guys. I'd never tell you what to do. But those people planned that breakfast three months ago. It's a big deal for them. A really big deal. And you're the only van that can go back."

Foote: "I hate to see a grown man cry. Let's go."

McClary: "Hey, thanks. Thanks a lot."

Foote: "No problem, Lou. We're all pretty hungry anyway."

And so, once again, Van Two turned around and headed back up the road, away from its destination, toward an obligation.

10:12 A.M.

Vans Three and Four had parked in the town of Culbertson, population 821. Inside Van Four, Jarvis' blister was being drained by Ron Kiser. Pat Connelly walked over to say hello to Assistant Chief of Police Charles Reese, one of the drivers of the support van. Their discussion would eventually trigger an upheaval.

Connelly: "We were just casually talking about the run and Reese said, 'Hey, we're either missing or just barely making a lot of dinners and breakfasts along the way. We're losing the goodwill effect of this relay. Something's gotta be done.'

"He asked me, as coach, 'What do you suggest?' And I said, 'We could run a couple alternate routes. Or we could all slow our pace to 90 minutes for a couple turns. Or we could throw out the watches and not time for a couple of turns. That would slow everyone down for sure.'"

Throw out the watches. It was a volatile idea — but not a new one. Connelly and Alex Shearer had been espousing it for years.

In fact, they led a small faction on the team, known as "The Rebels," which believed in a no-clock, no-time concept. Shearer was its most articulate spokesman:

"Timing makes no sense for two primary reasons. First, this is a team effort, and the clocks cause internal competition, which causes stress and injuries. Second, the clocks don't really tell you anything about how well one runner is performing vis-à-vis another runner.

"Look at it this way. You've got guys ranging in age from 28 to 54, running all kinds of terrain under all kinds of weather conditions, at all hours of the day. And many times they're not even running 10 miles — they're running 9.6s all the way up to 10.6s.

"How in the world can you possibly tell me some guy is running better than another? You can't. But at the end of the relay, they tally up all the times and average them, and they list them next to each guy's name on a big trophy that's put on display at the Police Academy. And for time immemorial, those times are there for everyone passing through those hallowed halls to see. And there isn't a runner — not one runner — who wants to be number fourteen on that damn trophy. And no runner should be number fourteen on the trophy, because number fourteen worked and trained and sweated as hard as everyone else, maybe more. But all that effort is transformed into one lone number on the bottom of a list. It's just not right."

But the clocks remained "on" primarily because one man wanted them on. Bob Burke — the originator and director of the LAPD relay runs—believed the clocks were an indicator of performance. "Not a perfect indicator," he'd argue, "but an indicator. After thirty legs or so, terrain, weather and other factors tend to balance out. And after two or three weeks of this type thing, I want to look at a piece of paper and know how I did. And most of the other men feel the same way."

How the other men felt was academic, because the LAPD relay team was not run by committee. It was run by one man — soft-spoken Policeman-Two Bob Burke, whose power here held sway over sergeants, lieutenants, even assistant chiefs of police.

Assistant Chief George Beck: "This is Burke's baby. Christ, he invented the thing. If he says, 'Run to Montreal backwards,' we run to Montreal backwards. We don't do anything unless Burke approves. We don't change anything unless Burke approves. Bob Burke is in total control."

But here in Culbertson, that control was beginning to slip away.

Connelly: "When I told Chief Reese we should think about getting rid of the clocks, he said, 'That's a helluva idea. I've been watching these guys pound themselves into the ground because of the clocks — Hickey, Murphy, Janowicz, Garcia, Jarvis, Mullens.' He asked me, 'What do you think?' I said, 'Throwing out the clocks will take the stress off. The guys are thinking more about their injuries and running than about meeting and talking with the people along the way. But this is a relay of goodwill. It's not a race. Throw out the clocks.'"

They agreed that Connelly should take the idea to team captain Chuck Foote. Connelly would later explain that strategy: "Foote was handpicked by Burke to be team captain. But he sees what's happening. He sees guys are hurting. That we're missing banquets. And all because of the clocks."

In Connelly's mind, if a united front of Connelly, Foote, Reese and Beck could be mounted against Burke, his power might be broken. But right now, Foote was the key.

11:28 A.M.   **Just inside the**
                                                 North Dakota border

While others talked about turning off the clocks, Bob Burke and two officers from the North Dakota Highway Patrol were studying a huge map, looking for alternate routes.

Long before the run began, Burke had decided that if the team got too far ahead of schedule, the men would burn off time by running extra miles. Under the plan, the team would shoot off the designated path to Montreal and run a loop of anywhere from 20 to 50 additional miles, depending on how much time was necessary to burn off. It was an ingenious plan. It would keep the team on schedule. It would keep the clocks running.

11:41 A.M. CURT HALL

Four days earlier, Curt Hall had carried the baton into Montana. Now he completed the 717th mile of the course mapped out across Montana and sprinted over the border into North Dakota.

1:48 P.M., Central Time   BOB HICKEY

Hickey felt the hand of the Lord as he blazed across hilly terrain. "Every time I came to a hill, I got a strong gust of wind. It was as though God was putting His hand behind my back and saying, 'Here you go, lifting me up by giving me a big blow of wind.'"

It had been another hectic day for the men of Van Two. Once again, they had darted back to a reception, gobbled down food, and exchanged hurried pleasantries with their hosts. Now, they were racing toward the hand-off point, more than a hundred miles from Wolf Point.

By coincidence, on its mad journey Van Two pulled into a gas station where Van Four was already refueling. Driver George Beck took a few minutes to chat with Charles Reese. The conversation turned to "The Schedule Problem." Reese quickly apprised Beck of his conversation with coach Pat Connelly. And Beck suggested that the team might solve the problem by simply slowing down. It was only a suggestion, but it would muddy the waters even more.

It was raining as Hickey surged past the halfway point of his sixteenth leg. "They were more like pellets than raindrops. They stung." Hickey would run his leg in 61:41 — his second fastest.

Van Two reached the hand-off point and parked beside Van One. As the runners and drivers traded jibes and stories, Beck made an observation: The team is going too fast. It would have to slow down. Burke said the problem was under control. He'd already figured out an alternate route to burn off some time. Beck signaled his approval with a nod. But for Alex Shearer, slowing down or alternate routes were like fried foods — tough to digest.

2:50 P.M. ALEX SHEARER

"I had some hills, but I just attacked them. I was in a very mean, aggressive mood because I found out that the course is being changed. Burke wants us to run longer. And Chief Beck says we should start running on our hands. My idea of a run is you pick out a point and try to get there as fast as you can. But suddenly we're going on another route, in another direction."

Inside Van Two

Janowicz: "We're about seven hours ahead of schedule. Whaddya think of Burke's idea of running alternate routes to get back on time?"

Clark: "We've got 1,700 miles to go. We shouldn't make any decisions yet about what we're gonna do."

Janowicz: "The thing is, we've got all level land ahead. Most of the guys are gonna run good times."

Clark: "Yeah, but you don't know how long we can all sustain our times. A lot of guys are hurting."

Chuck Foote listened, but he didn't say a word. He apparently wanted no part of the controversy, at least for the time being. It had been Foote's habit throughout his life to let events build before acting. Whether by design or by accident, he would stay above the tumult for now. If he saw the gathering storm, he didn't let on.

Shearer normally would have run his hilly course in 75 to 80 minutes. But he was pounding out his frustrations with sub-seven-minute miles.

"Snow White — AKA Larry Kramer — said he wanted to run with me, and I said, 'Good.' I felt so mean and aggressive, I wanted to punish someone a little. You know, you can't really punish a bad runner. They're unpunishable. They'll just drop out. But a good runner, like Kramer, you can punish, because he has a little pride and wants to stay with you.

"I love Snow White. And, as Oscar Wilde said, you always hurt the one you love."

For the first time in sixteen legs, Alex Shearer broke 70 minutes — 67:03. "You'd be amazed what Al can do when he puts his mind to it," Connelly had said. Shearer had put his mind and his venom into that one.

3:57 P.M.

As Bob Burke headed toward the town of Williston, "Burke's Boys," as Pat Connelly had derisively named them, were having something of a disagreement inside Van One.

Shearer: "It is ridiculous — super-ridiculous — to have to run further. I can remember another run when we had to go to some point in the desert, run down a road for a mile-and-a-half, and then come back, just to burn off time. Incredible."

Hickey: "That was the San Leandro run against Compton, and there was good reason for that, Al. There was a very active Black Panther Party movement in San Francisco at that time. Panthers had just killed two San Francisco policemen. And everyone was afraid if we went into the area, someone might try to sniper-shoot at us. So we only ran to San Leandro, instead of Oakland, as planned. And we had to make up the distance in the desert."

Shearer: "Okay, that's right. But this time we're just burning up miles because we're missing a few banquets along the way, and because they want to reach Montreal on July 4th. Who cares if we get there July 3rd?"

Rockwood: "Well, I can compare that to the Compton-LAPD run. L.A. won it by something like 36 hours. But they came in at two in the morning, and when Compton came in at nine in the morning a day later, the band was there, and there were helicopters, news media, city and police officials — everything. And nobody even knew L.A. was in the race. I was on the Compton P.D. We got all the fanfare even though you guys won. So I think it's kind of important to finish at a certain time."

Shearer: "This is the thing. You psych yourself to do a certain thing, and the next thing you know, instead of being rewarded, instead of them saying, 'Hey, that's great; you guys are way ahead of schedule,' instead of saying that, we're being punished. I realize that maybe Canadian officials are waiting for us, and certain events are scheduled, but I say so what? We're supposed to run as fast as we can, and they can adjust to it."

Bonneau: "I think it's important that we arrive in Montreal reasonably close to our ETA, mainly because of all the plans that have been made there. It wouldn't be fair to ask the guys to slow down, because I think everybody should go out and run the way he feels like running. So I think the only thing we can do is run extra miles . . . "

A frown crossed Shearer's long face.

Bonneau: "I know Al and I disagree about that but . . . "

Shearer: "I am disgusted with you. You're a treacherous little guy. You're selling me out."

Bob Hogue (Burke's closest friend and one of the drivers of Van One): "It sounds like Alex might be trying to organize a sort of rebellion here . . . perhaps an out-and-out rebellion."

Bonneau: "Well, he's that kind of guy. Look at his face. Just look at him. See the goatee. See the pointed ears."

Shearer: "Now, wait a minute. Let's knock that off, Bonneau."

Shearer put on a police commander's hat as he talked.

Bonneau: "Oh, I forgot. Alex has been elevated to a commander."

Rockwood: "He looks a little like Field Marshal Montgomery."

Hickey: "They're about the same age."

Bonneau: "Montgomery died, you know."

Hickey: "Yeah, they look remarkably similar."

Shearer: "Well, anyway, the thing is, it doesn't seem to make any difference what my views are on this extra mileage thing. We're going to run around like a gaggle of geese until we add some more time. And I say every one of the guys who is against me in this camper is a whip. You're a bunch of whips."

Kramer: "Who do you think you could win over to your point of view in this camper?"

Shearer: "Well . . ."

Hickey: "You know, we've got a saying in this camper, Larry, that if you're looking for sympathy, you'll find it in the dictionary somewhere between shit and suicide. Alex gets no sympathy here."

Shearer: "I'm not looking for any sympathy. Just reason. And besides, I never pointed this out to you guys, because you seemed so proud of your little saying, but sympathy comes after both shit and suicide in the dictionary, not between them.

"Anyway, there are only two possibilities to pull over to my side. One of them is Bonneau and the other is Rockwood. Hickey is kind of a Burke man, I would say. And although he may love and respect me, I think he would tend to stay with Burke. But Bonneau—if I could give him some good logical reasons for following me, he would follow. And Rockwood would follow because he's just wishy-washy. [Shearer laughed.] It's the truth."

But Rockwood wasn't laughing. He was furious. The beach buddies were starting to get on one another's nerves.

Then, for the first time during the debate, Shearer got an ally — a most unexpected one.

Hickey: "I'll agree with you, Alex, on one thing. When we went on this run, it was said basically that we would start at such-and-such a time and would arrive in Montreal hypothetically on the Fourth. But when you go without your family for 19 days, you don't give a damn about adding any distance. You just want to get the run over with. To hell with bands or whatever — we've done it. That's it."

Shearer: "Well, I guess I was wrong about Hickey. I thought he would be very loyal to Burke. But he's a man of reason."

The conversation then turned to another point — one which would prove decisive during the next 24 hours: Since it was the runners who had the most to gain or to lose by whatever decision was made, perhaps it was they who should make that decision.

A vote. It had never happened before. All decisions had been made by Bob Burke. The men of Van One were now, in fact, talking rebellion.

Shearer: "There was no vote on this running extra miles. If there was one, it was taken while I was out on my run. I don't see why there shouldn't be a vote. But let's face it. I'm going to do whatever the powers-that-be say to do. I can't just walk out there into the sagebrush or whatever the hell they have out there, and disappear. All I'm saying is that finishing at a designated time is not that big a deal. I've been on many of these runs before, and if you get thirty people to come out and watch you finish, fifteen of them are relatives, five of them are winos who couldn't get up off the ground, and the other ten are officials who were assigned to go out and meet you. That's all there is to it. I want to get to Montreal as quickly as possible and then fly home to spend time with my family and/or loved ones."

5:06 P.M.

After having 10 miles to ponder it, Bob Burke finally settled on an alternate route. It would burn off 39 miles, or about five hours.

So for the first time the team would veer off the main route and run a north-east-south loop. Van Three would begin running the extra miles shortly after midnight.

Inside Van Two

The runners and drivers of Van Two didn't know that Burke had settled on a plan.

Clark: "We could run up to the city limits of Montreal and stop and have a little party, and then run in at the scheduled time later on."

Murphy: "Or we could run extra miles."

Janowicz: "That's what we're probably gonna do."

Inside Van One, Bob Hickey was asked where he stood in overall time. "I'm probably among the top five. But I don't really know. I don't care."

6:18 P.M. DICK BONNEAU

Dick Bonneau scooted through the Dakota wheatfields at a seven-minute-per-mile clip.

When Bonneau had about a mile to go, Chuck Foote walked out of the van to get ready for the hand-off. He was treated to a bizarre sight. The runners of Van One were performing a rain dance, complete with nonsensical chanting. Alex Shearer threw his hands into the air and cried out, "Let Foote be touched by the spirit of rain."

Driver George Moore, from Van Two: "Should I get out my Model-A headlight and put a hex on 'em?"

Clark: "Yeah. Zap 'em."

The chanting continued: "Hiya, hiya, hiya."

Shearer: "Let Foote be drenched by the spirit of rain."

Chorus: "Hiya, hiya, hiya."

Shearer: "Let him be inundated by the spirit of rain."

Rockwood gazed over the wheatfields at Bonneau, who was now about three-quarters of a mile away.

Rockwood: "Wait a second. Hold it. We did it too loud. Our voices carried. It's raining on Bonneau."

Shearer: "We're getting our own runner wet!"

Clark: "Look at him. He's scurrying down the path like a little field mouse."

Foote: "Hurry up, Bonneau, before it starts raining here. I can run ahead of the rain."

7:27 P.M. CHUCK FOOTE

But even the fleet Foote couldn't run ahead of this rain. It was his companion for 62 minutes and 25 seconds, the time it took him to run 10.1 miles.

And for sixteen legs, Foote had also been unable to run ahead of Bob Hickey. (For some reason, most of the runners thought Foote was outpacing Hickey. Murphy, for example, called Foote "invincible." But in truth, Foote and Hickey were waging an epic battle.) The standings: Hickey (after sixteen legs), 65:34; Foote (sixteen), 65:37; Janowicz (fifteen), 68:04; Burke (sixteen), 69:49.

8:29 P.M. JIM MURPHY

Murphy ran past 10 miles of farmlands. "It was really funny. Thirty-five cattle saw me coming, and they kinda congregated and then took off with me. Horses just kinda turn around and look at you like you're crazy. But cows want to get into the act."

10:57 P.M. FRANK JANOWICZ

"Before I ran, I figured out my average. It was 68:04 for all the miles that I've run so far. So I says, 'I'm gonna run 68 or better on this leg.' I concentrated on staying on the balls of my feet, and I lifted my knees high. I ran about a 6:30 pace for my first seven miles."

Inside Van Two, Clark to Foote: "You ran another rocket pace there. You keep puttin' us ahead, and we'll have to run up through Siberia."

Janowicz ran to the outskirts of Stanley, North Dakota. "I talked to myself my whole 10 miles. I kept saying, 'Ball of my foot, ball of my foot, ball of my foot.' And I did it again. Ran the whole 10 up on my toes. I'm running right. I'm running right." Janowicz ran 10.1 miles in 67:04.

Inside Van Two, Clark and Foote continued their conversation.

Clark: "Two days in a row we gotta shoot our fannies back some place for a banquet. Something's gotta give."

Foote: "People were waiting for us. They made a lot of plans. It's really not that big a deal."

The storm was still gathering. Tomorrow it would hit. And tomorrow the team captain would act in a drama that had been years in the making.

They were opposites, these two.

Pat Connelly, a world-class runner and coach, articulate, confident, holder of two college degrees, a policeman-three after six years on the job.

Bob Burke, a poor to mediocre athlete all his life, so shy he failed his first oral examination to join the LAPD, nearly flunked out of the Police Academy because of English, no college background, a policeman-two after more than 20 years on the job.

When they first met, back in 1968, they became fast friends. Burke was one of those who worked hardest to get the near-sighted Connelly onto the LAPD. And so Connelly felt awkward when he pointed out to Burke in 1969 that it was too difficult for the men to run five-mile legs, three times each, on their relay race to San Diego. Connelly felt that the three hours between the men's runs wasn't enough time to recuperate. That was the first time Connelly challenged Burke. It was not the last.

They were opposites in background, opposites in philosophy. Their clash reached its apex during the relay of goodwill.

Burke: "I'm out here because it's something I have to do. I've never been good enough to do something by myself in anything I've tried. I was almost like a lost soul most of my life. I didn't have a spot. But then I created this type of running. I finally found my niche."

Connelly: "Look. I'm 38, and when I was 26 or 28, I set goals for myself. I wanted to run 10,000 meters in 27 minutes. I wanted to run the mile in under 4:08. I wanted to qualify for a national team. I trained hard. Now I can sit back and say I've reached at least some of my goals. And now I'm happy. Now I'm running for recreation, fun, fitness. I still like to compete for the department occasionally. When we ran against other departments, I went all-out. But I just don't feel the need to compete against the other members of the team on this relay. I think that's silly."

Burke: "Competition is part of this. It's healthy. Look, these guys are getting receptions, they're on radio and television, and they're getting their pictures in the paper. We have to earn people's respect. If we're just gonna walk or trot across the country, I don't think we've earned it. You know, a guy sees us, and he says, 'My God, you know how fast that policeman is running?' That's respect. You get it by giving of yourself. I shouldn't even say I expect it of the team. But I expect it of myself. I trained hard to bring my times down this time. And when I get back from this race, I can sit across from my wife at dinner, and I don't even have to mention it to her, but I am at peace with myself."

Connelly: "This just isn't in the same category as my past competition."

Burke: "To me it's like going to Mt. Everest or to the stars."

Connelly: "It's tough and demanding. But it is not a race. And it should not be a test of endurance or mental and physical capabilities."

Burke: "Nobody's ever told me this. If a man came up and told me this, I would say, 'Step off the team. We have room for somebody else — maybe not as good as Pat — but somebody who does want to give his all.'"

Connelly: "Look. A lot of these guys started running just five, 10 years ago. Most were in their 30s when they started. And they still have these goals to meet. Goals that I met as a runner back in the sixties. It's important for them to go out in these relays and run their best average, because they're still satisfying their needs. But my need is past, and it makes a big difference."

Burke: "Some people who are very good on the track can't put up with the mental punishment of this type of run and the 10,000 different physical and psychological things that come up. Hickey, Bonneau, Janowicz and I are running faster than Murphy, a top-notch national champion, and whipping Connelly, also nationally ranked. How do I explain it? Willpower, guts, body power. This type of running is entirely different than any other type of cross-country running. It's a great test."

Connelly: "We're teammates. This shouldn't be an internal test. But more importantly, this is not a true test of a runner. There's different terrain, different conditions. You can't measure performance."

Burke: "It all evens up. Our van took the first mountains, the Angeles Crest. We took the desert during the day. Then someone else took the flat."

Connelly: "This is a run of goodwill. Totally."

Burke: "I never think about bringing a message of goodwill

across the country. I think about my times, when I have to get
out and run. I can't even remember what city I ran through or
what time I ran. I concentrate on not damaging myself like some
of the other guys.

"We're not bringing the goodwill. It's these people who are
bringing the goodwill to us. We're not buying them food.
They're buying it for us. What they deserve is a good performance. And not everyone has put out as hard as he could. I don't
have to mention any names. It's obvious."

Connelly: "These people have gone out of their way for us. If
we took the clocks off, we'd pass through these towns on
schedule. And without the clocks, we'd reduce injuries."

Burke: "These guys knew they were gonna be timed. Before
the relay even Connelly said, 'I'm in great shape this time. I
don't want to have the worst times.' Everyone knew the clocks
were on. They've been on every time.

"Injuries? They're part of this type of racing. Guys run on
bloody feet. Have heat exhaustion. But these guys are a rare
breed."

Connelly: "This thing should not be made more difficult than
it is."

Burke: "There are people here who do not put out or suffer as
much as the others. But they cannot leave this thing alone. They
have to be part of this group. They're here because they do not
want to be left out."

Connelly: "Why do I go along? All I can say is I just can't sit
home and watch the other guys go, I guess. It's an ego thing. It's
like the grounded pilot on the aircraft carrier, when the doctor
says he can't fly the mission today. And he sits there and
watches the planes take off, and they're going without him.

"What makes us do it? The attention. The attention along the
way, on the department, at home."

Burke: "Nobody should gripe. They have no orders except to
run, period. They don't have to worry about money, logistics,
equipment or schedules. They've never had to worry about
anything except running."

Connelly: "Bob Burke won't let anyone help him, because
then people would get involved in some of the decisions, and he
doesn't want that. He tells you what camper you're in, who
holds the money, how much you get for meals, who's gonna be
team captain. He makes all the rules."

Burke: "My feeling about life, I guess, is a lot like I feel about
these runs. We argue — actually argue among ourselves about

why we're doing this. Every guy has a different reason. You know, God, country, the department.

"But my feeling is if you don't do it for number one first, you're not giving the straight scoop. I think every guy here has an ego. But he's not an egotist. He has to want to do it for himself. Then all the other reasons. And I don't think there's anything wrong with that."

Connelly: "I'm representing my department and my country on this run."

Burke: "These guys have their own reasons for doing this. But I'll tell you this: They'll look back, and they can always say, 'We did it. We did something that no one else has ever done and very few people could do.' And nobody will ever be able to take this away from them. Even if our accomplishment gets beaten a million times, we're still the first to do it, and that's a rare thing these days. Not many people walking the face of the earth can say that."

Connelly: "With Burke, running is ego. Strictly ego. He will do anything to be out of the ordinary. It's out of the ordinary to be able to say to people, 'I ran 15 miles today.' And that's why this relay is so important to him. It's out of the ordinary."

Burke: "I know it sounds corny, but I want to leave something behind. Some accomplishment, some record.

"It makes me feel bad to think I may be totally wrong. That I haven't discussed completely what this thing is about.

"Maybe they're so caught up in just being part of the team that these guys haven't sat down and figured out what they want from this. Maybe I'm wrong in making it so strenuous. Maybe I'm wrong . . ."

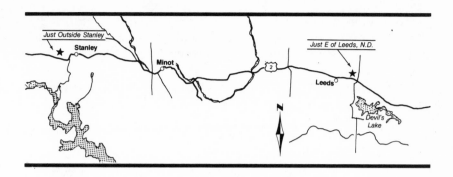

THE THIRTEENTH DAY
Saturday, June 26, 1976

12:10 A.M. BOB JARVIS

"Good riddance to the bastard," Bob Jarvis said, his cockiness returning. The "bastard" was the blister that had been tormenting him for days. Suddenly it was gone. "Kiser's magic worked," said the ebullient Jarvis.

Jarvis ran through Stanley, North Dakota, a town of less than a thousand. Despite the hour, at least fifty people shook his hand, slapped him on the back and yelled encouragement as he trotted through the two-block "downtown" area. Across the middle of the street, the residents had strung a huge banner: "Good Luck Runners."

1:20 A.M. CONNELLY-MULLENS-GARCIA-HALL

Two miles into his leg, Pat Connelly turned south. The man who wanted to burn off time by "throwing out the clocks" thus became the first to burn off miles by running the alternate route mapped out by Bob Burke. The 80-mile detour would be one of the toughest stretches of the entire relay — brutal hills, high winds, near-freezing temperatures.

"That was a bad run for me," Connelly said afterward, "because I wasn't getting closer to the finish and home."

For the second leg in a row, Frank Mullens barely broke 80 minutes. And he struggled over the tough detour to do that. But pride wouldn't let him slow into the 80s.

245

Eddie Garcia — his right knee aching — took the baton at 3:51 A.M.. He didn't like the hour or the alternate route. "I wasn't running toward our objective," he complained. "That added to the mental upset."

And it was just six degrees above freezing during Curt Hall's run, but there was one consolation — a breathtaking sunrise.

Showers, breakfast and a reception had been set up for Van Three in Stanley, the town Bob Jarvis had run through five hours earlier. Van Three couldn't attend, so once again, it was left to Van Two to carry out the mission of goodwill.

6:24 A.M.
Van One

Hickey, Shearer and Burke completed the alternate route.

Shearer: "I was still mad because of those extra miles they added on, so I attacked the hills. Ran with hostility. I ran the course in about 72 minutes. Normally I would have done it in about 80."

8:45 A.M.   Stanley, North Dakota

In Stanley, a Dixieland band entertained as the runners and drivers of Van Two sat down to a pancake and sausage breakfast hosted by city officials, the junior chamber of commerce, and the police and sheriff's departments.

Van One, which was carrying the baton, was some 70 miles ahead. Chuck Foote kept glancing at his watch. He was scheduled to run in less than two-and-a-half hours. He ate sparingly.

The hosts questioned their guests about the run, their jobs, themselves. This is what this relay is all about, Foote thought, trying to convince himself. But it was no use. There was no goodwill churning inside his stomach. He wanted to get the hell out of there.

9:47 A.M. JOHN ROCKWOOD

John Rockwood was back on the main route. The terrain was flat. Rockwood was running one of his best times.

Back in Stanley, first the mayor, then the chief of police, then the Jaycees and finally the sheriff's department, made presentations to the runners. Then, as tactfully as possible, the men of Van Two bid a hurried goodbye. They were 80 miles from the hand-off point. They had 90 minutes to get there. Dick Clark put an arm around Foote's shoulders.

Clark: "Don't worry. The worst thing that can happen is that we'll run out of gas, or get stopped for speeding, or blow a tire."

Foote: "If we do, Bonneau might take it to Montreal by himself."

Rockwood couldn't have asked for better conditions. "Great, just great," he said. "I did it in 67:12. One of my best."

On the road to Minot, North Dakota

Foote, inside Van Two: "Rockwood ran it in 67 minutes. Christ, this is gonna be close."

10:54 A.M. DICK BONNEAU

The terrain was ideal, and Bonneau laid down a sub-seven-minute-per-mile pace as he carried the baton toward Minot, North Dakota. When he entered the outskirts of that city, four miles into his leg, Van Two was 25 miles behind him. Adding to the tension, the route inside Minot had been changed, and now there was confusion over the location of the hand-off point. By the time it was cleared up, Bonneau was into his final two miles. Van Two shot up to the hand-off spot and parked. Bonneau was less than a mile and a half away.

12:01 P.M. CHUCK FOOTE

The usually unflappable Foote was mad as hell.

"First, we have to hustle our asses up here from Stanley. Then we have to figure out where the hand-off spot it. Once we get there, I gotta just jump out of the van and start running without a warmup. And then I get no music for the first five miles because the follow car has to get gas, and I get paced by Van Two. I have to listen to myself think for five miles. Man, it's dead out there without my music. I just ran as fast as I could."

Indeed he did: 60:14, which propelled him into the lead in overall average on the relay for the first time. After seventeen legs, Foote was averaging 65:18 per run; Hickey, 65:27. But at this point, it was small consolation to Foote. He was angry. The storm he seemed to be waiting for had broken — on him.

1:01 P.M. JIM MURPHY

"The blisters on my right foot started bothering me at five miles. By seven, the foot was supersensitive, and I kept hitting gravel.

It was all over the road. Every time I hit some, it was like an electric shock went through my system."

It took Murphy 70 minutes to complete his leg. And it took Kiser 60 minutes to treat Murphy's blisters. This time, though, the Mercurochrome solution was junked in favor of the pain killer Xylocaine. Ten minutes later, Jim Murphy was feeling great.

2:11 P.M. DICK CLARK

"Miserable run. I've never felt so bad. It was hot, and I was sweating like a horse. I had salt all over my body. I felt terrible."

As Clark crossed the Dakota badlands, Van Three pulled up beside Vans Two and Four, which were parked under a clump of trees, about two-tenths of a mile down the road from the next hand-off point. Chuck Foote, still upset from his morning ordeal, had just talked to Chief Charles Reese about the schedule problem. They agreed: The detour hadn't worked. Going into it, the team was seven hours ahead. Coming out of it, the team was still two and a half hours ahead. But now, one van later, the team was nearly three and a half hours ahead again.

Foote, the team captain, and Reese, the second-highest-ranking officer on the run, felt the only thing that made sense was to slow down. Otherwise the team might end up running 500 extra miles.

Reese did not bring up the possibility of throwing out the clocks, however; he was going to leave that task to Pat Connelly. But the idea was already on Foote's mind as he was met by Connelly outside Van Four.

Connelly: "He told me he had just talked to Chief Reese, and he said, 'Hey, we got to slow this thing down.' I said, 'Yeah.' He said, 'The only sensible thing is to throw out the clocks. Everyone will slow down automatically if they're not timed.'

"But we both knew it wasn't that easy. We still had to deal with Burke. We decided to talk to Reese."

Clark was now in the final four miles of his run. "A young lady drove up alongside me, got out of her car and ran with me for a block. She was wearing cowboy boots. She took some pictures of me. I gave her a little squeeze as I left her."

Outside Van Four, Connelly, Foote and Reese were holding a strategy session.

Connelly: "We went over the objective of the run once more,

and we agreed it was to meet people and carry a message of goodwill across the country. And so we said, 'Let's screw the timing. That's what's causing all the problems. The runners are competing against one another, and we're missing the whole point of the relay.'

"Foote asked me then, 'Hey, will your camper go for it?' And I said, 'I think so.'

"Then Reese said, 'Look, we have to tell Burke, and that's gonna be the most difficult part, because Burke definitely is going to be against it.' I suggested that Foote and I go to Burke, but Reese said no. Reese said Beck should be the one. He said Burke looks upon Beck as a kind of father figure of the team. Reese said he'd talk to Beck."

Clark felt as though he were trying to finish a marathon instead of a 10-mile run. "My legs felt like lead. My feet and knees ached. I'll tell you, a lesser man would have been crawling those last three miles. Geez, I didn't even get the music I asked for. I got some cowboy wailing the blues. That hampered my style even more."

Janowicz, inside Van Two: "There's rumors that we'll have to slow down. They're making us run more miles. Hey, we're athletes. We're competitors. You can't tell us to slow down. If we get to Montreal early, that's just tough luck. This is a race. I'm racing the clock. I'm racing everybody on this fucking team. I'm gonna run as fast as I can."

Clark was now two miles from the finish. "I just kept telling myself, 'One foot in front of the other, one foot in front of the other. Keep going, keep moving.' But it really hurt. Then, every so often, a slight breeze would come by, or a cloud would cover the sun, and that would cool me a little and keep me going. The good Lord was up there helping me out."

According to Connelly, the five runners in Van Three would line up against the clocks — and against Burke — if the issue came to a showdown. But only Shearer could be counted on in Van One, and only Foote himself in Van Two. Seven men. Only half the team.

Even an 8 to 6 margin against Burke wasn't enough. When you fire at a king, don't miss. A 9 to 5 margin would be lethal. Chuck Foote knew where the pivotal votes were. In his own van. He went to work:

"Look. We got a problem. We're going too fast, and we gotta slow down. The guys in Van Three agree. We're missing too many events. We're rushing all over the place. I think the best thing is to throw out the clocks, because if they're on, it's only natural to compete against them."

Janowicz: "Just because the clock goes off, I'm not gonna slow down."

Foote: "You'd be surprised what you'd do, Frank, if there's no watches. The clocks push you. Without the clocks, you'll slow down instinctively because there'll be no pressure to run a certain time. You'll only know that you're running comfortable, and time will become meaningless. Look, my idea is to turn off the watches for about 300 miles and see what happens."

George Moore: "But, like Murphy — he wears his own watch, and he's not gonna stop looking at it."

Foote: "But if he knows that no one else is recording times, George, then he won't be so concerned with his own pride, like he is now. He won't kill himself to run 80s and 75s. He won't come in with his heart pounding and blisters throbbing — pushing himself because he knows he's a better runner than that.

"We really have three alternatives: Run slower with the clocks, turn off the clocks, or run more miles."

Murphy: "Or go home."

Janowicz: "Okay. Look. I trained nine months to be one of the fastest guys. I can't see slowing down. I can't see turning off the watches. I want to know my times.

"If we get to Montreal early, one guy can bring the baton across the finish line, and then maybe the next day we can all run across the finish line together."

Foote: "It's not just that, Frank. The problem is this: Along the way, people have been setting up receptions and dinners for us. We're four, five, six hours early. They can't switch all their plans around in four hours.

"This is not really a race, Frank. It's a run of goodwill. And if we're gonna spread any kind of goodwill, we're gonna have to talk to these people, not rush in and rush out. They went a long ways out of their way to do something for us — total strangers. The least we can do is get there within a reasonable time of when we should be there."

There was silence. Janowicz pondered Foote's words. Finally he spoke — slowly, deliberately:

"I spent nine months of hard-ass training for this. I was up at five o'clock every morning, five days a week, running 10 miles. Hard-ass fucking training.

"But what you're saying is true, Chuck. We're supposed to be spreading goodwill. The only alternative is to turn off the clocks."

Frank Janowicz — the most unlikely of converts — had been converted. The margin was 8 to 6.

3:26 P.M. FRANK JANOWICZ

It was hot and humid, and Janowicz was fatigued from the start, but he realized this might be his last leg with the watches on, so he ran hard. His head bobbed, his shoulders rolled, and his feet pounded across the Dakota badlands.

Inside Van Two, Foote went to work on the still-uncommitted Murphy and on Clark. He was unable to sway Clark, who felt the team would not automatically slow down simply because the clocks were turned off. And Clark injected yet another point into the debate: He wanted the team to run extra miles to break the distance record set in the Washington, D.C., to Los Angeles relay — a relay Clark had missed.

Murphy agreed with Clark — but with reservations:

"I think we should go for a new record — say, 4,000 miles. That would be just one extra leg per man. But if we start running extra miles all over the place, I might not fucking make it."

Clark: "Well, I think we should go for the record."

Foote: "I agree, but by the same token, I think we should turn off the clocks. We have to get on schedule, and guys are hurting. By taking off the clocks, people won't push themselves as hard. They can slow down with grace. No one will know how slow anyone is running."

Murphy: "I agree. I think knocking off the timing would probably be the best thing."

And with that, the margin was 9 to 5. The king was vulnerable.

Janowicz was about three miles into his leg as Van Two crept alongside him on its way to the next hand-off point.

Clark: "Heeeeeey, Frankie, baby! Go get 'em!"

Janowicz waved the baton.

Murphy: "The guy's hurting, and he's going out and killing himself. He's just started, and you can already see it on his face. He's in sheer agony, because he wants to run a fast time to keep in the top five, to keep in contention. It's stupid. What are we doing? We're killing ourselves. We're not enjoying the trip."

Foote: "You're right."

Murphy: "Chuck, I think what we should do is go to the nearest airport, fly back to Los Angeles, contact Vogue campers, see if we can get the new mobile homes, and start the whole thing over again."

Foote: "Yeah, right."

Clark: "I think we should spend four hours in a brothel."

Murphy: "Hey, we've been trying our best and haven't been too successful."

Clark: "And that way we'd be so ruined, we wouldn't be able to pick up time. We'd be losing time. We'd get to Montreal in August."

A freak event was occurring at the hand-off point. Van Three, which would receive the baton from Janowicz, was parked there. But so were Vans One and Four. And with Van Two on its way, it appeared that for the first time since the relay began, all of the team members, with the exception of the man carrying the baton, would be together for something other than a reception. It was ideal — ideal for a confrontation.

Van Two pulled beside the other vans and parked. Moments later, Assistant Chief George Beck emerged, grim-faced. His mission — discuss the time problem with Bob Burke. As he walked slowly toward Van One, he spotted Burke and waved. Burke smiled. He had no idea what the chief had on his mind.

The two men shook hands and walked to a nearby tree, where they could get shade and privacy. Beck said he was carrying a message from Reese, Foote and Connelly on behalf of the team: The clocks should be turned off, he said. There were injuries. There were missed receptions. The detour hadn't worked. He didn't want to bring this message, but he had been asked by Reese. It was difficult for him. Burke said he understood Beck's position. Appreciated it. But, he said quietly, the clocks would stay on. The assistant chief flinched, then turned and walked away from Policeman-Two Bob Burke.

Moments later, Burke spotted Connelly.

Connelly: "He called me over and just laid into me. He said, 'Hey, why are you going over my head to Chief Beck and telling him to come to me?' I told him I didn't do that. I told him, 'I wanted Chuck and me to see you, but Reese said Beck should do it because he's closer to you.'

"Then Burke said it isn't right for any of us to ask the guys to slow down or take the clocks off. And I argued, 'Well, then why did Lou McClary and Rich Wemmer and Julia Nagano go to all that work planning these activities at certain times if we're gonna miss 'em all? And if it was going to be a race, why didn't you inform all the guys who were running?"

"He said watches have been on in every relay and if there was gonna be a change, it should have been made in Los Angeles. We argued back and forth, and finally I said, 'Look, everyone's here. Let's explain both sides and put it to a vote.' Well, Burke couldn't say no to that." Connelly quickly told the other runners there would be a vote.

The Rebels were taking dead aim at the King.

Janowicz rumbled on, his legs "dead," his breathing labored, his body exhausted. "But I was still battling the clock. I told the drivers I would be highly pissed off if I wasn't timed. They assured me I would be. I wanted to break 70 minutes."

3:40 P.M.
Van Two

Inside Van Two, the conversation turned to injuries.

Murphy: "I'm hurting, but I'll make it. I'll make it if I have to crawl. But that's the thing: Why should I have to crawl? Look, you guys all know my primary goal at the start was to be number one. But I think now most of us agree, our primary goal is to finish in one healthy piece. Nothing else makes sense."

Clark: "Okay, but anybody who's really hurt has really done it to himself . . . like Janowicz . . ."

Murphy: "Hey, that's why policemen have sergeants. It's a fact of life. We need supervision. And that's why sergeants have lieutenants, because sergeants are constantly disappearing and not supervising the men."

Sgt. Clark ignored the remark.

Murphy: "I think a good piece of ass would take care of everything for everybody."

3:45 P.M.
Van Two

Connelly: "Hi, fellows. We're gonna vote on the three alternatives."

Foote: "Summit meeting, guys. Let's go."

The runners gathered in a circle under the burning North Dakota sun. Only Janowicz, who was running, was not there.

The drivers and support people — even the assistant chiefs of police — stood aside. This was a private matter.

Chuck Foote opened the meeting:

"Look. Obviously we have a problem 'cause we're running so damned fast. As I look at it, there's three things we can do: We can run more miles, we can turn off the clocks and run without times, or we can deliberately slow down with the clocks still on. No matter what we do, I think we should get to Montreal reasonably close to when we said we'd get there."

Foote knew he had nine sure votes against the clocks. He decided to back off for a moment and try to pick up a tenth. He threw a bone to the wavering Clark.

Foote: "Now, I don't think it makes any sense to go 3,845 miles and run short of the record. I think we should also go for a new distance record. So what are we talking about?"

Burke: "Well, right now, we're going about 3,810."

Foote: "So we're talking about 60, 70, 80 more miles. That's not too big a problem."

Garcia (very annoyed): "Well, that takes care of our problem."

Foote: "Hey, wait a second. Wait a second, Ed."

Garcia: "I think I'll just sit in the camper and shit while you have your meeting."

Foote has miscalculated. He thought the distance record could be used to persuade Clark. Instead, it had angered Garcia, who didn't relish the thought of running extra miles on his damaged knee.

Foote switched back to the main issue: "Wait, wait. Let's talk about this thing. Too many of us are hurting. But we're not competing against another team now. We're doing it against one another. With fourteen of us, it's obvious that somebody's gonna be last and somebody's gonna be first. I think we're all grown-up enough to say, 'Hey, who gives a damn?'

"Now we can either purposely go out and run slow and take our time. Or we can take off the watches — throw 'em out. I say let's try just one go-round, two go-rounds without the clocks. Let's see if it puts us on schedule. If it doesn't, we'll have to come up with something else, okay? I also think we should run the extra miles for the record. That's all I've got to say."

Clark: "I'd like to go for the record."

Shearer: "Why?"

Clark: "We're pretty damned close to it. Why not?"

Shearer: "But why?"

Clark: "Why not?"

Shearer: "Why first?"

Connelly: "Yeah, why do we wanna go for the record? Who wants to go for the record?"

Clark: "I'd like to go for the record. Probably Eddie would, and Murphy — since we weren't part of the world-record team."

Foote: "And I don't know whether we'll ever try this again."

Connelly: "Wait a minute. Did this start out as a race to break our old record? Or did it start out as a Bicentennial Relay of Goodwill? We're supposed to go out and meet people on the streets, representing our department, our city, the Bicentennial, our nation. It doesn't say on that sign up there, 'A Relay Record Race to Montreal.'

"We're defeating our purpose by running ourselves into the ground. This is supposed to be enjoyable, so we can go out and meet these people."

(At this point, Hickey quietly turned and left the circle to return to his camper.)

Connelly: "You're supposed to have smiles on your faces and enjoy it. But you're fighting for your times, you're fighting for your sleep, you're fighting for your meals, you're fighting to make receptions."

Foote: "I agree."

Connelly: "There's guys under a lot of stress on this team 'cause they've gotta prove something to themselves, to prove that they're better than their peers. It's not working. We're carrying a message of goodwill. That's the objective of this relay. I'm for stopping the timing for that reason."

Bonneau: "We're meeting our obligations of the relay the way we're running right now, Pat."

Connelly: "No, we're not."

Foote: "The last three days, our van has had to shoot back to fill commitments and pick up the pieces for everyone. The whole thing's getting out of hand."

Bonneau: "By adding mileage, we can still make our commitments and still go over the record."

Foote: "But if we keep adding mileage in order to keep our commitments, we might end up running 300 or 400 extra miles. Guys are tired and hurt already. I say let's break the distance record by a couple of miles and throw out the clocks."

Murphy: "We're injuring ourselves because we keep running every leg as fast as we can. You can't do that for three weeks."

Foote: "If you slow down, you've also got more time to rest in between legs."

Beck walked over to join the group: "What are the plans? Let's vote."

Clark: "It doesn't have to be any one thing in particular. It can be people kinda backing off and relaxing a little bit more, and maybe also adding a little bit of distance."

Connelly: "I also think the clocks can stay on for certain guys, like Burke. He wants to run 'em all under 70. That's his goal. And I say, go ahead and keep your times."

Bonneau: "There's only about three or four guys that I can see that are fast enough to be in competition with each other anyway. Let them time themselves if they want to."

Connelly: "You know how two weeks after the relay that list comes out from the athletic club and it says who had the best average — one through 14. All of us have an ego. All of us are competitors. And I don't wanna see my name down there in eleventh place."

Foote: "That's right. We're a team. We're not supposed to be in competition with each other."

Connelly: "No one's gonna beat Chuck Foote's time. And he's the one who says throw out the timing."

Foote: "Why do I wanna be in competition with you guys? You know, you're my friends. I don't care if I'm number one or number 10. It doesn't make any difference to me. Now, if we were competing against another police department, I'd run my nuts off. Every time."

Jarvis: "Alex, Burke and myself have been on every one of these runs. And for just about all of us, this is probably the last one. And I wanna remember it as a good relay. I've enjoyed every one. I don't wanna have to say on the last one, 'Jesus Christ, I couldn't make it, I couldn't finish.' Let's enjoy the damned thing and not compete with one another."

Hall: "Damned right!"

Clark: "Where's Hickey?"

Shearer: "Probably sleeping."

Hall: "What's Janowicz think?"

Foote: "I asked him before he went out. Frank says he's worked his ass off for nine months. And he said, 'Chuck, when I came into this thing, I wanted to be among the top five guys.' He says timing is very important to him. But he said he'll go along with throwing out the clocks for the sake of the team. But if Frank wants to be timed, we'll time him. And at the end, he'll be able to say, 'I averaged 66 or 67 or whatever.'"

Connelly: "Okay. I move we throw out the timing."

Hall: "I second that."

Foote: "Okay, let's vote. Raise your hands. Those in favor?"

Nine hands shot up. Burke, Bonneau and Rockwood remained motionless. There was no need for their vote. The matter was decided. The Rebels had taken aim. The King was dead.

Foote: "Okay. Let's notify the follow car. No more timing."

For several moments, there was total silence. After thirteen years, Burke's absolute rule had been broken. He stood to the side — calm, expressionless. His overthrow had taken place without a word of opposition from him. A tension hung over the circle of twelve runners. The King had fallen, but there was no jubilation. Probably because if nothing else, Burke had been a benevolent ruler.

Finally Clark broke the tension: "Somebody tell Janowicz to slow down. He hasn't heard, and he's killing himself."

Everyone laughed. Even Bob Burke.

Moments later, the runners took a second vote: They decided to run extra miles in order to set a new world's record. So it was official: The clocks were off, but the run for the record was on.

Janowicz finished his seventeenth leg in 69:01 and Van Three, where the revolt against the clocks had originated, took the baton.

4:35 P.M. - 11:10 P.M.
Van Three

The five runners of Van Three ran slow and relaxed. Instead of holding the baton for the customary six hours, they held it for just over six and a half. Each man expressed relief that the clocks, and the pressure, were off.

As Van Three carried the baton, Bob Burke sat outside Van One and discussed the rebuke he'd just been handed. Why hadn't he spoken up at the meeting?

"As I was listening to the guys around me, I decided that if I gave my feelings, it would split the team right there. I listened to the tone of their voices, to what they were saying. They were hostile. So I decided to back off.

"We're out here to promote friendship and goodwill between ourselves and the people we're meeting along the way. We wouldn't even have it among ourselves if I spoke up. So I said nothing and let the vote go the way it did and let everybody feel good."

Did he feel betrayed?

"No. I feel saddened. Stopping the timing takes something away. You could almost say my feelings were hurt, which is a little boy speaking. But I've got to take it and let it roll off my back, or we could have a disaster."

Shortly before midnight, Curt Hall ran through Leeds, a small farm community in the northeast corner of North Dakota. "It was like the Fourth of July," Hall said. "They shot off fireworks and roman candles. About a hundred people were out there — a lot of schoolchildren and older people. Everyone was hollering and shouting and cheering. It really made me feel good, feel proud to be part of the team. That's what this run is all about."

Then Hall sheepishly made a confession:

"By the way, off the record, it was my fastest run so far. I know the clocks are off, but I timed myself. I ran it in about 65 minutes."

That, too, apparently was still what this run was all about.

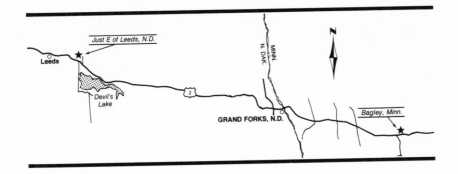

THE FOURTEENTH DAY
Sunday, June 27, 1976

11:10 P.M. BOB HICKEY

Bob Hickey had left the "summit meeting" in disgust before it was half over. Later, he ordered the follow car to time him. It did. And Hickey blazed over "the flattest course I've run since the relay started" in 64:01.

12:14 A.M. ALEX SHEARER

Shearer never wanted to be timed anyway, so there was no question when he took the baton: The clock was off. About a mile into his leg, his lower esophagus, which hadn't troubled him in days, began to hurt. "It felt like that ball was back in there expanding," he said. "It would come on about every 400 yards, then go away for about 200." Shearer thought he could shake it, but the pain kept returning. By the three-mile mark, he was in agony.

Back in Van One, Bob Hickey sat on his bunk, scribbling a letter to his wife. He was too upset to sleep. He hadn't even showered. Hickey had said nothing at the team meeting. But now, eight hours later, he put his pen aside for a moment, and his bitterness poured forth.

"I walked away from that meeting because I was too uptight. I didn't think the meeting or the vote was justified. The big squawk was that we're getting to these towns faster than we

259

should. Well, it was set up originally that if we got far ahead of schedule, we'd take deviation routes to burn off time. We also knew that on every previous run there had been a sense of competitiveness, and that some guys were going to push a little bit harder than the others. They [the Rebels] complained there were injuries. Of course, there were injuries. There's always been injuries. That's part of this type of run."

Out on the highway, Shearer was cold and sick. The pains were coming more quickly and lasting longer. He tried to alter his breathing, taking two quick breaths and pushing the air out hard and slowly. But the tightness remained. Shearer, who liked to downplay his miseries, was now telling the follow car that he had a "very serious problem."

In Van One, Hickey directed his wrath at Pat Connelly: "On all these runs, I've always made Connelly my competition. He was one of my teachers, so it was a teacher-student thing. I've never been on his level as far as AAU competition was concerned — on the track. But I felt that out here on the highways I could compete with him. And you know, in six years I've never lost to him out here. But now he's turned off the clocks, and it just takes everything out of it. I don't know what kind of average he had, but I know he wasn't one of the top runners.

"You know, every relay for six years it's been suggested that we shouldn't clock the guys. And it's funny because the best runner on the team, Pat Connelly, always makes the suggestion. And yet he's the one who puts out the least.

"I don't know. This type of run — it was just the thrill of knowing that out here on the highway I had a chance of competing against really great runners in my park and not in theirs, and possibly beating them."

Shearer was now halfway through his leg. He tried massaging his chest and coughing hard to get rid of the pain in his esophagus. But the pain worsened.

Hickey continued: "I'm like the defending champion on these runs. I've had the best overall average per leg each time except when I was injured in 1972. This time when they stopped the watch, I was in second place behind Chuck Foote. I'd averaged 65:27 for every leg since the start." (All the other runners still thought Foote held a wide and invincible margin over Hickey at this point. But Hickey was acutely aware that only five seconds per leg separated him from Foote after eighteen legs by Hickey and seventeen by Foote.) "I didn't have the fastest average, but I was going for it," he said. "That was my goal." (Once again, Hickey had flip-flopped on his goal for the run.)

Shearer had two miles to go. The pain was excruciating. When it hit, every 20 to 25 seconds, he doubled over, gripping his chest. But he never contemplated stopping. "I've never stopped before," he said simply. "I really saw no reason to do it now."

Inside Van One, Hickey finally answered the inevitable question: Why was he talking now instead of at the meeting yesterday?

"I'll tell you. I've been a supervisor for nearly seven years. And I know when policemen get together, and they've got something they want to do, they're going to do it. Sometimes you don't like it, but there's nothing you can do about it. That's why I walked away."

Shearer ended his run and handed the baton to Bob Burke. He didn't bother cooling down. Instead, he climbed quickly into the van and called Van Four.

Shearer: "I need something for my chest. It's tightening up again."

Van Four: "Roger. We'll tell the doctor. You'll get your medicine C.O.D."

Moments later the medicine arrived.

Shearer: "It was Dilatin, Mylantin, Maalox, or something like that. I don't know. It was liquid in a little green bottle. I shook it and drank it. I didn't care what it was. I was hurting."

Shearer was also bewildered. He hadn't eaten any fried foods in a week.

1:36 A.M. BOB BURKE

A few hours earlier, Van One had received two words of advice from a member of the North Dakota Highway Patrol: Stay alert. The officer explained that a lot of folks in these parts liked to go into Leeds on Saturday night and tie one on. The danger came when the drunks headed home.

Back in Van One, Uncle Alex summoned the strength to read his nephews one quick story. It concerned brotherly love — a brother's love for his sister.

Shearer: "Disgusting story. Just disgusting."

Rockwood: "Just 'cause you weren't close to your sister . . ."

The two drunk drivers were drag racing. They were traveling at least 80 miles an hour. Both apparently were oblivious to the swirling blue lights ahead.

J.P. Nelson and Larry Kramer, who were in the pacer behind Burke, spotted the cars simultaneously. They thought they were going to be killed. Nelson, the passenger, grabbed the mike and hollered to Burke to jump off the road. But before Burke could react, the two cars swerved around the pacer and nearly hit him.

Burke: "They missed me by inches. Then just kept going. Never saw 'em again."

Burke finished the leg without further incident in just 68 minutes. The clocks would remain on for Bob Burke.

2:44 A.M. JOHN ROCKWOOD

John Rockwood decided to test the Foote timing theory, which held that if a runner were not timed, he would automatically slow down, because he would have nothing to push him.

"I looked at my watch at the start and finish," Rockwood said. "I wanted to see how fast I could run — how much I could push myself — without pressure from the clocks. I thought I could run in the low 70s. A nice relaxing 73 would have been great. I thought I was doing it. But I ran 79:01. I was depressed. I felt I kind of let myself down, because I didn't push myself like I should have.

"I found I can't just go out there and go for the fun of it and push myself into the 60s or low 70s. I need a motivator. I need the clocks. They keep me going."

Rockwood would be timed the rest of the way.

4:03 A.M. DICK BONNEAU

"I had a long stretch of flat highway that seemed endless. A lot of guys like the flat, straight shot, but I don't. It really bothers me psychologically. It seems like you're running 20 miles instead of 10. I would rather have some hills and curves and things like that."

Bonneau ran with the clocks on. His time was 71 minutes.

Hickey, Burke, Rockwood and Bonneau would be the only runners to be timed officially the rest of the way. However, a number of runners would time themselves secretly. And one of the "closet timers" would turn out to be a most unlikely one.

5:14 A.M. CHUCK FOOTE

"I ran very, very slow — probably about a hundred minutes. Even the mosquitos were passing me."

6:21 A.M. JIM MURPHY

"It was a beautiful, leisurely, sunny morning run. No problems. The new system of no clocks made it real nice. I think I'll finally be able to recover and feel like a human being again."

In Van Two, the conversation was about the future.

Foote: "I don't think we're ever gonna do this again."

Janowicz: "Nope."

Clark: "I don't know what you could do to top this."

Foote: "I know Bob would never coordinate another one. In fact, a long time ago, he said, 'This is it.'"

Beck: "And nobody else would go through the work he's gone through."

Foote: "So this is it. We really ought to try to savor every day of it. We've only got a week left."

7:51 A.M. DICK CLARK

"Chief Beck ran along with me the first two or three miles. Gave me a little career counseling session. Lot of white clouds in the blue sky. Beautiful. Serene.

"Ran past a lot of black snakes and ground squirrels. I also stampeded a herd of cattle along the road.

"I didn't feel any pressure at all. Just jogged along. I didn't know what my time was, and I didn't care. The new system is working. It's a good deal."

9:17 A.M. FRANK JANOWICZ

Frank Janowicz normally approached his 10-mile legs like a warrior going to battle. And after seventeen battles, he had enough wounds to qualify for a Purple Heart. But now, even Janowicz was caught up in the new spirit. "I just ran along real relaxed. For the first time, I enjoyed looking at the scenery."

Back in Van Two, the "new" Janowicz did not go unnoticed by his teammates. As the van passed him on its way to the next hand-off point, Janowicz waved and smiled.

Clark: "Look at him. He's going bananas."

Murphy: "He's actually enjoying himself."

Clark: "There's nothing bad about feeling good, is there?"

Murphy: "No. But I guess for some guys there might be."

Janowicz was philosophical about his transformation: "I proved I can average sub-70-minute legs out here. So I feel I've accomplished what I set out to do. I don't have to punish myself anymore."

Vans Two and Three were parked at the next hand-off point, waiting for Janowicz. The runners and drivers had gathered in small groups outside the vans, chatting and joking.

Frank Mullens talked about those "damned clocks":

"I was pushing myself, tearing myself down. I was getting pretty damned tired. But I had set personal time goals. And at the meeting I said to myself, 'Wait a minute. Do I want to turn the clocks off or not? How will I know that I accomplished the thing I wanted to accomplish?' But I realized the most important thing is to spread goodwill.

"And I also realized I've accomplished what I want to accomplish. I can judge my running from my first sixteen legs. And I know my times wouldn't get worse, because the worst is over. So I'm satisfied. I think most guys are."

Down the road, two cars approached — a gold Chevrolet Monte Carlo and a late-model station wagon. The station wagon pulled beside the vans and stopped. A man with a microphone and a young woman with a television camera got out. Moments later, the Monte Carlo parked. The man inside jumped out and waved at the runners.

Visitor: "Are you the policemen from Los Angeles?"

Murphy: "Yes."

Visitor: "Well, I'm Art Linkletter."

The runners laughed.

Murphy: "Yeah. We know."

Linkletter was in the area for a three-day Bicentennial celebration at nearby Devil's Lake. When he heard about the run, he said, "I had to offer my best wishes."

The news team accompanying him—Chuck Bondlie, the news director of Channel 8 in Grand Forks, and his camerawoman, Julie Haalandi—was going to cover his appearance in Devil's Lake. Now they decided to do a quick feature story on the run, too. Bondlie held a mike, and Haalandi began shooting film, as Linkletter talked with Bob Jarvis.

Linkletter: "Are you on any kind of natural foods?"

Jarvis: "No. Just eating what we can. We eat a wide variety and lots of food."

Linkletter: "Are you going to stay for the Olympic games?"

Jarvis: "No. Most of us will just stay a couple of days and fly back."

Linkletter: "Yeah, we need you. There's a crime wave, you know."

Jarvis: "That's right."

Bondlie: "Thank you, Art Linkletter."

Linkletter chatted with the runners and drivers for a few minutes, wished them well, and then headed down the road. Jarvis couldn't believe his good fortune:

"He said to come and see him sometime. So I'm going to do it. You never know — he might be able to help my career. That one incident could do it. But it's remarkable. Here we are, in the middle of nowhere, and we meet Art Linkletter. It's crazy."

Janowicz was in his eighth mile when the follow car told him he was going to be filmed and interviewed. He decided to take it easy until the camera crew arrived, and then "turn on the speed to make it look good."

Julie Haalandi was waiting with her camera as Janowicz entered his final quarter-mile. When he spotted her, Janowicz made his move. Haalandi's camera caught his final sprint and hand-off to Jarvis. She continued filming as Janowicz walked dramatically down the highway, taking deep breaths, hands on hips, ostensibly oblivious to the camera. Haalandi and Bondlie approached Janowicz for an interview.

Bondlie: "What are your living accommodations like?"

Janowicz: "Well, I'm in Camper Two, which is called Canadian Club. We've got the Lone Ranger, Tonto, Batman, and Mercury."

Bondlie's eyes widened. He wasn't sure he was hearing right. Janowicz realized he needed to elaborate.

Janowicz: "Those are nicknames. We got various nicknames for each other."

Bondlie: "Oh, I see."

Bondlie was a veteran newsman, but with Frank Janowicz, he found himself groping for another question.

Bondlie: "So you're on the Los Angeles police force? Whaddya do?"

Janowicz: "I work recruitment division, and my primary job is to increase females."

Bondlie's mouth dropped open.

Janowicz realized his answer was a bit confusing. He tried to elucidate: "I work affirmative action, plus I teach a physical fitness class every Saturday morning at our Police Academy, which [sic] the class is to help prospective candidates become physically ready for the academy."

Bondlie was now desperate. He needed at least one coherent 20-second statement for his feature story. He tried again: "Do you have any doubts about making Montreal by July 4th?"

Janowicz: "No doubts at all, 'cause this is my third run. I've been on runs from Mexico to Vancouver, Canada, and from Washington, D.C., to Los Angeles, California, two years ago. So we're gonna make it. It's just a coast now. We're over halfway."

Bondlie smiled. Finally he had something usable for the six o'clock news.

As Bondlie and Haalandi piled their equipment into their station wagon, Clark sauntered up to Janowicz, who was feeling 10 feet tall after his interview.

Clark: "I was standing next to that camera lady while you were running."

Janowicz: "Yeah, I really turned on a burst of speed for her."

Clark: "Well, I'll tell ya. She saw you pounding down the highway, and she said to me, 'Boy, doesn't he look tired after 10 miles?' "

Janowicz looked at Haalandi, who was now waving goodbye to the team. Janowicz waved back weakly. He was devastated: "I'm surprised she'd say that. I thought I looked fresh. Well, shit. From now on, I'm running comfortable."

Clark: "You'll be ready for 'em next time, huh?"

Janowicz: "Yeah, I'll be ready."

1:24 P.M. FRANK MULLENS

Grand Forks, North Dakota, was ready. Radio and television had blared the news all day that the Los Angeles Police Department's Bicentennial Relay of Goodwill would be passing through the city that afternoon. Hundreds of people were on the streets as Mullens entered town. He was joined by a member of the Optimist Club and a 15-year-old boy and a 15-year-old girl. The follow car played the Olympic Theme.

Mullens slowed his pace to nearly nine and a half minutes a mile. Suddenly, he was propelled back in time: "It was just like my days in baseball with the big crowd and everything. The same old ego trip. I was thrilled, absolutely thrilled. All along the way, people were welcoming me."

About two miles into the run, Mullens and his companions were joined by a seven-year-old boy. Mullens slowed down even more.

"I told the youngster, 'You know, you could be a good runner.' And he said, 'Do you really think so?' And I said, 'No question about it. You're going to be fantastic.' Then he got this real serious look on his face, and he said, 'You know, I don't know why I'm doing this.' And I just looked down at him and laughed, and I said, 'That makes two of us.'"

Mullens crossed the bridge that marks the North Dakota-Minnesota border. His companions wished him luck and dropped out. He ran another two miles and handed the baton to Eddie Garcia. "That was my best leg so far," said Mullens. "It was great."

2:56 P.M. EDDIE GARCIA

"It was miserable. My knee just throbbed. The clocks didn't make a damned bit of difference for me. I would have been in misery, no matter what."

The runners of Van Two should have been sleeping, but instead, they rendezvoused with the other campers for a huge party at the Westward Ho Motel in Grand Forks. The police department there had arranged for two rooms where the runners could shower, shave and relax. And they had set up an elaborate buffet beside the pool. It had been planned as a dinner buffet but was rearranged as a luncheon, because the team was still running two and a half hours ahead.

Still, the no-clocks policy was working. When the clocks were scrapped just a day earlier, the team was three and a half hours ahead of schedule and gaining time with each run. But now the trend had been reversed, and so had the mood.

All afternoon, the runners ate, drank, swam, joked, and traded camper gossip.

4:22 P.M. CURT HALL

Twelve miles east of Grand Forks, Hall ran into a fierce hailstorm. "The wind was blowing in my face. Hail was hitting me from all directions. My feet were slipping on the wet pavement."

But in Grand Forks the sun was still shining and the party continued. Ron Kiser, camera in hand, decided to stage a sequel to his John Day "streaker" epic. He offered instant stardom to three young ladies who were lounging around the pool.

Scene one: The "actresses" enter one of the hospitality rooms with Dick Clark and John Rockwood.

Scene two: The five of them are in bed, only their heads and bare shoulders exposed.

Scene three: Officer Jim Murphy peeks in the window, breaks open the door and confronts the frolicking hussies and their clients.

Scene four: Instead of making the expected bust, Murphy has

a sudden change of heart, rips off his clothes and jumps into bed, too.

Epilog: Murphy and the others were all wearing bathing attire.

Rating: Strictly "G."

As Hall slipped and slid along flooded Highway Two, Van Three stopped at a gas station to fuel up.

Mullens: "Eddie, I'm going into the rest room to brush my teeth. Wait for me."

Watkins: "Gotcha, Frank."

About 10 minutes later, Watkins climbed into the van, looked around and asked if everyone was there. "Yeah," a chorus replied. Watkins pulled out and headed toward the next hand-off point.

Moments later, Mullens emerged from the rest room — teeth meticulously brushed and flossed. But he was a man without a home.

Mullens: "I asked the kids who worked at the gas station, 'Where's the camper?' And they pointed east. They said it went thataway. They were laughing. So I thought they were kidding. I walked to the corner and looked down the street, but no camper. I figured, 'They'll have their little joke and come back.'"

But the van didn't come back. Mullens walked over to a middle-aged couple who was getting gas. "I asked them if they saw the camper that was in here a few minutes ago. They said, 'Yes, it went over that bridge.' And I said, 'I'm supposed to be in that camper.'

"By now the kids at the station are laughing like hell. They thought it was the funniest thing in the world. I thought, 'Okay, I'll get on the road and start hitchhiking.' A couple of cars went shooting by. They must have thought I was some kind of idiot out there in a running suit with my thumb out.

"Anyway, the couple that was getting gas pulled up to me, and the guy said, 'Jump in. I'll take you up there.'

"We were driving down the road, and he said, 'How far do you figure they're ahead of us?' I said, 'They've got at least six miles.' And he steps on the gas, and he's just ripping down the highway about 85 miles an hour. Very cool, though. I said, 'Boy, you look like you're a pretty good driver.' And his wife said, 'He ought to be. He used to be a race driver.'"

About 15 minutes later, Van Three came into view. Mullens waved out the window at Eddie Watkins.

Watkins: "Look at that guy. He looks like Frank Mullens."

Garrison: "He really does."

Watkins: "Hey, wait a second." Watkins turned halfway around. He saw Mullens's sleeping bag atop his bunk. "Frank, are you back there?" he yelled.

No answer. Eddie Garcia, who had been sitting up front with the drivers, walked back and shook the sleeping bag.

Garcia: "Christ! That *is* Mullens out in that car! We must have left him behind!"

Everyone burst into laughter. But in the car, Mullens was visibly disgusted.

For days, a debate would rage between Mullens and his campermates about that incident.

They: "It was a mistake."

Mullens: "I'm not sure they didn't do it on purpose. But they won't cop out to it."

Jarvis: "All I know is we all decided from now on we better check and make sure Frank is with us all the time."

A few minutes later, Van Three picked up its final runner, Curt Hall, and headed toward the town of Bemidji, where it would take the baton again the next morning. But en route, publicist Lou McClary radioed to tell the van that a tiny community called Bagley was planning a late dinner for the team at its police-fire station. The van decided to stop there.

6:53 P.M. ALEX SHEARER

"It was another miserable run. It was raining, and my chest was still tightening up. Bob Hogue ran along for support. I tried everything to get rid of the tightness, but nothing worked. Then, about halfway through the run, I swallowed a fly. I thought I was going to die."

Hogue: "He started coughing and choking and spitting. I thought he was having a heart attack. But when he started swearing, I knew he was okay."

8:20 P.M. BOB BURKE

"It stopped raining when I took the baton, and there was a beautiful sunset. The clouds were absolutely gorgeous — green clouds. You could have taken a spoon and reached up there and had a parfait right out of the clouds. I don't know how you couldn't believe in God after seeing something like that."

As Burke ran through the town of Mentor, Minnesota, Van One, with Bob Hogue at the wheel, picked up a conversation on its C.B. radio.

Hogue: "They were talking about the run and trying to figure out what was going on. So we broke in and explained. One guy asked how it was being financed, and I told him through private donations, mostly from businessmen in Los Angeles. Well, this guy thought that was absolutely great. And he said, 'I want to support you guys. When you enter Mentor, check the city limits sign. There'll be some money there.'

"When we got to the town, we stopped and checked. There was a dollar bill attached to the sign."

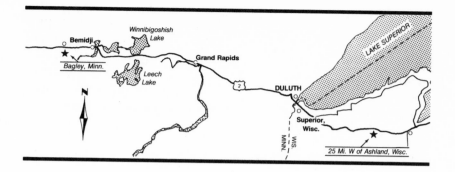

THE FIFTEENTH DAY
Monday, June 28, 1976

Bob Burke: "Chuck Foote has been acting a little sheepish about the whole timing thing. I see it in the way he approaches me. It's like a little puppy dog going to its mama now."

Shortly before his nineteenth leg, Chuck Foote took a deep breath and walked over to Van One to chat with Bob Burke. The father-son camaraderie was strained. There was an uneasiness now between these two old friends. And that uneasiness was exacerbated when Burke told his team captain that there was no sense in going for a new long-distance record, because everyone was running too slowly to add extra miles.

Burke then zeroed in on Van Two: "You're dragging your feet. You're leaving Camper One to carry the entire load."

Burke delivered his message quietly. But it hit Foote like a baton across the forehead.

Bagley, Minnesota

Bagley, Minnesota is Middle America. Most of its 1,600 residents live in small, old, but well-kept homes. The business district is several streets of weather-beaten stores and restaurants. The tourist area is two motels. All of this is protected by a five-man police force, which shares its surprisingly modern quarters with the city fire department.

In a subterranean area below the main station, there are showers and a recreation area. On this night, the recreation area had been transformed into a reception center for the LAPD runners.

The party began shortly after midnight. It lasted for three hours. During that time, scores of townfolk and cops from three nearby departments dropped in to welcome the runners. And newspaper reporters from Bagley and outlying towns arrived with pads and pencils to conduct interviews. Night life had come to Middle America.

12:44 A.M. JIM MURPHY

As Murphy began his run, a dense fog began to envelop the area just east of Bagley. This was Indian country — hostile Indian country. The fears weren't imaginary here: A few days earlier, Indians had ambushed a police car and shattered the windshield with shotgun pellets. A gun battle ensued. The suspects had gotten away.

Now, as the fog continued to roll in, the local sheriff and two of his deputies rode lookout duty ahead of Murphy. They aimed their flashlights into the heavily forested area that lined both sides of the road, fighting to pierce the ever-thickening fog. Then they rode back to where Foote and Clark were standing.

Sheriff: "I wouldn't recommend sleeping in this area. In fact, you fellows ought to think about bunching up your campers and driving through here convoy-style."

Clark: "How much farther have we got before the reservation ends?"

Sheriff: "About 25 miles. We'll keep checking ahead for you."

Bagley

As usual, Bob Burke was at work in his camper — this time trying to figure out who would drive the vans back to Los Angeles once the team reached Montreal. Several people had expressed interest, but always with an "if" or a "but." Burke made a mental note to pin down some drivers, and then headed for the party.

Burke: "Everyone was eating and talking and laughing. I started talking to this policeman, an elderly guy who had a farm outside the town with a couple hundred acres. And we talked about his farm and the law enforcement problems here in Bagley and back in L.A. He wanted to come to Los Angeles and see the Police Academy.

"That's the first time I had really talked to any policeman in the whole two weeks of the run. And I realized then that I'd been missing a big part of this run. I think I was wrong — this run really *is* a vehicle of goodwill. There in Bagley, I finally was enlightened to that."

Murphy: "The run was eerie. Heavy forest, dense fog. I expected any time to see a UFO come down and land. It looked like something right out of a movie. Real weird."

Back in Bagley, Frank Janowicz kept a promise to call his wife shortly after 11 P.M., Los Angeles time. Bea Janowicz had shattering news.

"She told me I'd been transferred out of Recruitment Division to Hollenbeck. That means I'm back on the street. No more nine-to-five job. No more civilian clothes. I gotta wear a uniform. I don't wanna go back to wearing it. I gotta work some miserable shift — probably morning watch, probably Tuesday and Wednesday off.

"But the worst thing is I'll be back on the street. I've worked it. It's harder after you've been there and left. All the beefs, all the scum. There's nothing in the street but trouble."

Frank Janowicz will never get a commendation for being subtle. His transfer depressed and angered him. To make matters worse, all promotions had been frozen because of budget problems, and he'd go back on the street as a policeman-two — the lowest possible rank.

"I've met all the requirements to be promoted. But my sleeve will be bare. No stripes. I'm losing money, too. But the main thing — I'll look like a dumb shit out there without any stripes. It's embarrassing and demoralizing. And the street — they say it's the backbone of the department, but all it gets is the shit. Anybody who works patrol and doesn't think he's a fool, well . . ."

When most people think of cops they think of street cops. They do not think of physical training instructors or teachers or athletic directors or recruitment officers or police commission investigators. Radio, television, movies, newspapers, magazines, novels — all have packaged cops as knights in blue, jousting with the modern forces of evil.

That battle is waged in the streets. And so the street cop has become a glamorous figure; his mission, a mission of glory. But there is really nothing glamorous or glorious about busting hookers and pimps, battling male "mentals" armed with chains, raiding a Black Panther headquarters, or rescuing babies caked

in three days of their own feces and covered with maggots —
rescuing them from their own mothers.

Cops approach this agonizing human drama from different
perspectives. But it is the drama itself that binds all of them —
whether they work in Los Angeles, Bagley, Boston or Brussels.

Connelly: "You can be a doctor or mailman and not like it, but
still do it. But police work is one job that's not safe for you if you
don't like it. And if it's not safe for you, it's not safe for your
partner or for the entire community. You just shouldn't be out
there."

Jarvis: "I'm not in the field right now. But in April, we didn't
have a class at the Academy, so I went to Hollenbeck to work
juvenile gangs. I hadn't been on the street in eight years. And I
had one fear I'd never had before — the fear of being shot . . .
killed.

"You know, years ago it used to be that the gangs used chains,
fists and clubs. Now it's knives, shotguns and high-powered
rifles. They'll set up ambushes, and they'll kill a policeman if
they can. I'm talking about kids as young as 12 years old.

"And the laws have changed in eight years. You just don't
kick somebody's butt like you used to.

"I'm glad I'm not on the street anymore. I'd probably end up
in jail myself."

Shearer: "I worked the street for about seven, eight years back
in the fifties. It wasn't that dangerous then. Never had to choke
anyone out. No one ever tried to choke me out. I never shot
anyone. No one ever shot me.

"I took a little acting in college, and it came in handy back
then. Police officers really are actors anyway. A lotta times a
policeman doesn't have as much going for him as people think
he does. That's where acting comes in. You have to talk people
into doing things they really don't want to do. You can get
people to like you in a hurry, and then you say, 'C'mon, get in
the car,' instead of having to get them into a choke-hold or
something.

"That's the way I operated. We had a lotta fun in those days."

Burke: "Sometimes, when I worked the street, I had to be
forceful with someone I was arresting. To me, it was justified. To
someone else, it might have been brutal. But I can tell you — in
those days when cops could be good and tough on the beat,
you'd be able to go downtown with your family on a weekend
night and be safe and enjoy it. Now you can't. Someday it will be
safe again. But it will take very strong policemen to do it.

"You're paying a policeman to take your bumps in life, your physical bumps."

Garcia: "I've been on the street. I've gone through that phase. I've paid my dues. I liked it. Thrived on it. And I'm glad I was there. But there are other things that I want out of life other than playing cops and robbers. Sure, I wanna go back on the street, but as a field supervisor. There you have to play both roles — policeman and management."

Hickey: "I don't like being a field supervisor. I wanna go back to the street. I wanna be a policeman. I'm not doing the things I wanna do — stopping people I think need help, stopping to help someone with a flat tire . . . what I call public relations.

"Ideally, I would like to get involved in our Policeman Bill program, working with little kids, letting them know that the policeman is their friend."

Hall: "When I joined, [William] Parker was chief and there was no public relations. He believed that a cop is a cop. When he died, the department became more public-relations minded.

"That's all that teaching program is to me — public relations.

"A cop, to me, should wanna be on the street. That should be his first instinct. I've taken the examination for Sergeant and other promotion tests, and I've always scored in the upper ten percent. I've turned down a number of promotional opportunities. I'm just happy on the street, and I want to stay there for the foreseeable future."

Garcia: "I sure as hell wouldn't want to have an attitude like that. You have to be a more well-rounded individual to be a professional police officer. Staying out there in the field is remaining at the same level and not developing. I intend to go as far as I can in this job.

"I taught for two years. I loved it. Right now, my desire is to train recruits — train them to be the best possible police officers.

"I'm not saying Hall is wrong, because many individuals feel the way he does. And the more people who feel like Hall, the more chances I have of promoting."

Murphy: "There are about 7,400 men in the Los Angeles Police Department. And fewer than 2,000 are on the street. Ideally, every one of us should be there, because our job is to stop crime, catch criminals, and you can't do that except on the street.

"The problem is the street can become very demoralizing. Remember, the police officer is the one who sees the crime firsthand. He sees the victim, and he sees the criminal in the raw, so to speak. But months later, when the criminal goes to court, all the jury sees is some well-dressed guy with his hair neatly cut and combed, defended by some slick-talking attorney. And very often the guy gets off on some technicality.

"Sometimes you feel like you're just spinning your wheels out on the street."

Jarvis: "If I had any job to choose on the department, it would be right at the academy. I can stay in shape. It's a nine-to-five job. Weekends off. Holidays off. And I'm not getting shot at."

Hall: "When I came on the department, I thought nobody stayed at the academy more than two years. But I see Jarvis — eight years there — he couldn't possibly know anything about the street."

Clark: "The street is a negative environment. You see terrible things. Disgusting things. And it tends to make a police officer very skeptical and distrusting and cautious of his fellow man.

"An officer has to realize he is dealing with only a very small percentage of the population. He is not dealing with the large percentage that silently supports him and pays his salary. But he can forget that and get a very jaded view of humanity.

"That's why a lot of guys are recycled off the street into various jobs or find outlets — like running. The negativism can build up, and you just have to flush it out of your system."

Foote: "Working the street is a different kind of accomplishment than say, teaching. You hardly ever see the end product.

"I remember once pretty early in my career, my partner and I were going down Sunset, and a woman comes up and blows her horn. Her baby had stopped breathing. The mother was terrified. The baby was starting to turn blue — just a little one, about seven, eight months old.

"I had kids myself. And all of a sudden you've got someone else's kid plopped into your lap, and you've gotta save its life or watch it die. It's a terrifying feeling.

"I gave the baby mouth-to-mouth resuscitation as we raced code-three to Central Receiving Hospital. Right away, it started to get its color back.

"When we got to the hospital, some doctors grabbed the kid and rushed it to Children's Hospital.

"I found out later we'd saved the baby's life. But the mother never came back to say hi, goodbye, thanks — nothing.

"That's the street."

2:04 A.M. DICK CLARK

Spared from Indian attack and UFO landing, Murphy completed his leg in about 80 minutes. He handed the baton to Dick

Clark, who dedicated his run to Pecos Bill. Clark didn't know it, but he ran his leg in under 70 minutes. "Because of Burke's comments about our van, I really picked 'em up and put 'em down. The pressure was back on because of those statements."

And there was still pressure because of the Indian threat. The sheriff and his deputies had now covered the entire road through the reservation.

Sheriff: "There's nothing out there that we could find. But we'll keep riding along with you, just in case."

Like Murphy, Clark cut through the eerie fog. "You could see two images of yourself ahead because the headlights of the pace car reflected into the fog. Two people would be jogging in front of you. It was a weird feeling."

3:12 A.M. FRANK JANOWICZ

"My transfer and Burke's comments pissed me off. I told the follow car, 'I wanna be timed.' I took all my frustrations out on that run. I hit about a six-and-a-half-minute-per-mile pace and just pushed myself."

Van One had left Bagley and was now parked beside Van Two on the Indian reservation. All the runners and drivers, with the exception of Alex Shearer, were sleeping. Shearer walked outside the van, where he met Dick Clark, who was still cooling down from his run. The sheriff approached.

Sheriff: "I'm glad to see another van is here. It's safer that way."

Clark: "But we'll be leaving for the next hand-off point pretty soon."

Sheriff (to Shearer): "You guys should stay with 'em. Stay together. Believe me, it's safer."

Shearer nodded. The sheriff turned and walked down the road again, shining his light into the dense forest. Shearer told Clark to come with him. They entered Van One. And without warning, Shearer went berserk.

Shearer (shouting): "We've got to get them before they get us! We've got to kill every one of them! Wipe out the red menace! Take no prisoners!"

First Rockwood, then Hickey bolted awake.

Shearer: "Kill, kill, kill! I, for one, will show no mercy to the Red Devil."

Burke, Bonneau, Kramer and Hogue were awake now too, staring at Shearer.

Shearer: "Kill every man, woman and child! Kill the red beast! I've had it! I've had it!"

Shearer stomped around the camper, exhorting his campermates to battle. They were now all wide awake, laughing.

Suddenly, Shearer stopped, climbed into his bunk and went to sleep.

Janowicz: "I could see my shadow in the fog in front of me. I ran right through it. The first time I did that, it spooked me. I thought, 'Christ, I'm on an Indian reservation and maybe that's the Great Spirit comin' at me.'"

Janowicz ran his 10 miles in 64 minutes.

Later, as he cooled down, the sheriff walked up to him.

Sheriff: "The reservation ends in a couple miles. You're safe. It's daytime. They won't attack now. Good luck."

4:16 A.M. BOB JARVIS

Jarvis ran over rolling hills into the beautiful resort town of Bemidji. Lush forests and small glistening lakes cover this section of Minnesota, but Jarvis's thoughts were elsewhere: "There's still a lot of problems on the run. Everybody's getting pissed at everybody else. Everything's falling apart. Burke is upset with everybody except in his camper. And his camper is upset with everybody because Burke's upset."

10:30 A.M.   30 miles east of Bemidji

The rebellion of two days earlier had left its scars. Burke was still angry at Connelly and Foote for "going behind his back" on the clocks issue. And he felt the team was running too slowly.

Most of those inside Van One were sympathetic to Burke and were barely on speaking terms with the men of Vans Two and Three.

(There was one exception. Alex Shearer was on good terms with all his teammates, including those in Van One, where any hostility toward him should have originated. Shearer had been the only member of his van to vote against the clocks. And he was a charter member of the "rebels." But it's difficult to dislike Shearer. And to make himself even more lovable, he drew a skull and crossbones on a sailor hat and quickly donned it whenever the timing matter was rehashed. Shearer had added another character to his one-man repertory company — "The Mutineer.")

There was uncertainty in addition to the hostility. It still was not clear whether the team would try to break its existing cross-country distance record or run the number of miles originally set out.

So a second "summit meeting" was held — this time in humid woods in northwestern Minnesota.

Burke: "We cleared the air. I found out that Foote and Connelly didn't plot behind my back, that the whole issue of the clocks was brought up by the brass, and that Beck was just supposed to relay their opinion to me. No ultimatum or anything. Beck misunderstood. I misunderstood. Everyone also said they're still gonna run as hard as they can, but comfortable. So everything's okay."

Connelly: "We resolved our differences. There were a lot of misunderstandings."

Foote: "This whole thing about the record — it just shows you that sometimes you're so wrapped up in something, you just can't think clearly. We all had forgotten that the distance record set on the D.C. run was with thirteen men. This run is over different terrain with fourteen men. So anything we do on this relay will be another world's record."

Hall was the only runner who didn't attend the meeting. He was running past woods and streams. "I love this type of country. It's basically the kind I was raised on in Texas. And I remembered years and years back. It was like going home."

2:26 P.M. JOHN ROCKWOOD

"That was my fastest run — 63:57. It was humid, but I kept getting a breeze, and it was a little overcast, so that broke it up. I just got a good relaxed pace going and kept it up."

3:30 P.M. DICK BONNEAU

"That was worse than the desert. The humidity was miserable. I felt real sluggish. Every step was a struggle. I was dehydrated, exhausted."

Bonneau labored toward the hand-off point to the strains of the "New World Symphony." Bob Burke greeted his sweat-soaked campermate by tossing pebbles at him.

Bonneau: "You know what they say on this team — you'll find sympathy between shit and suicide in the dictionary." As Shearer had pointed out, you won't, but then you wouldn't find it on the team either.

5:40 P.M. JIM MURPHY

The runners were now nearing Grand Rapids, and the countryside was speckled with farms and small towns. "People kept

coming out of their houses, lining the streets, waving and shouting and shaking my hand. They would say, 'God bless you . . .
we're with you.'"

In Van Two, one of the "closet timers" revealed himself. It was
the man who probably more than anyone else had swung the
team against the clocks.

Clark: "Everything seems to be straightened out with Burke.
We can run nice and easy again."

Foote: "Yeah. Remember that one I told you I ran in 99?
Actually it was about 67."

Clark: "Hmmmm . . ."

Foote: "And I ran this one in 64.13."

Clark: "Wait a second. Are we keeping time again?"

Foote: "It doesn't make any difference to me. I didn't know
the pace car started the watch."

Clark: "Hmmmm . . ."

Foote: "The pressure is off. Let's just have a good time for the
last eight legs."

Clark: "Yeah."

6:50 P.M. DICK CLARK

The sun was setting as Clark took the baton. It was cool and
humid, and the air was thick with gnats.

Inside Van Two, the runners and drivers were relaxing when
there was a knock on the door. It sounded like a bear was trying
to get in. George Moore unhooked the lock, and the doorway
was filled with 6-feet-6-inches, 325 pounds of humanity.

Visitor: "I'm in charge of this county — St. Louis County."

He laughed and looked around. "You're from L.A., huh?" He
numbing.

Visitor: "I'm in charge of this county — St. Louis County,
Minnesota."

He laughed and looked around. "You're from L.A., huh?" He
laughed again, a heavy, hearty, contagious laugh.

Murphy: "How many men in your department?"

Sheriff: "Let me put it this way: You know those two-man cars
you fellas ride around in in L.A.?"

Foote: "Yeah."

Sheriff: "Well, those two-man cars carry twice as many cop-
pers as there are on the entire St. Louis County Sheriff's Department. The department is standing right here, fellas."

He burst into his tremendous laugh again. The camper
seemed to shake.

Janowicz: "You on 24-hour call?"

Sheriff: "Yeah. They really keep me hopping. That's how I keep my shape."

This time everyone laughed.

Foote: "How much territory are you responsible for?"

Sheriff: "I figure about 350 square miles."

Janowicz: "You get a lot of drunk drivers?"

Sheriff: "Yeah, a lot of 'em. Better be real careful out here, in fact. I take 'em into Duluth, about 50 miles away."

Foote: "Fifty miles? You drive a drunk 50 miles, he's gonna sober up before you get there."

The sheriff laughed: "That's true. A lot of times those guys are stone sober. I mean, Kojak never had a problem like that."

Everyone laughed again.

Sheriff: "But I'll tell you one thing: You fellas can't get away with what we can out here. I mean, we can use a more direct approach. For instance, I had this one guy who was giving me a hard time, and I really didn't have any circumstances for an arrest. So I finally told him, 'You can either stay here, or you can end up a swamp mystery.' The guy got the drift."

The sheriff entertained the camper for another half-hour and then headed out.

Sheriff: "Hey, good luck. You're an inspiration to us all. Everyone in law enforcement is proud of you. If I could shed a quick 200 pounds, I'd run along."

8:06 P.M. FRANK JANOWICZ

Janowicz ran toward the town of Proctor. "All along the way, people kept coming out of their houses to wave at me. Women in nightgowns actually came out. People took my picture. About five people wanted my autograph. Some kids ran along with me for a block or so. Their parents would yell, 'There's the runner. Go ahead and run with him.' And they'd shout, 'God bless you, good luck.' We're like TV idols. We're like supertype people."

Back in Van Two, a second "closet timer" revealed himself.

Murphy: "I had a great run. I could've run that one in the mid-50s. I was flying."

Clark (innocently): "What'd you run it in?"

Murphy: "Sixty-four."

Clark glared at Foote, then at Murphy: "Are we timing again?"

Foote: "Nah. I think there's just somebody new in the follow car that turned the watch on."

Murphy: "I think it's Reese."

Clark (sarcastically): "Chief Reese? Well, we'll just have to discipline him severely. I'll reprimand him for that." Then he paused. "Funny. He didn't turn the watch on for me."

9:14 P.M. BOB JARVIS

"I ran into Proctor. The entire town was there to greet me. Two, maybe three hundred people."

The Moose Lodge in Proctor had set up a last-minute reception for the runners. Spread out on five tables was coffee, tea, fresh pastries, ham, tuna, and egg salad sandwiches. The head of the lodge kept apologizing: "I wish we could have given you guys steak dinners, but we didn't have enough time to prepare 'em."

It had become something of a tradition during these relays for Pat Connelly to run one all-out 10-miler. As he put on his favorite pair of running shoes inside Van Three, Connelly turned to Frank Mullens and told his old friend, "I feel great. I think I'm gonna go out and do one now."

For the first and only time during the run, Connelly left the camper early and warmed up. Then he radioed the follow car: "I wanna be timed."

Connelly was ready.

A television camera crew from Channel 2 in Duluth filmed the hand-off as Connelly snatched the baton from Bob Jarvis.

10:38 P.M. PAT CONNELLY

"I knew I was gonna go. I felt edgy all day. My feet felt light, as though I could run over eggshells without breaking them. I took off, and the pace car was just sitting there, talking. And I was around the corner and a half-mile away and they said, 'Where the hell's Connelly?'"

Connelly ran his first mile in 4:55. His first two in 11:05. "I wasn't feeling any pain or discomfort at all. I said to myself, 'I'll hang on for five and see what happens.'"

At five, his time was 27-flat.

"I said, 'Well, two times 27 is 54 minutes. I'll see if I can hang on for another three.' Between five and eight miles, I ran over a bridge which connects Duluth with Superior, Wisconsin. I was flying. Two kids on bicycles followed me through Superior, and we talked for three miles about the run. Then two guys from the local Optimist Club jumped in and tried to run with me, but there was no way they could keep up. I gave them a greeting and kept moving."

Connelly ran his first eight miles in 43:45. He had a shot at the sub-55-minute leg.

"But at eight miles, I hit an upgrade. That disappointed me. But I kept the pressure on. Kept pushing myself."

At 10 miles, the follow car called out his time: 56:40.

Until that moment, Frank Janowicz's charge down the Angeles Crest had been the single fastest leg on the relay (56:54 for 9.8 miles). Connelly ran another six-tenths of a mile before he reached the hand-off point. His total time was 60:25. Only he and the pace car knew how fast he had run the first 10 of that 10.6 miles. Connelly wanted it kept secret: "It's not important for me to have the fastest leg, but I don't know what kind of an effect it would have on Janowicz if he found out he didn't. It might destroy him."

11:38 P.M. FRANK MULLENS

Mullens ran two miles to the outskirts of Superior, across flat, comfortable terrain. But at the two-mile mark, he hit a massive upgrade that would continue without letup for the next eight miles. At the five-mile mark Mullens was struggling. His good friend, Rudy DeLeon, was in the pace car.

DeLeon: "Frank, how would you like some company out there?"

Mullens waved to signify, "Okay."

DeLeon jumped out and joined Mullens.

Mullens: "Rudy really helped me. Pulled me along. We cussed the hill, like we always do, and kept saying, 'When's this damned thing gonna end?' We had a pretty good time out there, considering."

DeLeon: "Two elderly runners, cussin' and swearin'. But let me tell you: Frank ran eight miles of that thing. He is very, very tough."

Van Two

The runners of Van Two were still hungry as they bid goodbye to their hosts at the Moose Lodge in Proctor. They hopped in the van and traveled to Superior, where they found an all-night restaurant called the Via Duct Bar and Cafe. The runners were wearing their sweatsuits, and a patron, who had been at the bar for some time, recognized them. He was a huge man with a bright red face and bloodshot eyes that testified to his regular patronage at the Via Duct.

Drunk: "You guys are the runners, aren't you?"

Murphy: "Yes, we are."

Drunk: "Well, can I buy you a drink? Won't break training, will it? A beer. Four beers for my friends here."

The bartender walked over and drew four beers.

Bartender: "You're the guys who're running to Montreal?"

Foote: "Yes."

The bartender summoned his daugher, a 10-year-old with long blonde hair and shy green eyes.

Bartender: "This is my daughter. And these are the police men we heard about on the radio, who are running across the country."

Girl: "Can I have your autographs?"

Foote: "You sure can. How old are you?"

Girl: "Ten."

Foote: "I have two children. A little girl and boy. They're both younger than you."

Girl: "Do you call them on the telephone when you're away?"

Foote: "I sure do."

The girl ran to the back of the bar and returned moments later.

Girl: "Here."

She handed each runner a key chain and can opener. The bartender drew four more beers, and the runners ordered hamburgers, French fries, and small salads.

Drunk: "I am buying that food."

Foote: "No, no. We'll get it."

Drunk: "I insist."

Clark: "Let him get it if he wants."

Drunk: "I have been a patriotic person all my life. You people are patriots, right?"

Murphy: "Right."

Drunk: "And you're police officers from Los Angeles, right?"

Murphy: "Right."

Drunk: "Well, then, this is the least I can do for my country."

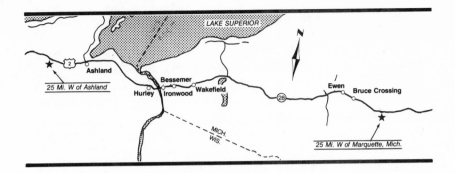

THE SIXTEENTH DAY
Tuesday, June 29, 1976

4:06 A.M. — 9:52 A.M.
Van One

The five runners of Van One felt so good running their twentieth leg in the rain past Lake Superior that they cut another 40 minutes off the projected 75-minute-per-leg pace.

Now the team was again more than three hours ahead of schedule, and there was talk about running extra miles either later this day or tomorrow.

11:04 A.M. JIM MURPHY

Just before noon, Jim Murphy crossed the border into Michigan. The Bicentennial Relay had covered 2,865 miles through ten states. Inside Michigan, two state police cars and two cars carrying a delegation from the Michigan Fraternal Order of Police joined Murphy. Until then, with only rare exceptions, the runners had been restricted to the extreme right-hand side of the road. But here, the state police swung into the middle of the road and motioned Murphy to get behind them. The runners would travel in style through Michigan.

12:18 P.M. DICK CLARK

Dick Clark ran through the small towns of Wakefield and Bessemer. "I had a fan club out there! People honked and yelled and waved. About ten people took my picture. Incredible! Seems like everyone knows we're coming."

In Van Two, the enthusiasm was contagious.

Murphy: "In the city, we're kind of like front line troops. We forget what this country really is. These are the people whom we in the cities are really fighting for."

Foote: "There are good people in the city, too, Jim. We just don't see many of 'em."

Janowicz: "We see the dirtbags, the scum. That's who we see."

Foote: "It would jade Mary Poppins."

Murphy: "She'd get raped."

Between Wakefield and Bessemer, two youngsters on bicycles joined Clark. "One of them said, 'You're just doin' this 'cause you like to get your picture in the paper.' And I said, 'I always get my picture in the paper. I'm bionic.'

"I think he believed me."

Back in Van Two, Murphy was still enthusing over Middle America.

"For the last five miles of my run, the streets were lined with people. They were waving. Friendly. Really good people. I think we're tying the country together, going through these states. We're touching these people — their pioneer spirit, their desire to excel. We're helping them show how they feel about their country."

Janowicz: "I think the people do think we're like the pioneers."

Murphy: "We're seeing the fruits of all our hard work. We're really something to these people."

Janowicz: "Heroes. Starlets."

Murphy: "Our running is a bond between ourselves and the people we're sworn to protect across America. Their response to us is an incredible experience."

Van Three pulled up beside Van Two as Clark handed the baton to Janowicz.

Foote: "How are things in Pigpen Three?"

Jarvis: "I'll tell ya, I'm in the greatest camper on this run. The guys are terrific. They're very considerate. I got accused of making too much noise last night when I was spreading peanut butter on my sandwich. And they said I was munching my banana too loud, too. Just unbelievable. Makin' too much noise eatin' a banana. Can you believe that?"

1:30 P.M. FRANK JANOWICZ

Rain was coming down hard as Janowicz carried the baton through Ironwood, a lumber town of 8,700.

"I hate the rain," Janowicz complained. "When I was in the service in Florida it rained by the week, not by the day. I don't like looking at it, living in it or running in it."

Back in Van Two, Clark was becoming obsessed with the surreptitious timing he felt was going on. He camouflaged his concern in offhanded questioning: "What'd you run your last one in, Mercury?"

Murphy: "Sixty-three-fifty-eight."

Clark: "I thought we weren't being timed anymore."

Foote: "We aren't. It's just that someone in the pace car is timing us, that's all."

Clark: "Well, he's not timing me."

Foote: "Hmmm . . ."

Janowicz battled hills and a strong headwind with the same determination you'd expect of him at a perilous moment on duty. His eyes were squinted, his forehead creased in a slight frown. Mountains. Wind. Fatigue. Tight calves. Sore groin. They were mere hindrances. They could not deter Janowicz.

In Van Two, the delegation from the Michigan Fraternal Order of Police was chatting with the runners and drivers. They mentioned it would be nice if some of the runners could backtrack about 20 miles to Wakefield, Michigan, for a dinner where the team was scheduled to receive an official proclamation from the governor. The delegation received some nods and grunts, but they left without getting a commitment.

Beck: "I don't give a shit about the proclamation. Let's go eat."

Clark: "And do laundry."

Laundry. In the scheme of things, it came only after running, eating, and sleeping in importance to the runners.

It was often a tedious chore that required being at the right place (a town) at the right time. Often times it was done at the wrong place at the wrong time.

Shearer: "During the San Francisco run, our van pulled into

Livermore [in Northern California] at about two in the morning, and someone said, 'We gotta wash our clothes.' And I said, 'Yeah, okay. But as long as we're doing it, we might as well have a party.' So we went to this laundromat, opened a bottle of wine, and had a party while we washed our stuff. Well, we got a little silly. I mean, Foote and I started dancing — together. A couple of guys started singing. And we put Burke in a dryer. We were very tired, and very silly.

"Anyway, this cop car goes by real slow, and someone says, 'Hey, there go the cops.' But we kept dancing and singing, and Burke's going around in that dryer. Then another cop car goes by. And I say, 'Hey, something must be up.' But we just kept on partying.

"Well, about two minutes later, about ten cops come screeching up, and a bunch of cops come charging into the laundromat yelling, 'What's going on here?' We say, 'Oh, we're from the LAPD, and we're running to San Francisco.' And they just look at us and start laughing. And one of them says, 'Oh, we weren't expecting you so early.' And there's Burke just sitting in that dryer in the fetal position.

"The cops just shook their heads and left."

Pat Connelly entered Van Two: "We're three hours ahead again. We gotta slow down."

Clark: "Now you tell us. Most of us just ran pretty good times."

Connelly: "Well, all our runners are gonna run about 90-minute legs."

Murphy: "What's Van One gonna do?"

Connelly: "Continue to burn it."

The team had been due in Wakefield for the dinner and proclamation from the governor at precisely 4:07 P.M.. That event had now been rescheduled for 5 P.M.. But at that hour, the team would be about 35 miles east of the city. Finally, it was decided that Van One would make the trek back to Wakefield.

3:09 P.M. PAT CONNELLY

It was chilly as Pat Connelly headed through Michigan's Upper Peninsula into a flat, sparsely populated, wooded area. He was joined by two runners, Mal Frisk and Bob Nick, who had already run 10 miles with Bob Jarvis.

Mal Frisk, who was in his mid-50s, was a former lumberjack and copper miner who looked like he could tear a tree out by its roots and mine the earth with his bare hands.

His friend, Bob Nick, was 39 — a residential manager for lakefront property in the area. By his own account, he had been an overdrinker and overeater until he decided to start running and change his ways. Neither man had been running very long, but both had already run marathons. They were big, strong, hearty men — products of America's diminishing wilds.

Connelly: "Bob was quiet. Didn't say much at all. But Mal — he was unbelievable. He kept telling me how tough he was. He said he worked in those lumber mills and copper mines all his life and talked about all the fights he'd been in. He told me a couple weeks ago three guys jumped him on the highway, but he kicked the hell out of 'em. Tough guy, very tough. He could eat the bark off a tree.

"I asked them if they run in the winter. And Mal says, 'Oh, it's great out here when it's two degrees below. Snow flurries. Boy, I'll tell you, you feel like flyin'. And I said, 'You're crazy.'

"Then Mal starts giving me a history lesson. He points to this house and says, 'See that up there? It belonged to an old policeman. That old sonofabitch shot and killed my dog 25 years ago. And then he committed suicide. He's been dead 25 years, but I still hate the sonofabitch. Shootin' my dog.'

"He said, 'See that house over there? That used to be a whorehouse. This whole place used to be a mining town — diamonds. All torn down now. Then a lumber community. Now it's copper.'

"They asked me what I did on the LAPD. And I told them I worked juvenile, taught at a high school. They wanted to talk about patrol, and they asked if I'd run into some pretty hairy things. I told them I could handle just about anything at work, except child abuse, child neglect — anything involving kids.

"I told them about this one time where this woman had her 11-month-old baby on her lap while she was sitting next to the driver in a car. She musta weighed about 280 pounds. Enormous, a beast. She rear-ended a car — and her weight just shoved the baby right into the glove compartment. Killed him. That just kept botherin' me.

"And I told 'em one time I went on this call — a woman said a baby had been left alone. So I went there and knocked, and I heard a cry. I guess I woke the baby up. I kept knockin', and the baby kept cryin'. So I stood back and kicked the door down and went inside. And here's the baby in a highchair in the living room. He's tied in the highchair with an apron. What happened, the mother was going to Vegas, and she'd hired a three-day babysitter. The mother had a plane to catch with her boyfriend.

So she just wrote a note for the sitter, and left a bowl of porridge or something in front of the baby and took off. Never bothered to call. Well, the babysitter got in a car accident on the way over and didn't make it. And that baby spent two-and-a-half days in that highchair.

"Well, here were two rough-tough guys who thought they'd heard and seen everything, and they couldn't believe their ears. They didn't know such things existed. I told them one last story. The only time I really got close to getting in trouble on the job.

"My partner and I were told there was child abuse at this house. The neighbors had complained about it. We knocked on the door, and this lady says, 'Nah, you can't come in here.' Well, we could come in there, because she had said she was alone, but we heard a baby crying, and that's our p.c. — probable cause — to go into the house.

"She wouldn't let us in, so I stood back and kicked the door open. I go inside. There's dog shit all over the floor. The furniture is a mess. There's old newspapers and magazines all over the place. That's the living room, okay?

"I go into the kitchen. Here's drawers half pulled out. Food running over the sink. Food on the stove that's boiled over, mildewed and rotten. Here's dog food all over the floor, scattered where she feeds her dogs, about six dogs. The sinks are full of dirty dishes that stink, okay?

"I go down a hallway into a bedroom. She sleeps on a mattress. Her clothes are all over the floor.

"I go down the hall and into a second bedroom. And there's the baby — I would say about 13 months — tied by a rope to its crib. The rope has cut into his skin. No sheets — just a plastic mattress. The baby had crapped in his diapers. And the shit has crusted. It's hard. All over him. There are tremendous sores all over him, blister deep. The cuts, caused by the rope, have healed and scabbed, but the rope has torn the scabs off, over and over again, all over the hands.

"There are several empty liquor bottles. This woman is feeding her child — her baby — gin, bourbon, vodka straight to stop it from crying when she goes out with her boyfriends at night.

"The baby is thin, emaciated, head is swollen — not from being hit, from what I could tell — but from the alcohol.

"Here I am, untying the baby, and she's grabbing the baby saying, 'Hey, you leave my child alone — you have no right!' And I grabbed her by the collar and took her and threw her clear across the room. She banged her head against the wall and went down on the seat of her pants. The impact almost knocked her out.

"She reported me for unusual force, and the department took the complaint.

"You know, I coulda done a lot more than that. I really related to that child, 'cause I had a year-old child at that time. And that poor thing looked up at me with these great big eyes, held his hands up, crying, his arms extended toward me. That baby knew I was there to help. Knew I was someone who loved it. And I took that child in my arms.

"My partner clapped the cuffs on that old bitch, and we hauled her down to the station. We took the baby to juvenile hall. I checked, and the baby was put in a foster home four months afterwards. He had brain damage from the alcohol.

"I couldn't erase that baby from my mind. When I got home that night, my wife said, 'What's wrong?' I sat her down and told her the story. I cried. I couldn't help it. The tears just came. I was so wrapped up in that thing. Right there in the San Fernando Valley. The white San Fernando Valley. These things go on. Right next door. The guys couldn't believe it."

5:36 P.M. FRANK MULLENS

As Mullens took the baton, just west of Ewen, Michigan, two more local runners joined in. One was Bob Olson — a 2:48 marathoner — 45 years old, who owned radio station WMPR in Hancock, Michigan. The other was John McClary, a young doctor who had just started long distance running. Both were members of the Hancock Long Distance Running Club. They had heard about the run on the radio and had driven 100 miles to participate.

As Mullens and his four companions started running, the heavens suddenly opened up, and torrents of rain cascaded down.

Mullens: "We talked about everything. About halfway through my leg, the two guys who had run with Connelly dropped out. Bob and John forced me to run harder than I normally would have. I hadn't run one under 80 in three days, but they drove me into the mid-70s.

"Then about nine miles out, a young fellow from a Frostie Freeze came running out and handed us all some ice cream cones. I ate the ice cream but threw the cone away. That ice cream bothered me for the last mile. I needed it like I needed a hole in the head. But how could I turn it down?"

9:04 P.M., Eastern Time CURT HALL

Curt Hall took the baton about 10 miles east of Bruce Crossing — a gas station and a lamppost on the Michigan landscape.

Pat Connelly walked along the road to where Van One was parked, waiting for its runner to take the hand-off from Hall. Bob Burke sprang out of the van.

Connelly walked over to his old friend and adversary, and Burke draped one of his lanky arms around him. They walked together for a few moments.

Connelly: "We weren't attacking you with that vote, Bob. We're all with you. God knows you worked hard. None of us'd be here if it wasn't for you. It was just something we did for the team."

Burke nodded. Here in the rain forests of Michigan, peace between these two men was finally at hand.

Curt Hall wound his way across northern Michigan. A sheriff's car led the way. It darted about 150 feet ahead and waited. Hall sprinted, trying to catch it. It was a game. But Hall aggravated his sore ankle playing it. After six miles, he was limping.

During his last four miles, people kept coming out of their houses to wave and shout encouragement. A few teenagers ran beside him, shook his hand, and asked for autographs.

At the hand-off point, Connelly was talking with Alex Shearer.

Connelly: "These receptions have just been overwhelming. The people are thrilled about the whole thing."

Shearer: "Yeah. It has been pretty incredible."

Connelly: "And it's gonna get even better. Just wait 'til we get to Sault Ste. Marie on Thursday. We haven't seen anything yet. The Canadian government's got big things planned."

Shearer: "Well, I'm going to put my best possible image forward."

Bonneau: "You mean you're gonna stay in the van?"

Shearer: "Now cut that out, Bonneau. You've been mouthing off this whole trip. I might just send you back before we reach Canada."

Rockwood: "It would serve the munchkin right. He threw that magic set we gave him all over the place, because he couldn't figure out any of the tricks."

Shearer: "He did? Well, no Uncle Alex story tonight for Bonneau."

This was a time of euphoria. The clocks controversy was over, and the wounds were healing. For most, the running was becoming routine. And even for those who were injured, there didn't seem to be any real concern about making it to Montreal.

Euphoria — not realism — was the prevailing mood now.

10:27 P.M. BOB HICKEY

Bob Hickey took the baton between Sidnaw and Baraga counties in the middle of Michigan. About an hour earlier, his blisters had once again been injected with a 5 percent solution of Mercurochrome. And about 20 minutes earlier, he had received a challenge from Rudy DeLeon and J.P. Nelson. They decided to start running and see if Hickey could overtake them during his leg. As they began, it was announced that Hall had 2.2 miles to go. Actually, he had 3.3.

Hickey: "It was daylight when I started out, even though it was after ten at night. But then it got dark, and I couldn't see in front of me.

"At about two miles out, I got a gradual uphill, and I started to feel some pressure right between my big toe and second toe in the ball area of my left foot. It started throbbing. I tried to rotate my weight, left to right, to keep the pressure off. But I kept my pace — in fact, I pushed it a little bit because I wanted to catch DeLeon and Nelson.

"My foot got progressively worse. I didn't know what was happening. I thought maybe I'd stepped on a rock and bruised it or something. At nine miles, the pace car told me I was under 59 minutes. I couldn't believe I was running that fast. My last mile was all uphill, long and steep. I kept trying to see if Rudy and J.P. were ahead of me, but I couldn't see 'em. My foot was just throbbing, but I stepped up the pace and finished in 64 minutes.

"I found out later they finished just 200 yards ahead of me. And they had a three-and-a-half-mile head start."

11:32 P.M. ALEX SHEARER

The pain in Alex Shearer's esophagus had disappeared during the past 24 hours. But shortly before his run, Shearer made an error. "A very, very, very serious error. I not only ate fried foods, I ate them three hours before my leg, and I ate everything in sight — chicken, shrimp, French-fried potatoes."

The meal was guaranteed to maim. It did.

"It was the worst pain yet in my esophagus. It got so bad, I would actually double over in the road for five or six seconds until it would go away. I was running real slow, but then I got mad at myself, and I started stepping out. I actually was under six-minutes-per-mile there for a while. But that pain would come back about every 400 yards or so, and I would just double over."

In the follow car, Larry Kramer and Rudy DeLeon were concerned. They radioed ahead to warn Van One that it might have an emergency. They asked the van to check to see if there were a hospital in the area.

Inside Van One, Bob Hickey's left foot felt as though it were on fire.

Hickey: "God, it hurts. Feel it. Feel how hot it is."

Bob Hogue: "It is hot. Feels like it has a fever. You better soak it."

Hickey soaked the foot in ice water for about a half-hour and then took a shower. When he got out, his foot felt as if it were ready to explode. He soaked it again and lay down.

Shearer's esophagus kept tightening up, doubling him up in pain five, ten, twenty times now. There was near-panic in the follow car. Van One was monitoring its frenzied description. A call went out to "Doctor" Kiser in Van Four. Meanwhile, Shearer started coughing, and that caused him to lose stride. The pain came again, and this time he nearly fell to his knees. When the pain subsided after about 10 seconds, Shearer shot down the road as fast as he could — at a sub-six-minute-per-mile pace. He wanted to get this over as quickly as possible.

Hickey was in agony. He buried his face in his pillow and cried. "I was too embarrassed to cry aloud," he recalled. "I just endured it. The guys thought I was sleeping. But I was wide awake — my face in my pillow, crying."

Shearer finished and handed the baton to Bob Burke. "They told me to go over and see the doctor [Kiser]. I said, 'Absolutely not. I won't go see that guy. He's not a doctor. And besides, if he wants to see me, he can come see me."

Despite his own pain, Hickey hobbled over to Van Four for his old friend.

Shearer: "Hickey got this pill for me. I don't know what it was. I wasn't even gonna take it. The only reason I did was 'cause I didn't want to hurt Hickey's feelings. So I took the pill, took a shower, and went to sleep."

Hickey, his mission of mercy done, climbed back into his bunk, sank his face into his pillow, and cried in quiet agony for the next two hours.

12:55 A.M. BOB BURKE

"We shouldn'ta had that fried food. I caught this mountain about halfway through my run. I got about three-quarters of a mile up, and there was no holding back. It just came up. That dinner was a mistake."

Tell it to Shearer.

Back in Van One, Uncle Alex announced there would be no dramatic reading from *Penthouse* this night: "Uncle Alex just wants to tell all his nephews that he is very sick, but he'll be all right tomorrow, and he'll read them an extra story then. One other thing: Uncle Alex is through forever and ever with fried foods. He's gonna dine on pablum from here on out."

2:12 A.M. JOHN ROCKWOOD

"I ate the same garbage everyone else ate. It upset my stomach. And my legs were awfully heavy. I ran up and down hills my entire 10 miles. I was so tired, I felt like my feet were gonna fall off."

3:34 A.M. DICK BONNEAU

Dick Bonneau was lucky. He had enough time to fully digest the dinner that had wreaked so much havoc on his teammates. He glided through a heavily forested area in under 70 minutes.

Back in Van One, Bob Hickey sat up and touched his fever-ridden foot. "It's infected," he told himself. "The damn foot is infected."

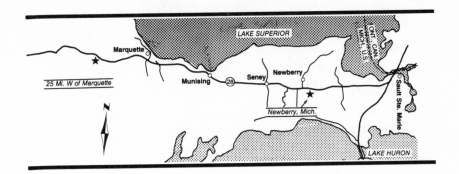

THE SEVENTEENTH DAY
Wednesday, June 30, 1976

7:11 A.M. MURPHY-CLARK hand-off

Murphy: "I had been a little bored through my run 'cause it was early in the morning, and we went through side streets. So I was thinking of ways to put a little life into the thing. And there was Dick Clark standing out in the road, waiting for the baton. And I thought to myself: What would it be like if I didn't have the baton? What would Dick do? So I put the baton in my pants, in the back. And as I got closer, I could see this expression changing on Dick's face. Like, where's the baton? When I got to him, I yelled, 'Dick! No baton! No baton! It was ripped off!'"

Clark: "Well, I thought maybe he'd dropped it, because I'd thought about dropping it when I ran over a bridge or something — and what would they do — fly in another baton? Just thinkin' about crazy stuff like that. You're carryin' that stupid piece of metal for so long."

Murphy: "He completely froze. Later he told me that he was looking around for a stick, 'cause he knew he had to carry something. I wish I had a picture of that expression on his face."

Clark: "When old Mercury came chargin' down the hill with no baton it kinda stunned me. Then I got the idea he was probably trying to mess with my mind. And finally, at the last second, he reached back and handed it to me."

Murphy: "Dick got a look of relief on his face. Then he does two pirouettes. And as he pulls out of his second pirouette, in the direction that he's running, he slams right into Chief Beck, who's holding a cup of hot coffee. It rained coffee for about 30 seconds."

7:30 A.M.
Van One

Hickey: "I couldn't sleep. I kept hoping that Van Four would come by with Kiser, so I could tell him that my foot was really bothering me, and that I didn't know what to do about it. Finally, Four pulled up. I went over."

Dick Clark, accompanied by Chief Beck, ran toward the city of Marquette.

Clark: "When we got into Marquette, this guy from the local radio station started runnin' with us, interviewing us. He had this big long cord, and he kept lookin' back over his shoulder, 'cause he knew he was gonna get to his short leash. He asked a couple of quick questions, and his cord ran out. End of interview."

8:25 A.M.
Van Four

Kiser: "Before the last leg, I had told Hickey to run easy, because his foot was already extremely tender and sensitive.

"But when he came to me in the morning, his foot was a mess. He had a blister, a callus and a stone bruise, one on top of the other. And they were in a critical location — on the ball of the left foot next to the big toe. That particular location takes a lot of shock. I knew that in order to keep him running, there was gonna be a lot of pain. What I tried to do was keep the skin on the blister. If he lost that skin, there's no way he could run.

"I drew out some fluid from the blister and then injected a solution of Xylocaine to numb the area. I had to go very deep."

Hickey: "When he inserted that stuff into my foot, it felt like something had exploded inside me. I broke down.

"Then I told him I had problems sleeping. So he gave me a sleeping pill and a muscle relaxer. And I went back to the camper. The pain was slightly relieved. I fell asleep."

Kiser: "That foot is damned sore — a lot of pain in a very critical area. But if I was taking bets right now, I'd say he'll be ready to run his next time out."

Clark: "The chief and I are running along, and this mailman starts running with us. And in the follow car, George Moore starts singing over the loudspeaker: 'Neither sleet nor snow nor foggy days can faze the post office . . .' or something like that.

"The mailman told me he had a heart attack a few years
before, and he started distance running for therapy. He said he
runs about five miles a day. He had his track shoes on with his
uniform."

Beck: "Then we ran past the police station, like we do in every
town, and some officers were out there to greet us."

Clark: "And across the street there was this big church, and
they sounded the bells as we went by, which was kinda nice."

Beck: "I ran six miles, then jumped in the pace car. That was
enough."

Clark: "I ran past this big prison. There was this beautiful
flower garden. And as I'm goin' by, George Moore broke into
chorus again over the P.A. system — 'If I Had the Wings of an
Angel.'"

8:35 A.M.
Van Two

Murphy: "I think I'm turning into an alcoholic. It's just after
eight-thirty in the morning, and I'm drinking beer."

Foote: "That's okay. We don't have any wine."

8:37 A.M. FRANK JANOWICZ

"I ran along Lake Superior, I guess. Some big lake. I felt real
good."

Murphy, inside Van Two: "We're supposed to burn off time,
so we all run nice and easy — 75-80-85-minute legs. And now
Janowicz is out there burning up the highway . . ."

Clark: ". . . making up everything we lost."

Foote: "Look at that scenery. The trees, the lake — beautiful."

Clark: "It's unbelievable. I can't tell the difference between
looking out the window at Lake Superior and looking out the
window of my apartment at the Pacific Ocean. I thought you'd
be able to see the other side of Lake Superior. But you can't."

Dick Clark wandered over to Van Three to pay a visit. As he
entered the camper, he was singing, "Good morning, good
morning." Bob Jarvis, who would take the hand-off from
Janowicz in a few minutes, was the only man awake. He was
putting on his running shorts.

Clark (in a whisper): "Don't you need a jock supporter?"

Jarvis: "I never wear one. Just flow freely."

Unidentified: "Ssshhh!"

Jarvis (in a whisper): "My campermates. I can't eat a banana. I can't make a fuckin' peanut butter sandwich. I can't even whisper. Let's get the hell out of here."

11:09 A.M. PAT CONNELLY

"They told me we're four hours ahead of schedule and that we gotta slow down, so I ran as slow as possible — ridiculously slow. I ran 10-minute miles. Almost had to walk."

Connelly finished his run in slightly over 100 minutes. "I broke Foote's record of 99 (which in reality was an unreported 67). Now I hold the slowest time of the team and the fastest. That certainly proves I don't have an ego problem."

12:09 P.M. FRANK MULLENS

Late the night before, Norma Harger, a trim, vibrant woman who's "closer to 50 than 40," got a call from her friend, Bob Olson, the marathoner who'd run with Mullens and Garcia. "He told me the LAPD runners were coming through my hometown, Munising, sometime Wednesday morning, and that I ought to run with them. I've been running religiously for several years. So here I am."

Here she was with three of her five children — Sheila, 10; Lisa, 15; and Kirk, 14 — running with Frank Mullens toward Munising, Michigan, population 3,677, on the banks of Lake Superior.

· In Munising, Bob Jarvis decided to call home:

"I knew this trip was gonna cost me money, and sure enough — my wife just told me I had an offer from Columbia Pictures to shoot a part in a movie this Friday. It was a good part, too. It woulda paid about $700. My wife told them, 'He's not here. He's running to Canada.'

"Just great. Here I am, thousands of miles from nowhere. Hollywood's a long way from Munising, or wherever the hell I am. But I'm gettin' back as fast as I can. First plane out of Montreal, I'm goin' back."

When Mullens and his new-found friends entered the outskirts of Munising, the city's police chief, Doug Myron, joined them, as they passed under a sign that proclaimed, "Welcome to Munising." Myron was a huge man — at least 6-foot-3, close to 300 pounds. Later Mullens would say: "I was afraid that chief of police was gonna drop over." But the chief hung in, running the middle four miles of Mullens's leg.

Several hundred people gathered along the route in Munis-

ing. There was the usual applause and cheers of "Good luck."
But near the end, someone in the crowd bellowed, "Take the
chief all the way — get him out of town."

The police chief dropped out as Mullens and the Harger family
ran into the open spaces outside Munising.

Mullens: "She told me her kids hold this family relay record
up here. Four of her kids — the oldest ones — ran a quarter-mile
each. Total was 3:57. The youngest kid was 12. Oldest, 17. Quite
a family. Great gal."

Norma: "We talked a lot about eating. I said that probably was
the most difficult thing for them because of their irregular
schedule. I told him our family eats lots of carbohydrates and
food low in animal products; that we get our protein from other
sources. He told me he eats anything he can get his hands on —
that he's hungry all the time."

Chief Myron stopped in the same restaurant in Munising
where Van Two was now eating breakfast. He was invited to join
them.

Chief Myron: "I've been reading [Joseph] Wambaugh's
books. Enjoy 'em. I wonder — how is he regarded out there?"

Beck: "Turncoat."

Foote: "Depends on who you talk to."

Beck: "If you ask me, you're ruinin' my breakfast."

Myron: "That's interesting."

Beck: "I hate the sonofabitch."

Myron: "His books are interesting. The last one I think I read
was *The Onion Field*."

Clark: "Well, that is a good book."

Beck: "He did a good job there. But his novels — I'm unhappy
with them because he consistently portrays policemen as being
either psychos or crooked or suicidal. You know, there's never
in his books — in any of his books — been a policeman that lived
a normal family life. None."

Myron: "Yeah. That's true."

Beck: ". . . and I resent that. You know, like *The Choirboys*. His
entire theme seems to be that the pressures of police work in a
large city are so great that human beings can't seem to tolerate
them. And that's not true."

Several months later, Chief Beck's name would be splashed
across television, radio and newspapers in Los Angeles, just like
one of Wambaugh's choirboys. His statements in that small cafe
in Munising would suddenly take on new meaning — and irony.

3 P.M.
Van Three

Frank Mullens was famished. He grabbed a bowl, poured in some Cheerios, filled it to the brim with milk, sat down on a trunk near the driver's seat and began to eat. Pat Connelly, Mullens's coach, friend, and occasional tormentor, slid behind the wheel.

Mullens: "You drivin'?"

Connelly: "Yeah."

Mullens: "Well, take it easy, for Chrissakes."

With that, Connelly revved the motor once and then jammed his foot on the accelerator. The van lurched forward. So did Mullens and his bowl of cereal. Cheerios and milk splattered on his shorts and leg.

Mullens: "Damn it, Connelly! Don't you know how to drive?"

No answer.

Connelly careened onto the highway.

Mullens: "Jesus, Pat! How'd you ever get on the police department?"

No answer.

Connelly wound his way down the highway. The only problem was that the road was straight.

Mullens: "Christ, Pat! Your depth perception must be shit!"

No answer.

Mullens juggled the bowl of cereal, trying to eat quickly, before he lost more of it into his lap. There was a red light ahead. Connelly hit the brake as if he were trying to avoid a catastrophe. The bowl of cereal landed squarely on Mullens's bare chest. He was irate.

Mullens: "Pat, you're the worst fuckin' driver in the world!" No answer. "I can't believe you're on the department!" No answer. "They wouldn't dare trust you in a patrol car." No answer. "Do you have somebody drive you when you go on vacation?" No answer.

Mullens gave up eating. He tried to wipe the cereal and milk off his chest. The light changed to green.

Connelly: "You looked good out there, Frank."

Connelly gently pressed his foot to the accelerator, and the huge van moved out smoothly.

Mullens: "What the hell are you talking about? I'm tired and hungry."

Connelly: "I drove by you. You were striding along good. Your muscles looked relaxed. You looked like you had full command of all your tools. You looked great."

Mullens started to perk up: "I don't know. That was tough for me. I was tired."

Connelly: "Well, that might have been tough for you, but I've been coaching a long time, and when we drove by you, you looked good. You mighta felt bad, but boy, you looked good."

Connelly pulled the van over to the side of the road. Mullens sprang to his feet. His fatigue and hunger had vanished.

Mullens: "I'm gonna take a shower."

Two 15-year-old boys from Munising joined Eddie Garcia and drivers Rudy DeLeon and Eddie Watkins as they ran through barren stretches east of Munising. It was over 90 degrees — the hottest day of the year in this part of Michigan. The five runners traveled along at a leisurely nine-minute-per-mile pace. The object at this point was to keep the baton as long as possible to burn off time. (Bob Burke had also mapped out another alternate route of about 20 miles to burn off additional time.) The team would reach the Canadian border the next morning. The crossing was scheduled for precisely 6:43 A.M.. The Canadian government had been alerted, and big ceremonies were expected. It was critical that the team reach the border on time.

Mullens was riding high as he emerged from the shower. Connelly knew his pep talk had propelled him there. Now he figured it was time to bring Mullens back down.

Connelly stared grimly at Mullens as he dried himself. Mullens was smiling and humming a tune. Connelly continued to stare. Mullens stopped smiling. Then stopped humming. He was feeling a bit uneasy. Then Connelly, his face expressionless, his tone grave, told Mullens:

"You know, I took a look at your medical report on the clipboard over in Van Four. And according to that, you shouldn't even be here."

Mullens: "Whaaa . . . ?"

Connelly: "I mean, your heart's supposed to be bad. You can't hear. You can't see . . ."

Mullens: "Connn . . ."

Connelly: "You've got an injury to your right leg from way back. Your back is bad from that baseball accident. And you're old — I mean, you're nearly 60, aren't ya? What're you doin' here?"

Mullens: "Damn you, Connelly! Damn you! Don't go talking about my age that way."

Mullens pulled on his sweat pants and stalked to his bunk at the rear of the van. He was "back down."

Up the road, a more serious scene was being played out. Bob Hickey was scheduled to run in about two hours. But his foot was swollen with infection. The pain was intense.

Minutes earlier, while Hickey was sleeping, Ron Kiser had stopped by. Like a doctor breaking bad news to a patient's family, he told the men in Van One that Hickey's condition was grave. Kiser explained the extent of the injury — a blister, callus, stone bruise, infection. And then, he issued the prognosis:

"He might — I repeat, might — not be able to run."

The statement stunned the runners and drivers.

Twenty minutes later, Hickey awoke and gingerly tested the foot. The pain was excruciating. But it was nothing compared to his mental anguish. He got up slowly and hobbled out the door. Van Four was parked about 75 feet away. Hickey walked the distance torturously. Once inside the van, he sat down and Kiser began to inspect the poisoned, bruised foot.

Garcia and his companions finished. Garcia's knee ached. He put his arm around DeLeon, his old commander at Hollenbeck, and squeezed his shoulder.

Garcia: "Thanks for running with me. It helped keep my mind off the pain."

DeLeon: "Hey, you're a great runner. It's my honor. Take care of it, now."

DeLeon walked off to the support vehicle to shower. Garcia sat down on a huge rock and drank a beer.

"There's a great man," he said, pointing at DeLeon. "That man has handled more controversy than anyone on the department, including Chief Davis. Hollenbeck's a tough division. All those gangs down there.

"You know, his philosophy is that there's a job on this department for every officer — no matter how messed up he might be. That's why he ends up with so many psychos. He'll take 'em. He'll rescue 'em.

"I mean, this man's had so much controversy — the East L.A. riots, Wambaugh's books, and he really did have to deal with the real choirboys. He keeps things cool in East L.A. He knows everyone. He's respected by everyone. He's one of the most respected officers on the force. Indispensable. Believe me, if we had more DeLeons, L.A. would be a better and safer place. Believe me."

3:06 P.M. CURT HALL

The runners of Van Three were averaging nearly 90 minutes per leg, and Hall was under pressure to maintain that average. But he had a problem. His right ankle was sore and swollen from his long-ago motorcycle accident, and the pounding and jarring of a slow pace would do the injury more harm than good.

"What I'll do is take a little detour through the woods along the way and maybe add a couple miles to my leg," Hall said. "That way, I can run a faster, more comfortable pace, and keep the stress off the ankle, and at the same time burn off some more time."

Hall had company on his run. Norma Harger's oldest son, 17-year-old Greg, had just gotten off work. Despite his age, he was already a veteran of five marathons. Hall and Harger ran past a heavily wooded area. Their pace was about eight minutes-per-mile.

Inside Van Four

Ron Kiser carefully measured a solution of Xylocaine. The hypodermic needle glistened under the lights of Van Four. Kiser inserted the needle into the bruised area. He wanted to make certain he numbed just the affected region and not the entire foot, which was now badly swollen.

Chief Charles Reese and AAU official Andy Bakjian watched as Hickey gently tested the foot. He winced: "My God, it hurts!"

Hickey took two steps and stopped. His face was white.

Bakjian: "Bob, I wouldn't run on that foot. You could ruin yourself."

Hickey: "No! No! I gotta run! I can't, I can't . . ."

Hickey's eyes filled with tears.

Bakjian: "What do you say, Ron?"

Kiser: "It's up to Hickey. That Xylocaine will take effect shortly. But my advice is — pass."

Hickey glanced down at his infected foot. He tried to step on it again. The pain shot through his body.

Bakjian: "Look, Bob. You can pass one time. All you have to do is take the baton from Hall, walk two feet and hand it off to Alex."

Hickey: "But then Alex will have to run my 10 and his 10. He's been sick. He might not make it. It's too much of a burden. Too much . . ."

Bakjian: "Alex can do it. He . . ."

Hickey: "Look. I'm gonna try."

He limped out of the camper.

Hickey: "I was very upset. I didn't want to be the first runner ever to drop out of his assigned leg. I decided to change into my running clothes and get ready. I was determined I was gonna run. I thought to myself: 'If I pray hard enough, maybe I can put this thing out of my mind. Tell myself that the pain isn't really there. I could overcome it.'"

Hickey struggled back to Van One and started to dress. And pray.

The Xylocaine needed time to take effect. The word went out from Kiser to the follow car: Tell Hall to slow down.

Hall and Harger spotted a narrow dirt path off the main highway — a perfect detour.

Hall: "Let's take it."

Harger: "Okay."

They darted off the main road before the follow car knew what had happened. The path was cut through a thick forest. Oarflies assaulted them. The hot sun added to the discomfort.

Hickey dressed and carefully laced his Nike running shoes. As he stood up, the pain shot through him again. He started to cry. Bob Burke was the only other person in the van.

Hickey: "I'm really hurtin', Bob."

Burke: "Look. There's no problem. If you can't run . . . look, why don't you go out and see if you can walk on it."

Hickey nodded and hobbled out of the camper.

Burke was really suggesting two things when he suggested that Hickey try to "walk." Hickey was a race walker — rated among the top twenty in the United States. There was a chance that he could "walk" — heel to toe — in a respectable time, say 90 minutes. The pressure on the foot would not be as intense from race walking as running. But Burke was also suggesting that Hickey merely walk if the race walking became too painful. Perhaps a combination of the two would work. Hickey gave it a try.

Jack Garrison and Rudy DeLeon were stunned. They couldn't believe Hall would suddenly ditch them. They swung the pace car around and headed up the dirt road. About three-quarters of a mile in, they spotted the runners coming back toward them. Garrison tried to negotiate a narrow u-turn as the men waved and shot past him. The dirt was soft on both sides of the road. The wheels spun and churned up the sand. Garrison swore softly. The pacer was stuck, three quarters of a mile up a dirt road, off the main course, in a forest in the middle of Michigan. DeLeon swore loudly.

Bob Burke had no real illusions about Hickey's condition. He knew he and Shearer had better prepare to assume a massive burden. He went to Alex.

Burke: "I don't think he's gonna make it. Under the rules, he's gotta at least touch the baton. So why don't we do this? He can take the baton from Hall and hand it to you. You run 15 miles, and then I'll take over and run your last 5 and my 10."

Burke and Bakjian — without consulting one another — were thinking along the same lines. But Shearer had some reservations.

Shearer: "Okay. That means Hickey would not be disqualified because he ran at least part of his leg, right?"

Burke: "Right. But he would have to run his entire 10 miles next time out or he would be disqualified."

Shearer: "Right. And since I would be running only five miles of my own leg, I would have to run my full 10 next time or be disqualified, too."

Burke: "Right."

Shearer: "Well, I'd rather not face that. I mean, I'd rather run my full 10 this time. In other words, I'll run 20 this time. I'm ready. I know I can do it."

Burke: "Look, Alex. You've been sick. It's hot out there. There's no sense in trying to run 20. Let's split it. Fifteen-fifteen."

Shearer shrugged: "Okay."

As DeLeon and Garrison struggled to free the pace car, Hall and Harger turned onto the main highway. With no car to protect them, the runners headed toward the oncoming traffic.

Hickey tested his foot for 10 minutes. "I asked God for help. I walked and limped and prayed. But I just didn't have the strength."

Hickey climbed back into the van. Burke and Shearer were there waiting for his decision.

Hickey: "I can't do it. I want to, but I just can't. There's too much pressure. I can't even walk."

Hickey sat on his bunk, buried his face in his hands and wept.

Burke: "You sit this one out. Take care of that foot, and you'll be ready for your next one."

Hickey: "I just wanna get out of here. I wanna get on a plane and go home. I've let down the team."

Burke: "You haven't let anyone down. You've got an infected foot. It coulda happened to anyone. That's what this type of racing is all about. But you can't play around with an infection. It could ruin ya. It's just not worth it. You've run a great relay. And you'll be back."

Hickey shook his head. Tears rolled down his face. His anguish was overwhelming. Burke gently put a hand on Hickey's shoulder as Shearer walked outside. Now it was just Hickey and Burke.

Hickey: "I prayed, Bob. But I was too weak. Too weak."

Burke: "You'll be back. You'll be back."

Burke turned and walked outside, too. Kiser, Bakjian and Reese approached.

Kiser: "Shearer says Hickey isn't gonna run."

Burke: "No, he isn't."

4:42 P.M. HICKEY-SHEARER

On a desolate stretch of highway in northeastern Michigan, Bob Hickey lined up five yards behind Alex Shearer, waiting for the hand-off from Curt Hall. AAU official Andy Bakjian watched, to make certain the rules were not violated.

Hall trotted to the hand-off point, handed the baton to Hickey, who limped the five yards to where Shearer was standing, and handed off to his campermate. The exchange had been made. And so had history. Bob Hickey had just become the first LAPD runner ever to miss a scheduled leg.

Shearer began his unprecedented 15-mile run. And Hickey began to slowly make his way back to Van One.

Driver Bob Hogue joined Shearer for his long run. But 50 feet down the road they got a jolt.

Kiser: "All of a sudden, Rudy DeLeon, who was driving the pace car, stops, 'cause there's Hickey. Hickey's running up the road. RUNNING! Running after those guys with a bottle of water. And here he is pouring the fuckin' water on them. *Running!* And Rudy says, 'Shit, he sprinted up there.' And he says to him, 'What about your foot?' And Hickey says, 'Well, it's sore but you know, it isn't that bad.' Well, shit no, it isn't that bad 'cause it's filled with Xylocaine.

"So there he is — fuckin' sprinting around and then fuckin' around in the pace car (which had picked him up). And from Van Four, I got on the mike and said, 'Get your ass out of the car and get into your van and soak your foot.' And he says, 'Oh yeah, I'm going to as soon as we finish.' And I said, 'When's that?' And he said about an hour-and-a-half. And I said, 'Fuck it!' And he makes these mumbling noises. And I said, 'Don't give me that! I've told you to soak it for a week-and-a-half. If you don't take care of that foot, you're gonna have trouble.' What am I supposed to do? You know, if he doesn't answer the call the next time, he's out. Out of the race."

Hickey ignored Kiser's admonition and settled into the pace car beside his astonished friend and commander, Rudy DeLeon.

On the road, Shearer and Hogue were on a gradual but steady incline.

Shearer: "We were both a little upset because of that hill. It went straight up for about five miles. But the final 10 were the straightest and flattest run that anyone could possibly have. Just perfect.

"On a 10-miler, I usually start out slow and then pick it up through the middle and build. You know, climax. But on this, we just tried to hit it all the way through — a steady, constant pace. But that has a tendency to fatigue the legs. And that's what happened. By eight miles, my legs were tired. And it was a little warm."

In the pace car, DeLeon tried to comfort a now-distraught, depressed Bob Hickey.

DeLeon: "He was very emotional, very upset. You know, I've known Bobby since he was a kid. He grew up across the street from my mom and dad. I first became acquainted with him in a working relationship 16 years ago, in accident investigation. And now, of course, he works with me in Hollenbeck.

"He just kept staring out the window and saying he let the team down. That those guys were running for him. That he was the first one to drop out. He was very upset about that. He kept saying, 'Why did it have to be me? Why did I have to be the first one?' And I talked about fate and circumstances. And I told him, 'You didn't let anybody down. Nobody feels that way. This isn't that type of team.'"

But DeLeon was not quite accurate.

Bonneau: "There were about four or five guys — and Hickey's one of them — that were in such fierce competition with each other that they ran the risk of injury. It's hard to fault a competitor when he does the best he can. But this is a team race. You've gotta think of the team first."

Mullens: "He's depressed. Yeah. But he was one of those who

was running too fast. He hurt himself. Don't feel sorry for him. Feel sorry for the guys who have to pick up for him and run 15 miles now."

Connelly: "Suddenly we're running 15-mile legs because one guy went too fast and got injured. And really, he hasn't hurt himself as much as his teammates.

"I'll tell you one other thing. I think he shoulda walked. I don't mean race-walked. But walked. It's his 10 miles. He should do it."

Jarvis. "No comment."

Janowicz: "Kiser kept telling him to soak his foot and to slow down. But Hickey wouldn't do it. Murphy had injuries, and he had enough sense to back off. Hickey didn't."

Murphy: "He gets a thought, he sets a certain goal, and he's gonna do it, come hell or high water. But sometimes you just have to swallow your pride and back off. Maybe he figured even if he lost a foot he'd still finish. But an infection — that puts it completely beyond the control of mind or body."

Kiser: "The next thing you'll see is a red line running up his leg. Sure. Blood poisoning. His fuckin' leg and groin will start swelling. Then he'll fuckin' be in the hospital. He's a big boy, and if he doesn't want to take care of himself, well . . ."

But there were kinder words, too. Ironically, the kindest came from the two men most directly affected by Hickey's injury — Alex Shearer and Bob Burke.

Shearer: "Hickey's Hickey. You can't change personalities. He's gonna run the way he wants to. He ran that way the first time I took him out with me in the Police Olympics in 1967. And he'll run that way 'til the day he dies. And it's no problem.

"Look. The team has run thousands of miles. Any of us could have been injured."

Burke: "Hickey's never dropped out before, so they can't say he was running too fast, because he's always run fast, and nothing happened before. If anybody does look down on a guy that does what Hickey did, then he doesn't belong on the team. But I don't think anybody is looking down."

A little more than two hours after they began, Shearer and Hogue glided toward the hand-off point — the Beatles' song, "The Long and Winding Road," blaring from the pace car behind them.

Shearer: "It really wasn't that bad. I could have gone 20. And I'm glad to do it for Hickey. What the heck. He'd do the same for me. Any of these guys would."

6:52 P.M. BOB BURKE

As Bob Burke began his 15-mile run, he was joined by a Michigan state patrol car. Sgt. Earl Johnson interviewed Burke and then fed the information to radio station WNBY in Newberry, Michigan.

Burke: "I hit some pretty tough hills right away. But I figured the old man [Shearer] did it, so that was my incentive right there."

Radio station WNBY: "We interrupt Boots Randolph's 'Alligator Annie' for this bulletin. Sgt. Earl Johnson of the Michigan State Police tells us the Los Angeles Police Department relay team is now passing through Seney. The man running is Police Officer Bob Burke. Now one guy has a foot injury. He got it this morning. I told you before that they're running 10 miles at a time. Well, to make up for this guy's injury, they're running 15 miles at a time now. I'm told they get about 16 hours of rest between runs, which isn't a heckuva lot when you consider all the blisters and things you have on your feet when you're running 15 miles at a time. True? True."

Inside Van One, John Rockwood was talking to Dick Clark: "Man, my feet felt heavy last night. All that fried food really messed up my stomach."

From the rear of the van, Shearer chortled.

Rockwood: "Yeah. That's the last time I'm gonna eat fried foods before I run. That was the worst."

Shearer chortled again.

Rockwood: "I don't think you have anything to laugh about, Alex."

More chortling.

Rockwood (to Shearer): "All I know is that when you were running last night, all I could hear was 'Get an ambulance up here! Send for the rescue helicopter! Send for the medics! Alex isn't gonna be able to make it! Alex is dyin'!'"

Clark: "What was the general feeling inside the van?"

Rockwood: "Our unanimous reaction was to tell him to shut up, run and quit sniveling."

Shearer: "Typical."

Bob Burke headed toward the second detour he had mapped out — toward two small towns, Dollarville and Newberry.

Radio: "They're at McMillan now, so they're moving right along. They should be at Newberry within the hour. They make better time than my old car used to do. If you want to see them, go to the high school. You could line up and cheer them along. This is a Bicentennial thing. And what I'll do — I'll put a long record on. And when you hear that long record, you'll know that I'm watching them go by, too."

Bob Burke rolled past the 10-mile mark in just under 80 minutes. He was maintaining a steady, comfortable pace — one that would bring him to the hand-off point in just under two hours.

Burke approached one of the myriad hills on the course. He lowered his arms to his sides, gently shook them, took a deep breath, and then headed up, never breaking stride. Each hill lasted no more than two-tenths of a mile. Burke came over the top of the latest one and then lowered his arms again, letting the decline carry him along. His running appeared almost effortless.

Radio: "I thought you might be interested in hearing from two members of the relay team that will be running through Dollarville within the next hour or so. In our studio now are Sgt. Dick Foote . . ."

Clark: "No, no, no. Dick Clark."

Radio: "Oh, there we go."

Foote: "I'm Officer Chuck Foote."

Radio: "Okay. So we've got Sgt. Dick Clark and Officer Dick Foote . . ."

At about the 12-mile mark, Burke suddenly turned and shouted at Hickey in the follow car, "You should be soakin' your foot right now."

Hickey, "I will, Bob. I promise I will. When I get back."

Inside Van Four, Bob Hogue was being treated for blisters and Shearer for mosquito bites. Ron Kiser, Rudy DeLeon, and Chief Charles Reese rounded out the group.

DeLeon: "Janowicz came to me at three-thirty in the morning. He said he'd just called home and found out he was going to Hollenbeck and wanted to know if he could have Sundays and Mondays off. [Laughter] I said, 'Shit, is that all?' I said granted, yeah — granted." (Laughter)

Shearer: "Is it?"

DeLeon: "No way. [Laughter] He'll get morning watch." (Laughter)

Radio: "Let me ask Sgt. Chuck Clark . . ."

Clark: "That's Dick Clark . . ."

Radio: "Right. Sgt. Dick Clark — what is your endurance? How far could you run right now before you'd have to stop?"

Clark: "I imagine I could run 20 to 30 miles if you gave me enough hours to do it in."

Radio: "How do you like running through the Upper Peninsula as compared to Los Angeles? Do you notice one big difference right away."

Foote: "Sure. You've got a lot more mosquitos." (Laughter)

Radio: "How about the clean air? Little bit of difference, isn't it?"

Foote: "Really, Los Angeles gets a kinda bad rap about its smog. It isn't that bad. You get used to it."

Radio: "Okay. We're talking with Officer Chuck Foote and Sgt. Dick Clark of the Los Angeles Police Department. They're on a goodwill tour. They left Los Angeles on the 14th of June. And they're expecting to be in Montreal in time for the summer Olympics."

Foote: "It's not really for the opening of the Olympics, 'cause we'll all be back in Los Angeles long before they open."

Reese, inside Van Four: "Hickey's in the follow car, huh?"

DeLeon: "Yeah."

Reese: "We oughta just rope that sonofabitch in and make him soak his foot."

DeLeon: "Yeah."

Radio: "Okay, Sgt. Johnson tells us the second runner to go 15 miles is almost finished. He says they're nearing Watson's Hill. They're getting close. So go on out to the high school, and let's give the team a big welcome. Now, let me ask one last question and then let's open this up to our listeners if they want to talk to Officer Dick Foote and Sgt. Dick Clark. Let me ask you this: Do you plan to take in the entire Olympics, from start to finish?"

Foote: "No. Not really."

Burke was on the final 400 yards of his 15 miles. His mouth was open. Sweat rolled down his face. His eyes were zeroed in on John Rockwood. The pace car was playing John Denver's "Country Road." All the runners and drivers of Van One were there to greet him.

Hogue: "Attaway, Bobby. Attaway."

Shearer: "Bobby who? We're here to see Hickey. And we all

want to see the driver of the follow car, to see if he's still sane after being with Hickey for 30 miles."

Bonneau: "Attaway, Bobby!"

Shearer: "C'mon, Burke. It's time to start partying."

Burke reached the hand-off point and handed the baton to Rockwood. The small reception committee burst into applause. Burke seemed to be almost delirious.

Bonneau: "Want a beer?"

Burke: "Yes, thank you."

Burke walked over to a nearby farmhouse, where a puppy was barking and wagging its tail. He knelt down and started petting the mutt. He tried to appear in control. But he was dizzy and exhausted. He had been running hard since the Angeles Crest. Dealing with a multitude of problems. Under constant stress. This 15-miler had drained him, emotionally and physically. After downing his beer, he would take a quick shower and then sleep. He hoped to sleep for hours.

8:42 P.M. JOHN ROCKWOOD

"I ran the detour route through an area where there are supposed to be more black bears than anywhere in the United States. Larry Kramer ran along — sort of as a companion and bodyguard."

Radio: "Sgt. Earl Johnson tells us that two new runners are on their way now. The last guy has finished his 15 miles in just under two hours. Can you believe that? Could you do that? Fifteen miles in less than two hours! The new runners are up on Watson's Hill, and that's about three miles from our radio station here. Now if you want to greet the runners, go to the high school and wait there. The runners will be passing there within the next 30 minutes. Maybe 20 minutes, the way these guys run. Let's have a big turnout."

Rockwood and Kramer ran through the tiny town of Dollarville and headed toward Newberry, where at least 400 people had gathered at the high school. Scores of teenagers, parents with young children, elderly people — all waited on the lawn of the high school.

Along the route, families gathered on their porches and lawns. The American Legion hall emptied to greet the runners, as did the tiny Methodist church. Dozens of people were riding bicycles to the high school now, and at least 40 cars were trying to get there, too. It was perhaps the biggest traffic jam in the history of Newberry, population 2,334.

Rockwood and Kramer climbed Watson's Hill — a steep up-grade that separated Dollarville from Newberry. They headed toward the high school.

As the runners came into view, the crowd erupted into a chorus of cheers, applause and whistles. Rockwood waved the baton and smiled. Dozens of people grabbed his hand and slapped him on the back. Larry Kramer kept yelling to the throng, "He's the runner, he's the runner!"

The cheering continued for nearly five minutes. Rockwood and Kramer slowed their pace as they headed for the hand-off point, about a mile away. Some members of the crowd began to run with them. Others hopped on their bikes or into their cars and trailed behind. The procession wound its way through Newberry. People waved from their porches and lawns.

When Rockwood handed the baton to Bonneau, he was surrounded by well-wishers, including at least twenty giggling, squealing teenage girls.

Bob Burke, who had been exhausted a few minutes earlier, was suddenly exhilarated. He and the other runners mingled with the townfolk.

Old man: "You know, this is the biggest thing to hit this town since the tornado 15 years ago."

Burke invited some of the people into Van One. There, sitting dejectedly, soaking his foot, was Hickey.

Burke: "This is where we live, cook, eat, sleep. This is our home for three weeks."

Local resident: "What's he doing?"

Burke: "Soaking his foot. He got an infection."

Local resident: "Oh, he's the one who couldn't run. Heard about that on the radio."

Hickey pulled his still-swollen, infected foot out of the water and started to dry it.

Burke: "Keep soaking it."

Hickey plunked his foot back into the bucket.

Local resident: "You gonna be able to run tomorrow, son?"

Hickey: "I hope so. I think the swelling is going down. It feels a lot cooler."

The cops and the people of Newberry and Dollarville traded goodwill for another 20 minutes. Then Van One slowly pulled away toward the next hand-off point.

9:57 P.M. DICK BONNEAU

"I took the hand-off about halfway through town and then ran down a little detour highway about two miles to the main highway. All along the way people kept waving and wishing me well. I was a little sad, though. I knew this would be my last run in the United States. And I was sorry to leave after all the great receptions — especially the one in Newberry."

Ten minutes after Van One pulled out of Newberry, the city resembled a ghost town. Not a soul was on the street. Only one restaurant remained open — a small diner. The town had stayed open far past its bedtime — waiting for the runners. And now, totally spent, it fell into a sound slumber.

Bonneau finished his 10 miles and handed the baton to Chuck Foote. After a quick shower, Bonneau and the other members of Van One gathered around Uncle Alex for some bedtime stories.

Shearer: "Uncle Alex and one of his nephews had to run extra far today, so he is very tired. But he will still accommodate the literary instinct of his nephews by reading some bedtime stories."

Chorus: "Yippee! Hooray for Uncle Alex!"

Bonneau: "All heart."

Shearer: "Shut up, Bonneau. Okay, our first story deals with a one-legged transvestite who is deeply attracted to maimed World War Two veterans . . ."

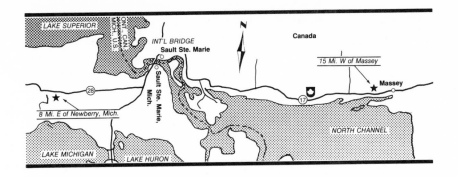

THE EIGHTEENTH DAY
Thursday, July 1, 1976

The Bicentennial relay had now covered 3,130 miles, and the team was less than 70 miles from the Canadian border. First Foote, then Murphy, then Clark ran along Highway 28 toward Sault Ste. Marie, Michigan, and the International Bridge, which connects it with Sault Ste. Marie, Canada.

2:47 A.M. FRANK JANOWICZ

Highway 28 was cut through a dense, primeval forest. Frank Janowicz — with Johnny Mathis's "Chances Are" breaking the silence — thundered down the highway, seemingly oblivious to the serenity and beauty around him.

In Camper Two, the runners were too excited to sleep. The border was just 20 miles away, and they and the other runners would cross it together. But the talk now was of their just-completed twenty-third legs.

Murphy: "I thought this one was gonna be flat, but it was all uphill."

Clark: "Mine, too."

Foote: "Hey, wait a minute, guys. We ain't in the middle of no mountains. What the fuck is this 10 miles uphill?"

Murphy: "It was a steady grade . . ."

Clark: "There was an incline all through it . . ."

Foote: "Here are you guys runnin' through the middle of a molehill, and you're makin' it into a mountain."

Out on the highway, Bob Jarvis, barely awake, stumbled out of Van Three into the cold. There, alone, motionless, he waited for the hand-off. He stared blankly down the road at Janowicz, then turned, wrapped his arms around his chest, jogged a couple of steps in place and stood shivering, ready to begin his twenty-third 10-mile run.

As Janowicz closed to within 200 yards of Jarvis, the pace car called out his mileage: "Nine miles. Somebody up there must be watching over ya."

But Janowicz was in no mood for charity. He might run 9.7 or 9.8 miles, but not just nine.

Jarvis watched Janowicz close to within 25 yards of him, then slowly he extended his left arm behind him for the hand-off and gazed blankly ahead. Every move, however simple, seemed to take a maximum physical effort.

Janowicz charged to the hand-off point, but instead of handing off, he sprinted past Jarvis, bellowing as he did: "It's only nine miles!"

For a moment, Jarvis stood frozen, stunned. This had never happened to him before in any relay. He watched the slowly disappearing figure of Janowicz and exploded: "Run the whole way, Janowicz!" His voice grew louder, his pitch higher. "Run across the goddamn border!" Louder and higher. "Take the fuckin' thing to Montreal!" Jarvis kicked at the dirt. He was wide awake.

Van Three had set up incorrectly on faulty orders from Van Two. Suddenly the drivers of the two campers, who were parked just 50 yards from one another, were on the two-way radio "conversing." Sgt. Eddie Watkins of Van Three was as angry as he was outranked by Assistant Chief of Police George Beck of Van Two. Pat Connelly recalls their spirited exchange:

"Eddie started yelling into the two-way: 'Goddamnit! I'm tired of this shit. Can't you ever set up right?' And the chief says, 'Who am I talking to?' And Eddie says, 'You're talking to Eddie Watkins, and I'm tired of this shit.' The chief is listening to this, and he says, 'You wanna get out and fight? You wanna have fisticuffs?' He was kidding, you know. But he was upset. He'll remember it."

Jarvis hopped back into Van Three, which sped ahead one mile and parked. Once again, Jarvis jumped out of the van and waited for the hand-off. This time it came.

Janowicz: "I'm not gonna stop no one mile short for nobody. I don't give a damn who's out there waitin' for me. A tenth or two, I don't care. But not a mile. That's horseshit."

As the team approached the Canadian border, the strain of 18 days of running, irregular hours and cramped quarters was having a telling effect. At first it seemed only Janowicz, in his volatile way, had expressed the increasing pressures. But now almost every team member was moving toward the edge. Small differences — such as gradual inclines versus mountains — became battlegrounds at 3 A.M. Hickey's injury, mileage, distance, the clocks — all were contributing to a mounting tension.

As Bob Jarvis carried the baton over gentle rolling hills toward Sault Ste. Marie, Pat Connelly, a perennial tease and practical joker, plotted to test the nerves of his teammates just a bit more.

5:17 A.M. PAT CONNELLY

Pat Connelly would lead the team over the International Bridge into Canada.

"I was a little ticked off at Janowicz for passing Jarvis and because of the exchange between Beck and Watkins. When I got the baton, I just put my head down and took off. It was six miles to the border. I hit the first five in 31 minutes."

About three miles into his leg, Connelly charged by the thirteen other runners who were preparing to join him at the International Bridge.

Connelly: "I just ripped by — didn't even say hello. They were hurrying like mad, getting their USA sweats on, trying to get ready. They knew I was going fast. Someone said, 'God, slow him down. He's gonna get to the bridge before we do.'"

Ten minutes later, at the five-mile mark, Van Three passed Connelly on its way to the assembly point near the bridge.

Connelly: "Bob Jarvis leaned out the door and yelled, 'You better slow down! We're gonna meet you and go across together.' And I says, 'Jarvis, I'm runnin' for time.' They're always screamin' about runnin' for time. 'So if you get out here, you better be ready to go.'"

Jarvis slammed the camper door and threw a tantrum, stomping his feet, pounding the wall and screaming, "Damn him! Damn him! He's goin' too fast. I know he's not gonna slow down for us. He's gonna make us run too fast."

Frank Mullens joined in the panic: "Christ, he's not gonna slow down. Damn Connelly. Goddamn him, anyway."

By now the camper was in an uproar. The drivers radioed the other campers. The panic spread. And for good reason. Most of the men had just been awakened for this unprecedented "team" run. They were tired and tight. Their common fear was that they'd pull every muscle in their legs if they were forced to run a six-minute-per-mile or better pace.

Moments later, dressed in their blue AAU-USA sweats, the runners gathered at the base of the bridge, waiting worriedly for Connelly.

Hickey: "And here came Mr. Connelly, hot to trot. He just shot by us. I was real upset. I didn't know how I was gonna keep up with him on my bad foot."

Connelly: "They saw me coming full-throttle, probably at a five-minute-per-mile pace. And they all had their hands in the air trying to stop me.

"I shot past 'em, ignoring 'em. I went maybe 10 yards and then stopped and looked back. They were just standing there, kinda stunned. Then they all joined in.

"We jogged about an 11-minute pace over the bridge, but I still heard all kinds of moans and groans back there: 'Slow down. We're straggling now. Wait for Hickey.'"

Hickey: "We couldn't get him to slow down his tempo right away. I was in a lot of pain. I felt like I was gonna pass out. Honestly, as much as I love that man and respect him, I coulda killed him on that bridge."

Connelly's pace was not, in fact, 11 minutes-per-mile. It was closer to nine minutes, and that was too fast for most of the runners. At one point, team captain Chuck Foote pulled alongside Connelly and hollered, "Slow down!" Connelly yelled back, "I can't go any slower."

Moments later, Dick Bonneau and John Rockwood shouted at him, "Slow down! Slow down!" Connelly turned around angrily: "It was you guys who wanted the clocks on." He kept his pace steady at nine-minutes-per-mile."

Across the bridge the Bicentennial relay moved. There was little goodwill.

Connelly was out front. Hickey lagged far behind — occasionally sprinting, trying to catch up. And between them were twelve angry men, complaining, yelling and pleading with Connelly to slow down.

Connelly: "Finally, I just stopped and waited for them."

It was Pat Connelly who just a couple days earlier had told of the excitement he and his teammates felt about the prospect of crossing an international border as running ambassadors of the United States. Now, during a leg marred by disharmony, there was disillusionment, too.

The runners were greeted by one lone customs guard, who ran halfway across the bridge with them. On the other side, there was a scattering of minor government officials and virtually no press. But it wasn't Canada's fault. Somehow Bob Burke had misread his own schedule. The team had arrived one hour early. The few Canadian officials who were there tried to regroup. They held a brief welcoming ceremony, and a few reporters and camera crews hurried to the scene.

Connelly: "We come all this way, and we're greeted by a customs guard. It was more amusing than exciting, I guess. Welcome to Canada."

The first time the LAPD relay team crossed a national border was during the Tijuana to Vancouver run.

When the team arrived in Mexico, it was greeted by fifteen of Tijuana's finest. The Mexican cops were a colorful group. The chief wore a gray pinstriped suit and sunglasses. His men were dressed in black pants, maroon shirts, and each carried a different type of gun—one a .45-caliber pearl-handled revolver.

The hosts quickly formed an escort and led the LAPD through the streets of the border town at breakneck speeds — up to 80 miles an hour by some accounts.

The relay started at Tijuana's boxing arena. Members of Mexico's national basketball team ran with the LAPD's two lead runners. The second runner was Alex Shearer:

"Each of these guys would run one mile at a time. Then a new one would come in—like the Pony Express. The first few runners were carrying this flare, which was supposed to be something like the Olympic torch. But burning pieces from the flare kept falling on their hands, so they finally gave that up.

"Anyway, they kept sending in these fresh runners, and by the fourth mile, I was getting real tired. One guy ran ahead of me, and this police official drove up and motioned for him to get back.

"Finally I crossed the border with this one guy. And he goes two, three, four miles with me, and then he says something in Spanish and disappears."

Connelly: "That guy had to be picked up at four miles and taken back. He was trying to leave the country."

6:32 A.M. FRANK MULLENS

Frank Mullens took the baton on the streets of Sault Ste. Marie, Canada. At the border, team captain Chuck Foote called a meeting. The subject: Bob Hickey.

Hickey: "Chuck told the team that if I passed again or couldn't complete my next leg, I'd be out. But then he said it'd be nothing to be ashamed of, 'cause everyone knew about the problem with my foot. They all gave me a lot of encouragement. Really made me feel good. Kiser asked me how I felt. I said the swelling was down a little, but it still felt like there was a balloon in my shoe. He said, 'You'll make it.' I said, 'I don't know.'"

As Frank Mullens ran through the streets of Sault Ste. Marie, a patrol car pulled up beside the pacer.

Local cop: "Welcome to Canada."

Garrison: "Thank you. We're really glad to be here." Then he paused. "Tell me, how do you really feel about all this?"

The local cop's smiling face suddenly turned serious. "It makes me feel really proud to be a policeman. You're representing your country, but you're also representing policemen everywhere. We're living your experiences vicariously."

There was silence for a few moments, and then the local cop made a request: "There's a driveway that runs off the main street in front of our police station. Would you honor us by running through that driveway?"

Garrison relayed the request to Frank Mullens.

Mullens: "By all means."

The drivers and runners of Van One gathered at a restaurant on the outskirts of Sault Ste. Marie for breakfast. After the team ordered, Bob Burke asked Bob Hickey to walk outside with him.

Burke: "Look, Bob — I don't even know how to put this. But for the sake of the team, I think you should pull out. Do it 'cause we're so close to the finish. It's not being unmanly. You'll still be a member of the team, no matter what you decide.

"But I've been watching you walk. I can tell you're hurting. You've only got four more legs. That's nothing. But you could permanently damage yourself. And another thing — if you drop out after one or two miles, and Alex's chest acts up, and he can only go a couple, I'll have to run 26 miles — a marathon. I can do that. I'd be willing to do that. But I think it's unnecessary to put that kind of pressure on yourself and the team.

"So I'm saying — don't think you have anything to prove. You've done an incredible job for the team. You'll still be a part of the team. But I think you should stop running. It's too dangerous."

Hickey turned and walked a few steps. His eyes filled with

tears. He could feel his foot throbbing. The heat and swelling of the infection told him Burke was right. Slowly he turned and faced Burke.

Hickey: "I know what you're trying to say. But I'm sure I can do it. I soaked the foot twice last night. I'm gonna see Kiser in about an hour, and he's gonna treat it. I think I can race walk on it, take the pressure off the infected ball of the foot and put it on the heel. I wanna try anyway."

Burke: "I'll say a prayer for you, Bob."

Hickey: "I . . ."

That's all Sgt. Hickey was able to say. He turned and walked toward the highway. This time there was no pillow in which to bury his face.

Mullens turned onto the driveway that circles in front of the police building. There fifty policemen had gathered on the steps to show their respect for their fellow officers.

Mullens: "Instead of just running around the driveway and saying hi, I decided to run up the stairs and shake their hands. Well, I got up about two steps, and I tripped. Fell flat on my face."

Garrison: "All the officers ran down to help him, trying to grab him and pick him up."

Mullens: "One guy reached over to pick me up, and I accidentally hit him in the head."

Garrison: "By now, Frank is about three shades of red. But he did shake everyone's hand."

Mullens: "My big appearance, and I fall on the fucking steps. Can you beat that?"

Mullens regained his composure, ran the last couple of miles through Sault Ste. Marie, and then headed onto the King's Highway, the road that would take the team to Montreal.

Traffic on the highway was especially heavy. It was Dominion Day, Canada's equivalent of the Fourth of July. In addition, Lou McClary's publicity had not preceded the team this time. The result was a stream of angry drivers who didn't quite understand why they were being held up by a man in shorts, running in front of a car traveling eight miles an hour. Countless motorists honked their horns or yelled or swore as they drove by Mullens.

Finally he had enough. He ran off the highway onto the shoulder, which was covered with soft sand and loose rocks. Ideal conditions — for an injury.

7:51 A.M. EDDIE GARCIA

Garcia took the baton in what should have been idyllic surroundings — Lake Superior to his right, tree-covered rolling
hills to his left, and just off the road to both sides, grassy
farmlands, with houses neatly situated on spacious plots, and
cattle and horses lounging and grazing in the sun. But it was not
idyllic. The traffic continued to speed by. And unlike Mullens,
Garcia could not afford to tempt fate on the soft shoulder.

Garcia: "I was shocked by the drivers. They were going extremely fast. Just barely missed the follow car and came extremely close to me. I felt very uncomfortable. However, I was
determined to run on the pavement because of my sore knee."

Van One drove along the King's Highway and radioed ahead
for Van Four's location. The support camper said it was parked
about 30 miles ahead. A half-hour later, Van One pulled up
beside it. Bob Hickey hobbled over to see "Doctor" Kiser.

Three times during the past 12 hours, Hickey had soaked his
foot, trying to reduce the swelling and infection. About 90 minutes before Hickey's next scheduled run, Kiser took over.

The pain had never been worse for Garcia. It felt as though
daggers were being thrust into his right knee with every step.
For the first time the pain slowed him down. He tried running on
his heels to take the weight off the knee. But he only succeeded
in aggravating his left arch. Each step sent shock waves through
his fatigued body.

"I could barely tolerate the pain on that one," he said afterward. Then he drew his boxing analogy: "I'm in the final
rounds. Four more legs and it's over. I've come too far. There's
no way I'll let my opponent beat me now."

9:12 A.M. CURT HALL

Just minutes before he took the baton, Curt Hall received a
message from Ron Kiser: Slow down to permit maximum treatment for Hickey's foot.

In Van Four, Kiser soaked Hickey's foot for a half-hour in
water that Hickey described as "almost unbearably hot." Next
Kiser upped the dose of Xylocaine from 1 to 5 percent, shooting
it directly into the infected area. Then he inserted a specially
built foam rubber cushion between the ball and toes of Hickey's

foot to relieve some of the pressure there. And finally, he issued a warning.

Hickey: "He told me that I would have to be extremely careful. Otherwise, I could damage my foot. He asked me if I planned to run. I said no, I'd race-walk it. It would be easier, because the pressure would be on the heel and not on the ball of the foot where the infection was located. I walked out of the van and tested it. The Xylocaine hadn't taken hold yet, and there was still a lot of discomfort."

Curt Hall finished his first five miles in 36 minutes. The information was relayed to Kiser, who sent back a terse order: Slow him down.

Hall: "I came up these hills, and I decided the only way I could really slow it down was to turn around and go up the hills backwards. I managed to con Rudy DeLeon out of the follow car to run with me. And we carried on a conversation for the next five miles. We could look each other in the eye and talk. I ran about a nine-minute pace, which is the equivalent of six-minutes-a-mile goin' forward."

By now, Lou McClary had contacted many of the radio and television stations in the area, and the run was being explained to the Canadian people. They responded warmly. Waves and greetings replaced the earlier anger. People began to gather on their lawns and alongside the road to welcome Hall. "They came out and wished me good luck. It was very nice runnin' in Canada."

Ron Kiser stood by the side of the road, assaying the terrain Hickey would challenge in about 10 minutes.

Kiser: "Okay, Robert. Now listen. Take care. Take your time. No rush. I'll be in the follow car."

Hickey paced back and forth, testing his foot and thinking. He knew as soon as he touched the baton, he had to go 10 miles. Otherwise the pressure would be on Shearer. Yesterday, as planned, Shearer had completed just five miles of his own leg, in addition to Hickey's 10. If Hickey dropped out this time, Shearer would have to run the remainder of Hickey's leg, in addition to his own 10. Theoretically that could mean a 20-mile run for Shearer if Hickey dropped out immediately.

And if Shearer were unable to run — if, for instance, his chest spasms returned and forced him to quit — Bob Burke would then have to run the remainder of Hickey's leg (10 at most),

Shearer's leg (also 10 at most) and his own: A possible 30 miles total.

The whole process could have a snowball effect, literally wiping out runner after runner. There were just three days left in the relay, but its fate could very well be decided in the next 90 minutes.

Every team member with the exception of Hall, and Connelly and DeLeon, who were in the pace car, gathered at the hand-off point.

Hickey: "They gave me some pill, and I just feel pretty good. I'm floating right about now."

Curt Hall jogged slowly toward the hand-off point. Johnny Mathis's "Chances Are" rose softly from the pace car loudspeaker.

Chorus: "Attaboy, Curt. Nice goin', Curt. Go get 'em, Hickey."

Jarvis: "We're all here to see Hickey walk his little heart out."

10:33 A.M. BOB HICKEY

Bob Hickey took the baton and began race-walking over roller coaster terrain.

To most people, race-walking is an abberation of athletic motion — the walkers thrusting their arms behind their back, shooting their legs straight forward, knees unbent, heels driving into the ground, then pushing off with the toes, the rear end making the exaggerated motions of a spastic streetwalker. It's difficult for the uninitiated to tell whether the walker is moving smoothly or whether he's struggling. But in Hickey's case, it was apparent: He was in trouble immediately. His arms were flailing, as if trying to do the job by themselves. His shoulders were tense, his foot movements irregular and uncertain.

"I just couldn't get adjusted to the way the foot felt," he said later. "My shoe felt like it was full of cotton. And I wasn't used to walking. I hadn't race-walked in a long time."

After a quarter of a mile, it didn't seem possible he could last 10. He was pushing himself. Hurting himself. His jerky movements made him look like a man possessed.

One-and-a-half miles out, Hickey hit a steep incline, his first real test. His arms began swinging wildly for momentum. He struggled to bring them up and back. It is arm movement that gives walkers their power — without it, there can be no leg drive. Hickey struggled to coordinate his legs and arms. And at the same time, he continued to rotate his damaged foot, trying to keep pressure off. Hickey's foot was virtually numb from the

Xylocaine, and that was dangerous. He had to be careful not to come down on the injured area, and thus inadvertently compound an already serious injury. Pain is nature's way of saying beware, but at this point Bob Hickey felt no pain. He was playing a high stakes game with his body.

Hickey drove his elbows and shoulders back, and went up the hill like a little tin soldier, wound to double speed. A car shot by and the driver waved. Hickey broke his stern concentration for a moment and waved back. In the pace car, Ron Kiser and Rudy DeLeon laughed.

DeLeon: "A showman to the end."

Hickey reached the top of the hill and began a gradual decline. He was moving with neither grace nor form. But he was moving — at about a nine-minute pace. By two miles, he had gotten his rhythm. "From two miles on, I knew I could do it," he recalled. "I actually began to enjoy it."

The cycle of hill-decline-flats was to be repeated over and over again, as Hickey waddled his way along the King's Highway.

"A lot of people slowed down their cars and shouted encouragement to me," Hickey said. "They yelled, 'Hang in there . . . keep on truckin' . . . hey, walker, that's the way to go.' I could also see some people laughing as they went by, 'cause they're not used to seeing people race-walk."

Hickey reached the five-mile mark in 45 minutes and 45 seconds, a 9:09-minute-per-mile pace. He was now "locked in" — there was no real effort involved any more. He took hill after hill. His legs, which were wobbling slightly at the start, became straight and strong. His arm swing, smooth and relaxed. "That walk," Hickey would recall later, "was my longest time out on the road, but it went by a lot faster than a lot of my runs did."

Hickey finished his walk in 92 minutes and 45 seconds. Only a small number of people in this country could run 10 miles that fast over any type of terrain.

John Denver's "Country Road" played on the pace car's loudspeaker as Hickey handed the baton to Alex Shearer. The runners and drivers of Van One cheered.

Hogue: "Attaboy, Bobby. You okay?"

Hickey (gasping, barely audible): "Oh, yeah. Yeah. But I'm pooped. Oooh. Aaargh . . ."

Hickey, his hands on his hips, walked about 20 yards down the road, then turned around and walked back, trying to cool down and retrieve his breath. He was soaked in perspiration.

Unidentified: "Hey, Bobby — what'd they give you before you went out there?"

Hickey: "Ahhh . . . argh . . . I know last night Kiser gave me some muscle relaxers. And a pill. Boy, I was really sleeping. I just coulda kept on sleeping. And he woke me up with cold water this morning. And right after I got out walking, I felt pretty good. I don't know what it was."

Unidentified: "How's the foot feel?"

Hickey: "The ball's pretty inflamed. But I don't put as much pressure on it walking as I do running. I'm just tired. I haven't walked in a long time."

Dr. Kiser walked up to his prize patient.

Kiser: "Okay, let's go back now."

Unidentified: "Will he be able to run tomorrow?"

Kiser: "He could have run today."

Unidentified: "Run today?"

Kiser: "But we don't need it. We didn't have to have a run out of him. He came in here with a 92:45. That's all we needed. We don't even need that."

Unidentified: "You gave him a muscle relaxant and a sleeping pill last night?"

Kiser: "I didn't give him anything last night."

Hickey: "Hey, you guys gave me . . ."

Kiser: "He took it himself." (Laughter)

Unidentified: "Muscle relaxant and a sleeping pill?"

Kiser: "Right."

Unidentified: "Bobby, congratulations."

Hickey: "Well, thank you very much. It's just a thrill to be back on the team. That was my biggest concern."

12:06 P.M. SHEARER-BURKE

Alex Shearer and Bob Burke, who had run 15 miles apiece their last time out, were prepared to run anything from 20 to 30 miles this time, depending on what Hickey did. Now each did their 10, took their showers and went to sleep. The fatigue and pressure of the past three weeks — and particularly the past 24 hours — had drained them.

Once before, Shearer and Burke had been victimized by Bob Hickey.

The incident occurred in 1968, during the team's first cross-country relay. The LAPD was battling an eight-man team from the Los Angeles County Sheriff's Department. The run was from Los Angeles to San Diego, 125 miles. Each man was to run three five-mile legs, a brutal pace because of the short rest (about three hours) between runs. To make matters worse, the relay began after work on a Friday night.

The lead changed hands throughout that night, with one team, then the other, seemingly headed for victory.

With two legs to go, Alex Shearer took the baton. He had about a half-mile lead.

Shearer: "Hickey was directing me, and he told me to go down this street. Well, right away I start hearing these mumblings from the pace car, 'Jeez, I think he might have gone the wrong way.' Then Burke (who was in one of the vans) picks up from the sheriff's two-way that I had gone the wrong way. And I hear Hickey talking to Burke, and I am about ready to kill Hickey. I'm mad as hell. And here comes the pace car up alongside me, and I'm ready to smash Hickey, and he looks out at me with these two big eyes, and he says, 'I'm sorry, Alex, but you're going the wrong way.' And I just said, 'That's okay, Bob.' I mean, he just looked like someone's puppy dog."

By now, Shearer had gone more than a mile out of his way. He turned and began chasing the San Diego runner. With about a mile to go, he saw him 200 yards ahead. Shearer began to sprint. "And then I heard this sheriff's deputy yell to their runner over their pacer's loudspeaker, 'Don't let that old man pass you.' And that just made me more mean and irritable."

Shearer passed the deputy and handed the baton to Bob Burke, the team's anchor man. Burke should have had a comfortable lead, but now he had to run his third and final leg all-out. He fell 800 yards behind at one point. But with 200 yards to go, he caught his rival and beat him. The margin of victory was 13 seconds.

2:38 P.M. — 5 P.M. ROCKWOOD-BONNEAU

As the team moved further and further away from Sault Ste. Marie and into the Canadian countryside, it again began to outpace the publicity machine of Lou McClary.

Rockwood: "The cars were flying by me — 60, 65 miles an hour. And the reception was very cold. I told someone, 'Hey, if the rest of Canada is like this, I wanna see about getting a bus out of here as soon as we get to Montreal.' This is for the birds."

Bonneau: "A lot of drivers were honking like they wanted me to get the hell out of the way. I think everybody on the team was a little surprised. We were getting a very cool reception from the Canadian people."

Inside Van Three, Jack Garrison was still fuming at the reception his van had received on the open highway six hours earlier: "About one out of twenty motorists go by and smile. Tremendous. These people can hang it in their ear."

Hall: "It's a big holiday here. We're just in their way. In small towns they'll be friendlier. They don't have the pressure. It'll be just like the U.S."

Garrison: "I don't believe it."

8:38 P.M. FRANK JANOWICZ

"About the second or third mile out, this guy in a station wagon was gettin' irritated. He kept honkin' his horn. Then, all of a sudden, he passed the follow car on the right and went over the gravel past me and yelled something. He missed me by about six inches. He was going 20 or 30 miles an hour, which means he coulda done damage on me.

"My first impulse was to kill him — get a gun and blow him right out of the car. At that time I woulda done it. No doubt in my mind. He woulda never done that again. I wished at the time I was carryin' a gun.

"I'm not sayin' I woulda killed him. I woulda beat the hell out of him. I woulda punished him so that he never did that again."

Welcome to Canada.

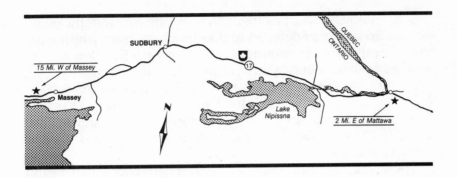

THE NINETEENTH DAY
Friday, July 2, 1976

11:16 P.M. PAT CONNELLY

Pat Connelly ran past a Dominion Day celebration in the town of Massey. "About 150 people were there, including the mayor," Connelly recalled. "When I came by, they applauded and screamed and yelled. It was almost like being back in the U.S.

"Then at the outskirts of town, I noticed Frank Mullens in a phone booth. I knew he was talking to his wife. They live about two miles from us, so I told him to have her hang up and call my wife and tell her that I'm about one mile into one of my legs in Massey, Canada. He did, and that was nice, because my wife could visualize me running with about an hour to go."

Serious running can put a tremendous strain on a marriage. Running requires spartan principles: dedication, discipline, sacrifice. And a spartan lifestyle: correct diet, plenty of sleep, long hours of training. It also requires a profound understanding from the nonrunning mate. Otherwise, the intense commitments and training can become battlegrounds.

It is virtually impossible to explain the "need" and the joys of running to someone who has never run. It's like trying to explain love to someone who has never loved. Or a belief in God to a nonbeliever. The uninitiated in these instances is being asked to take a leap of faith — or at least a leap of understanding. Most of the wives of the LAPD runners do not run themselves. But most have taken the leap of faith.

Joan Connelly, who has spent "half my life with a stopwatch," is one. So is Suzie Foote, a big booster of the team who would meet her husband in Montreal. And of course Sue Burke, who worked so many hours with her husband planning the run. Gigi Murphy loves to see her husband win races, and realizes it takes "constant training, which I don't mind." Vi Mullens supports her husband's running, though tortured by the pain he put himself through for this and previous relays. And Ginger Shearer backs Alex "100 percent."

There are two running wives—Bea Janowicz, who began running for her police reserve training, and Nina Hall, who has run a half-marathon. Both encouraged their husbands. Nina would be the only wife besides Suzie Foote to meet the team in Montreal.

Dawn Hickey felt her husband had "overextended" himself with his coaching, college work, and running. And Marlene Jarvis has "her own life," according to her husband, and is "not very interested in my running."

The other runners were either separated or divorced.

Virtually all of the married runners said they would not run if their wives didn't at least tolerate their training. In most cases, however, the wives were supportive. They realized running kept their husbands in top physical and mental condition. And they knew too well about the negative outlets used to relieve the tensions of police work.

Running might be time consuming, but most of these wives felt it was time well spent.

12:20 A.M. FRANK MULLENS

After 19 grueling days on the road, Frank Mullens was near exhaustion. He rarely spoke to his teammates anymore. Virtually all his energies were focused on sleep, food and summoning the strength to run his next 10 miles.

His sleeping conditions with Eddie Garcia in the "coffin" were intolerable. Even on his best nights — or days, as the case might be—he claimed to sleep only sporadically and two or three hours at most. Connelly disputed that, saying his old friend was sleeping at least twice that long. But in his mind, Mullens "knew" he was getting little rest. And that's where such things matter—in the mind.

As Mullens took the baton for the twenty-fourth time, he was in a state of acute fatigue. He wasn't ready for what was about to happen.

"I was running along this real nice area—farmlands, neat

little houses. About three miles along, Eddie Watkins says on the pace car loudspeaker: 'Frank, we've treated you all right on this run, haven't we?' I acknowledged him by waving the baton. He says, 'When we came through Grand Forks we set up a nice reception for you.' I waved the baton. 'Munising?' I waved the baton. 'John Day?' I waved the baton. 'All those places, we treated you real nice, huh, Frank? Great, 'cause we have one more surprise for you.' Eddie paused for a few moments, then blurted out: 'The camper can't get started. Battery's dead. It can't get to the next hand-off point. It can't contact Van Four. What I'm saying Frank — you might have a long run tonight. A very long run.'

"I could see myself running all night, forever and ever."

About 15 minutes later, Van Three made contact with Van Four, which sped over and mechanic George DeWitt remedied the situation with jumper cables. Eddie Watkins was informed, but he decided to withhold that information from Mullens. He thought he'd have some fun instead.

Watkins (at the five-mile mark): "Frank, we calculate you're only 453 miles from Montreal. At your pace, you'll be there Sunday at noon. Steady she goes."

Mullens: "I didn't know whether to laugh, cry or die. I mean, it was one-thirty in the morning. No relief anywhere."

Watkins (at the six-mile mark): "Frank, you're closing in on Montreal. The only problem is you might have to go it alone for a few hours, 'cause J.P. (the driver) and me might pull off the road for a snooze. It gets very tiring driving this car."

Mullens was too tired to acknowledge anything. He began to set his mind on running perhaps 15 miles. He could do that, he thought. Fifteen. Yes. If the terrain stayed flat, he could do it.

Watkins (at the seven-mile mark): "Attaboy, Frankie. "Lookin' real good. Strong. You'll be in Ottawa before you know it, and Montreal is just a hop, skip, and a jump. Boy, will those guys be surprised when you carry it in all by yourself and get all the glory."

Mullens was in no mood for glory. His legs were growing heavy. His breathing labored. His body drained. He kept throwing one foot in front of the other. Hoping for some good news from the loudspeaker. Hoping the terrain continued flat. Hoping his body didn't fail him.

The night was quiet. There was no traffic, no other signs of life. Just a 54-year-old Los Angeles police lieutenant, running along a dimly lit highway, a car creeping slowly behind.

Watkins (at the eight-mile mark): "Frank, you are eight miles into your journey without end."

Mullens was now wrapped in thought — confusing thought. One moment hope — "I can do 15." The next moment depression — "I'm very tired." The next moment despair — "I really could be running all night."

But moments later the uncertainty ended. Van Three came roaring down the highway, its horn signaling its triumphant recovery.

And 20 minutes later, Mullens was back inside the van, gulping down grapefruit juice, eating a peanut-butter-and-jelly sandwich, and relating his adventure to Pat Connelly. Mullens concluded: "Eddie is a funny guy. Without him, I think we all woulda cracked up long ago."

Connelly had sat expressionless throughout Mullens's 10-minute account. Finally he responded: "Frank, I don't understand you. Haven't you any consideration for your teammates? I mean, here it is, two in the morning, and you think it's real funny, what happened. We couldn't get any sleep while all this was going on. You had it easy out there, joking around with Eddie. But how about thinkin' about us, sitting here in the camper, unable to sleep?"

With that, Connelly walked back to his bunk, crawled in and closed his eyes. Mullens, open-mouthed, watched in disbelief.

1:52 A.M. EDDIE GARCIA

"The twenty-fourth was my worst leg of the entire relay. I was physically tired. Emotionally tired. My right knee was killing me. It was two-thirty in the morning. And the receptions through Canada had been less than we had expected. We felt unwelcome. I thought, 'What the hell am I doing here?'"

Shortly before the run, Garcia applied heat to his sore knee. "I'll be glad when this is over," he said. "But if I had it to do over again, I'd do it. Just for the experience. Just what it's taught me about myself. How much I can take physically and emotionally. What my talents are under adverse situations."

Garcia removed the hydrocollator from his knee and limped toward the shower. Suddenly he turned. His eyes — sad and pained — reflected his ordeal. "I've put myself through hell, man. Pure hell."

3:20 A.M. CURT HALL

Hall had been awakened about 20 minutes before his run. "I was still a little woozy when I got the baton. At about four miles, my system finally began to work. I had to jump off the road and get my business taken care of. Even so, I ran that leg in about 84 minutes."

4 A.M.
Van One

The alarm beside Bob Hickey's bed jolted him from his slumber just two hours after he had crawled under the covers and one hour before his twenty-fifth run. He moved groggily through the dark camper to the radio.

Hickey: "Camper Four, this is Party Time One. Come in."

Kiser: "I hear ya, Party Time. I'll be right over."

Moments later, Kiser arrived with his medicine chest. First, he carefully re-inserted the custom-built pad he'd made for Hickey's shoe. Then he shot a 5 percent solution of Xylocaine into Hickey's foot. And then, for 10 minutes, they discussed strategy. Finally, they decided that Hickey would race-walk again but that he'd test his sore foot by running the last 50 yards of every mile.

4:51 A.M. BOB HICKEY

Hickey began his leg 23 miles west of Sudbury, population 97,741, home of Canada's Big Nickel — an imposing monument to the city's nickel industry, one of the largest in the world.

"I was ready to go," Hickey recalled. "I wanted to walk faster and better than yesterday." And he did.

"A couple of miles out, a carload of people yelled and whistled at me and gave me all kinds of encouragement. Then I went up this hill, and I was just ready to break out of my walk into a jog, but they were still cheering my walking, so I just stayed with it and really pulled on that hill. They had all gotten out of their car — I think seven of 'em — and they were standing on the top of the hill, clapping and screaming. When I got to the top, I shook hands with each of them.

"Every mile after that, I broke into a slow jog for 40 or 50 yards. It wasn't bad going from a walk to a jog, but back again to a walk is very difficult, because you have to get your hips back into the movement, into the rhythm."

About halfway through Hickey's leg, a police motor escort arrived from Sudbury. A motor sergeant and two officers rode ahead of Hickey.

"They kept looking back and shouting encouragement. They'd been told I was injured and had to walk."

With a mile to go, two more motorcycle officers joined the

escort. Once again, Canada was beginning to warm up to its American visitors.

Sudbury, Ontario, Canada

Because it had been months since Bob Hickey had race-walked, his body was sore — particularly his shins, hips, and back, which take tremendous shock from the rigors of race-walking. "But my foot felt good, and that's all I was worried about.

"When I finished," he recalled, "I was totally exhausted. I felt like I'd just finished a 35-kilometer walk [21.7 miles]. But it was a good exhaustion. Not the kind where you think you're gonna die."

Hickey was invited to take a sauna and shower at the Sudbury police station. Minutes later, he was luxuriating in a wood-tiered sauna, dousing himself with cold water and drinking liberally from a nearby hose. Later, he took a long, leisurely shower and shaved for the first time in three days.

"I actually felt halfway human," Hickey said.

Alex Shearer passed the biggest smelting operation in the world — the International Nickel Company of Canada iron ore plant at Copper Cliff, just outside Sudbury. One of the smokestacks reaches 1,250 feet into the usually gray, polluted Canadian sky. Sulfur fumes pour constantly from that smokestack — a signal of industrial power and environmental disdain.

"One of the motor officers asked me if the sulfur fumes bothered me," Shearer said. "I told him no. I guess the air in Los Angeles prepares you for anything."

7:46 A.M. BOB BURKE

Burke carried the baton past the "Big Nickel" into Sudbury, and the warm Canadian welcome that had started anew on Hickey's leg continued.

"Sudbury was when I first started to notice people honking and waving and giving the thumb-up and all that. The reception was real nice in Sudbury."

And for good reason. Publicists Lou McClary and Rich Wemmer had been able to alert the local news media about the run, and Sudbury's radio stations were carrying bulletins nearly every half-hour.

Meanwhile, radio and newspaper reporters had gathered at City Hall, where the team was being honored by the mayor, chief of police and other city dignitaries. The mayor handed Pat Connelly a memorial nickel, which was to be presented to Mayor

Tom Bradley of Los Angeles. Then each team member — including support personnel — received plaques.

8:53 A.M. JOHN ROCKWOOD

Rockwood ran through the suburbs of Sudbury. All along the way people lined the streets, greeting him with waves and cheers. The coldness of the day before was quickly fading from memory.

As Rockwood finished his run, he glanced to his right. There, outside a freshly painted blue house between two trees, hung an American flag — about four-by-six feet. A black woman in her late 30s and her three daughters stood on the porch waving at Rockwood. He waved and started toward the house with Bob Burke, who had already talked to the woman.

Burke: "They just moved here from New York and read about the run in the newspaper about a month ago. She said she and her daughters decided to sew an American flag and hang it out for us."

Burke and Rockwood approached the porch.

Burke: "This is John Rockwood, who just got through running."

Woman: "You are amazing. I don't know how you can do it."

Rockwood: "It's a lot easier than it seems. A lot easier than all the work that went into that flag."

Woman: "Oh, I just felt I had to do something!"

Burke: "It's just tremendous. The team wanted me to thank you."

Woman: "Thank you. And good luck the rest of the way."

10:11 A.M.
Vans One and Two

For the next 70 miles, past farms and one-street business districts, the runners were embraced by their Canadian hosts.

Bonneau: "From Sudbury on, people were all over the place, wishing us well. It was fantastic."

Foote: "Marvelous run. People waving. Honking horns. Fantastic."

Murphy: "Great run. People ran up to me and shook my hand. I felt great."

1:30 P.M. DICK CLARK

As Dick Clark ambled across the Canadian countryside, Chuck Foote, Jim Murphy and Frank Janowicz talked about the relay — their strategies, their mistakes and their triumphs.

Foote: "I've run in every one of these since the San Francisco run, and each one has taught me something. But the last run — the Washington, D.C., relay, really prepared me for this one. That was our longest, and by the last three or four legs, I was exhausted. Just ppphhhlllfff . . . So I knew going into this one that you don't immediately go pour on the coals, because you risk serious injury. I did it before, and it screws you up. You go out and run under control and build."

Janowicz: "That's right. Chuck's one of the smartest runners. He just went out easy and got stronger. I blasted everything like a fool. I shoulda knew better, too. 'Cause I've been on these runs before. But I had this ego thing. If you can defeat ego, you've got it made."

Murphy: "You see, Frank, basically Chuck was an asshole. He knew all the secrets, but he kept them to himself until now. So while all of us were hobbling around like a bunch of cripples, he was gliding along in comfort. We're suffering, and he's going first-class. He's an asshole."

Everyone laughed. Better than anyone else, Murphy knew how Foote had tried to share his "secrets." The problem was that Murphy, Janowicz, Hickey and the other "walking wounded" hadn't wanted to listen.

With three miles to go, Clark was joined by Assistant Chief George Beck. Usually relaxed and easygoing, Beck had not been his usual self on the trip. He was preoccupied. His closest friends knew why, and they were concerned.

There had been telltale signs of his preoccupation during the trip. Time and again, Beck had set up at the wrong hand-off point, precipitating countless arguments with both Vans One and Three. Some of the officers had seen him immersed in thought late at night, obviously mulling over his problems, unable to sleep. The great escape these relays invariably provided hadn't come. Instead, the relay had become a prison of sorts for George Beck. His problems were too overwhelming.

Beck is a tough, proud, persevering man. In 1968, doctors took out one-third of his stomach. Cancer. They told him he "wasn't gonna make it." They gave up. Prescribed nothing. But Beck and his wife prescribed exercise.

"As soon as I got home from the hospital," he recalled, "I started walking to the corner, which was about a half a block away. Then my wife would help me back. I'd have to sit down three or four times. But one day, I made it all the way on my own."

Within a year, Beck was jogging. His body was getting stronger. The doctors were dead wrong. The cancer which they said would eat away and destroy George Beck had been defeated.

Since 1969, Beck had run two miles every day. That had seemed enough until this trip. "What these guys are doing is contagious," he said shortly before he joined Clark on the King's Highway. "I'm gonna run more miles when I get back. I'll have to set aside more time. Two miles just doesn't do it anymore." This time out, Beck ran three miles.

It was raining hard as Clark and Beck reached the hand-off point. The run, and the companionship of Clark, had taken the chief's mind off his problem. But the respite was brief. The problem was still there. Montreal was getting closer. And so was Los Angeles. And the trouble that awaited him there.

2:57 P.M. FRANK JANOWICZ

The ego dies hard in some men. Frank Janowicz had vowed to himself to run all his legs in Canada in under 70 minutes. At least he was healed. He could handle his latest dare. He pounded over the King's Highway in just over 67 minutes.

6:53 P.M. FRANK MULLENS

Frank Mullens carried the baton across an unpopulated stretch of Canadian countryside. Rain was now pounding down. But Mullens was ready for it. Perhaps too ready. He had on a T-shirt, a pullover running shirt and a sweatshirt. The rain drenched layer after layer. By the end of his 10 miles, he was carrying an extra 10 pounds.

Mullens had now run 250 miles in 19 days. Every 10-miler was now a war — a war of survival.

"But I can see the barn," he said. "I'm almost there. It's almost over."

8:19 P.M. EDDIE GARCIA

Ron Kiser had built foam rubber pads for Eddie Garcia's right shoe to cushion the shock to his sore knee. "And that finally did it," Garcia said. "For the first time in I-don't-know-how-long, I felt good. Real good."

Garcia's old captain at Hollenbeck, Rudy DeLeon, decided to run along. He thought he'd be able to help take Garcia's mind off his pain. He and Garcia had no way of knowing Kiser's pads would work so well.

DeLeon, in his mid-50s, was a plodder. He could keep up with

an injured Garcia. But Garcia wasn't hurting now, and so De-
Leon had to push himself. As they ran through the cool Canadian night, the two Chicano cops were serenaded by another
Chicano — Freddy Fender — whose south Texas twang swelled
from the pace car's loudspeaker.

Garcia pushed the pace to a sub-eight-minute-mile. DeLeon
knew how depressed Garcia had been about his injury. And so
he said nothing about the pace, which was becoming more and
more difficult to maintain. Garcia breezed along. DeLeon gritted
his teeth and kept going.

DeLeon was a driver. On countless occasions he had said the
runners were the stars of the team. There was no way he was
going to slow one of them down.

Garcia didn't know how fast he was running. Only when his
time — 75:06 — was announced by the follow car did he realize
the strain he had put on DeLeon.

9:34 P.M. CURT HALL

Curt Hall ran over rolling hills. A light rain splashed across his
face. His pace was seven minutes per mile.

Back in his camper, Garcia put in a call to Van Four.
Garcia: "Is El Viejo [the old man] there?"
DeLeon: "Yes, I'm here."
Garcia: "El Viejo — are you okay?"
DeLeon: "Fine. Fine."
Garcia: "I'm sorry I ran so hard. I didn't know."
DeLeon: "Don't worry. You've got enough on your mind. I'm
   a tough old bear. No young cub is gonna kill me."
Garcia: "Good night, El Viejo."
DeLeon: "Good night, Eddie — and thanks."

Hall was into his last two miles. The rain had turned into a
refreshing drizzle. The night air was warm.

Off the road, ahead to his right, was a small farmhouse. As
Hall drew closer, figures moved off the porch toward him. A
minute later, he was surrounded by three adults and five children.

Family: "We knew you were coming. Heard about it on the
radio. Waited for an hour. Good luck. God bless."

Hall stopped and shook their hands. There, on a lonely stretch
of highway in Canada, the rain and gentle breeze their only
witness, Canadian hosts welcomed the American messenger of
goodwill.

Welcome to Canada.

whirled around and fired blindly. He caught my dad in the face."

The bullet smashed through the left side of Officer Hickey's face, just beneath the eye. It shattered the cheek, severed the mastoid gland, and exited through the back of the neck. The bullet missed the brain by a distance equal to the thickness of a piece of paper.

Officer Hickey managed to get off one round as he crumpled to the pavement. The shot went wild. The suspect escaped. Hickey lay on the street, bleeding, slowly dying for 15 minutes.

Hickey was on the critical list for 10 hours. Finally, his condition stabilized. The doctor told the family he'd make it.

But Officer Hickey would never work again. For over a year, he would have no equilibrium. He would be unable to climb even one step. The wound would leave him deaf in the left ear. And according to his son, "he still goes through periods of despondency."

Bob Hickey is 99 percent his mother — gentle, religious, caring. He is the antithesis of the tough, stereotype street cop that was his father.

But when he talks of "the incident," there is a transformation.

What would he have done if he had caught the man who shot his father?

"I would have killed him," he says coldly. "I would have done it with my hands."

At the six-mile mark, a young couple pulled off the road ahead of Hickey, snapped his picture, and wished him good luck. It was nearing midnight as Alex Shearer dragged himself from Van One and stood at the base of a steep hill, waiting for the hand-off.

Hickey: "I saw Alex there, but I thought the camper lined up a little short, so I decided to run the hill."

Hickey flew past the startled Shearer and the other runners and drivers who had gathered at the hand-off point.

Bonneau: "Everyone just shook their heads and said, 'I don't believe it.' I think he did it as a goodwill gesture to Alex for those 15 miles Alex ran for him a couple days earlier. But it was so silly, because everyone has to run 10 miles anyway. And a little hill at the beginning doesn't matter at all."

Hickey later received a stern lecture from Bob Burke about the necessity of handing off at the designated point.

Hickey had run 10.5 miles in 71 minutes and 35 seconds, which meant he ran a sub-70-minute 10-miler. He was ecstatic.

But at least one of his teammates was disgusted.

Connelly: "He wouldn't give the baton to Alex. Can you believe that? You know, toward the end of every relay he does some psycho thing like that. And I think everyone's still really upset with his pulling out of that one leg — because everybody's got injuries. He drops out. Then he comes back the next day and race-walks a 90 or something, testing it. Then he runs a 71. Watch. He'll be in the 60s the rest of the way.

"If his foot was that bad, how could he come back that fast — in two days? It doesn't stand. There's no sense to it."

One explanation for Hickey's incredible "recovery" might be found in Ron Kiser's medicine cabinet. Perhaps you can fool Mother Nature — with Xylocaine.

1:14 A.M. BOB BURKE

"An Ontario Provincial Police car escorted me through a beautiful forest. The officer told me I was running through the biggest moose area in Canada. And of course, as soon as he said that, I thought I heard something snortin' behind me."

2:28 A.M. JOHN ROCKWOOD

"I got it on the other side of moose country. Lotta hills. Thought I was on a roller coaster.

"I felt pretty heavy on that run. Legs were tired. But in the back of my mind I just kept thinking: 'One more (10-mile leg) to go. Just one more.'"

Most of the runners were trying to figure out who would carry the baton into Montreal. The consensus was that one of the last runners of Van Three, on their twenty-seventh leg, or one of the early runners of Van One, on their twenty-eighth leg, would draw the honor.

4:55 A.M. - 9:30 A.M.
Van Two

Van Two carried the baton through lush forests and sweeping farmlands. The first three runners — Foote, Murphy, and Clark — took it easy, enjoying the scenery and serenity of their twenty-sixth leg. But Frank Janowicz was still battling the clocks and himself. He wanted to leave no doubt that he was the fastest runner. (He still didn't know that Connelly had run the fastest 10-miler.)

And so, under ideal running conditions — cool weather and flat terrain — Janowicz ran perhaps the fastest five miles of the relay — 25:45. If he maintained that pace, he had a chance for a spectacular 52- or 53-minute leg.

But at the five-and-a-half mile mark, he began to crumble. "I just ran out of power. Every step was agony. By seven, my thighs and calves were like lead. At eight, it started to get real warm. And I hit a hill. I got dehydrated. My legs got rubbery. I finished on brute strength. That's all. Just brute strength."

Janowicz ran his 10 miles in just over 61 minutes. He had dropped from a five- to a seven-minute-per-mile pace for his last five miles.

12:18 P.M. FRANK MULLENS

Frank Mullens had slept six hours. He claimed it was two. The joke in the camper was that Mullens was being awakened every two or three hours and was running half the legs assigned to the five runners of Van Three, but that in his fatigued state, he didn't realize what was happening.

It might have been a joke to his teammates, but Mullens felt as though he had run 1,000 miles during the past three weeks. Now, mercifully, it was all coming to an end.

Mullens ran his twenty-sixth leg through a silent drizzle over hilly terrain in 76 minutes. Afterward, he sat in the van, eating. The running and living conditions had done a lot of things to Frank Mullens. But they had not dulled his appetite.

1:34 P.M. EDDIE GARCIA

It was another painful run for Eddie Garcia. The pads, which Ron Kiser had built and inserted to cushion Garcia's sore right knee, began to lose their effectiveness at about the four-mile mark — just as Garcia entered the town of Renfrew, population 9,048. Once again, the Canadian people halted their daily routine to welcome their American guests. Despite his pain, Garcia's lined face broke into a broad smile. He waved the baton, shook hands, returned greetings.

Back in Van Three, Mullens was sitting on a cooler, munching on his second peanut-butter-and-jelly sandwich, when Pat Connelly walked over.

Connelly: "We don't have any water left for a shower."

Mullens: "I don't care."

Connelly: "You don't care? Well, I do. You stink. You know, I read somewhere where old men just ordinarily smell bad. Something about their cells dying. You add that to a 10-mile run and wheww! You gotta get a shower."

Mullens put down his sandwich.

Mullens: "What the hell are you talking about, Connelly?"

Connelly: "It's true. Ask your doctor sometimes. He'll tell

you. Or maybe he'll hide it from you. Or maybe he's as old as you, and he won't admit it. But it's a fact. Old men have this weird odor, 'cause their cells are dyin'. And because their senses are going, they can't smell it. That makes it even worse. They think nothin' is wrong, but they're stinkin' up the place. That's what I really admire about Eddie . . ."

Mullens: "Wait a second. Garcia? He's never complained about anything. Hell, you're crazy, Connelly!"

Connelly: "Poor Eddie. His knee. Those lousy sleeping accommodations with you. And then the Old Man Smell Syndrome. Poor Eddie. He'll have nightmares about this. He might even qualify for a psycho discharge from the department 'cause of it. He won't say anything. He's holdin' it all in. But it's eatin' him up."

Mullens tossed the remainder of his sandwich into the trash.

Mullens: "Damn you, anyway, Connelly. You know all those miles you've run since you were a kid — I think they've scrambled your brain."

Connelly: "Maybe so. Maybe so. But my senses are still solid. And I can detect the smell syndrome. I'm gonna sit on the other side of the van."

Garcia was now east of Renfrew, running along a lonely stretch of highway sandwiched between broad stretches of farmlands, rain pounding his fatigued body. "I just kept thinking: 'One more to go. One more to go, and it's over. It goes to a decision, and I win.'"

3 P.M. CURT HALL

Curt Hall carried the baton through farm country, with nothing to break the monotony but the realization that Montreal lay less than a day away. Tomorrow at this time there would be no more running, no more pace car, no more hurried meals and irregular sleeping hours. Tomorrow at this time it would be over.

It was on everyone's mind. The all-consuming thought. One more 10-miler. Just one more. And then Montreal. And glory. And a hotel room. And a hot bath. And a warm bed. And sleep. And French-speaking ladies. And fancy restaurants and classy nightspots. And glory. And an overwhelming sense of joy and accomplishment.

4:15 P.M. BOB HICKEY

Just as Connelly had prophesied, Bob Hickey was back in the 60s. He ripped through the first mile of his twenty-seventh leg in

six minutes, then gradually slackened his tempo to a comfortable six-and-a-half-minute-per-mile pace.

Hickey ran his leg in 65:40.

5:21 P.M. ALEX SHEARER

"I ran hard, attacking the hills and pushing myself. I just wanted
to get it over with."

But Shearer was ambivalent.

"I thought to myself, 'Thank God, it's ending.' But I also felt
sad, because it was ending. Maybe for good. I've felt so close to
these guys for so many years, and I knew this probably would be
my last long relay with them.

"All of these have been more than just runs. But this one will
always be special, because it was the last one."

Back in Van One, publicist Lou McClary was collecting money
for a team party in Montreal.

McClary: "I'm collecting five dollars from everyone, Bob."

Hickey: "I'm not going to be able to go. My parents and
daughters are coming in, and I'm spending the time with them."

McClary: "Hey, bring them along. It's a team party. Everyone
on the team should be there. Give me five bucks, and bring them
along."

Hickey: "I'll stop by if I can, but I doubt it."

Hickey did not contribute toward the party. His teammates
were upset. But Hickey had his reasons: "I've been away from
my family for 19 days. And they're far more important than
anybody else here is to me. If I stop by the party, it will be for a
very short period. Just to say hi. And then I'll get back with my
own group, who I feel more relaxed with."

Even now, after three weeks of the most intimate kind of
sharing, Hickey still didn't fit in with his fellow police officers —
the same men he said he'd die for.

7:51 P.M. JOHN ROCKWOOD

Rockwood figured this would be his last run. His feet barely
touched the ground as he floated toward Ottawa, the capital city
of Canada, which was less than 15 miles away.

Inside Van Two, Chuck Foote was trying to figure where he'd
take the baton. He and the other members of Van Two had just
learned that the route had been changed from Highway 17 — the
freeway into Ottawa — to Highway 17B, a main surface street.

Foote: "I thought, 'Doggone. I'm gonna be aced out of Ottawa. Not see a soul and run through trees and barbed wire and that sort of thing again.' I hadn't run through a town since we left L.A., and here on my last leg, with a chance to run through Ottawa, I was gonna lose out on that one last chance."

Meanwhile, Van One had taken Highway 17 into Ottawa — the wrong route — and suddenly Rockwood was running without prospect of making a hand-off. The seven-, eight-, and eight-and-a-half-mile marks flew by. Then so did the camper, which had corrected its course.

At the nine-mile mark, Rockwood burst into a sprint.

"I figured, 'This is it.' I'm so happy it's over."

9:08 P.M. DICK BONNEAU

The sun was sinking below the majestic Ottawa skyline as Bonneau began what he also thought would be his last and most memorable run. The scene was breathtaking. Six patrol cars from the Ontario Provincial Police and eight motor officers — their sirens and lights alive — escorted Bonneau through the crowded streets of Ottawa, a city of 300,000.

Just 17 hours earlier, at four in the morning, Bonneau had been tired and sluggish as he ran across a barren stretch of Canadian soil.

Now, his adrenalin pumping, his legs lifting effortlessly, he was buoyed by the huge, enthusiastic crowds that lined Ottawa's main thoroughfares shouting, "Bravo, bravo!"

"I really can't describe my feelings adequately," Bonneau would say later. "It was simply my best run."

His time was 65:15. But emotionally, it was a four-minute mile.

10:13 P.M. CHUCK FOOTE

It would have been a normal, lazy summer weekend evening in Ottawa. People were sitting on lounge chairs outside their homes, enjoying the first cool of evening. Others were strolling along the streets, heading for restaurants or theaters, or simply relishing the calm. The parks were crowded with families and lovers. The city was serene. But the electricity of Bonneau's run had switched on large sections of Ottawa. Now — despite earlier doubts about whether he'd run in Ottawa — it was Chuck Foote's turn.

"I took the baton right near the Parliament Building — a gorgeous old gothic structure that looked like it came right out of England. People were all over the place, minding their own business, and then all of a sudden they'd see those police cars and hear those sirens, and they'd start waving and shouting things in French."

At this point, Foote was escorted by four patrol cars and the pace car. As he wound his way through the streets of Ottawa, the night grew darker and the lights and sounds of his escort grew more pronounced.

"I ran by the Royal Canadian Mounted Police facility [the national headquarters], and all the brass and the inspectors and officers were lined up outside. I stopped completely and shook hands with the commissioner and his assistant. Then we roared out of there and headed onto the streets again. There were people everywhere. I kept waving the baton and saying hello, and they kept shouting back and waving. I mean, it was 10 solid miles of this. Just fantastic. I didn't even know it, but I was running a six-minute-per-mile pace. Without even trying. It was so exhilarating.

"Then I ran past the Ontario Provincial Police headquarters, and here's all these officers — about 150 of them — lined up on one side. And as I'm coming up, they all snapped to attention and saluted. Chills just ran down my spine."

Foote was now just a short distance from Alexander Bridge, which connects Ottawa with its sister city of Hull, across the Ottawa River in Quebec province.

"I was just about to cross the river, and here comes these motor officers. There must have been ten or twelve of them, screaming up this side street. Scared the life out of me. I mean, they were blowing their sirens and slamming on their brakes. And I whirled around. I thought they were gonna run over me. And zoom! They go shooting past, and block off all four lanes of the freeway into Hull. Unbelievable. I mean, all four lanes! I said, 'Hey, fellas. I only need one little lane.' They probably didn't understand me anyway."

All traffic from Ottawa into Hull came to a complete standstill as Foote cruised along the freeway, protected by the motor officers, riding ten abreast behind him.

Five minutes later, Foote reached the city of Hull.

"I think I ran through the red light district of Hull. There were streetwalkers all over the place. I thought, 'Jeez, I'm in downtown L.A.'" The pimps and prostitutes seemed unconcerned at the massive show of law enforcement in their neighborhood. They watched passively as the police entourage roared by.

The red light district gradually gave way to aging tenement

buildings and rundown stores. People sitting on apartment steps and children playing on sidewalks were rocked to attention by the motorcycles thundering through their neighborhoods. Several youngsters tried to run along with Foote but gave up after a few steps. From the streets, people shouted, "Bravo!" and tried to communicate in French. For the next three miles, Foote was embraced by the French-speaking people of Hull. At the end he was ecstatic.

"That one run made the first 26 worthwhile. It was something I will never forget."

Foote paused a moment, then continued. "You know, when Bob Burke asked me to run this time, I really had to think about it. I'd be away from my family and all that. But I thought about the Bicentennial theme and the fact that this could be the last time we ever do this. I thought, 'This is gonna be a once-in-a-lifetime thing. And I might regret it the rest of my life if I miss it.'

"Now I won't have any regrets."

11:13 P.M. JIM MURPHY

Van Two was convinced it was running its final leg. And so, as Jim Murphy began his twenty-seventh run, the van drank champagne in honor of its first finisher, and Dick Clark proposed a toast: "Viva la Foote!"

Murphy ran through five more miles of Hull. "And at every corner there were six to eight people. They had their thumbs up. They were smiling and shouting. It was fantastic."

The motor cops roared ahead of the main escort, blocking off intersection after intersection. The electric shock that began in Ottawa had rolled across nearly 20 miles of urban Canada. Now, five miles into his run, Murphy reached the outskirts of Hull, and entered a rural setting.

"The crowds continued, but my mind started to wander back. I thought about when I had run just six or seven legs and how depressed I was. I thought about my heel blister and how tired I felt. And how I just couldn't imagine actually getting ready and running twenty more times. Putting on my socks. Putting cushions in my shoes. Rubbing linament on my legs. Stretching. Getting out of the camper in the middle of the night, in the desert, in the mountains. The same routine. Over and over. After a while it got so close together, it seemed like I'd just finished one leg and had to get ready for the next one. And then I thought, 'This is the last one.'

"It was a great feeling knowing that each step I took was not going to be repeated. And that I'd accomplished something very special in my life."

12:22 A.M. DICK CLARK

"I remember being about a quarter of a mile from the end and seein' Janowicz standin' there. I just hauled off and really started lifting. When I handed the baton to Frank, I jumped up in the air and let out a war whoop that you wouldn't believe. 'Cause that was it for me. I'd made it.

"There wasn't a soul out there. And after I calmed down, I walked down the road and tried to get my thoughts together. I said, 'Thank you, God. Thank you.' And then I said, 'Phil, we made it. It's over.'"

1:36 A.M. FRANK JANOWICZ

"It was a depressing run, 'cause there were no people. I woulda liked to have people cheering me on my last leg. It was two in the morning, and not a soul in sight.

"The run was a gradual uphill all the way. But I figured I probably deserved it, 'cause my first ten were all down."

And so, Van Two finished as it had started — at night. Now only the brief climactic run through Montreal remained. But here, off a dark Canadian highway, the members of Van Two celebrated their victory. They talked and drank and joked and reminisced.

Would they ever run in this type of relay again?

Foote: "Sure."

Murphy: "Yeah."

Janowicz: 'Don't ask me now; but I'm sure I would."

Clark: "I don't think so."

What was the toughest part?

Unanimous: "The living conditions. The uneven hours."

The party continued into the early morning hours. No one wanted the exquisite feeling of triumph to end.

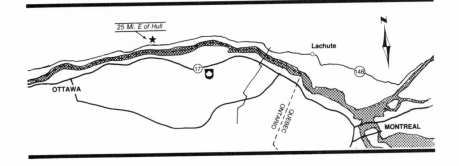

THE TWENTY-FIRST DAY
Sunday, July 4, 1976

There are men who can live — indeed, prefer — a life without hills or valleys. But there are others who require challenge, regardless of the risks.

Each of the runners in the Bicentennial Relay of Goodwill had accepted a monumental challenge and responsibility on this run, because any failure could never be purely personal. It involved too many others.

Driven by that obligation to self and teammates, each man had succeeded. And each had watched his comrades succeed. Such victories are precious.

The final triumph was less than 12 hours and 100 miles away. Fittingly, it would come in the city of Montreal, which would turn briefly from its Olympic obsession to welcome fourteen cop-athletes — men whose dedication, message and victories over the past three weeks were a perfect prelude to the courage and skill soon to be displayed by other great athletes in the city's magnificent stadiums and arenas.

2:45 A.M. BOB JARVIS

"I ran through some little villages. People were still up at 3 A.M.. They were hangin' out windows, wavin' at me. I took it real easy. Didn't overextend myself. But I was glad to get it over with."

This was the end of the line for Bob Jarvis, one of the charter members of the LAPD relay team.

"I'm all through," he said. "I've been on every one of these relays. There's no reason to go anymore."

Before the relay, Jarvis had said he would have foregone the run if he had been offered a good movie or television role. But once it began, Jarvis had worked hard to maintain harmony. It was he who broke up the fisticuffs of Garcia and Hall. And it was he who had delivered an eloquent plea for sanity and peace from both sides during the summit meeting over the clocks.

Now, as he moved toward the stationary figure of Pat Connelly, he felt sad. In past relays, the other runners and drivers had always greeted a campermate completing his last run. It was a tradition. But only one man — Pat Connelly — was there when Jarvis finished his leg. And he had to be; he was taking the hand-off.

In the desolation and darkness, Jarvis summed up his feelings in two words: "Fuck it."

3:58 A.M. PAT CONNELLY

"That's all he said. I mean, on all the past relays, you had a comradeship that developed. Everybody felt a sense of accomplishment. But it wasn't felt in our camper this morning."

Connelly took the baton across a primarily barren stretch of Canada, broken briefly by two small towns. His pace was swift — 61 minutes. His attitude, jaded.

"I've had it. I'm ready to go home. If there were a plane out tonight, I'd go tonight." (There was a plane out that night. Alex Shearer was booked on it.)

Would he run again? "As of today, definitely not. But then I've always said 'no' after one of these runs.

"There were so many ups and downs on this relay. But I'm sure as time goes by, I'll forget all the downs and remember all the ups. But after my last leg, all I felt was sadness. The only person out there to greet me was Frank Mullens, who was taking the hand-off.

"I gave him the baton, and I said, 'Good luck, Frank. Last run! Atta way to go!' And I jogged with him about a half-mile.

"That's the way it should be done."

4:59 A.M. FRANK MULLENS

The physical and emotional demands of the last three weeks had exacted a terrible toll on Frank Mullens. But now, as he covered his final 10 miles, he, too, reflected on the past 21 days. And his reflections differed at least in one way from Connelly's.

"I think of all the trips I've made, this was the most compatible group of guys I've ever been with. There was just tremendous camaraderie.

"But the running! After a while, it seems like all I ever did my whole life was run. You get to be a robot. Somebody shakes you and says, 'Hey — get dressed and get ready to run.' You say, 'Okay, which way?' And they point you in the right direction."

Would he run in another relay? "After my last one, I told my family, 'That's it.' But then Burke came up with this one. And it had the Bicentennial theme. And the Olympic theme. And I said, 'One more.' I just couldn't break away from the guys. I couldn't let them go without me. My daughter just about came unglued. She didn't want to see me put myself through the agony that I have to go through to get in shape. Seventy, eighty miles a week training. Tired. Irritable. Cranky. So I promised everyone this would be my last one. And it will be. I have to be fair to my wife. I have to ease up on my running."

And then, almost as an afterthought, Frank Mullens got to the crux of the situation:

"The run took a lot out of me. I'm getting old."

6:19 A.M. EDDIE GARCIA

Eddie Garcia, his right knee throbbing, carried the baton toward Lachute, Canada, the last "big" city before Montreal.

"I won the match," he'd say after his twenty-seventh and final leg. "I didn't k.o. my opponent, but I finished. I ran every mile."

Garcia and Jim Murphy were the rookies on the team. It was inevitable, perhaps, that they found the greatest meaning in the relay — meaning the others had found long ago. Murphy had discovered himself. And Garcia:

"In terms of testing myself physically — in terms of endurance, training, and conditioning — this was by far the ultimate. I've never experienced anything like it.

"To know that I was able to do it—it's something I'll relish and reflect about the rest of my life.

"A situation like this breaks you down physically and mentally. It gets you to look at yourself. You forget all the fantasies and illusions you had about yourself. You look at the raw you — for better or for worse.

"Myself? I'll think about those living conditions — that coffin up there with Mullens. It was like being in one of those tiger cages in Vietnam. If there's one thing I'd never do again, it's put myself through that fuckin' . . . that bunk again. No ventilation. No light. Christ, I'll have nightmares about that.

"I'll think about getting up and straining myself physically and psychologically every 16 hours for three weeks. I feel I put myself through a tremendous stress situation, and I came through. I feel a sense of reward.

"Still, I never realized how really close the guys are. After being with them on this relay, I can assure myself that we're probably gonna be close from now until doomsday. We won't be going over to each other's houses for coffee all the time — nothing like that. But that mutual respect and admiration will always be with us. We went through a unique experience together and survived.

"I was an outsider before this run, but now I'm part of this group, part of this experience."

Would he do it again? "You know, for the last few legs I was thinking, 'I put myself through this for what? For absolutely what?' But I'm sure in a coupla weeks I'll forget all about the bad parts and remember all the good parts.

"Yeah. I'd probably do it again."

Garcia's tense, pained face suddenly broke into a grin. Twenty-five yards ahead stood Curt Hall. His hand outstretched. This easy-going Texan was the antithesis of Garcia. But there was now a bond between these two men that seemed unthinkable three weeks ago at the academy, when they came to blows.

"Attaboy, Eddie! Attaboy!" Hall yelled as he took the baton. From across the way there was a whoop and a holler. A man sprinted toward Garcia, and they embraced. "You did it, man! You did it! Great. Great." Bob Jarvis hugged his campermate and fellow P.T. instructor. They had argued, bitched and joked for 21 days. Sometimes their verbal jousting had bordered on the vicious.

But now, just outside Lachute, they were rejoicing in their common triumph. It was a shared victory that very few men ever know.

6:59 A.M. CURT HALL

The team had no idea what kind of reception awaited it in Montreal. But it received a miniature preview in Lachute, 45 miles west of its goal.

Curt Hall picked up the baton about three miles outside Lachute and was joined by two provincial policemen. As the three men entered Lachute, firecrackers popped, and a crowd of 200 people gathered on both sides of the city's main thoroughfare, cheering and applauding.

"It looked like the whole town was out there," Hall said.

Hall had started the relay with a battered ankle and shoulder — the result of his on-duty motorcycle accident. Now, three weeks and 270 miles later, the shoulder was still sore and the ankle weak. But overall, he felt better than at any time during the run. He had reached his goal. He had conditioned himself on the run. "I'd like about a three-day rest, and then I'd love to run a good 10-mile road race," he said.

Hall reflected on the past three weeks. "The running was not the hardest part for me. In fact, I could keep doing this for another month, easy. I wouldn't particularly want to. But I could.

"No, the hardest part was just bein' away from home and the schedule and the living conditions. My whole internal system was in an uproar. I had bowel problems all the way. And then, of course, the cramped quarters with six other guys. Sometimes it was a relief just to get out there and run. You know, I'd almost say, 'Can I run now?'"

Would he do it again? "Oh, yeah. Sure."

8:09 A.M. BOB HICKEY

Bob Hickey carried the baton past a scattering of houses and gas stations toward Montreal. The air was warm and moist.

"The first five miles were fantastic, but then the heat got to me. I said, 'I can't go anymore. I can't push anymore.' But there were a lot of people along the way, yelling encouragement. Those people didn't know me from beans. But they took time from their routines to photograh me and wish me luck. They kept me going."

It had been a rough 21 days for Bob Hickey. He had been forced to run the last one third of the relay without his great motivator and yardstick — the clocks. He had suffered through the excruciating pain of blisters, calluses, a stone bruise, an infection, and the mental anguish of becoming the first LAPD runner to drop out of an assigned 10-mile leg.

Now it was all drawing to a close. And Hickey tried tngs in perspective:

"I find it very difficult to cope with a lot of policemen's attitudes. It gets me uptight. Like the way they treated Bob Burke over the timing."

Hickey paused a moment and then reflected on the greater problem — the problem that had nagged him ever since he joined the department more than a decade and a half ago.

"I'm from a police family. My dad was a cop for 17 years. And he was one of the boys. My father-in-law was a cop for 32 years.

And he was one of the boys. And my brother-in-law is a police sergeant. And he's very much one of the boys. I just never fit in. This is the closest I've ever been able to, and it's mainly because of Bob Burke. He acts as a shield for me.

"I just don't have the attitude of most cops. I was pulled out of the field for about a year-and-a-half once because I wasn't aggressive enough. Now I'm a supervisor, and it's hard because I have to watch other people do the job."

Hickey's voice trailed off. It was as though he suddenly realized he was a square peg trying to fit into a round hole.

"This is my last run," he continued. "I don't mind the running aspect. It's just that I don't like being away from my family this long. My wife is very tolerant. Very understanding. But to be honest, before I left she said we're gonna have to sit down and talk when I get home. Because after the job and coaching and my training, we don't have any time together.

"I work morning watch. I've slept with Rockwood for three weeks now. That's probably more than I've slept with my wife in two or three months. It's not fair. Not to me or my wife. So this is my last relay."

Again Hickey paused. And then, once more, his ambivalence about his fellow officers poured forth:

"I knew this was gonna be my last run. And I wanted to prove something. I wanted the best overall average. When they turned off the clocks, it was a relief to some of those guys, but it was frustrating to me, because I'm competitive.

"But all my pain — the infection — everything was worth it. This was a team accomplishment. And I'd go through hell for my teammates."

9:09 A.M. ALEX SHEARER

As Alex Shearer took the baton for his final leg, Van One was parked at a gas station, filling up for the trip into Montreal. A boy in his early teens was cleaning the windows of the van when he spotted the huge sign adorning its rear: "Los Angeles Police Department Bicentennial Relay of Goodwill."

Boy (to Bonneau): "Los Angeles? Isn't that in Florida?"

Bonneau took the boy to the side of the van, which had a huge map of the United States and southern Canada on it. The route of the relay was etched in a dark line from Los Angeles to Montreal.

Bonneau: "Here's Los Angeles, down here in the state of California. And over here is Florida, about 3,000 miles east."

Boy: "I never was any good at geology."
Bonneau slapped the boy on the back and chuckled.
Bonneau: "Yeah. I bet your best subject is geography."

The temperature was reaching into the high 80s. The terrain
was the same as it had been throughout Canada — mostly flat
with some rolling hills. Shearer was tired.

"Tired. Very, very, very, very tired. The miles seemed so long
on that last one. It was a very tough run. I was just very happy to
see Bob Burke standing in the road there."

What was the hardest part for the Second Oldest Man of the
Highway? "You know, once you get on the road, it's like one
long day, without any form or meaning. I couldn't tell you
where I ran or when.

"But the toughest part is the preparation — the long hours of
training, month after month. And leaving home. You know,
there's a lot of people who don't like to see you go. Wives, and as
I've said many times before, loved ones.

"But seriously, I like to be home. When these things are over,
I'm the first one to fly out. I'll be gone tonight. I'll be home by
9:30. Everyone else is staying a couple of days at least."

Would he do it again? "No. This is the end for me."

The past three weeks had not been easy for Shearer. He had
suffered agonizing chest pains and a painful toe "operation."
Nonetheless, he had kept Van One and the rest of the team loose
with his Uncle Alex stories and fine assemblage of wines. Now
he confessed some truths to himself.

"You know, I love to run. I've enjoyed myself on every relay. I
enjoy running at the beach, in races. But this run has been an
effort for me. It's been tough. I have no idea really . . ."

But Shearer did have an idea. After a moment of reflection, he
faced reality.

"It's been two years since the D.C. run. You know, I'm 47
now. And that could be it. It just seems like it was a lot harder for
me this time than ever before. It really was."

Age had made its move on Alex Shearer.

10:27 A.M. BOB BURKE

Bob Burke was on the outskirts of Montreal. "I kept running past
groups of people — fifteen to twenty at a time. They were
standing off the road. Many had just come out of their homes.
As I went by, they shook my hand or touched me. And they
were saying something in French that I couldn't understand. So

I asked a motor officer who was escorting me, and he said they were yelling, 'God bless you,' and 'Happy birthday, U.S.A.' It made me very proud."

The receptions continued through Burke's first five miles. Then, slowly the populated area gave way to rolling grazing land. There were no people to witness the final 10-mile run of the gentle warrior.

"This is it. I'm retiring. I've done just about everything I've ever wanted to do in running. The dreams I've had are fulfilled. Now I want to put as much into my family as I've put into these relays.

"It's time to break away from my toys."

11:35 A.M. JOHN ROCKWOOD

John Rockwood thought his final run had taken place the night before. But as the team drew closer to Montreal, it became apparent that he would have to put on his worn running shoes once more.

The sun marked off high noon in the eastern Canadian sky as Rockwood ran his final 10 miles toward Montreal. The blisters of his first run up the Angeles Crest, the dehydrating heat of the Mojave, the psychologically crushing run through Bishop, California, were distant memories. Now, as he cruised through the suburbs of Montreal, he sorted out his thoughts.

"The hardest part of this type of thing is just surviving in that camper for 20 hours a day for 21 days. You're tired, irritable, and you've got seven different personalities to cope with. I can see why they're so selective in submarines when they put people together for long stretches of time."

Would he run again? "The Vancouver run was my last run. The Washington run was my last run. And this one will be my last run."

For seven miles, Rockwood moved through the suburbs of Montreal — mostly farm houses and open spaces. And then he spotted the bridge that would carry him into Montreal. After 21 days and more than 3,800 miles, the baton was finally passing into Montreal.

Rockwood was on the bridge now, and ahead of him, to his right, he saw a crowd — perhaps 400 to 500 people. There were police officers, news camera crews, reporters, photographers, children, working people, housewives, a half dozen patrol cars, motorcycle cops, and twenty men in jogging suits.

As Rockwood drew closer, the huge throng began to vibrate. At first, the vibration was low, contained. Then it grew. And as

Rockwood passed, it exploded. The police cars and motor bikes screeched ahead of him, clearing the road. The twenty runners, from the Montreal Police Department and the Quebec Provincial Police, fell in behind him. The pace car played the Olympic theme. Rockwood, exhausted from his three-week ordeal and unexpectedly thrust into a twenty-eighth leg, was suddenly rejuvenated. His legs were light, his breathing easy, his adrenalin pumping.

"I was starting to fly. I'd look back over my shoulder to see if everyone was still with me. But every time I did they were right there. So I knew I had twenty runners with me, not just twenty gaggling policemen."

Indeed he did. All twenty were marathoners. Most had run the Boston Marathon.

The mass of men, escorted by steel and rubber, wound through the streets of Montreal, greeted like conquering heroes. The Canadian cops remained a few feet behind Rockwood at all times — leaving the glory to him. And then the hosts began to sing "Happy Birthday." Rockwood was startled: "What do you mean, 'Happy Birthday'?" The cops quickly clarified themselves: "Happy 200th birthday."

And so it went. A sea of armor and men, a continuous chorus of "Happy Birthday," crowds of people moving along the street, waving and smiling and yelling.

But the original excitement that had lifted Rockwood was beginning to subside. The pain of nearly 280 miles under the most arbitrary conditions was overtaking him now.

"I didn't want to slow down, because I kind of felt that would make me look bad in the Canadian runners' eyes. So I asked the follow vehicle how much farther I had to go. They said seven-tenths of a mile. And I said to myself: 'Good. I can start my kick and cruise in for the last seven tenths.' So I started picking it up, and then I started thinking: 'This is my last seven tenths. It's all over now.'"

But the follow car was wrong. Rockwood had a mile and seven-tenths to go. He was notified.

"I almost died. That extra mile at that pace nearly killed me. I ran the 10 miles in 65 minutes. I was completely exhausted. The only thing that kept me going were the news photographers, the TV cameras, the people cheering, and those twenty guys behind me. There was no way I could slow down."

And then at 12:40 P.M., Rockwood handed the baton to Dick Bonneau, who would log the final miles through Montreal. Rockwood put his hands on his knees, gasped for breath, and listened as his heart pounded against his sweat-soaked USA T-shirt.

But at least it was over.

Chuck Foote approached.

Foote: "Got some news for you, John."

Rockwood (whispering, gasping): "What?"

Foote: "Everybody's gonna run the last three miles through the city together."

Rockwood couldn't talk. He could barely move. He climbed slowly back into Van One. He was dizzy. Nauseated. The van began to swirl around him. The nausea welled up. Darkness began to fall. He lay down on the floor. Bob Hickey soaked towels and put them over Rockwood's head and legs.

In the rear of the camper, Bob Burke and Alex Shearer were still recovering from their just-completed runs.

Shearer: "I feel terrible. Weak all over and nauseous. I don't think I'm gonna run that final three."

Burke: "I feel lousy, too. I think I'm gonna have to pass, too."

Two, three minutes passed. Chuck Foote entered the van. Only Hickey appeared to be among the living. The others lay or sat passively, staring blankly, trying to regain lost strength.

Foote surveyed the carnage. "We're running in two minutes," he said. "Let's go."

The men responded like robots. First Rockwood climbed to his feet. Then Burke rose and walked forward. Shearer followed. Hickey, ever the housekeeper, remained behind a few moments. He folded the wet towels, put them away, and tidied up his bunk.

12:50 P.M. DICK BONNEAU

Bonneau had been running for 10 minutes through the crowded streets of Montreal toward the downtown area when he was joined by his teammates. In two weeks, the greatest marathoners in the world would travel this same route in search of Olympic gold.

Like many of his teammates, Bonneau said the living conditions had been the toughest part of this run. And like many of them, he said this would be his last long-distance relay.

These were the last miles then for Bonneau and many of his teammates.

"The final leg was one of the proudest moments of my life," he would say later. "For two days, we were trying to figure out who would run through Montreal. It just happened as a stroke of luck that it was me."

Now there were thirty-four runners, a herd of patrol cars and motorcycles and the omnipresent Turtle winding through downtown Montreal. The crowds grew larger and larger. People hung out of high-rise buildings, waving and shouting. Others gathered along the streets.

Again the Canadian hosts sang "Happy Birthday." And then they cried out in unison: "Hip, hip, hooray for the LAPD!" The people along the way clapped and cheered. All that was missing was the ticker tape.

The entourage deviated several times from the Olympic route to pass by law enforcement agencies. At each one the Canadian cops filed out of their headquarters — fifty or sixty officers lining both sides of the street. And as Bonneau passed, the men snapped to attention. The pace car blared Sousa marches and the Olympic theme.

Connelly: "I had such a feeling of pride. I jogged up beside Bob Burke and put my arm on his shoulder, and I said, 'This is really great.' That's all I could say. Neither of us could say anything else. We felt such emotion."

Then the Canadian cops got an idea. They began taking off their department T-shirts and offered them in exchange for the shirts worn by the LAPD. The exchange was spontaneous and lighthearted. Only Clark refused to go along.

Clark: "That really irritated me. Here we had these $10 USA shirts, and we're exchanging them for 50-cent T-shirts that said CUM on them [Community Urban Montreal]. You know, if they said 'Montreal Olympics' or something — fine. But those crummy things — we got robbed. And I also figured, 'Shit, these guys are gonna steal our thunder, too. After running 3,885 miles, everyone's gonna think *they're* the LAPD and *we're* the locals."

The Canadian runners paired up with their American counterparts, and the exchange of T-shirts went on. Several cops approached Clark and offered to exchange shirts, but he was adamant. No way. Now Clark was the only LAPD runner still wearing the USA colors. Another Canadian cop offered to exchange. No. Another. No. The runners continued through Montreal. The crowds grew larger and noisier.

Bonneau pranced ahead, his 5-foot 7-inch frame erect and proud. Behind him, a mob of thirty-three runners. Despite the appearance of mass confusion, the Canadian cops had a leader, whose job it was to keep them behind Bonneau at all times. Every so often an exuberant officer might sprint toward the head of the pack, only to be flagged down by the leader. This was the

LAPD's show. And despite the exchange of T-shirts and Clark's fears, the Canadian cops were not going to steal their guests' triumphant arrival in Montreal.

The bitterness, disillusionment, and fatigue that existed before Montreal were gone now.

Burke moved toward Pat Connelly and grabbed his hand. Chuck Foote moved through the runners, patting them on the back and congratulating them.

The huge mass wound its way toward the Montreal City Hall and the American Consulate, where the consul-general, champagne, photographers and a proclamation waited.

City Hall would be it. The end. At least a thousand people were gathered there.

The crowds along the streets were now two and three people deep as the team moved toward its climax. And suddenly it was over. A tremendous roar rose from the steps of City Hall. Cameras flashed and reporters, with their mikes and camera crews in tow, pushed forward. Even the foreign press, which would cover the Olympic games, was there.

The roar became thunderous. The cops were overwhelmed. And the words of Bob Burke came back, rising above the tumult: "I want to leave something behind. An accomplishment. Very few people can claim that. And if that accomplishment is beaten a million times, you still did it. You were there first.

"These guys will look back and say, 'We did it.' And nobody will ever be able to take this away from them."

The runners fell into the crowd. Clark was finally persuaded to give up his T-shirt. The reporters pressed forward. Interviews. Congratulations. Hugs. Kisses. Relief. Exultation. Triumph.

Murphy: "It was the perfect ending. A classic. A classic. This is the way it would be on TV, in the movies. Perfect. It's just what you dream about. It's like you won the Olympic marathon and ran into the arms of the waiting . . ."

Foote: "It was the best of possible endings . . ."

And no one would ever be able to take it away from them.

THE FIRST DAYS BACK

One night shortly after the relay, one of the runners was ordered into an interrogation room by his supervising sergeant. And there, for an hour, the sergeant questioned, chastised and threatened the officer about his running. The scene would be repeated every night for weeks. The sergeant accused the officer of trying to use his athletic skills to get by on the job, get close to the brass and promote. And he issued a warning: "I'm gonna get you thrown off the department if it's the last thing I do."

If police work fosters a brotherhood of closeness, interdependence and sharing, it also demands a certain conformity. Like any fraternal order — which the police department most certainly is — the LAPD is uncomfortable with men who bring more glory to themselves than to the group.

It was felt by many officers that the runners did bring glory to both themselves and their department. But some felt otherwise — that the relay was an exercise in self-glorification. Their emotions ranged from jealousy to outright hostility.

When the LAPD relay team returned to Los Angeles, there was little overt hostility. It's difficult to criticize a group of men who had just represented your department and country and who had performed a spectacular athletic feat, as well. But there were no parades or plaudits at police headquarters at Parker Center either.

To many, the runners had violated the group's norms. They had excelled far beyond comfortable limits.

The award for outstanding athletic performance on the LAPD in 1976 went to the softball team for playing 24 straight hours.

Tuesday, July 6, 1976   The Police Commission
ALEX SHEARER

True to his word, Alex Shearer had returned home Sunday night. He took one day off to be with his family — who apparently were also his loved ones. And then he returned to his duties with the police commission.

During the day he handled a few problems and then wondered out loud how his fellow officers had been able to get along without him for three weeks.

Friday, July 9, 1976   Robbery-Homicide Division
FRANK MULLENS

Frank Mullens returned to robbery-homicide at 8 A.M. and was mobbed by his fellow officers. Uppermost in their minds: The John Day streaker.

Within a short time, Mullens was back in the old grind: Phones ringing, radios blaring, mountains of paperwork.

There was one consolation: There were no bank robberies this day.

Monday, July 12, 1976   The Police Academy
PAT CONNELLY

Pat Connelly was on loan to the academy during the summer while school was out. On this day, he began his first assignment: Monitoring and recording all testing of the department's physical fitness program.

For Connelly and the others at the academy, their return was something of a letdown. There were a few handshakes and congratulations, but the department's brass did not acknowledge the team's return. The tumult and shouting of Montreal would have to suffice.

BOB BURKE

Bob Burke walked stiffly into his small office at the Los Angeles Police Academy and dove into the mass of paperwork that had accumulated over the past four weeks. He worked on the department's athletic program, as well as the Police Olympics, and began tying up the loose details of the Bicentennial relay. At midday he checked in the shotguns that had been taken on the run. By five o'clock he had balanced the books on the relay, and he went home.

JOHN ROCKWOOD

John Rockwood returned to the Police Academy and began working on a reevaluation of the department's self-defense program. Specifically, the obstacle course which recruits are required to run. Rockwood's job: Determine if there was any correlation between the obstacle course and the real-life situations officers face in the field. Rockwood prepared a questionnaire to be sent to field officers to determine how often they climb walls, jump fences, run through parking lots filled with cars and so forth.

DICK BONNEAU

Dick Bonneau had wanted to work vice. But at 8 A.M. on Monday morning, he, too, found himself back at the Police Academy. The staff work there was overwhelming. He was told he would have to say at least through September. All day Bonneau, an expert in the legal nuances of searching suspects, worked on revising the statewide standards in that area.

BOB JARVIS

Bob Jarvis's first assignment was to take a physical training test — the same one he would later administer to police officers who had been on the job for two years or longer. The test was to determine how much the officers had retained from their recruit training at the academy.

Jarvis dashed 150 yards across a flat course, shot at hidden targets, hurdled two fences, climbed a wall, walked across a six-foot beam, hopped over hedges, climbed through an eight-foot conduit, and then sprinted across the finish line. After running 273 miles in 21 days, it was a breeze.

CHUCK FOOTE   Juvenile Division

Chuck Foote was assigned to child abuse. His partner quickly briefed him on their case: Incest, involving a father and his 11-year-old daughter. Foote's reaction: "I'd like to kill him — but of course, I can't do that."

Foote and his partner decided to investigate the suspect's request for reduction of bail from $10,000 to $5,000. They feared that the suspect, a Mexican national, would flee across the border if released.

The man had given the judge a letter saying he'd worked at the Brown Derby restaurant in Los Angeles for three years and therefore was a solid citizen deserving of bail. The officers checked the Brown Derby on Wilshire Boulevard. The suspect had never worked there. It was now lunchtime, but Foote's partner was on a diet and didn't want to eat. All he wanted to do was work. Foote was famished. He was also the junior officer. So he deferred to his superior. The officers skipped lunch and went to the Brown Derby in Hollywood. Yes, the suspect had worked there as a waiter — but for just three months. One last Brown Derby to check — this one in Beverly Hills. The man had worked there, but for only two months. He had been fired. The manager said he was a "bum."

One final detail. They stopped by the home of the suspect's wife. She said he'd told everyone in the family he would go to Mexico if released on bail. Let him go, she said. I don't hold any ill-will against him. He's sick. I don't want him back. We have been married 18 years.

Foote and his partner congratulated each other. They had just made certain that a child abuser would go to trial and not be given the chance to flee the country.

It was 6:30. Foote returned home. He hadn't eaten since seven that morning. But he felt fulfilled.

JIM MURPHY   Hollywood Division

Usually after a long vacation, oficers are assigned to desk work, the jail or courier duty. The department realizes its officers need at least one day to readjust to the job. Jim Murphy was not granted such a respite. He was back in the field immediately, patrolling the area around Griffith Park and the Greek Theater. He handled a dispute between a landlord and tenant. And then he got a call, "Vehicle versus dog. No traffic cop available. Handle this call." Murphy did, but when he arrived, there was no car, no dog, no reporting person, no witnesses — nothing. He walked around a few minutes and chatted with some people, asking them if they'd seen anything involving a collision between a dog and a car. No. Then he was approached by an elderly woman who complained about cars speeding into Griffith Park along a narrow road where scores of youngsters normally play. Murphy told her how to file her complaint with the traffic coordinator of the LAPD.

As they were talking, a car sped by, heading toward the park. Murphy excused himself, jumped into his patrol car and took chase. He cited the driver for doing 41 miles-per-hour in a 25 mile-per-hour zone. An hour later, Murphy's first day back on the job was over.

Wednesday, July 14, 1976   Hollenbeck Division
FRANK JANOWICZ

After a two-year hiatus, Janowicz returned to Hollenbeck Division. He was greeted warmly. Asked about the run. Congratulated. At roll call, he was identified as the Six-Million Dollar Man who could run down any suspect in the barrio.

Still Janowicz was depressed. He was back where he had been two years ago. "Same officers, same people I put in jail, same crime problems. It was like I'd never left."

Janowicz and his partner cruised the streets of East Los Angeles. "Patrol — I knew what it was going to be like. I've done it long enough. A lot of things change on the department. But not patrol. Not the street. It's always the same bullshit."

Monday, July 19, 1976   The Police Academy
DICK CLARK

Dick Clark and Eddie Garcia had driven the "Turtle" back across the country. Now, after being away from his job for five weeks, Clark returned. The vacancies in his situation simulations unit had been filled — without his having been consulted. He met the new people, talked briefly with his commanding officer, and wrote a unit progress report covering the past two weeks — weeks he hadn't been on the job.

BOB HICKEY   Hollenbeck Division

Bob Hickey was bombarded with questions about the run and finally ended up giving a 10-minute presentation during roll call on morning watch. Afterward, his fellow officers surrounded him, shaking his hand and telling him how proud they were of his performance.

Hickey was temporarily assigned as watch commander, which meant he was in charge of the station itself — approving reports, making decisions on bookings and recording each incident that occurred in the field and at the station.

Hickey authorized the transport of a juvenile offender to nearby Downey, where he was wanted by authorities. He also authorized the booking of a drunk, the detention of a runaway who was later taken home, and approved the arrest of a man who was stopped for a routine traffic violation, but ended up being booked for possession of marijuana and carrying a concealed, fully-loaded .22-caliber pistol.

Through the night he read various reports — mostly burglaries, some domestic disputes. Nothing serious.

For Hickey it was frustrating. Being a supervisor in the field and watching other officers do the work was bad enough. Sitting inside the Hollenbeck station and shuffling papers was pure torture.

Monday, July 26, 1976   The Police Academy
EDDIE GARCIA

Eddie Garcia worked all day with representatives of a private company that had been hired by the department to determine whether the LAPD's height and weight standards were valid. The department was facing a number of court challenges from groups who claimed the standards were being used to prevent women from joining the force.

Garcia read the raw data of earlier testing. The conclusions were obvious: There was a correlation between an officer's size and strength and the number of altercations that officer had in the field. There was evidence that during an arrest, a suspect under stress often felt angered and humiliated when ordered about by a smaller person. In that emotional state, the data suggested, many suspects challenge smaller officers. Conversely, bigger officers, by size alone, were more apt to intimidate their suspects and thus got involved in fewer altercations.

Garcia, by no means a large man himself, had been involved in more than his share of battles in the field. He read the data with acute personal interest.

EPILOGUE

Bob Hickey and his wife had their "talk" when he returned from Montreal, but little in his life changed. He completed work for a bachelor's degree, continued coaching his girls' track team, and like most of the other team members, continued running. On the job he found himself even further away from the street work he loved. He was put in charge of communications at police headquarters at Parker Center on the daywatch. That made him more determined than ever to retire from the LAPD when his 20 years were up and to return to the street with another department. By early 1978, he'd already lined up a job with the Irvine Police Department, near his home in Orange County.

Within a month of Dick Bonneau's return from Montreal, he got his wish — he was transferred to the vice squad in the tough, vice-infested Rampart Division. In December of 1977, he remarried. And by early 1978, he had passed all the tests for sergeant and was awaiting promotion.

His divorce final, Dick Clark's personal life settled down, too. On the job, he was transferred from Training Division to Juvenile Division and finally to the predominately black Southwest Division, where he was made a field supervisor.

371

Shortly after the run, the Los Angeles City Council decided that the LAPD's teaching program in secondary schools was a "frill" and cut off the funding. Pat Connelly was transferred to uniform patrol on the streets of the West San Fernando Valley. And Chuck Foote was transferred to Training Division at the Police Academy, where he helped set up continuing education programs for officers.

Jim Murphy was transferred from Hollywood to the Rampart Division. A month after the relay, his wife, Gigi, gave birth to a daughter. And during 1977 and early 1978 he set seven American records for his age group, including 8:58.1 for 3,000 meters and 15:01 for three miles, both new standards for 38-year-olds.

Curt Hall clung to his love affair with the bike, patrolling the streets of West Los Angeles. He cut down on his intense pre-relay training (up to 140 miles a week) and began running for fun. His new schedule gave him more time to enjoy his other hobbies — sailing and scuba diving.

On December 6, 1976, Frank Mullens talked a young gunman into releasing a hostage he'd been holding for two hours atop the tallest building in Los Angeles. The incident earned Mullens the LAPD's highest citation — the Medal of Valor — one usually reserved for front-line street cops.
In early 1978, Mullens retired after 29 years on the force and became an investigator for the California State Bar.
And he kept running.

Alex Shearer stayed on with the police commission, helping people "cut through the red tape." He was joined there by Frank Janowicz, who displayed the same singlemindedness in getting off the streets of Hollenbeck as he had in pounding over the highways of the Bicentennial relay. When he returned from Montreal, Janowicz applied for virtually every vacant desk job on the department. He finally got one — a quiet assignment with the police commission.

On the LAPD, the saying was, "Rudy DeLeon *is* Hollenbeck." In 1977, he realized a long-time dream for his division — the completion of a half-million-dollar youth athletic center, built with private funds and donated materials and labor. It gave the young people of East Los Angeles an alternative direction for their energies and aggressions. By early 1978, DeLeon was about to be promoted to commander, a rank that would have automatically moved him out of Hollenbeck Division to police headquarters downtown. In an unprecedented move, the LAPD tried to create a commander's job for DeLeon in East Los Angeles so that he could stay where he was needed most.

In the midst of this, Gov. Jerry Brown offered DeLeon a position on the powerful state parole board. After much soul searching, DeLeon left the LAPD and his beloved Hollenbeck and took the job.

In the fall of 1976, Assistant Police Chief George Beck made headline news in Los Angeles. He was busted one rank and suspended 10 days in connection with the release of raw police files on the Skid Row Slasher murder case to a motion picture studio. In January of 1978, when Police Chief Ed Davis retired, Beck was automatically considered for the job — a formality. His career had been ruined by the scandal. But Beck, who had started running during his bout with cancer, completed a marathon during his bout with notoriety.

John Rockwood, Bob Jarvis, Eddie Garcia, and Bob Burke remained at the Police Academy.

Jarvis picked up minor acting parts here and there, but still waited for his "big break." Garcia made progress in his carefully plotted police career, passing the preliminary exams to become a sergeant. Rockwood concentrated his energies on recruits and reservists.

Bob Burke put away his "toys" and got down to the nuts and bolts of planning football games, volleyball tournaments, track and field meets, and the sundry sports related to his job as an athletic director. In early 1977, Burke contemplated retirement and went so far as to turn in the paperwork. At the last moment, he decided to stay on.

Late that year, with Montreal a distant memory, Burke received a letter from a fire brigade in Victoria, Australia. We've got a team together, it said, and we'd like to run 4,000 miles around our continent. Could you help us?

Don't, one of his co-workers told Burke. If they succeed, they'll break your record.

Burke ignored him and painstakingly compiled a package of information for the firefighters on financing, transportation, food, public relations. He shipped it off in early 1978.

But the letter had unlocked Burke's toy chest. By mid-January he was talking about another relay. This one in Australia. This